BISHOP'S UNIVERSITY
1843–1970

BISHOP'S

UNIVERSITY 1843–1970

CHRISTOPHER NICHOLL

Published for
Bishop's University
by
McGill-Queen's University Press
Montreal & Kingston • London • Buffalo

© Bishop's University 1994
ISBN 0-7735-1176-8

Legal deposit second quarter 1994
Bibliothèque nationale du Québec

Printed in Canada on acid-free paper

Canadian Cataloguing in Publication Data

Nicholl, Christopher, 1922–
Bishop's University, 1843–1970
Includes bibliographical references and index.
ISBN 0-7735-1176-8
1. Bishop's University—History. I. Title.
LE3.B52N43 1994   378.714'66   C94-900180-5

To those who have built and
sustained Bishop's University
during 150 years
this volume is
respectfully dedicated

CONTENTS

ILLUSTRATIONS		ix
ACKNOWLEDGMENTS		xiii
PREFACE		xv
ABBREVIATIONS		xvii
PROLOGUE		3
1	THE FOUNDERS	13
2	PRINCIPAL NICOLLS: THE YEARS OF HOPE	30
3	PRINCIPAL NICOLLS: THE YEARS OF TRIAL	53
4	THE SMALLEST DIMENSIONS	89
5	THE END OF THE BEGINNING	128

6	THE REIGN OF PRINCIPAL McGREER	164
7	TRANSITION	213
8	THE WINDS OF CHANGE, 1960–70	249
EPILOGUE		295
APPENDIX ONE	THE ACTS RELATING TO BISHOP'S UNIVERSITY	299
APPENDIX TWO	THE CONTEXT OF THE BATTLE FOR THE CHARTER	312
APPENDIX THREE	THE FACULTY OF MEDICINE	317
APPENDIX FOUR	ENROLMENT STATISTICS	348
NOTES		351
INDEX		367

ILLUSTRATIONS

George Jehoshaphat Mountain, ca.1845   15
   Conference Room, McGreer Hall
Lucius Doolittle, ca.1850   19
   Conference Room, McGreer Hall
Edward Hale, ca.1870   24
   By H. Sandham; Old Library, McGreer Hall
Jasper Hume Nicolls, ca.1850   32
   Principal's Office, McGreer Hall
Henry Hopper Miles, 1867   34
   McCord Museum of Canadian History, Notman Photographic Archives
John Samuel McCord   48
   McCord Museum of Canadian History, Notman Photographic Archives
Thomas Cushing Aylwin, 1861   51
   McCord Museum of Canadian History, Notman Photographic Archives
The University of Bishop's College, 1859   54
   McCord Museum of Canadian History, Notman Photographic Archives
Bishop's College and Bishop's College School, 1862   67
   McCord Museum of Canadian History, Notman Photographic Archives
Richard William Heneker, 1900   78
   By Robert Harris; Old Lodge
Thomas Kennedy Ramsay, 1870   85
   McCord Museum of Canadian History, Notman Photographic Archives
Richard W. Norman, 1872   85
   McCord Museum of Canadian History, Notman Photographic Archives

Joseph Albert Lobley O. Howard *The Montreal Diocesan Theological College* (Montreal: McGill-Queen's University Press 1963)	92
Thomas Adams, 1901 By M.B. Schreiber; Principal's Dining Room, Dewhurst Hall	101
The Stigma Group, 1890 Bishop's University Archives	108
Bishop's College and Bishop's College School, 1895 Bishop's University Archives	116
Robert Hamilton *The Mitre* 10, June 1903	119
James Pounder Whitney *The Mitre* 10, June 1903	129
Waiting for the governor general. Jubilee Convocation, 1903 Bishop's University Archives	130
John Hamilton, 1925 By Horne Russell; Hamilton Staircase	133
A.F. Cecil Whalley's study, ca. 1905 Bishop's University Archives	138
Richard Arthur Parrock Bishop's University Archives	141
Frederick George Scott, Belgium, 1915 McCord Museum of Canadian History, Notman Photographic Archives	151
Grant Hall Bishop's University Archives	155
Francis Reginald Scott, B.A., 1919 *The Mitre* 26, June 1919	160
Arthur Huffman McGreer, 1935 *Bishop's '36*	165
The campus, 1923 *The Mitre* 30, no. 4, June 1923	167
The Bishop's Candlesticks, 1926 Bishop's University Archives	180
Frederick Edmund Meredith *The Mitre* 33, no. 2, 1925	183
Students' Executive Council, 1934–35 Bishop's University Archives	186
Philip Carrington, 1935 *The Mitre* 43, October, 1935	188
Robert Ernest Alfred Greenshields Bishop's University Archives	191
Edward Boothroyd, ca.1941 *The Mitre* 52, May 1945	202
William Rothney, ca.1938 Bishop's University Archives	202

Basil Jones, 1947 Bishop's University Archives	204
George Hugh Alexander Montgomery McCord Museum of Canadian History, Notman Photographic Archives	211
Arthur Russell Jewitt *Bishop's '51*	214
John Bassett, 1950 McCord Museum of Canadian History, Notman Photographic Archives	216
John Henry Molson, 1949 McCord Museum of Canadian History, Notman Photographic Archives	218
William Bridges Scott, 1954 Bishop's University Archives	220
Harry Norton Bishop's University Archives	223
Breaking ground for the Norton residence, 1949 Bishop's University Archives	224
Norton Dining Room, ca. 1951 Bishop's University Archives	226
Albert Lincoln Kuehner, 1960 *Quad, '65*	232
Arthur Nicol Langford, ca.1965 Bishop's University Archives	232
Charles Lapslie Ogden Glass *Quad '67*	250
Intercollegiate Football Team, 1964 Bishop's University Archives	252
Bruce Coulter, 1983 Bishop's University Archives	255
Tartuffe, 1966 Bishop's University Archives	262
Arthur Motyer in Centennial Theatre, 1967 Bishop's University Archives	264
The Knight of the Burning Pestle, 1967 Bishop's University Archives	264
Chancellor Abbott and Celia Franca. Inauguration of Centennial Theatre, 1967 *Quad '67*	274
Anthony William Preston, 1968 Bishop's University Archives	282
John Herbert Price Bishop's University Archives	286
Jeffrey Jefferis, 1960 *Quad '65*	289
Philip Scowen, 1956 Bishop's University Archives	289

Chancellor William Mitchell 292
   Bishop's University Archives
Aaron Hart David 319
   McCord Museum of Canadian History, Notman Photographic Archives
Francis Wayland Campbell 320
   By William Raphael; Principal's Dining Room, Dewhurst Hall
Bishop's Medical Faculty, 1872 328
   The Canadian Illustrated News 6, no. 2, 20 July 1872
Western Hospital, 1902 328
   McCord Museum of Canadian History, Notman Photographic Archives
Octavia Grace Ritchie, 1888 337
   McCord Museum of Canadian History, Notman Photographic Archives
Maude Elizabeth Abbott, 1890 338
   McCord Museum of Canadian History, Notman Photographic Archives

End Papers
Bishop's College and Bishop's College School, 1865
   By W.S. Hatton; Principal's Dining Room, Dewhurst Hall

ACKNOWLEDGMENTS

Acknowledgments for generous assistance in the location and preparation of the illustrations are due to the following: Christopher Turner of the photographic laboratories of Champlain College, Lennoxville Campus; Nora Hague of the McCord Museum of Canadian History, Notman Photographic Archives; Anna Grant, Coordinator of Archives and Special Collections, John Bassett Memorial Library; Christine Ljungkull, Gallery Coordinator at Bishop's University; and Joyce Coulter, Arthur Langford, Arthur Motyer, Phyllis Preston, George Rothney, Harry Scott, Philip Scowen, and Catherine Wark.

PREFACE

This history has been written to mark the 150th anniversary of the founding of Bishop's University in 1843. It is my hope that, in making available to the members of the Bishop's community the record of their goodly heritage, the history may serve to reinforce their confidence in the value of sound and liberal education.

This book could not have been written without the help of a great many people, whose contributions I am happy to acknowledge. My greatest debt is to Professor Robin Burns of the Department of History at Bishop's University, who encouraged me to undertake the project, and who has been both patient and unsparing in his efforts to contain my enthusiasms and to direct them along fruitful paths. Anna Grant, responsible for the care of the Archives and Special Collections in the John Bassett Library, has unfailingly and cheerfully responded to my demands on the University's archives throughout the five years during which the work has been under way. The Bélanger-Gardner Foundation has been generous with funds for travel to several sources of original documents and for the typing of the several drafts of the work, which has been completed with great skill and patience by Mrs Linda Nyiri. I take particular pleasure in having responded to the wish of the late Dr Gérard Gardner that his generous benefaction to Bishop's University should stimulate the writing of the history of the English-speaking community in the Eastern Townships.

I have also been encouraged by the interest and ready collaboration of a number of other men and women. For their help in dealing with particular periods and questions, I am grateful to Pamela Miller, Conservator of the Archives, and Nora Hague of the Notman Photographic Archives, both at the McCord Museum of Canadian History; the staff of the Archives of McGill University; the librarian of Rhodes House, Oxford; Canon Anthony Capon, Principal of the Montreal Diocesan Theological College; Monsieur le professeur Philippe Sylvain de l'Université Laval; and, from the Bishop's community, Principal Emeritus Anthony Preston, Professors Arthur Langford and Eivion Owen, and C.H.M. Church (B.A. '29), sometime Com manding Officer of the COTC at Bishop's.

Drafts of the work have been read by Professor Burns, Professor Emeritus Jeffrey Jefferis, and James Sweeny. Their painstaking and often trenchant comments have pruned the text of a number of errors and a tendency to discursiveness. I am also grateful to Frances Rooney for her scrupulous editing of the manuscript. For the final text, I take full responsibility. I have sought to give as complete an account of the history of Bishop's University as the available resources permitted, but it will be obvious to the reader that the choice of material and the emphases attached to certain developments have been influenced by my experience and by my view of the essential character of a university.

ABBREVIATIONS

A.A.	Associate in Arts
APEW	The Association for the Professional Education of Women
Association	The Bishop's College School Association
AUCC	The Association of Universities and Colleges of Canada
BALC	The British American Land Co.
BAUT	The Bishop's Association of University Teachers
B.A.	Bachelor of Arts
BCS	Bishop's College School
B.D.	Bachelor of Divinity
B.ès A.	Bachelier ès Arts
B.L.S.	Bachelor of Library Science
B.Sc.	Bachelor of Science
BUFA	The Bishop's University Faculty Association
CAMC	The Canadian Army Medical Corps
CAUT	The Canadian Association of University Teachers
CEGEP	Collège d'enseignement général et professionnel
CIAU	The Canadian Intercollegiate Athletic Union
CLC	Compton Ladies' College
COTC	The Canadian Officers' Training Corps
CPI	Council of Public Instruction
CPR	The Canadian Pacific Railway
CPSLC	The College of Physicians and Surgeons of Lower Canada

D.C.L.	Doctor of Civil Law
D.D.	Doctor of Divinity
D.D.S.	Doctor of Dental Surgery
D.E.C.	Diplôme des études collégiales
F.R.S.	Fellow of the Royal Society
l'École	l'École de médecine et chirurgie de Montréal
ELPSI	English-language post-secondary institutions
M.A.	Master of Arts
M.D.C.M.	Doctor of Medicine, Master of Surgery
MDTC	The Montreal Diocesan Theological College
McG.Corresp.	McGreer Correspondence, Bishop's University Archives
MGH	The Montreal General Hospital
M.Sc.	Master of Science
Mus.B.	Bachelor of Music
NCCU	National Conference of Canadian Universities
RAF	Royal Air Force
RCNVR	Royal Canadian Naval Volunteer Reserve
RNC	Royal Naval College (Dartmouth or Greenwich)
RORS	Rules, Orders and Regulations of Bishop's University
School	Bishop's College School
SEC	Students' Executive Council of the Students' Association of Bishop's University
SL&A	The St.Lawrence and Atlantic Railway
SPCK	The Society for Promoting Christian Knowledge
SPG	The Society for the Propagation of the Gospel in Foreign Parts
UGEQ	l'Union générale des étudiants du Québec
Union	The Young Mens' Protestant Educational Union

BISHOP'S UNIVERSITY
1843–1970

PROLOGUE

Bishop's University is older than Confederation. In 1992 Canada celebrated 125 years of the union of British North America. A year later, Bishop's celebrated its sesquicentennial—its 150th anniversary.

The University was founded to serve the English-speaking community in the territory which at present forms the province of Quebec, and until very recently Bishop's has depended almost entirely on Quebeckers for financial and moral support. Since Quebec's English-speaking community has been and remains unique in the Canadian experience, it is necessary to set the scene with a description of that community and the environment in which it was developing during the decade which began in 1840.

THE SEED BED

In 1840, 27 years before the confederation of the provinces of British North America, the total population of Lower Canada* was approximately 640 thousand, 525 thousand of whom were French-speaking.[1]

---

* Lower Canada became Canada East in 1841 and Quebec in 1867, but the earlier title remained in use until long after Confederation.

From these figures it is evident that English-speakers were very much in the minority; but because the province was a British colony, and because they controlled the levers of power, the English-speakers had been a dominant minority.[2] They were not uniformly distributed over the settled area of the province. In 1844 most of them lived in and around the cities of Montreal and Quebec, and in that region south of the St Lawrence River and west of the city of Quebec known as the Eastern Townships, in which land could be held in freehold tenure.

By 1840 reliable transportation had been established by steamboat between Quebec and Montreal during the ice-free months. Everywhere else in the province communication depended upon the rudimentary road system. Except for a very few, which had been constructed for military purposes but had not been maintained, the roads had been cleared by local initiative and were frequently impassable to wheeled traffic during the summer months. The most reliable and convenient modes of transport were by sleigh in the winter and on horseback during the summer, and, on a few roads, by stage coach. Most settlers travelled, of necessity, on foot. Under these circumstances communication between "English" communities was difficult, and they developed quite distinct characteristics.

The enterprise of the merchants of Montreal had made the city the commercial metropolis of the Canadas. Prosperity founded by the fur traders of the Northwest Company had been reinforced by the growth of industry, and Montreal had become a funnel through which exports from the Canadas (and even from Vermont) reached Great Britain under the mercantile system which accorded preferential tariffs to Canadian produce transported in British ships. English-speaking Montreal was then essentially an entrepreneurial and trading community and increasingly the site of the banks and other financial and commercial institutions which controlled the development of the Canadas.

The prosperity of the city of Quebec also depended upon the mercantile system. Timber from the forests of the vast area drained by the tributaries of the St Lawrence was exported from the port of Quebec to Great Britain. However, the leaders of the English-speaking community of that city had a vested interest in the British connection over and above commercial interest. Quebec had been the seat of the governor-general and the centre of military and political power since the seventeenth century. After the departure of the officers of the French government and most of the seigneurs following the treaty of 1763, the Roman Catholic Bishop of Quebec and the Superior of the Seminary of Quebec had become the cultural as well as the spiritual leaders of the French-speaking majority in Lower Canada; and it was to Quebec that Jacob Mountain, first Anglican Bishop in the Canadian colony, was appointed in 1793. Though political power was by 1840 being gradually diffused into the hands of elected assemblies, there was in Quebec still a ruling society of government place-holders—members of the Executive and Legislative Councils, the British military garrison and the civil service—whose perquisites, reinforced by marriage with the daughters of the wealthy timber merchants of the city, enabled them to live in a style very similar to that of the gentry in England. They tended to look upon the wealth of Montreal as parvenu, and they abhorred the rising power of elected politicians.

The population of the Eastern Townships was of a very different character. The region was (and is) one of the most beautiful in Canada—approximately seven million acres of rolling, mostly arable land, cut by streams and rivers which offer abundant potential water power, and enjoying a healthy and comparatively mild climate. In 1844 the largest community in the region was Sherbrooke, with a population of 800.[3] Roughly 59 percent of the 48 thousand Townshippers had been born in Canada, 21 percent in the British Isles and the remainder in the United States,[4] but a great many of the native born were the children of immigrants from America. As yet, the French-speaking population was very small. The habitant was accustomed to seigneurial tenure and the provisions of the code civil respecting the inheritance of property, and there was as yet no provision in the region for a right of tithe for Roman Catholic parishes.

With the exception of a very few, who either brought some capital with them or possessed enough influence in Quebec to obtain a large grant of land from the Crown, these men and women had settled on virgin land. The principal occupation in the region was farming, mostly at subsistence level. In order to farm the settlers had to clear the land, but except for the lumber required for their houses and outbuildings, the trees of the forest had been mostly converted into potash, which found a ready market as fertilizer in the more settled areas. In general the immigrants from the United States had come from pioneering communities and were better prepared for life on the frontier than were those from Great Britain. They had built most of the water-driven grist mills, fulling and carding mills, and saw mills which served to meet the needs of the region, and many of the merchants to whom the settlers almost inevitably became indebted were of American origins.

Until a few years before Bishop's University was founded, dealings in land were the principal source of capital in the region, and enterprise was severely restricted by the lack of money in circulation. In 1833 a group of British capitalists incorporated themselves as the British

American Land Company (BALC) and obtained a grant from the Crown of nearly a million acres of Townships land at bargain prices against an undertaking to provide the infrastructure, in particular roads and bridges, necessary to stimulate development. Further stimulus was provided in 1836 by the establishment in Sherbrooke of a branch of the City Bank, which had been founded in Montreal in 1831 by a group of merchants, mostly of American origins and backed by American investors. By 1840 an entrepreneurial class was beginning to emerge and to challenge the agricultural interests for political influence.

Following a recommendation of the Durham Report, Upper and Lower Canada were joined in 1841 to form the Province of Canada. Though the eight members of the new Legislative Assembly who represented the Townships were now part of an English-speaking majority, this majority usually split along party lines. The French-speaking members from Lower Canada rapidly discovered that if they voted as a bloc, they held the balance of power. Dual appointments in the civil service and hyphenated ministries were the inevitable result, of which the most famous was the Baldwin-Lafontaine government. Under these conditions the Townships members could count on the support of the majority in the Assembly only if their initiatives obtained the support of all parties in Upper Canada. Unhappily, the most intense divisions among Upper Canadians during the 1840s were generated by the question of support from public funds for educational institutions which were under denominational control. The early development of Bishop's University, founded as an Anglican institution, was therefore strongly affected by the predominance of the concerns of Upper Canada in the minds of the English-speaking members of the assembly of the "united" province. Nor was local political support for an Anglican educational initiative by any means unanimous. Political allegiance was, naturally, strongly influenced by religion and by cultural ties. Many Townshippers still looked to their American cousins for religious and cultural leadership. When the termination of the mercantile system by the British government during the 1840s led to a commercial depression, strong support developed in the Townships for the proposal by a number of Montreal merchants that Canada should be annexed to the United States.

EDUCATION IN LOWER CANADA

Perhaps the most important aspect of the environment in which Bishop's University was founded was the education available to boys and young men who wished to enrol as undergraduates. The development of education at the primary and secondary levels in Lower Canada had been strongly influenced by the power of religious communities to control the curricula in the schools and by the concern of the French-speaking members of the Legislative Assembly to defend their "nation" against assimilation by the English-language culture which was increasingly dominant in North America. However, in 1840 the role of the state in secondary and post-secondary education was marginal, and the health of educational institutions at these levels depended almost entirely on the initiative and the resources of the communities concerned.

Under the French regime the supreme authority governing education in the colony had been the bishop (though the Jesuits claimed the protection of Rome). The clergy and the religious communities founded schools in which the curriculum conformed to the instructions of the bishop; and the role of the state (i.e., the king, acting through the governor and the intendant) was limited to reinforcing the authority of the bishop and providing endowments, chiefly in land, for the support of education.

Under this regime a number of parish schools—*les petites écoles*—had been established in which children were taught to read, write, and count, to memorize their catechism and "se former aux moeurs honnêtes des plus sages et vertueux chrétiens qui vivent dans le monde."[5] At the secondary level, the Jesuits had founded their college in Quebec in 1635. Its curriculum was inspired by that of the Collège de LaFlèche, one of the most famous of the French classical colleges, which numbered among its alumni François de Montmorency Laval, first Bishop of Quebec. By 1760 several feeder schools—*les écoles latines*—had been established in the environs of Quebec and at Montreal, which taught the first years of the classical curriculum. The teachers in all these schools were members of religious communities, and their aim was to educate men for the liberal professions, in particular for the priesthood and the teaching and missionary communities of the Roman Catholic Church.[6]

Following the signing of the Treaty of Paris in 1763 the officers of the French colonial government and many of the seigneurs and other leaders of the community returned to France, but the Church remained. Though the link between the civil and religious authorities had been broken, the devotion of the clergy enabled perhaps forty of the *petites écoles* to carry on until 1774 when the Quebec Act restored much of the Church's authority. When the pope disbanded the Society of Jesus in 1773, the Seminary of Quebec and the Sulpicians of Montreal founded classical colleges to replace the Collège des Jesuits.

The tradition of education which the English-speaking governing class brought with them was also a tradition of private and religious initiative. Neither in England nor in Scotland had education been considered to be a responsibility of the state. Most of the grammar schools and universities of Great Britain had been founded by private initiative, frequently with pious intention, and sometimes with endowments recovered from the dissolution of religious houses. Only a few borough councils had used public funds in support of schools.

Canada enjoyed no such heritage of English-language schools, and not many English-speaking immigrants could afford private tuition for their children. Many of them had come from New England, where primary schools were supported by taxes—at first under municipal law and after the revolution under state law. They began to petition the government for a system of state-supported schools.

However, Lower Canada was not New England. Political power was for the moment concentrated in the hands of the English-speaking population, but the great majority of the inhabitants were French-speaking Roman Catholics. That education might be dissociated from religious instruction was not at that time conceivable. Indeed the first of the instructions to governors-general, that to Murray in 1763, had combined references to religion and education in the same paragraph. As long as schools were the result of private initiative the religious divisions of the population could be accommodated, but the intervention of the state as co-ordinating authority and principal source of funds would require discussion and compromise among the several religious constituencies. Such a dialogue proved difficult to achieve.

When Jacob Mountain was consecrated first Anglican Bishop of Quebec in 1793, he immediately began to press the governor and the Executive Council for funding for schools. As a prelate of the established state religion of England, he found it natural that he should lead an initiative for the development of a system of state-supported schools in a British colony. The Roman Catholic hierarchy disagreed. They had been pleased to be allowed to retain the endowments which supported their own educational system, but they were accustomed to exercising authority and were unwilling to share that authority, in a matter as important as education, with a government whose majority owed them no allegiance. There were also a number of English-speaking Protestants who were not prepared to accept an Anglican Establishment in the colony.

Nevertheless, Mountain at first enjoyed a measure of success. The most effective spur to action proved to be "the mischiefs which may arise of sending youth for education to Foreign America, a necessity which at present certainly exists and to which I know some worthy and prudent parents reluctantly submit."[7] While Dorchester was governor general, the bishop was unable to move the government to action. In 1796 Sir Robert Milnes was appointed lieutenant governor of Lower Canada; he proved willing to submit a proposal for a state-supported system of elementary schools to the Executive Council. With their approval he consulted the colonial secretary in London. The minister gave the proposal a very favourable reception, and suggested to the governor general that income from Crown lands might be employed in support of the scheme. This financial carrot proved sufficient to enlist the support of the primarily French-speaking Legislative Assembly. In 1801 an act establishing the Royal Institution for the Advancement of Learning was passed and given royal assent.

The new Royal Institution was to control all state-assisted education. Though it was technically separate from the government, the governor was to appoint all its members, and he had to give his assent to all its acts—specifically, to the nomination of schoolmasters and the location of schools. From the administrative point of view the school system thus established was a highly centralized one, but the act was permissive rather than prescriptive. No school was to be placed in a parish unless a majority of the parishioners requested it. School properties were to be provided by local initiative and maintained by local assessment. What the schools were to teach was not stated, nor was any provision made concerning the language of instruction or religion. Furthermore, all private schools and all schools run by religious orders were exempt from control by the Royal Institution. This provision gave the Catholic majority liberty to continue as before if they wished to do so.

Citing Bishop Mountain's hope "that the inhabitants might be persuaded by degrees to embrace the Protestant religion"[8] and the expectation cherished by some members of the Executive Council that the schools would provide means to anglicize French-speaking Canadians, the nationalist schools of French-Canadian historians have attacked the scheme as one designed to assimilate the *habitants*. However, in the discussion and debates which preceded the passing of the bill, education and not anglicization had become its purpose.[9] In practice it proved possible for French-speaking parishes to appoint French-speaking teachers, for the Roman Catholic curé to act as Visitor (an official whose duty it is periodically to inspect the workings of an educational institution), and for the Roman Catholic religion to be taught and practised. As Louis-Philippe Audet noted in his study of the history of education in Quebec, "Il nous semble, en effet, que si les chefs religieux et civils du Bas-Canada avaient accepté cette loi et décidé de l'utiliser comme nos parlementaires le firent pour le gouvernement responsable, ils auraient tôt ou tard amené les choses au même point de contrôle démocratique et auraient réussi à obtenir un système d'écoles gratuites bien avant l'époque où ils les obtinrent en réalité."[10]

As it was, by 1825 elementary schools under the aegis of the Royal Institution had been established in 82 communities, of which 6 were in the Eastern Townships. However, the Roman Catholic hierarchy, led by bishops Plessis and Panet, steadfastly refused to lend their imprimatur to the work of an institution whose titular head was the Anglican Bishop of Quebec and a majority of whose governing body was Protestant and English speaking. In truth the hierarchy held a very particular view of the goals of mass education. The Protestant position, that the individual Christian's understanding of the Bible must be the guiding light of his or her religion, required being able to read. The Roman Catholic position on the other hand was that the Church had unique authority to interpret the Bible for the faithful. Literacy was therefore not necessary for everyone, and it might, if it led to the reading of books not acceptable to orthodoxy, even place the souls of the faithful in danger. These positions were fundamentally incompatible, and they led inevitably to two distinct publicly financed systems of schools.

In 1829, after prolonged negotiation involving the Royal Institution, Governor-General Lord Dalhousie and Bishop Panet, a bill to accommodate this incompatibility was presented in the Legislative Assembly by Vallières de St Réal. He was generally regarded as the most brilliant and scholarly lawyer in Lower Canada. Sometime speaker of the Assembly and trustee of the Royal Institution, he had played an active, independent, and generally moderating role in the politics of the period, in opposition to Louis-Joseph Papineau. As a young man Bishop Plessis had been his tutor, and he had the confidence of Bishop Panet. The bill provided for two committees, one Roman Catholic and one Protestant, for equal numbers of Catholic and Protestant members, and that the Anglican and Roman Catholic bishops should alternate as president of the Royal Institution. Inexplicably,[11] after the bill received second reading, Vallières changed his mind and moved to defer further consideration of it until the next session.

This cleared the way for those who wished to substitute the Legislative Assembly for the churches as the authority responsible for elementary education. This party achieved their goal during the same session by persuading the Assembly to pass the Syndics Act, which provided grants from the provincial treasury to establish elementary schools. Since these grants, in particular those for the payment of school masters, were more generous than the terms offered by the Royal Institution, the schools established by the Institution began to transfer their allegiance. During the next five years the Institution disappeared as an instrument of popular education, and the number of schools under the Assembly rose to some 1500, providing Lower Canada with a publicly financed school system.[12]

These new schools were under the management of elected trustees. Though after 1830 the curé of the parish was eligible for election, the Assembly schools escaped direct episcopal authority, and they were never accepted as better than a "*pis-aller*" by the Roman Catholic hierarchy. Nevertheless, so homogeneous were the French-speaking majority in matters of religion that in practice the Church retained complete control over the curriculum in the French-language schools. But where the language of instruction was English the impossibility of reconciling the doctrines of the several Protestant denominations made the Assembly less and less willing to subsidize avowedly denominational schools, and the teaching of religious doctrine ceased to be a primary function of the English-language school system.

By 1840 then almost all the English-speaking children of school age in the counties of Sherbrooke and Stanstead had access to elementary level education subsidized by the government—though the level of education offered and the competence of the teachers varied widely. Publicly financed education was supervised by a Department of Public Instruction, under a superintendent who was in theory not subject to political influence. However, under the hyphenated ministries which resulted from the Act of Union of 1841, one deputy superintendent of public instruction was appointed for Upper Canada and one for Lower Canada. Naturally, the first incumbent in Canada East was French-speaking, the founder of Collège l'Assomption, Jean Baptiste Meilleur. Furthermore, the governor-general now acted on the advice of his Canadian ministers, and the English-speaking minority could no longer count on sympathetic treatment of its educational institutions by the government. In the long run this was a healthy development, since it forced the English-speaking community to assume direct responsibility for its schools and universities, but the medicine was difficult to swallow, especially for the Tory constituency from which most of the supporters of Bishop's were drawn.

Education at the secondary level had suffered from the conflict between the Legislative Assembly and the Executive prior to the rebellions of 1837 and 1838. After the Assembly had obtained control in 1832 of the revenue from the Jesuit Estates, it cut off the grants which had been made from that source to support the grammar schools in Quebec and Montreal directed by the Royal Institution. Unlike the situation in Upper Canada and the Maritimes, no endowment in land had been provided in Lower Canada for non-Roman Catholic secondary education. In consequence the grammar school in Quebec had closed by 1840, and that in Montreal was struggling. In the Townships there was the Sherbrooke Academy, founded in 1827 by the Reverend W. Brown, to which John Sanborn, newly graduated from Dartmouth College, went as principal in 1842. A "seminary" at the secondary level had been founded in Stanstead in 1829 with some financial help from the second Anglican Bishop of Quebec, C.J. Stewart. Originally staffed from Scotland, it developed a strong Wesleyan connection. In 1836 Lucius Doolittle, the Anglican missionary to Lennoxville, had founded his grammar school there and installed a graduate of Cambridge University as its first master. All the major educational influences in the English-speaking community were therefore represented, but though these schools were receiving small grants from the government, none of them could be said to be firmly established.

Hopes for collegiate education in the English language had rested for over 25 years on the attempt by the Royal Institution to give effect to the will of James McGill. In 1813 he had left a bequest of £10,000 and an estate on the slopes of Mont Royal to enable the Royal Institution to found a university or college. A royal charter had been obtained in 1821, which stated that McGill "College shall be deemed and taken to be a University capable of conferring bachelor's, master's and doctor's degrees in the several Arts and Faculties."[13] However, as McGill's historian has remarked, the intervening years had been

> years of much litigation but little progress. The Burnside estate remained a farm, poorly cared for, as land which suffers from absentee landlords so often is. It belonged legally to the Royal Institution, which had its corporate existence several days' difficult journey away in Quebec City. The governors of the College were a group of men so important in their various offices that it was almost impossible that they should ever all be brought together in one place to effect the college's business.[14]

In 1840 buildings to house the Faculty of Arts were at last under construction, but it was not until September 1843 that the first three students matriculated and the Faculty* was brought into being.

---

* In the text, "Faculty" refers to a faculty of a university, "faculty" to the body of teachers. Similarly, "Classics" indicates a department or faculty of a university, "classics" a subject.

CHAPTER ONE

THE FOUNDERS

Bishop's University owes its foundation chiefly to the energy and initiative of two remarkable men, G.J. Mountain, third Anglican Bishop of Quebec, and Lucius Doolittle, missionary priest to Sherbrooke and Lennoxville under the auspices of the Society for the Propagation of the Gospel in Foreign Parts (SPG).

BISHOP MOUNTAIN

George Jehoshaphat Mountain was the son of Bishop Jacob Mountain. The family was descended from Huguenots who had settled in Norwich, England, where George Mountain was born in 1789. He travelled to Quebec with his family at the time of his father's appointment in 1793, and there he spent what seems to have been a happy and stimulating boyhood. At the age of 15 he was sent back to England to study for entrance into Trinity College, Cambridge, from which he was graduated B.A. in 1810. The next year he returned to Quebec to prepare for Anglican orders. He was ordained priest in Quebec Cathedral in 1814, and married Mary Hume Thomson, daughter of a long-established Quebec family. He devoted the rest of his long life to ministering to the spiritual needs of Anglican Canadians as Rector of Fredericton, Rector of the Parish of Quebec, Archdeacon of Lower Canada, and from 1836 bishop of a diocese which for many years had stretched from the Gaspé coast westward sixteen hundred miles to the Red River settlement. As president of the Royal Institution and first principal of McGill College he also found time to develop the educational initiatives of his father.

Mountain's portrait hints at a delicate constitution, and he fell gravely ill several times during his ministry. Nevertheless he visited every mission in his diocese at least once, and many annually, during his 27-year tenure. His journals give a vivid account of the difficulties of transport and the hardships of the life of a settler at that time. As well as covering great distances by sail, canoe, sleigh, on horseback, and on foot during his visitations, he exercised a fearless personal ministry to the sick during the terrible epidemics of cholera in Quebec in 1832 and of "ship fever" among the immigrants at the quarantine station on Grosse Isle in 1847.

His correspondence shows Mountain to have been a devout and moderate churchman who held that religion must appeal to the intellect as well as to the emotions. He believed that the United Church of England and Ireland had managed to successfully combine catholic order and evangelical truth, and he deprecated what he regarded as constituencies within the church—Tractarians and evangelicals—perhaps because they tended to challenge episcopal authority! His relations with his French-speaking opposite numbers in the Roman Catholic church appear to have been ones of mutual respect. Apart from providing French-speaking clergy for immigrants from the Channel Islands and one or two small Protestant congregations in the diocese which asked for his protection, he made no effort to proselytize the French-language community. When he died, a writer in the French-language newspaper of Quebec noted: "Le nombre de citoyens de toutes les classes et de toutes les croyances qui assistaient aux funérailles était immense. Le Lord Bishop Mountain avait conquis par sa bienveillance, sa charité et ses nombreuses vertus sociales et religieuses le respect et l'estime de tous."[1]

Mountain was nevertheless a staunch defender of the primacy of the Church of England in ministering to the religious and educational needs of the non-Roman Catholic population of the colony. Though as first principal of McGill College he had opposed religious tests for members of faculty and undergraduates, he found it natural that his church should retain ultimate authority over the institution. In politics he was an old-fashioned Tory, believing in an ordered society in which people should labour cheerfully in the stations to which it should please God to call them. He was generally charitable in his judgments of people, but he had little sympathy with the aggressively egalitarian democracy which was being promoted by many members of the Reform Party. For him, the voice of the people was not the voice of God. That Governor-General

George Jehoshaphat Mountain, ca.1845

Lord Elgin should appoint, and invariably act on the advice of, a Reform government Mountain felt to be an act of betrayal, and he found it indefensible that a Legislative Assembly which continued to recognize the rights of the Roman Catholic clergy to their tithes and endowments should devote so much time and energy to stripping the Church of England of its right to the income from the Clergy Reserves.

THE MISSIONARY CHURCH

Though considerable land, the so-called Clergy Reserves, had been set aside in the Canadian colony to provide an endowment to support a Protestant clergy, the rate of settlement in those areas of Lower Canada where land could be held freehold had been so slow that these properties were generating no revenue. At the time of Mountain's consecration as bishop stipends from the government for the Anglican clergy in Lower Canada were limited to the bishop, the Parish of Quebec, the Anglican rectors of Montreal and Three Rivers, and to the lifelong tenures of the incumbents. All other congregations in the diocese were ministered to by some 40 missionaries, most sent out from England under the auspices of the Society for the Propagation of the Gospel in Foreign Parts (SPG), and almost all supported from a grant made by the society to the bishop.

The SPG had been founded in 1701 as a corporation of clergy and laymen of the Church of England working to provide missionary clergy for the American colonies. When the American Episcopal Church broke off into independent life in 1783, Canada became the principal focus of the society's activities. The first Anglican mission in the Townships had been established in 1808 in St Armand by Charles James Stewart while he was working as an SPG missionary.

During the first quarter of the nineteenth century a large proportion of the society's funds had come from the British government. In 1833, as a result of a vigorous campaign by Dissenter members of Parliament, this support was terminated. When Bishop Mountain sought the support of the society for Bishop's College, its funds came entirely from individual subscriptions and collections in some 1,700 parishes of the Church in England.[2] By 1840 then, though the bishop still claimed the support of the British and Canadian governments for the Church of England in Canada, the missionary church in fact owed very little to either government. Unlike the Diocese of Toronto the Diocese of Quebec was receiving no income from the Clergy Reserve funds. It was not until 1845 that a surplus from the income received by the provincial treasurer from the Reserves was made available to the diocese, permitting the appointment of ten additional missionaries. Furthermore, when the Clergy Reserves were finally secularized by the Legislative Assembly in 1855, Lower Canada received only £15 thousand by commutation of the life interest of clergy dependent upon the Reserves fund, as compared with £222,620 recovered by Upper Canada.[3]

To offer one's services as a missionary in the wilds of Lower Canada required truly remarkable faith and zeal. As the population of the diocese increased under the pressure of immigration from Britain, the supply of ordained clergy from England began to fail, and the bishop had to find means for the training of young aspirants in Canada. It was also becoming evident that if the Anglican Church was to take root in Canada, it must generate a Canadian clergy. In response to this need, Mountain wrote the SPG in November 1840 to enlist their support for a project to convert the parsonage house at Three Rivers, which had been built as a small Recollet monastery, into a theological college. The rector, the Reverend S.S. Wood, was a graduate of Cambridge, and the bishop judged that he and one other clergyman would be able to provide adequate instruction for the small number of candidates for ordination.

LUCIUS DOOLITTLE

News of this plan rapidly reached Lucius Doolittle in Lennoxville. Born in Vermont in 1800, Doolittle had moved to the Townships as a youth and engaged in business in Hatley, a few miles south of Lennoxville, with an uncle. At the age of 18 he became acquainted with the Reverend Charles James Stewart, under whose influence he began to prepare for ordination. Before being admitted to studies in theology, candidates were required to demonstrate an ability to translate texts from the original Latin and Greek—for example, the works of the Fathers of the Church and the Epistles of the New Testament. In 1824 Doolittle matriculated at the University of Vermont, financing his studies during the next three years by teaching intermittently at the school supported by the Royal Institution at Hatley. In 1827 he was nominated for an SPG studentship, and left the University of Vermont without taking a degree to read theology with the Reverend Thomas Johnson, the missionary at Hatley. The next year he was ordained by C.J. Stewart, who had become second Bishop of Quebec. After four years' work at the mission of Chaleur Bay, during which his health was seriously affected, he was posted back to the Townships, where he served as a missionary to Lennoxville for the rest of his working life.

The first principal of Bishop's College, Jasper Nicolls, described

Doolittle as "my Father Confessor in all matters."[4] He was also a many-talented entrepreneur, about whose activities frustratingly little is known. He was an excellent man of business, acting as agent for the University of Vermont and for Bishop Stewart among other clients in the dealings in land which were their principal source of income at the time. With the capital thus generated Stewart was able to help his pioneer congregations to build churches and schools. Though his income from the church never exceeded the meagre stipend of a missionary, Doolittle was comfortably established in Lennoxville by 1840, and he was to be a generous benefactor of the college, leaving on his death in 1862 an endowment of £300 currency a year for bursaries for divinity students.[5]

Among Doolittle's achievements had been the establishment in 1836 of a grammar school for boys in Lennoxville. The school was initially housed in temporary quarters immediately adjacent to the parsonage, but from the beginning Doolittle meant to provide instruction to university entrance level, and the first schoolmaster was a Cambridge graduate, William Willis. In 1839 the school received a grant of £100 from the commission for the Promotion of Education, and his report to them for the 1839–40 school year reported a teaching staff of three for 23 pupils.[6] In 1841 he succeeded in recruiting, as master of the school, Edward Chapman, a graduate of Cambridge who had been teaching at the High School of Quebec. Enrolment increased, and the next year, to provide boarding facilities and increased classroom space, Doolittle leased a large house on the south-east corner of the village square which belonged to Thomas Austin. Austin was a considerable landowner, who had been a member of the special council which governed Lower Canada for two and a half years following the rebellion of 1838.

THE SITE

When Lucius Doolittle learned of the plan to establish a college at Three Rivers, he immediately set about persuading the bishop to expand the scope of the project to include a faculty of arts and to move the site of the institution to the Eastern Townships.

Though still isolated from the main lines of communication in Lower Canada, the Townships were nevertheless the seat of a largely English-speaking and Protestant population, greater than that of Montreal and Quebec combined, which was as yet provided with only rudimentary educational institutions. The bishop was persuaded that

> A College which, although its primary feature is the training of aspirants to the Ministry, comprehends a general course of academical instruction in preparation for any other profession in life, with

Lucius Doolittle, ca.1850

a school engrafted upon it, affording both classical and commercial education—all with the best prospects of efficiency and yet upon the most moderate scale of expense—may well be expected to retain within the Province a number of youths belonging to respectable families, who would otherwise be sent to form their minds and principles among our republican neighbours [and thus to] form a nucleus for the creation of an important influence over the moral, political and religious character of the rising population.[7]

Doolittle and his supporters also hoped that the college would persuade more of the immigrants pouring through Quebec to settle in the Townships.

Although Mountain recognized that the St Lawrence River valley with its numerous and tenaciously French-speaking and Roman Catholic population was not very fruitful terrain for an Anglican college, Three Rivers had possessed one important advantage in that a building with adjacent chapel sufficient to the needs of the theological students was available and could be adapted at small cost. Doolittle and the Townshippers countered by mounting a campaign for subscriptions of £25 currency, each of which would entitle the subscriber to nominate one student for four years free tuition at either the school or college level. Since a skilled tradesman earned five shillings a day,[8] £25 was a very considerable sum. Nevertheless, they obtained a hundred pledges, nearly all from the residents of the region. The list of subscribers included men from many walks of life and from every interest in the community. Conspicuously missing from the list was Alexander Tilloch Galt, who was about to become commissioner of the British American Land Company. It is difficult to understand why one whose career was so closely linked to the development of the region should have done little for the college, either at the time or later on when he was an influential minister in the government.[9]

The promoters of a site in the Townships for the college now felt confident that they could offer the bishop a building adequate to the needs of the expanded project advocated by Doolittle. However, the exact location of the site remained in dispute. Several of the more prominent members of the group lived in Sherbrooke, and they hoped that the bishop would choose a site in that town. Some owned land there, which would increase in value as the community developed. It was also confidently expected that the BALC, which had large holdings in the town, would donate to the college a "conspicuous and commanding site" of 50 acres on the east bank of the St Francis River, opposite the town.[10] Doolittle, on the other hand, was determined that the college should be established in Lennoxville.

With a population of over three thousand by the end of the decade, Sherbrooke was on the verge of becoming the commercial and industrial centre of the region. The establishment of the City Bank branch and the head office of the Sherbrooke and Stanstead Mutual Fire Insurance Company had provided much needed sources of capital. Under A.T. Galt's energetic promotion numerous factories were being built to exploit the abundant water power available from the falls on the Magog River. Galt and several other local entrepreneurs were vigorously promoting the building of a railway from Montreal to Portland, Maine, which would provide the region's producers with means to transport their products rapidly to the St Lawrence and to an ice-free port on the Atlantic ocean. The town obviously had a promising future. Lennoxville, on the other hand, was a peaceful village three miles upstream from Sherbrooke with no particular ambitions for development, but several members of the group felt that the tranquillity and beauty of its setting were better adapted to the needs of an academic institution.

Bishop Mountain was very ill during much of the winter of 1841–42, so he appointed a committee of residents of Quebec City (some of whom also owned land in the Townships) to study the matter and make recommendations to him. The committee in turn commissioned Mr Willoughby, a clergyman from Montreal, to visit the proposed sites and report on their respective advantages and disadvantages. He strongly recommended Sherbrooke. After prolonged and heated discussion the committee finally decided in favour of Sherbrooke.[11] However, the bishop had not sufficiently recovered to be able to act, and in the meantime it became evident that the BALC was not going to donate a site in Sherbrooke. In March 1842 Lt Col William Morris, one of the Lennoxville party, made the decisive move by purchasing 40 acres at the junction of the St Francis and Massawippi rivers. These he subsequently transferred to the bishop and his successors "for ever, upon trust ... for the creation, establishment, maintenance and support, and for the exclusive use and benefit, of a College in connection with the Established Church of England and under the superintendence, direction and control of the Bishop ... this done and passed at the residence of the Reverend Lucius Doolittle."[12] This land forms the core of the present university campus.

THE PROSPECTUS

Doolittle had invited the Bishop to meet a number of the Townshippers "at the Lennoxville grammar school" earlier in the winter. At this and subsequent meetings, a prospectus was drawn up for the Diocesan College of Canada East, to be circulated to prospective supporters.

In this prospectus the essential character of the institution was clearly stated. Though it was to be only "in part of a theological character," the first two members of the faculty, including a principal, were to be "clergymen of the Church of England in full Orders, and graduates of some university of repute in the British Dominions," and the Bishop was to retain ultimate authority over the institution's development. A grammar school was to be attached to the college, and "every care to be taken to establish the internal economy of the College and School upon such a plan and system as will be calculated to ensure correct, prudent and moderate habits among the students." A chapel was to be built "in which morning and evening prayers will be daily read, and the attendance of pupils and students will then be required. No exclusive character, however, will attach to the Institution as respects the religious profession of those who shall be admitted for their course of study." Attendance at public worship (on Sundays) was to be governed by instructions from parents.[13]

His service as president of the Royal Institution and first principal of McGill had given Bishop Mountain first-hand knowledge of the difficult gestation of that institution and of the antipathy of influential Montrealers to initiatives from Quebec. He was therefore at some pains to mollify them. In a circular sent out in 1842 he wrote, "The College, in the first instance, will be on a very limited scale; and although it is to be expected (as it is also to be desired) that it will grow with the growth, and strengthen with the strength of the country, no apprehension need be entertained of its interfering with the interests of the grander institution [McGill] in the populous, wealthy and comparatively ancient city of Montreal."[14]

THE ACT OF 1843

Bishop Mountain's project now possessed land and reasonable prospects of a building. The next step was to provide it with a corporation recognized in law (see 7 Vict., Chap. 49, Appendix One). The bill submitted to the Legislative Assembly in Kingston for this purpose sought to establish a governing body composed of trustees and the College Council, all of whose members were appointed by the bishop and none of whose decisions was final until approved by the bishop. One of the earliest supporters of the project had been Edward Hale, grandson of one of Wolfe's senior officers at the Plains of Abraham and son of the honourable John Hale of Quebec, who had been a member of both the Executive and Legislative Councils of Lower Canada. After five years as private secretary to his uncle, Lord Amherst, then Governor-General of India, Edward Hale had returned to Canada and settled in the Townships, becoming a considerable farmer, landholder and entrepreneur. In 1839 he had been appointed a member of the Special Council. When elections for the first Legislative Assembly of the newly united Province of Canada were held in 1841, he stood for the Sherbrooke County constituency and was elected. It was therefore to him that Bishop Mountain confided the task of piloting the bill through the legislature.

This he did with exemplary diligence and patience. Once it was clear that he was willing to cede the right to grant degrees (which was at the time the subject of intense political debate in Upper Canada), there was no opposition in principle to the bill in the House, but in the manner of deliberative assemblies the members haggled interminably over the name of the college. The petition had been presented in the name of "The Diocesan College of Canada East." By the time it had cleared the first committee, the projected institution had become "The Diocesan College of the Protestant Episcopal Diocese of Quebec." Returned to the House, the bill was held up again by the objections of a member who was known to be at odds with the bishop. Almost despairing, and "being a little quizzed about my Illegitimate Bill,"[15] Hale managed to have the bill referred to a special committee, where common sense at last prevailed. The committee reported in favour of the bill and proposed the name "Bishop's College"—thereby earning the gratitude of generations of graduates! The bill was duly passed by the Assembly and it received the royal assent on 9 December 1843, the official birthday of the college.

Under the presidency of the bishop, the college was to be governed by two bodies, the trustees, who were to be responsible for the financial affairs of the institution, and the College Council, in which was invested the responsibility for the immediate internal government of the college. The trustees were also assigned a watching brief over "matters relating to doctrine, morals, good order or discipline which require correction," with the responsibility of notifying the Visitor (the bishop) so that he might "investigate the truth of any charge thus brought to his notice."[16]

The first trustees were the Honourable A.W. Cochran, Ezekiel Elliott, the Honourable Edward Hale, the Reverend Christopher Jackson, Lt Col William Morris, the Reverend Charles P. Reid, the Reverend George Slack, and Hollis Smith. Cochran was a resident of Quebec who had been a valued counsellor to the bishop for many years. The son of the first president of King's College, Windsor, in Nova Scotia, he was keenly interested in education and had been a member of the board of the Royal Institution since 1823 and its president from 1834 to 1837. Several times a member of the Executive Council, he had held at one time or another most of the senior positions in the civil service in

Edward Hale, ca.1870

Quebec, and his knowledge of the workings of the bureaucracy was invaluable. It is hardly surprising then that when Edward Hale wrote to the bishop to suggest that the trustees of Bishop's College might be nominated by some form of election, it was Cochran who replied that "it has always appeared to me safer and better for the Church, and for the Institution as holding an important connection with the Church, that it should be as much as possible in deed as well as in name a Bishop's College."[17] Elliott was a successful farmer who had made a generous donation of land to the college. Hollis Smith was a local entrepreneur who became an associate of Galt. Born in the United States and raised a Baptist in Hatley township, he had by 1843 become an Anglican and been fully integrated in the British-American Conservative Party in the Townships. The three clergymen were those among his flock in whose financial acumen the bishop had the most confidence, and Jackson and Reid had been members of the original building committee. The College Council will be introduced later.

THE FIRST BUILDING

In the meantime the bishop had been soliciting support for the expanded project from the SPG and the Society for Promoting Christian Knowledge (SPCK) in England. One of the provisions of the prospectus, that "no exclusive character will attach to the Institution as it respects the religious profession of those who shall be admitted,"[18] proved unpalatable to the board of the SPCK. The bishop dispatched an emissary, the Reverend H.D. Sewell, to London to plead differences between the Eastern Townships of Lower Canada and England which made a degree of ecumenical co-operation essential to the success of the venture. As the bishop had written, "When the project was first put forward, there were many persons calling themselves dissenters who avowed their belief that no other body than the Church could carry it through, and who therefore cordially agreed to give their support upon terms which left them no voice whatever in the control and management of the Institution and no privilege except that of the education of their youth."[19] In the event, each of the societies contributed £1 thousand to the endowment, and the SPG promised another £300 annually for bursaries for theological students. Neither society would, however, agree to provide annual grants for faculty salaries.

The delay in obtaining financial support from England had caused some of the subscribers to decline to pay their instalments; but now the bishop felt able to sanction the beginning of building operations. He had been keen to have a building of some dignity in Collegiate Gothic, built of brick but with stone sills and trim. The general plan had been drawn up by J.G. Howard, a prominent architect in Toronto, and the details had been filled in by a local draftsman. The plan foresaw accommodation for 40 students, with a hall or refectory, lecture rooms, and apartments for two professors. The bishop was also determined to add a chapel as soon as funds could be raised.

To complete such a building in Lennoxville—two days or more by wagon from Port St Francis where the St Francis joined the St Lawrence over rudimentary roads which were often impassable in the spring and summer—made severe demands on the skill and enterprise of local tradesmen and industry. Stone for the foundation was quarried on the college land, and the bricks were manufactured locally. Sawn lumber was, of course, a principal source of revenue for local landowners. That the building took three years to complete was due not to shortage of materials or labour but to shortage of funds. The commercial depression of 1843 had caused a number of bankruptcies in the Townships. Many of the subscribers were slow to redeem their pledges, and the bishop feared that if he was too forthcoming with money from the societies' grants, some of them would conclude that their contributions were no longer needed. The first sod was turned during the summer of 1843, but it was not until 18 September 1844 that the bishop was able to lay the cornerstone, in the presence of as many of the trustees and local clergy as could be mustered for the occasion.[20]

In 1843 the building committee had already foreseen the possibility that it might be necessary to house the undergraduates temporarily in the Austin house. Within a year Thomas Austin was declared bankrupt, and Lucius Doolittle was able to buy the house on very favourable terms. When the construction of the college building was further delayed, the trustees, who by this time had accepted responsibility for the grammar school, decided to purchase the house from Lucius Doolittle on equally favourable terms. However, enrolment in the school continued to increase, and in the end, the principal and his ten pioneering students were housed, during the whole of the 1845–46 academic year, in makeshift quarters in a commercial building across College Street from the school.

In May 1845 Doolittle, who was on the point of sailing for England to recover his health, wrote to Edward Hale to report that the contracts let to date, to a total of nearly £1,428, would embrace only the walls, carpentry and joiner work. The subscriptions actually received amounted to just over £448, and it had been necessary to obtain a loan from the City Bank to meet the schedule of payments on the contracts.[21] During the next two years, the redemption rate of pledges increased; but in October

1847 the trustees were forced to recognize that £650 currency (corresponding to 26 of the original 100 pledges) would have to be assumed as a debt by the college. A further loan of £500 had to be obtained to pay for furniture, outbuildings and some clearing of the college property.[22]

FACULTY SALARIES — THE HARROLD BENEFACTION

There remained the problem of finding money with which to pay the faculty. Mountain's letters to the societies had emphasized that it was unlikely that grants could be obtained from a Legislative Assembly in which the majority of non-Roman Catholic members were strongly opposed to state support for denominational colleges. He sought the agreement of the SPG to change the designation of their annual £300 grant from bursaries for theological students to maintaining a principal or professor in the college. In return the college would provide free tuition, board, and lodging to the theological students. This would have enabled Mountain to offer a secure income to a prospective principal instead of one dependent upon enrolment and the prompt payment of students' bills. However, the most he could obtain from the society was permission to use that portion of the £300 which would be freed by the ordination of two of the students, about £100, toward salaries, and the society warned that they would not fund any faculty stipend for longer than three years from the date of the opening of the college.[23]

In these desperate circumstances it was with a very full heart that the bishop was able to report in April 1845 to the secretary of the society, Mr Hawkins (who had been a good friend to the venture), that "it has pleased God to put it into the heart of a very old friend of my father's, still living in England, to devise liberal things out of his liberal soul for the benefit of this Diocese."[24] The friend was Thomas Churchman Harrold, a medical man who was also a considerable farmer and landholder in the counties of Essex and Suffolk, and he placed at Mountain's free discretion the sum of £6,000. Mountain reserved £400 of this donation for the erection of a college chapel and allotted the rest to the endowment of Bishop's College.

Harrold is yet another source of frustration to the historian. A lifelong subscriber to the funds of the SPG and a generous benefactor of the society's works, he insisted on anonymity, refusing even the bishop's repeated requests that he allow his portrait to be painted and to hang in the college hall. The church adjacent to his seat at Little Horkesley in Essex was bombed during World War II, and the Essex County archives contain only a very scanty correspondence, which nevertheless suggests that he was a good steward of his resources.

The total assets of Bishop's College now amounted to some £10 thousand currency, land to the value of at least £500, a large house in Lennoxville assigned to the grammar school, and a partly finished college building which it was expected to complete using the balance due on the subscribers' pledges. This stands comparison with the £10 thousand in funds and perhaps £5 thousand in land left by James McGill to the college which bore his name—though the McGill land would become very much more valuable, and the financial resources of Montreal would greatly exceed those of the Eastern Townships.

THE FIRST PRINCIPAL

The bishop now felt able to negotiate seriously with prospective principals. He believed that "in the practical exhibition of Christian graces, no less than in sound scholarship and real elegance of classical attainments he (S.S. Wood) is not surpassed by any individual in the country."[25] To him moreover Mountain had already sent several prospective ordinands for their theological instruction. However, Wood had declined to consider the possibility of moving to Lennoxville. In 1835 he had also declined an offer of the principalship at McGill. Though Mountain had had other men in mind he had for some time been trying to interest his nephew, Jasper Hume Nicolls, in the post. Nicolls, the son of Major General Gustavus Nicolls and Heriot Thomson, had grown up in Quebec, where his father had been officer commanding the Royal Engineers. Sent to England to complete his education he had been graduated B.A. from Oriel College, Oxford, in 1840, was awarded a Michell Fellowship at Queen's (Oxford) in 1843 and ordained in 1845. Though John Henry Newman had been a fellow and tutor of Oriel during his undergraduate years, Nicolls' churchmanship had not been sufficiently influenced by the Tractarians to alarm the bishop, and he now offered his nephew the post of principal, at a salary of £300 a year, guaranteed by the income from the Harrold benefaction.

Jasper Nicolls knew the country he was being invited to, and he was fully aware of the magnitude of the task which would await him, but the only consideration which seems to have caused him to hesitate was the proposal to admit students who were not members of the Church of England.[26] Church privileges, in particular the religious tests imposed on prospective undergraduates at Oxford and Cambridge, were under heavy attack by the Whigs and Dissenters in Parliament, and Nicolls seems to have felt that it was not a time to yield on principles. However, the bishop's report of the support for the college from Townshippers of all religious persuasions and the opportunity afforded to mould the character of a developing community persuaded him.

The bishop wrote:

The whole concern, you see, will be to a College at Oxford or Cambridge what a £100 mission in the woods of Canada, with a wooden church standing incomplete, though used for Service, is to a snug English rectory with trim parsonage-house and its lawn and shrubbery overhung by the Gothic tower of its venerable temple. The inducement, as I am still anxious to keep before you, is that the first Principal may be the instrument in the hands of God of laying a deep and firm foundation for lasting good.[27].

Mountain had not misjudged the appeal which that opportunity would have for his nephew. Jasper Nicolls accepted the challenge.

CHAPTER TWO

PRINCIPAL NICOLLS: THE YEARS OF HOPE

Jasper Nicolls arrived in Quebec in August 1845, two months before his twenty-seventh birthday. After a thorough briefing by the bishop, and having renewed his acquaintance with many of the friends of his youth, he set out for Lennoxville, travelling by steamboat to Port St Francis and thence by stage coach to Sherbrooke.

FIRST IMPRESSIONS

At Lennoxville Nicolls found his college housed in the least unsuitable building which the trustees had been able to find (on the site of the present Roman Catholic church). Henry Roe, one of the first students, described the quarters in which the principal greeted his flock at the beginning of October:

> It was a curious rambling old place ... Mr Cushing's country store occupied the [south west] corner of the ground floor.
> Immediately to the right of the shop portion, facing the road to Sherbrooke, a door admitted you to the College apartments, opening into a room which served as our Common Room where we usually sat and studied together. Behind this room ... was our Dining Hall, sufficiently large, which also served as our Chapel. Out

of this room, at the south end, you passed by two steps up into
Mr. Nicolls' room ... a room looked upon us as sacred, into which
not one of us, I think, was ever admitted. Out of the north end
of the Dining Hall you passed into the kitchen. The bedrooms of
the students were upstairs, all of them small, the two or three
which were larger being cut into two cubicles each with a temporary
board partition running up some six or seven feet, with a piece
of hanging drugget for a door. One such cubicle was, I remember,
assigned to me, reasonably enough, as I was a mere boy ... and
all the rest of the students were grown men.[1]

The first students, ten in number, were a very mixed group. Charles Middleton, a young Englishman who had come out with Jasper Nicolls to prepare himself for ordination, was lying ill with typhoid fever when Roe arrived, and died shortly after the beginning of term. Charles Forest and Isaac Hellmuth had almost completed their preparation for ordination, Forest with S.S. Wood at Three Rivers, and Hellmuth in England and then with Bethune at Cobourg. Both were ordained at the end of their first year at Lennoxville. Thomas Ainslie Young and James Fulton had come from Quebec, Young after studying with S.S. Wood, Fulton after establishing himself as a druggist in that city. John Kemp and Henry Burrage were younger men, Kemp a brilliant scholar. Roe had matriculated at the age of fourteen as one of the first undergraduates of the McGill College Faculty of Arts. The loyalty of his guardians to Bishop Mountain appears to have prevailed over his personal preference in deciding that he should transfer to Bishop's. Two other members of the first class, Thomas Shaw Chapman and Frederick Robinson, were Townshippers who had been students at Lucius Doolittle's grammar school. They boarded in the village and went to the college for lectures and tutorials. All of the first matriculants were candidates for ordination.

In his memoir Henry Roe recalled the principal's "fresh complexion, rosy cheeks and general youthful appearance. Added to this was an air of shyness, almost amounting to bashfulness"—a reserve perhaps not surprising, considering the very close quarters in which he would have to live with his students. On closer acquaintance, Roe found him to be an uncommonly competent, patient, and devoted teacher and a gentle and transparently good man—from whom, according to another of the early matriculants, the less attractive opinions of the students were "studiously kept, from the very laudable fear of saying anything which might cause [him] pain."[2] Though generally light-hearted in his converse with students—his portrait, which suggests a capacity for observing the follies of academic life with amusement, has been a source of comfort for more

Jasper Hume Nicolls, ca.1850

than one of his successors—he was deeply religious, and uncompromising in the standards of behaviour which he set for himself, for his colleagues, and for the students. Like the bishop, he believed in an ordered society, and that "manners makyth man." He was repelled by the aggressively egalitarian democracy of the republic to the south, and he deplored the influence it had on politics in Canada. In a letter to his wife, describing a dinner at Lord Elgin's to which he had been invited, he referred cheerfully to one of the most powerful men in the Legislative Assembly and his wife as "a pair of cads."[3] It is not surprising that he enjoyed little success in soliciting grants from the government!

THE FACULTY

Nicolls' task of educating his somewhat heterogeneous flock was further complicated by the lack of endowment for faculty salaries and by the decision of Corporation in 1845 to assume responsibility for the grammar school.

Initially the principal was the only full-time member of faculty, and during the first winter he taught both divinity and classics. Henry Hopper Miles, a graduate of Edinburgh and Aberdeen in science and medicine, had been recruited as Professor of Mathematics. However, Edward Chapman had been engaged by McGill in 1844 as tutor and appointed in 1845 as lecturer in classics, so Miles had also to assume the principal responsibility for the school. This relieved the college of part of his salary, but left him with little time for college teaching.

Miles, who was also twenty-seven years of age (he was in fact one day younger than the principal), suffered in the eyes of the bishop from not being a graduate of an English university. Nevertheless, Mountain had judged him "an intelligent, steady sort of man, of exceedingly good attainments and most useful experience in tuition."[4] In fact, of course, his studies at Edinburgh and Aberdeen had given Miles a better training in mathematics and natural and moral philosophy than he would have obtained at Oxford. He served Bishop's loyally and effectively for 22 years as professor and vice-principal and for four years as headmaster of the school.

Fortunately for Bishop's, McGill proved unable to pay Edward Chapman's salary and he returned to Lennoxville in 1846 as part-time lecturer in classics and master in the school. Henry Roe described him as "the very type and model of a gentleman in all his feelings and instincts. No one was ever more charitably minded, more willing to make allowances for faults and to forgive failures than he, but anything like meanness, or untruthfulness or dishonesty or ungentlemanly conduct

Henry Hopper Miles, 1867

he could not endure."[5] Chapman was also an exceptional athlete, which reinforced his influence on school and college life.

The first lectures in chemistry were given by S.C. Sewell, a medical man from Montreal who hoped to become a candidate for ordination. Due to the commercial depression in Montreal, he had been unable to collect many of the professional fees due him and was in debt. Bishop Mountain, only too well aware of the meagre stipends on which his clergy had to live, would not accept him as a candidate until his debts were cleared up. Bishop's was unable to pay him for his lectures, and he finally moved to Bytown and re-established himself in a thriving medical practice. He had enjoyed teaching, and in 1854 offered to return to Bishop's as Professor of Chemistry and Mineralogy for a salary considerably less than he was earning from his practice. Unfortunately, the university was still unable to fund the position. Sewell's letters suggest that he would have added a valuable leaven of pragmatism to the curriculum.

ISAAC HELLMUTH

Perhaps the most interesting and certainly the most colourful of the original members of faculty was Isaac Hellmuth.[6] Born in Poland, he had been destined by his father for the rabbinate and educated in German schools and in the University of Breslau. During his university studies he had come into contact with a Christian missionary in Berlin and been persuaded to investigate the claims of Christianity. Learning of this, his father had turned him out of the house, and he had emigrated to Liverpool. There he lived for a time in a home for enquiring Jews which had been established by a group of energetic evangelical Anglicans. Under their tutelage he was baptised and confirmed in the Anglican communion, and employed as a teacher of other enquirers. He emigrated to Canada in 1844 intending to study for ordination with Bethune at Cobourg. However, he did not find there the evangelical enthusiasm of his godfathers, and he was attracted by the possibilities for conversion offered by the flourishing Jewish community in Montreal. In 1845 he called on Bishop Mountain to ask his advice as to whether this project was sufficiently promising to encourage Hellmuth to refuse an offer of full-time employment at a Jewish-Christian centre in New York.

The bishop thought him "a valuable man" and, with some misgivings as to his evangelical leanings, recommended him to Jasper Nicolls as a candidate for ordination and to the SPG for a bursary of £35. During the winter of 1845–46, the principal paid him another £30 out of his own pocket to teach the elements of Hebrew to the other students. Perhaps oddly, since they were men of very different personality and background, Nicolls and Hellmuth became firm friends.

The precise nature of Hellmuth's contribution to the academic life of the institution during the next eight years is difficult to evaluate. He was ordained deacon by the bishop in May 1846, and looked after the parish in Lennoxville during Lucius Doolittle's absence on sick leave that summer. The following January he married Catherine Maria, daughter of Major-General Thomas Evans, a prominent evangelical churchman of Montreal, and granddaughter of Isaac Ogden, a United Empire Loyalist. Corporation appointed him vice-principal during the principal's absence in England in 1847, but it was left to the Visitor to decide what this meant in terms of precedence over the other members of the College Council! Later that year, Hellmuth was appointed Professor of Hebrew and Rabbinical Literature, but contemporary correspondence suggests that these appointments were made so that he and his wife should have enough to live on rather than from any analysis of the needs of the college curriculum. In January 1849 the bishop licensed him to the mission of St Peter's, Sherbrooke.

During the next four years, St Peter's flourished under Hellmuth's preaching, and he was able to clear away the debt on the church building. He was also very active in evangelical circles in Montreal, and was among the candidates being promoted by those who wished the first Bishop of Montreal to be nominated from the clergy of the diocese. In 1849 he and his wife went to England to canvass the evangelical party on behalf of Bishop's College. They enjoyed considerable success, returning in 1850 with £1,000 for the endowment. Though he was highly regarded as a teacher and preacher, it seems obvious that Hellmuth's academic responsibilities did not weigh heavily on him. Miles and Chapman, on the other hand, were carrying heavy teaching loads in both the college and the school.

In 1852 the bishop was persuaded to act as sponsor for Hellmuth's application to the Archbishop of Canterbury for a Lambeth Doctorate of Divinity (D.D.).[7] Since the principal was "only" a Master of Arts, this raised some hackles, and Jasper Nicolls was encouraged to travel to England in 1853—ostensibly to raise money for the endowment but also to take his D.D. in course at Oxford.[8] He again left Hellmuth in charge during his absence, but before he could complete the examinations for his degree, he was forced to return to Canada to cope with Miles and Chapman in revolt. Unable to heal the breach, he was on the verge of offering his resignation as principal when Hellmuth himself resigned. Corporation, wishing to retain his influence for the college, appointed him a trustee, and this precipitated the first (but by no means the last!) flaming row in the governing body of the institution. At the relevant Corporation meeting, Chapman made formal objection to Hellmuth's appointment. Hellmuth offered to withdraw in a letter to the bishop in which he observed that "it has been my lot, in the midst of many blessings ... to suffer bitter persecutions."9 The nature of Chapman's charges is not revealed by any of the documents which have survived. Given his character, they would not have been trivial; but it seems likely that the motive force of the conflict derived from the precedence, and perhaps the remuneration, accorded Hellmuth, which, in the opinion of his colleagues, were not justified by his contributions to the academic life of the college.

The unpleasantness was papered over. Chapman resigned from the chair of classics and was appointed registrar, retaining his seat on the College Council. Hellmuth was granted a D.D. *ad eundem*10 in 1855, and was appointed general superintendent of the work in British North America of the Colonial Church and School Society, an evangelical foundation which succeeded in generating not a little dissension in the diocese of Quebec, to the distress of Bishop Mountain. Shortly afterward, Hellmuth was called by Bishop Cronyn to found a college for the training of clergy in the Evangelical tradition in the diocese of Huron. He went on to a distinguished, if controversial, career as second bishop of Huron and first chancellor of Western University, the antecedent of the University of Western Ontario.

FACULTY SALARIES

The principal and the bishop had thus cobbled together a faculty which, considering the isolation of the institution, was remarkably well qualified. Finding the money with which to pay their salaries would be a major problem during the whole of Nicolls' tenure. He made a good start in 1846, when he persuaded several Quebec merchants to subscribe a total of £100 per annum for five years to pay the salary of Edward Chapman as Professor of Classics. In March 1847 Nicolls sailed for England to try to raise funds for the endowment and to enlist the support of the SPG and the SPCK for a charter enabling Bishop's to grant degrees. Sickness confined him to his family home during much of his stay in England, and he returned to Canada in August without a charter and with the promise of only £700, much less than he had hoped for.

Fortunately, during the summer Thomas Aylwin, member of the Legislative Assembly for Portneuf, had moved that the government award a grant of £500 per annum to Bishop's College. Aylwin, a member of the Reform Party (at that time in opposition), had been a persistent critic of the act incorporating the college in 1843, but he had apparently been convinced of its usefulness and saw no reason why it should not share in the bounty being distributed to other colleges in Upper and Lower Canada—for example, Victoria College received a grant of £500 per annum from the date of its founding in 1841.

The report of the debate on Aylwin's motion makes interesting reading.[11] Samuel Brooks, member for Sherbrooke Town (and one of the original subscribers to Doolittle's project), spoke against the motion on the grounds that the institution had few students, was well endowed, and that he saw no justice in being obliged to pay for other peoples' education. Nicolls commented that Brooks had been converted to this point of view after his own children had been educated at public expense. Both Robert Baldwin and Louis-Hippolyte Lafontaine, the leaders of the Reform Party, intervened, Baldwin on principle, as being opposed to the granting of public funds to support denominational schools and colleges. Lafontaine's situation was a little more delicate. The Roman Catholic Church in Lower Canada had ample endowments and was empowered under seigneurial tenure to collect tithes, so it was not difficult for him to declare his opposition to grants of state funds in support of religion. On the other hand, many of the classical colleges in Lower Canada, attached to seminaries and sending most of their graduates into the Church, were receiving government grants. Lafontaine confined himself to objecting to the comparatively large amount proposed. Aylwin moved in amendment to reduce the amount to £250, and the amended motion was passed, along with grants to Collège l'Assomption, Collège de Joliette, and le Petit Séminaire de Ste Thérèse.

The trustees, who had had no prior notice of Aylwin's intention, were of course delighted to receive this manna. They decided to devote £100 of the grant to pay Hellmuth's salary, £100 to reduce the college debt and the remaining £50 to pay an assistant bursar, a relief for Lucius Doolittle, who had been performing the duties of bursar, without remuneration, since the days of the original subscription. Happily, the grant was renewed the following year and increased to £300 in 1850.

THE COURSE OF STUDY

In addition to providing for the training of clergy, Bishop Mountain's purpose in founding the college had been to provide "the blessing of a sound and liberal education" for the young men of the English-speaking community. How would the bishop and the principal have defined such an education?

First, as an education for life—"regarding man as always in infancy in this world, and under schooling for another"[12]—an education designed to develop character as well as intellect; in short, as a moral enterprise. Both Mountain and Nicolls belonged to the large body of moderate opinion in the Church of England which at that time perceived no conflict between religion and science, which regarded both faith and knowledge as necessary for salvation. In his 1860 convocation address the principal proclaimed his belief "that while man discovers, he discovers what God has made, what God *gives* him to understand. Universities, let us remember, are Christian institutions."[13] This commitment to an intellectual climate in which scientific knowledge and theology each revealed part of an integral truth was shared by most of the leading scientific scholars of the time in the English universities.

A liberal education, then, necessarily involved instruction in theology. *Sound* theological instruction conformed to the doctrines of the Church of England as expounded by moderate churchmen, who felt that piety without mental discipline tended to degenerate into extravagance and fanaticism, while learning without devotion gave no security against the snares of the world, the lure of the flesh, and the wiles of the devil. No religious tests were imposed on prospective matriculants, but undergraduates were required to follow courses in divinity and to attend services in chapel.

Perhaps the most lasting heritage left by Bishop Mountain was his belief in episcopal authority. Though he was a prime mover in the development of self-government in the colonial church, through the establishment of diocesan synods, he held that the bishop must have final authority. The act of 1843 gave him over the actions of the Corporation absolute veto—it was in truth *the bishop's* university. A century later Mountain's successor still expected to be consulted about any changes in the curriculum of the Faculty of Divinity. In Bishop's sesquicentennial year the Anglican bishops of Quebec and Montreal retain only their status as the Visitors of the university. As such they are the final arbiters of disputes between the members and committees of the university. Since by a very ancient tradition of common law there is no appeal from their decisions to the courts, they provide a valuable protection against external interference in the domestic affairs of the university.

The secular curriculum was designed to develop what were considered to be the two principal faculties of man as an intellectual being: language and reason. The case for the classics as the best means for the education of language was widely accepted in European and British universities. William Whewell, master of Trinity College, Cambridge, expounded most eloquently in 1837 the vision on which this case was based:

> The cultivated world, up to the present day, has been bound together, and each generation bound to the preceding, by living upon a shared intellectual estate. They have shared in a common develop-

ment of thought, because they have understood each other. Their standard examples of poetry, eloquence, history, criticism, grammar, etymology, have been a universal bond of sympathy, however diverse might be the opinions which prevailed respecting any of these examples. All the civilized world has been one intellectual nation... The authors of Greece and Rome, familiar to the child, admired and dwelt on by the aged, were the common language, by the possession of which each man felt himself a denizen of the civilized world;—free of all the privileges with which it had been gifted from the dawn of Greek civilization up to the present time.[14]

An anecdote of the life of S.S. Wood, rector of Three Rivers, gives a vivid illustration of the relevance of this "universal bond of sympathy" in the work of the founders of Bishop's. Mr Wood often accompanied the bishop on his visitations to outlying settlements under Wood's charge. Of one of these Mountain wrote, "I would you had heard how my companion, as we toiled along, beguiled the way through the midnight woods by repeating from his favourite poets, to whose works the conversation chanced to lead, I believe a hundred lines at a time, and favoured by darkness, which removed some of the checks upon his confidence, gave their full effect to many animated or touching lines."[15]

The second principal faculty, reason, was to be developed through the systematic study of mathematics. Again quoting Whewell:

Mathematics, in the shape of Geometry, holds its place as an element of great and incomparable value among the permanent studies of a Liberal Education [because] it offers to us examples of a solid and certain reasoning, by which the reasoning powers, and the apprehension of demonstrative proof, may be exercised, unfolded and confirmed.[16]

Since liberal education was particularly concerned with developing habits of mind, instruction was principally by tutorial sessions with "close and continuous supervision." The formal lectures which had become general in Continental universities were felt to be better adapted to speculative and innovative topics; in any case, Bishop's did not have the resources for such instruction.

A comparison between the texts specified for the undergraduate course in 1851 and those required for the pass degree at Cambridge suggests that Nicolls attempted to set a remarkably high standard. Such a curriculum would only have been accessible to well-prepared and strongly motivated undergraduates. In the announcement of the first session, dated 1 October 1845, candidates for admission were notified that they would be "examined in the Latin and Greek languages, in such books as they may have been lately engaged in reading, and will be expected to translate each language readily and to translate English into Latin: accuracy of scholarship and a thorough acquaintance with the fundamental rules and principles of the languages being required rather than extensive reading. It is further expected that they will be able to stand an examination in the earlier books of Euclid and Algebra; and they will be required to show a competent knowledge of the Bible, to translate the New Testament readily from the original and to answer questions from both the Old and New Testament."[17]

Despite these brave words contemporary correspondence makes it clear that not all the first undergraduates could have met these criteria. Competent teachers at the secondary level were very scarce outside Montreal and Quebec, and the desperate need for clergy exerted heavy pressure on the faculty to accept candidates whose lack of preparation greatly increased the labour of teaching them.

DOMESTICITY

In September 1846 the new building on the property at the confluence of the St Francis and Massawippi rivers was at last, if not complete in every detail, at least ready to be occupied. This first college building consisted of the five central bays of McGreer Hall but without the central tower and the stone steps and balustrade. Though supervising the work of the various tradesmen needed to finish the interior kept him very busy, Jasper Nicolls was delighted with his new kingdom. There would at last be proper classrooms and adequate living quarters for the undergraduates—though the provision for heating, by wooden flues from furnaces in the basement, would prove to be both inadequate to cope with winter in the Townships, and a serious fire risk!

Nicolls would also be provided with more adequate quarters and more privacy himself, which would permit him to pursue a personal project which his year "batching" on the upper St Francis had made increasingly attractive. In a letter dated 16 November, his father wrote: "You appear to me rather inclined to matrimony, which it gives me pleasure to see. Let therefore your female society be among the *good* and *estimable*, also don't be frightened at a woman because she may have two or three hundred or thousand of pounds!"[18]—But Jasper's choice was already made. During his school days in Quebec, he had been closely involved with his uncle the bishop's household and had often squired one or other of the

Mountain daughters. He had subsequently corresponded from time to time, from Oxford, with Harriet (christened Heriot) Mountain; and his visits to Quebec since his return to Canada had afforded opportunity for the friendship to ripen. During the fall and winter of 1846 he formally courted her.

Harriet hesitated, apparently fearing that she would not be able to hold up her end of the domestic intercourse in an academic household. A letter from a disconsolate Jasper during this interval reports that he had "left Hellmuth and his wife tête à tête, whence I had hoped bye and bye to be similarly placed with yourself. I hope they may enjoy my absence—one comfort for the onlooker—they are not *outrageously* affectionate, which somewhat diminishes the unhappiness one cannot help feeling in contrasting with your own position."[19] In January 1847 Harriet relented, and they were married on Nicolls' return from England in September. In 1848 Corporation authorized the construction of the Lodge (two floors but no verandah) adjacent to the west end of the college building to provide a home for the principal and his family. The marriage was a happy one. Its effect upon the life of the college may be judged by a letter, written from his missionary post, from one of the first alumni: "Certainly my reminiscences of Lennoxville are altogether pleasant; and among the most pleasant are those connected with your cheerful drawing room—Mrs. Nicolls puzzling her own head and ours with some wise conundrum or charade—Miss Katy frolicking with your humble servant, and yourself instructing and enlivening the whole."[20]

Not much else is known about undergraduate life during this period. The first debating society, the Quintilian, was founded at about this time, and a reading room association was formed in 1849, but no records of their early meetings have survived. The domestic economy of the college was governed by the College Council, heavily clerical in composition, and the bishop was frequently consulted. The question of whether it would be seemly for the college to tolerate dancing was referred to him in 1848, and he decided against it, fearing that "if our students go to dances, it will offend the prejudices of weak brethren and so hurt the Institution."[21]

FINANCIAL CRISIS AND RECOVERY

The number of undergraduates remained small—between ten and twenty—during these early years. Numbers in the grammar school continued to increase, but the college made no concession toward the teaching of "useful" subjects, and few of the parents who could afford the fees of the school were willing to contemplate a clerical career for their sons. One of the first trustees, the Reverend Richard Lindsay, wrote to the principal from his mission at Brome to point out that while it was obvious that the college must have the support of secondary schools, "there is scarcely a family in the missions around here that could afford to send their sons [to the grammar school] and instead of being a popular school with its hundreds, it is as Mr. Johnson terms, a penal settlement for Quebec and Montreal."[22]

Meanwhile the commercial depression due to the abandonment of colonial preference by the British government deepened, and the party in the Townships which favoured annexation to the United States became more numerous. In 1848 Isaac Hellmuth was dispatched to England to complete the canvass which had been interrupted by Jasper Nicolls' illness; he returned in 1849 with another £1,000 for the endowment. During that year, however, the college's financial position suffered a serious blow when the major part of the endowment, which had been invested in real estate in Montreal, suddenly ceased to produce revenue. As the principal reported to Ernest Hawkins, "We have had the misfortune to get our money into the power of a lawyer whom the distress of the country has brought out into his proper colours, and who apparently had the whole thing schemed beforehand and duped our representative in Montreal ... however, our capital is not lost. In four years it will come back to us."[23]

In the meantime, a deficit of £300 in the college's annual revenue had to be made up. Jasper Nicolls undertook another canvass of the merchants of Quebec and Montreal. He was greatly heartened by the response in Quebec, where a total of £245 per annum was subscribed for a period of three years. But Montreal proved to be stony ground. The merchants were feeling sorry for themselves, and many were flirting with the annexationist option. The clergy resented the tight control of the Corporation by the Bishop of Quebec. Montreal had been separated off as a new diocese in 1848, after persistent lobbying by Bishop Mountain, who had also organized the funds necessary to endow the new bishopric. Nevertheless, the new bishop, Francis Fulford, offered only lukewarm support. In order to try to counter the apathy of the clergy and the jealousy of those who feared that Bishop's would compete with McGill, Corporation in 1852 amended the act of incorporation of 1843 to make both bishops presidents of Corporation, with the provision that, in case of disagreement, the opinion of the bishop senior by date of consecration would prevail. Happily, over the next decade Bishop Fulford began to take a greater interest in the work of the institution. In November 1861 he spent ten days in Lennoxville as a guest of the principal and Mrs Nicolls, and he was sufficiently impressed that he wrote an enthusiastic letter to church authorities in England, expressing confidence in its future.

Fortunately the SPG, which had been given responsibility for dispensing the revenue from the Clergy Reserves, found itself at last able in 1848 to appropriate £300 currency from this source for Bishop's College. Over the next five years the economy of the province recovered, and payment of the interest on the endowment was resumed. In 1852 the society granted £1,000 from their jubilee (sesquicentennial) fund as an endowment in support of bursaries for divinity students. Two years later the bursar was able to report revenue from investments of £606 which, added to the government grant of £300 and the grant of £300 from Clergy Reserve funds, amounted in all to £1,206 currency per annum. The following year, as a result of the act secularizing the Clergy Reserves, the college received £4,400 in government debentures in commutation of the £300 annual grant from the Clergy Reserve Fund, and the annual grant from the government was increased to £450. For the moment, Bishop's was on firm financial ground.

THE BATTLE FOR THE CHARTER

The act of 1843 which incorporated Bishop's College did not grant the authority to confer degrees. The institution therefore laboured under a severe disadvantage as compared with similar institutions in Upper and Lower Canada. The bishop and the principal lobbied unceasingly to obtain a remedy for this deficiency, but unfortunately (for reasons which are elucidated in Appendix Two), the granting of university charters had become a very sensitive issue for both the British and Canadian governments.

Aware of the pressure toward the secularization of university education in Upper Canada, the bishop turned first to the new governor-general, Lord Elgin, who had arrived in Montreal (at that time the seat of the government) in January 1847. Elgin, who had taken a first at Oxford and been elected to a fellowship at Merton, was interested in philosophical questions, and had definite opinions on the nature and purpose of liberal education. He had been elected as a Liberal Conservative to the House of Commons in 1841, but had resigned the following year when he succeeded to the earldom. The Whig government of Lord John Russell had appointed him governor of Canada. He was 35 years of age, he spoke fluent French, and he found himself very much in sympathy with the Baldwin-Lafontaine administration which was formed in March 1848. He was, moreover, determined to be guided by the advice of his Canadian ministers.

Bishop Mountain had written Elgin within two weeks of his arrival to enlist his support in obtaining a royal charter conferring university status on Bishop's College. Elgin's ministers, embroiled in the turmoil in Upper Canada, advised him not to comply with the bishop's request, and Mountain was so informed on 22 March 1847. Undaunted, he dispatched Jasper Nicolls to London to enlist the support of Lord Lyttleton, who acted for the SPG; together they interviewed the colonial secretary Lord Grey. The secretary, however, refused to do anything about a university charter for Bishop's College without the advice and consent of the governor-general. Petitions to the legislature in 1848 and 1850 were equally unsuccessful.

The fact was that Elgin was alarmed by the situation in Upper Canada. He had grave doubts as to the wisdom of granting university charters to a multitude of denominational colleges, whose resources in his opinion would not in the foreseeable future be adequate to the role to which they aspired. From 1849 on, his attitude was also conditioned by the determination of Baldwin and the Reform Party to establish a provincial university under secular control in Toronto. Finally, Elgin was not interested in reinforcing the English-speaking community in the Townships. He had rapidly become aware of the strong support there for annexation to the United States, and he hoped that the rising tide of French-Canadian immigration into the region would convert it into a *cordon sanitaire* against American influence.[24]

In May of 1852 Elgin received a request from the directors of le Séminaire de Québec that he support their petition to the Crown for the grant of a royal charter to l'Université Laval, a French-language university for the Roman Catholic people of Lower Canada. L'abbé Louis-Jacques Casault, whose cherished project this was, had also needed to navigate shoal water before attaining his goal. There had been for several years a party, centred in l'Institut canadien, which was promoting a university under lay direction in Montreal. In their opinion, "Si la partie morale de l'enseignement appartient aux ministres de la religion, celle de la partie instructive appartient à la patrie, cette grande réunion de tous les intérêts."[25] However, this group was not sufficiently numerous or cohesive to be able to stand against the Roman Catholic clergy, who already controlled education at pre-university levels.

A more important obstacle was the redoubtable Bishop Bourget. He had hoped that the Jesuits, returning to Lower Canada in 1842, would be granted the revenues from the estates which they had forfeited to the

Crown in 1800. This would enable them to found a college which would be the nucleus of a Catholic university in Montreal. As well as "preaching for his parish," the strongly ultramontane Bourget had confidence in the devotion of the Jesuits to papal supremacy, whereas the Seminary of Quebec was suspected of liberal tendencies. Bourget's ultimate goal was to establish a provincial university, governed from Montreal by the Catholic bishops, which would be composed of a number of degree-granting colleges (similar in some respects to the present University of Quebec). He also wanted nothing to do with the government or the Crown.

Casault and the directors of the seminary feared that this rather grandiose scheme would generate opposition in both the provincial legislature and the House of Commons. They also feared interdiocesan jealousy. Finally, their financial resources, though large compared with the other Quebec dioceses, would not be adequate to cope with so large a project, and they could not count on financial support from the government. By patient and skilful diplomacy they succeeded in rallying the support of the bishops for a more modest proposal. L'Université Laval, named for the great seventeenth-century Bishop of Quebec who had founded the seminary, would be a child of the diocese of Quebec, and under the entire control of its archbishop.

Elgin was happy to support this project. A royal charter identical with the draft submitted by the seminary was granted, and at the request of Casault, dated 8 December, the Feast of the Immaculate Conception, which was the university's patronal feast day. The rapidity with which the British government responded is remarkable, since it was at the time rejecting Newman's proposal that a charter be granted to a Catholic university to be established in Ireland. It is also interesting to note that, although Laval was authorized by the pope to confer theological degrees in 1853, the entire confidence of the Vatican, in the form of a pontifical charter, was not obtained until 1876.

Since both Queen's University and the University of Trinity College had continued to operate under royal charters as institutions under denominational control, Elgin could no longer justify refusal to support the application of Bishop's College for degree-granting powers. He had no quarrel with the nature of the education which the college was attempting to provide. A memorandum, in his handwriting, of the course of study to be pursued for his degree at Oxford was remarkable, first for the broad and liberal spirit in which it was conceived, and second in that "Ancient History, together with Aristotle's Politics and the ancient orators were to be read ... in connection with Bible History, with the view of seeing how all hang upon each other and develop the leading schemes of Providence."[26] His brother, Sir Frederick Bruce, who was at

Oxford with him, recalled Elgin's opinions that "to reduce education to stuffing the mind with facts is to dwarf the intelligence and to reverse the natural process of the growth of man's mind" and that "the knowledge of principles as the means of discrimination and the criterion of those individual appreciations which are fallaciously called facts, ought to be the end of high education."[27]

These were exactly Jasper Nicolls' views on the nature and end of sound and liberal education. Elgin's opposition must therefore be attributed chiefly to his passionate belief in responsible government. The Anglican bishops had consistently sought the help of the British government to override the will of the elected Assembly, and Bishop Strachan, by his obdurate refusal to surrender any part of the endowment of King's College and by his ruthless political manoeuvring, had, in Elgin's opinion, alienated all parties, including a large proportion of the Anglican clergy and laity, of whom Robert Baldwin was one. The fate of the application from Bishop's had thus been largely determined by events which until 1852 had little relevance to the college's environment in Lower Canada.

That September Jasper Nicolls wrote to his wife that his most recent interview with Elgin and canvass of the ministers for Lower Canada had been more favourably received than previous campaigns. In October the governor-general invited Bishop Mountain to send him a copy of the proposed charter, which he then referred to the attorney-general. The latter reported favorably on its contents, and on November 11, the government advised Elgin to recommend to the imperial authorities that the charter be granted. On 18 January 1853 the long struggle for a royal charter was finally successful.

THE FIRST CONVOCATION

With its financial position restored, and the royal charter safely sealed, Corporation set happily about amending the Rules, Orders, and Regulations of the University of Bishop's College* to make provision for a chancellor, a vice-chancellor and a convocation which would govern the academic life of the institution and the conferring of degrees. The first chancellor was the Honourable William Walker, a member of the Legislative Council. Walker was a successful businessman from Quebec

---

* Until 1922 the institution continued to be generally known as Bishop's College. McGreer introduced the title "Bishop's University," which was legally adopted in 1958.

John Samuel McCord

City, the political spokesman for the commercial class, particularly for the timber interests. He had been a member of the Special Council which governed Lower Canada for two years following the rebellion of 1838, a deputy for Rouville (1842–43) in the Legislative Assembly, and very active in the commercial and financial institutions of the city. The first vice-chancellor was the Honourable Mr Justice John Samuel McCord of Montreal, an active churchman and philanthropist, and a close friend of Edward Hale's. The principal and the professors were to be ex officio members of convocation, together with "all Masters of Arts, whether by ordinary or extraordinary graduation," who made an annual payment of twenty shillings to the University. This latter provision of the charter became a sore point with the large number of clerical graduates who had to survive with their families on SPG stipends in missionary charges.

William Walker had agreed to become chancellor only as a temporary measure, and on condition that he did not have to perform the academic duties of the office. He referred to himself as a "paper" chancellor, but as Bishop Mountain observed he proved to be much concerned "with *papers* of consequence to the University"—the presentation of petitions to the government, and other political matters.[28] However, the first meeting of convocation consisted of ex officio members: the vice-chancellor, the principal and Professor Miles. They forthwith conferred the degree of M.A. on Lucius Doolittle (*ad eundem*, Doolittle having received an M.A. from the University of Vermont) and Edward Chapman (*honoris causa*, since Chapman had not yet proceeded to his M.A. at Cambridge) who then took their seats, and convocation thus constituted set about establishing itself on a broader base. Degrees *ad eundem* were awarded to some 25 clerical and lay graduates of recognized universities. Since several of the recipients were graduates of American universities who had actively discouraged young Townshippers from enrolling at Bishop's, the principal received angry letters from several alumni, but the principle of constituting the supreme academic body of the university from a variety of traditions was sound and praiseworthy. Less happily, the five oligarchs then proceeded to award to leading citizens a similar number of degrees *honoris causa*, many of which went to men who had little claim to learning or literary distinction, and several of which could be justified only on political grounds.

The granting of these degrees provoked an anguished protest from Bishop Mountain. He made no attempt to invoke the episcopal veto, recognizing the traditional autonomy of convocation; but, as he wrote, "with a dozen students and in the perfect infancy of our proceedings as a university, it appears to me that we should be very modest and sparing in the distribution of distinctions."[29] Mountain was especially pained to note among the politicians "a man thoroughly disreputable and noted for certain delinquencies which affect his character for honesty."[30] The blame for these excesses properly rests with the vice-chancellor, but Lucius Doolittle was also concerned that the first public meeting of convocation should have a good play in the press. The proceedings were totally out of character for Jasper Nicolls, and it is perhaps an indication of the wear and tear of nine years of struggle for survival that he was willing to defend these decisions to the bishop and the alumni.

Eight bachelors' degrees in Arts (B.A.) were also awarded in course, including one to Henry Roe, and two bachelors' degrees in course in Divinity (B.D.). To those early students who had been ordained without completing their studies in Arts, convocation offered the opportunity of taking a B.D. by examination. John Kemp and John Carry were the successful candidates in 1855. The other early students were recognized as "Alumni emeriti," but convocation offered them no certificate of study. In the wake of the prodigal distribution of degrees *honoris causa*, this was obviously not good enough. If students had left Bishop's without completing their studies in Arts, it was due to the acute need for missionary clergy and the fact that their financial support from the SPG had been granted to permit them to fill that need as quickly as possible. Most were serving in isolated communities where they had neither the time nor the facilities for further study. Many of them would have been satisfied with a simple Certificate of Studies in Divinity, sealed with the college seal. However, when convocation was seized of the question, it decided to grant an M.A. *honoris causa* in 1856 to each of the 18 ordinands who had not been graduated in course, either at Bishop's or another university.[31]

The first public meeting of convocation was held in Lennoxville on Wednesday, 27 June 1855. The proceedings were fully reported in the Montreal *Gazette*.[32] Unfortunately, the state of Bishop Mountain's health prevented him from being present on this historic occasion, and the Bishop of Vermont, whom he had invited to lend an international flavour to the ceremonies, was also prevented at the last minute from making the not inconsiderable journey from Burlington. Though (or perhaps because) their replacements had had little time to prepare their addresses, these were fully as long as was customary at the time.

The day began with a service in St George's, the parish church of Lennoxville, the college chapel being not yet completed. The Bishop of Montreal was the preacher (his sermon filled 55 column inches of type). The members of convocation "to the number of thirty or forty, attired in academic costume, then assembled at the college, whence they marched in procession to the large schoolroom in the village, at which

Thomas Cushing Aylwin, 1861

the ceremony of publicly conferring degrees took place." Principal Nicolls presented the first graduands for the B.A. in course to the vice-chancellor, and the new Professor of Divinity, J.H. Thompson, the first graduands for the B.D. This ceremony being concluded, the Bishop of Montreal addressed convocation (39 column inches of type). He was followed by Mr Justice Aylwin, who spoke extemporaneously (filling only 14 column inches) expressing, as his staunch and unfailing support of the institution entitled him, his joy "that parents would no longer need to send their sons out of the country, as he had been sent 30 years ago, in order to acquire a liberal education."[33] A member of the graduating class then read a shorter paper, the class valedictorian addressed the convocation, and the vice-chancellor declared convocation dissolved.

The day was brought to a close by a "picnic party" given by the inhabitants of Lennoxville to the students and the members of convocation at which, in the opinion of the *Gazette's* corespondent, there was present "such an array of well-bred beauty" as few places in the province could have produced.[34] The visitors were entertained again on Thursday by the hospitable gentry of the neighbourhood, and no doubt set out on the long journey back to the St Lawrence well content with their excursion.

The principal also had good reason to be content with the results of his ten years of unremitting labour. His fledgling institution was well housed and had survived its first financial crises and its first faculty fission. It had achieved official recognition of its status as a university, and had already provided the bishop with a considerable number of well-trained ordinands for the missions of the diocese. Supported by sound and well-qualified faculty, Nicolls could face the future with confidence.

CHAPTER THREE

PRINCIPAL NICOLLS: THE YEARS OF TRIAL

In 1852 the railway from Montreal had reached Sherbrooke and Lennoxville; the following year the junction of the St Lawrence and Atlantic (SL&A) with the northward-building Atlantic and St Lawrence was achieved at Island Pond, Vermont. A year later, a Quebec City consortium completed a railway from Levis to connect with the SL&A at Richmond. Sherbrooke was thereby suddenly connected by rail with the two major centres of population in Lower Canada and with Portland, an ice-free port on the Atlantic ocean.

The SL&A was the first Canadian railroad to traverse the Eastern Townships. Alexander Galt and his associates Samuel Brooks and Edward Hale had initiated the project, and Galt had been instrumental in determining the route for the line and, in particular, the choice of Portland rather than Boston as the terminus. His purpose was to provide markets for the industries he and his associates had been developing in Sherbrooke, and so to increase the value of the land and industries owned there by the BALC, of which he was still commissioner.

As a result, Sherbrooke and the region enjoyed rapidly increasing prosperity in the late 1850s. The establishment of the Eastern Townships Bank in 1859 provided another source of capital for development, and new ventures proliferated. Unfortunately, education, or at least the education which Bishop's offered, was not considered useful in this context, and enrolment languished, to the distress of the trustees.

The University of Bishop's College, 1859

THE NEED TO INCREASE ENROLMENT

During the period 1845–57, 72 students were admitted to the college, 21 of whom graduated bachelors of arts. Of these, 12 were subsequently ordained as Anglican clergy. In addition, two undergraduates of this period were graduated Bachelors of Divinity, and 19 more satisfied the Bishop of Quebec's examiners and were ordained without proceeding to a degree. During the academic year 1861–62, there were 16 fully matriculated students in residence in the Faculty of Arts and three Bachelors of Arts enrolled in the Faculty of Divinity. How did these figures compare with those in the other universities of the Province of Canada?

Since many of the surviving statistics were compiled with an eye to generating grants from the government, and many students included in these statistics were not present during the complete session, accurate comparisons are difficult to establish. According to Egerton Ryerson, six freshmen matriculated at the newly constituted University of Toronto in 1851, "and every one of the six having an endowed scholarship—a pitiful result indeed from an endowment of £9,000 per annum."[1] In 1848–49, the eighth academic year after the institution had been granted university status, there were 13 fully matriculated undergraduates enrolled in the University of Victoria College out of a total enrolment of 140 students reported to the legislature.[2] Queen's, 15 years after the university opened, awarded an average of five Bachelor's degrees in Arts each year during the period 1856–58.[3] From 1859 to 1862 this number increased to 12. The first two Bachelors of Arts were graduated from McGill in 1850, along with the first six graduates in Law. In 1852 that university finally achieved a new charter, and the new governors, judging the condition of McGill to be "unsatisfactory and almost hopeless," suspended operations for one year so that they could reorganize the administration, relieve the university of its "pecuniary embarrassments," reinforce the teaching staff, and appoint a new principal.[4] Five Bachelors' degrees in Arts were awarded in 1857.

The plight of the University of Bishop's College was thus by no means exceptional. The medical schools attached to the other universities of the Province of Canada were flourishing, but the Arts degree was evidently not highly prized at that time. Jasper Nicolls detailed some of the reasons for this in an address which he gave in January 1857 to the Young Men's Protestant Educational Union in Quebec City.[5] That he should give a public lecture was in itself an interesting development. The previous year, Bishop Mountain had been invited to address the Union, a novel experience for him, but one which he had enjoyed. He had observed the growing appetite for scientific and general information among the population, and regretted that his own clergy had not followed the examples of the ministers of the Kirk and the dissenting clergy in lecturing to general audiences on popular subjects. He perceived that here was a way to justify to the population at large the education the clergy had received and to convince the taxpayers that such education merited government support. Mountain wrote to the principal, urging him to accept the invitation of the Union to open the lecture series for 1857.

In his lecture, "The End and Object of Education," Nicolls noted that "though everybody wants to learn, almost everybody wants to learn as little as possible. Learning is not sought for its own sake, nor does a young man think (nor a young man's father in too many cases lead him to suppose) that he would become a greater and nobler being by cultivating the powers with which God has gifted him. The railroad or the counting house is open to him at an early period, and there he finds what both his own feeling of self-importance and desire to escape from control, and also his father's indoctrination, have led him to covet, immediate independence ... and even those whose aspirations are higher find too often what might be called the *learned* professions not only open their doors to them as soon as they knock for admission, but almost coax them to come in. While this state of affairs continues, we cannot become a great people."[6]

With a candour that cannot have recommended the university's cause to the power brokers of the government, Nicolls went on to express his opinion that "retired railway makers or railway speculators, retired merchants or retired and fortunate gold finders are not the men to legislate for a country which would be a great country, or to administer her laws ... we want men devoting themselves to these high purposes and callings and devoting themselves heart and soul to them from their youth ... men fresh and vigorous, able and prepared. It is learning and character, not wealth or station, which make a great man."[7]

These sentiments would have been heartily applauded by the heads of the other Canadian universities. There was, however, a growing debate about the content of the curriculum best suited to form the minds and characters of the future leaders of the country. The claim that the ability to read classical literature in the original languages was essential to the educated man was being challenged. In Europe, Whewell's "one intellectual nation" was beginning to break up, under the influence of the study of science and the "higher criticism" of biblical texts, particularly in the burgeoning universities of Germany. A "sound classical education" had come to be regarded in democratic circles in Canada as the education of a governing class, and therefore to be deplored. The idea that facility and elegance of style in English were best acquired as a by-product of translation to and from "dead" languages was felt to lead to much waste of time and intellectual energy.

When the "new men" who had taken over the governing of McGill in 1852 looked for a principal, they agreed that it was expedient that he should be a layman; and their choice fell upon William Dawson, who was the product not of a British university but of Pictou Academy and whose learning had been acquired chiefly by the independent study of geology. His friend and mentor, Charles Lyell, "regarded by most earth scientists today as the father of modern geology", had been so impressed by his published work that he had proposed Dawson for the chair of natural history at Edinburgh.[8] In his inaugural address at McGill in 1855 Dawson emphasized the primary importance of the study of English, "Which bids fair, like the Greek of old, to be the principal vehicle for the world wide diffusion of the highest ideas in science, in politics and in religion." He went on to claim that studies in science, "independently of their intrinsic charm, have in our day established a connection so intimate with every department of mechanical, manufacturing and agricultural art that without them the material welfare of nations cannot be sustained, much less advanced."[9]

Mid-nineteenth-century Canadians struggling to subdue their enormous and intractable land were continuously and intimately concerned with their material welfare; the curriculum Dawson advocated, which included modern languages, natural history, political economy, and career-oriented diplomas, was hailed as progressive and closely related to the practical needs of British North America by the leaders of business and industry and, increasingly, by legislatures.

In 1855 the Bishop's faculty consisted of the principal, who was also Professor of Classics, H.H. Miles, Professor of Mathematics, whose interests included natural philosophy and some applications, and J.H. Thompson, Professor of Divinity. The college was thus ill-equipped to respond to the public demand for a more practically oriented curriculum, a demand of which the trustees were aware, and which several of them supported. In 1854 they appointed a committee to solicit contributions "for the establishment of professorships and lectureships in sciences of practical utility, and for a library and museum."[10] The following year they prepared a petition to the government for a grant to enable them to provide for instruction "in Civil and Military Engineering, Chemistry and Mineralogy."[11] On the advice of their legislative lobby, they desisted from presenting their petition in return for an increase in the annual grant from £300 to £450. The £150 increase they designated as a salary for a professor of chemistry and mineralogy. However, at a period when

Queen's was paying (full) professors £375, Bishop's had no hope of attracting a competent man in a highly competitive field for less than half that amount. Another source of funds would have to be found.

The small enrolment in the Faculty of Arts, coupled with the comparatively restricted financial resources and political leverage of the Townships community, had worked continuously to the disadvantage of the college as it sought financial support from the government and the public. The trustees had considered several ways to increase enrolment. Broadening the curriculum was one alternative, but that would require a major increase in the endowment and might take many years. There was also some concern about the effect it might have on academic standards. Another alternative was to seek to reinforce the secondary schools in the region, so as to increase the number of young Townshippers who could qualify for matriculation.

The Bishop's trustees had taken over Lucius Doolittle's grammar school in 1845 in the confident expectation that it would be a source of matriculants for the college. This hope had not been realized. Very few of the parents who could afford the fees for the school were willing to contemplate a clerical career for their sons, and their sons, having spent their school years in Lennoxville, looked for wider horizons and a more exciting environment if they opted for post-secondary studies. From the beginning, Jasper Nicolls would have preferred that the grammar school be a separate entity, located not nearer than Sherbrooke. He perceived that daily contact between the older schoolboys, most of whom had no further scholarly ambitions, and the undergraduates would work to the disadvantage of the latter. He also foresaw, accurately, that the teaching resources of the college would be frequently raided to satisfy the needs of the school, which were difficult to predict from one year to the next since enrolment fluctuated widely as a function of the reputation of the headmaster and the efficiency of its boarding establishment. In 1854, the headmaster of the period resigned, and the trustees decided to close the school.

As an alternative means of increasing the number of students matriculating at Bishop's, the trustees had in 1852 appointed a committee to examine the possibility of granting affiliate status to academies and high schools established in the Townships by local associations. It was hoped to establish matriculation as the standard for graduation from these schools, and in 1855 Corporation decided that the eventual proceeds of the sale of the grammar school property in Lennoxville should be devoted to subsidies for affiliated schools. However, nothing seems to have come of this project. Later in the decade, McGill instituted a scheme of affiliation which encouraged academies to offer some of the Arts curriculum at a level satisfactory to the McGill faculty. This initiative proved very popular. St Francis College in Richmond was the first academy to be granted affiliate status, in 1858.[12] By the end of the nineteenth century the network of affiliated colleges extended to the Pacific coast and included institutions that have since become major universities.

Students in affiliated colleges would not, of course, have directly affected the 'body count' reported to the legislature. Bishop's had limited admission to candidates who had achieved or were at least capable of achieving matriculation (i.e., university entrance) standard. The university's reported enrolment suffered accordingly by comparison with the figures reported by institutions which admitted part-time students and men who did not aspire to a degree. Was there any way to generate a rapid increase in genuine aspirants for university standing?

During the winter of 1855–56 this question was canvassed in the correspondence between Bishop Mountain and the principal. Under the authority of the act of 1853 (18 Vict. Chap. 78), the secretary of state for the province had been attempting to obtain from the university, as an "Institution deriving in part its support from public moneys," a complete report of its "condition, management and progress."[13] The principal and the faculty feared this as a first step toward state control. Nicolls had been fiercely and publicly contesting the right of the government to request the report, and the faculty were preparing a petition to the legislature to have the universities formally exempted from the provision of the act. The bishop advised a more diplomatic approach. He believed that a significant increase in funding could only be obtained from the government. He reported that the "officials here of our own church, and men well affected towards us, told us when we pointed to Victoria College having double the allowance we receive, that at that college the returns exhibited, I think, 119 students."[14] Steps had to be taken immediately to find "means of adding to our numerical exhibition of persons in whose behalf the [government] grant could be made available."[15]

THE RESURRECTION OF THE GRAMMAR SCHOOL

In June 1856 a special meeting of Corporation was called to consider whether to open a junior department or to establish a collegiate school. Vice-Chancellor J.S. McCord proposed a scheme for a junior department or preparatory class of 20 pupils under the direction of a master who, assisted by the faculty of the college, would prepare all the students for matriculation. A new building for the junior department was considered essential to the success of the project. The principal, with the support of the faculty, moved in amendment that the projected junior department should be considered as a temporary expedient until means should be found to endow a completely autonomous school. The amended motion was approved. However, on further reflection the supporters of the vice-chancellor's scheme concluded that 20 pupils would not generate enough revenue to pay the salary needed to attract a competent master for the junior department. At another special meeting in February 1857 Lucius Doolittle moved, and it was resolved, that the proposed junior department be extended to admit an indefinite number of pupils of any age, in accordance with the original prospectus of the college.

It is probable that the trustees' decision to resurrect the grammar school was influenced by the steps the new governors of McGill had taken in 1852 to rescue the High School of Montreal from its financial difficulties. They had adopted that institution as "the High School department of McGill College"; and during the winter of 1852–53 they decided to build Burnside Hall, on the north-east corner of Dorchester and University streets, to rehouse both the Faculty of Arts and the high school.[16] However, that project was not a model Bishop's could easily follow. Almost all the students of the high school and most of the McGill undergraduates lived at home, so there was much less occasion for interaction between the two groups than there would be in the residential community at Bishop's. The McGill governors also had access to greater financial resources, and that together with the availability of part-time instructors in the much larger Montreal community enabled them to adopt the high school and reinforce the university faculty simultaneously.

In 1857 McGill had obtained an annual grant of £282 from the government for the high school. Perhaps the Bishop's trustees expected to obtain a similar grant for their "Junior Department." At any rate, they felt able to guarantee a salary of £250 per annum to the rector of the department, to be increased to £350 as soon as the fees from the scholars should permit. The rector was also to hold a chair in the college and to be a member of the College Council. Bishop Mountain commented that he would be on a better footing than the principal of the college.

These terms proved attractive to the Reverend J.W. Williams, a graduate of Pembroke College (Oxford), who was classical master at Leamington College in England, and he arrived to take up his appointment in August 1857. Williams proved to be an excellent choice—a sound scholar and competent teacher, and a strict disciplinarian who commanded the respect and, ultimately, the affection of the boys. By his third year in office, enrolment in the school had outgrown the accommodation available in the village.

In January 1860 a special meeting of Corporation was therefore called "to determine the site of the buildings about to be erected for the Junior Department and Grammar School."[17] A broadly based committee had been constituted in June 1857 to "bring before the public the need for new buildings";[18] but it had failed to report any progress at the annual meetings of 1858 and 1859. It was replaced in 1859 by a smaller committee with a mandate to "consider and report whether any and what steps may be taken to promote an enlarged sphere of usefulness to the public in the operation of the College."[19] This committee included R.W. Heneker, newly appointed a trustee, and destined to control the financial affairs of the institution for the next 40 years.

Heneker had replaced Galt as commissioner of the BALC. Born in Dublin, he had been trained as an architect and surveyor under Sir Charles Barry during the period when Barry was designing the Houses of Parliament and Westminster Bridge in London. In 1855, Heneker had abandoned his profession and set out to make his fortune in Canada. He proved to be a hard-driving and competent man of business, and he rapidly became the principal motor of industrial development in the Sherbrooke region. As well as being president of the Eastern Townships Bank and of the Sherbrooke Gas, Water and Electric Light Company, he worked hard to reinforce the cultural resources of the English-speaking community as French-speaking immigrants flooded into the region. He was for many years chairman of the Protestant section of the provincial Council of Public Instruction, and in 1887 he was a prime mover in the founding of Sherbrooke Hospital.[20]

In the course of the work of the 1859 committee Heneker found the college's accounts and financial affairs in a state which he regarded as deplorable, and the eventual recommendations of the committee dealt principally with the need to establish a more detailed accounting system and to exercise tighter control over the college's investments. Those recommendations responding more directly to the committee's mandate were strongly influenced by concern for economy and administrative efficiency. The key recommendation was that the junior department be incorporated with the college and carried on in buildings on the same site. An amendment by Professor Miles, that the school should be located on a separate site "at an inconsiderable distance from the present College buildings,"[21] was defeated, and the original proposal adopted, at a meeting of the Corporation in January 1860.

This motion together with Lucius Doolittle's motion in February 1857 sealed the fate of the Faculty of Arts. At that point it was absolutely essential, in order for the Faculty to reach maturity, that its teaching resources be reinforced to enable it to offer a more broadly based curriculum. In his address to the Young Men's Protestant Educational Union in 1857, Jasper Nicolls had identified those studies he held to be of primary importance—"which give [the student] knowledge of man in his various relations in private and public life, as a complete and independent being and as a member of various bodies." High on the list were history and drama, the latter in Nicolls' opinion "the truest exponent of the life and customs of the age it belongs to."[22] He also considered grammar, composition, and rhetoric essential studies, and he emphasized the value of the study of modern languages, which would yield "the almost incalculable advantage of enabling man to enter into the literature of other countries and compare together the minds of nations, one with another; for the characters of nations are as varied and peculiar as the idiosyncrasies of individuals."[23] Knowledge of the natural world, that is, the study of the sciences; Nicolls acknowledged to be useful, but he obviously considered it of secondary importance.

Neither the principal's desire to expand the range of humanistic studies in the institution nor the trustees' wish to "promote an enlarged sphere of usefulness to the public in the operation of the College"[24] was to lead to a reinforcement of teaching resources. Setting aside the advice of the principal and faculty, Corporation chose instead to attach first priority to the resurrection of the grammar school. As a result the limited resources of the community which supported the college were to be entirely devoted to this cause. Further, the schoolboys were to remain on campus, in frequent daily contact with the undergraduates, for another 60 years, requiring from the Corporation, the principal, and the faculty an expenditure of administrative and intellectual energy which they could ill spare, and which yielded a pitifully small harvest of matriculants for the college.

The committee further recommended that responsibility for the domestic economy of the institution be transferred from the College Council to the bursar, and that members of the faculty be required to take part in the instruction of classes in the junior department. Finally, the committee recommended that every facility be given for the admission of casual students "to adapt the College to the present condition of the population and to afford encouragement to persons already occupied in gaining their living to proceed to a degree."[25]

Though Corporation deferred consideration of these recommendations, they gave a clear indication of the direction in which the wind was blowing. They also suggest that the College Council, composed at that time entirely of members of faculty, had not coped successfully with its administrative responsibilities, which included all the details of supply and maintenance in connection with the boarding establishment. These had been greatly increased by the reappearance of the grammar school and aggravated by the fact that it was installed, temporarily it was hoped, in the old school building in the village. None of the faculty had had any business experience, and, superbly equipped though he was to give intellectual and moral leadership to the fledgling university, Jasper Nicolls had too optimistic a view of human nature to be a good administrator. By the end of the decade, the council's failure to maintain discipline and adequately supervise the boarding establishment had begun to affect the college's reputation.

LIFE IN COLLEGE

Before the resurrection of the school the council seems to have presided during the 1850s over a tranquil and hard-working community. Living conditions in college were spartan, but relations between faculty and undergraduates were close. Reminiscences written "forty years on" recalled the geniality and the gentlemanly character of Vice-Chancellor Hale and the members of faculty—"never lacking in that deference, even to a student, which preserves his self-respect and wins his affection"—the informality of the lectures and the interest of the professors in the progress of each student.[26]

The diary Louis Campbell Wurtele (B.A., 1857) kept during his final year in college[27] gives numerous glimpses of undergraduate life in a society in which "plain living and high thinking" were the norms. Wurtele came from a staunchly Anglican family in comfortable circumstances— his father was a considerable landowner and seigneur of Rivière David, near the Yamaska river east of Sorel—but he had been raised in a pioneer community and was equally at home repairing the haycocks on a Lennoxville farm or trapping and learning to stuff specimens for a museum of natural history in the college. Like most of his classmates, he was destined for the ministry, and he and his friends sallied forth on Sunday afternoons, on foot or on snowshoes, to teach Sunday School and Bible classes in the schoolhouses within a radius of three or four miles of Lennoxville. Opinions on religious doctrine were strongly held and frequently discussed by the undergraduates, and Wurtele was not above praying in chapel that the principal might "see the light" on some points at issue.

His account of the work accomplished by his class during the Michaelmas term, 1856 confirmed that the faculty had not yielded to the temptation to lower standards in order to increase enrolment. Under the influence of H.H. Miles, Wurtele developed a keen interest in natural science. He was persuaded that, in the context of the developing conflict between the biblical accounts of creation and the results of scientific observation and analysis, a sound grounding in science would lend authority to his ministry. Miles was a correspondent of Sir William Logan, the director of the Geological Survey of Canada, and through his influence Wurtele obtained field and laboratory experience in geology during the summer of 1857 and introductions to a post-graduate year of scientific study in London.

Outside the lecture room Wurtele and his friends organized weekly debates and worked under Principal and Mrs Nicolls' direction to develop a good standard of music in the chapel services. For other amusements, they swam in and paddled on the river in the spring and fall and ranged through the woods in the winter. Neither the quality of the food nor the housekeeping in college seems to have been cause for complaint—perhaps because Wurtele had been made very welcome in the home near Lennoxville of his friend Edward Towle (B.A., 1857), whose sister he was courting and would subsequently marry!

Discipline was not a problem. From the minutes of the College Council it appears that beer was served at dinner to those who could pay for it, and that undergraduates occasionally indulged to excess. More serious offenses included overdue return from one or more of the taverns on Wellington Street in Sherbrooke and, on one occasion, riding in a buggy with one of the female servants—though authority was at pains to impute nothing more than indiscretion to the offender. The principal resisted several attempts by the trustees to require members of faculty to take attendance at lectures and chapel. As an alternative, very much in keeping with his character, he asked each undergraduate to keep a record of his own attendance, and these were submitted weekly to Nicolls.

By 1860, however, the rapid growth of the enrolment in the school had increased the population which had to be housed and fed to over 100, and the council began to lose control of the household management. During the winter of 1860–61 undergraduate discontent with the conditions in residence boiled over. In the course of the Lent term there appeared the first (and last) issue of the "College Frying Pan," a printed broadsheet whose aim was "to place before the reader, as we see them, the hitherto irremediable wrongs of the resident students." "While we are proud of [the college's] standing as one of the first and best colleges in America, as unsurpassed in classical and mathematical knowledge in her professors and thoroughness in her course," the editors wrote, they had come to the conclusion that "learned men are fit only to be scholars and know very little of the practical parts of living men." The most immediate cause for complaint was the behaviour of the steward, Mr Fry, "a corpulent and burly man of sinister appearance, who rejoices in the possession of powerful lungs, whose strength he has enormously increased by constant altercations with his loving spouse." Fry, it was claimed, had replaced the College Council as the effective authority over the domestic establishment. Adverse comment was also made concerning the lack of punctuality of one of the professors and the impudence of the schoolboys.[28]

The bishops were not amused by this document, which they thought unseemly in an institution dedicated to the education of ordinands. The principal was required to read to the assembled undergraduates an episcopal reprimand and admonition. Nevertheless, the lightness of the culprits' sentence makes it clear that the complaints were in some measure justified. Shortly afterward Fry added injury to insult by assaulting an undergraduate when drunk on beer supplied by another, and he was dismissed. Nicolls steeled himself to be less merciful in his administration of justice, and the bishops added the vice-chancellor and two members of Corporation to the College Council. Professor Miles resigned from the council in protest and wrote to Bishop Mountain to urge that he be appointed a trustee. In practice, since the new members lived in Montreal or Quebec, the enlarged council could only be convened two or three times a year, when it heard formal reports from the principal, the rector, and the bursar. The week-by-week administration of the institution was presumably carried on by informal consultation among the local members, as before.

THE SHRINKING ENDOWMENT

The College Council attempted during the session of 1859–60 to revive the financial appeal. In March the principal canvassed the western area of the Townships lying within the Diocese of Montreal. Though the state of the roads finally forced him to desist before he had completed the task, he succeeded in obtaining new subscriptions amounting to $850 (£210 currency). Other members of the council had less success in the region around Sherbrooke and Lennoxville, but in May the principal and the rector raised $2,500 during a visit to Quebec, and they believed that more would be forthcoming. On the other hand, the committee that had agreed to assist the appeal in Montreal was of the opinion, reported by the Bishop of Montreal, that "the present time was in the highest degree unfavourable" for the prosecution of the appeal in that city.[29]

In an attempt to encourage a more generous response, donors of at least $500 were given the right to nominate a student for exemption from fees at either the school or college level. This "carrot," which had also been employed by the building committee in 1841, greatly complicated the financial statements of the institution. Such "donations" were in fact partly loans, which had to be carried on the books as liabilities. In some years, an appreciable fraction of the income from fees had to be charged to the redemption of these loans.

At the 1860 annual meeting of Corporation plans for the new school buildings were approved.[30] The building committee was authorized to proceed with construction and to procure the necessary funds, not to exceed $10,000, either *from the existing, funds of the college* or by loans, as the committee should see fit. By June 1861 the appeal had realized $5,850, but the committee had spent $21,732.[31] The deficit had been met by borrowing $10,000 from Edward Hale, $3,600 from the Professor of Divinity J.H. Thompson, and $2,000 from Lucius Doolittle. The committee was authorized to borrow a further $5,000, if necessary, to complete the work.

The buildings were finally completed in 1862 at a total cost of $30,825. The committee reported that $24,669 had been subscribed to the appeal, of which $13,979 had been collected, but a large number of these subscriptions were linked to exemptions from fees. In 1870 the college was still carrying nearly $13,000 as a liability in the accounts against exemptions from fees. In its efforts to respond to the growth of the school under the successful leadership of J.W. Williams, Corporation had thus appropriated about $16,000 of the college endowment, interest from which would provide the salary of one professor. Unhappily, Bishop Mountain died in January 1863, and in March Williams was elected to succeed him. He immediately resigned his rectorship, and he and his wife departed for Quebec, taking with them as housekeeper the matron of the school, Miss Thorne. The resulting dislocation had a serious effect on enrolment, and the accounts for the year 863 revealed an operating deficit of $3,000.[32]

In January 1865 Corporation resolved to send the principal and the Reverend Christopher Rawson, an alumnus, to England to appeal for £10,000 to restore and if possible increase the college endowment. In the prospectus drawn up for this purpose the Corporation justified its need for help by noting that, unlike many other universities and schools in the province, Bishop's had never received a grant of public funds for buildings or other nonrecurrent expenses incurred during the early years of such institutions. In addition, the grant toward operating expenses from the Superior Education Fund of the province had decreased from $2,000 per annum in 1857 to $1,500 in 1864. The authorities admitted the justice of the institution's claims, but they held out no hope of further funding for education which might make it possible to respond to them.

Bishop's College and Bishop's College School, 1862

In the event the appeal, in competition with others from more recently established and less wealthy colonies, fell on stony ground. The principal returned in September with a net subscription of £1,100. In the meantime the building committee had been authorized to spend another $4,000 to increase the accommodation in the new school building, so the endowment benefited little from the principal's labours.

Over the next three years the question of the operating deficit was continually on the agenda of the meetings of Corporation. An appeal to Episcopalians in the United States was mooted, but in the aftermath of the Civil War support could not be hoped for in that quarter. Meanwhile, Williams' successor as rector had come and gone, and a second incumbent was in difficulties. By the end of 1868 the institution's debt had grown to $24,300, and only the principal's salary, reduced to the minimum of $1,200 guaranteed to him by the trust deed of the Harrold benefaction, could be met from the endowment.

PENURY

As long as J.W. Williams had remained rector, the potentially disastrous consequences of Corporation's altered priorities had been avoided. The report of the proceedings of convocation in June 1863 was generally optimistic in tone.[33] Total enrolment in the school had increased to 150. The chancellor reported that the schoolboys had raised enough money to pay for the new bishop's episcopal robes. The valedictorian, Jérémie Babin, spoke eloquently to the undergraduates of the value of a Bishop's education: "Quand vous serez rendu maître des deux langues qui possèdent les plus riches trésors littéraires des temps modernes, que vous aurez appris à apprécier la sublime beauté des anciens et que vous serez armés de l'expérience de presque toutes les générations passées, il est évident que vous serez bien préparés à braver hardiment et avec succès les orages de la vie!"[34]

H.H. Miles, the vice-principal, addressed convocation, reporting at length on "our state as a working institution." Miles was chiefly concerned to respond to two veins of criticism to which Bishop's had evidently been subjected. The first referred to the small number of matriculants entering the college. He reminded his audience that, if Bishop's compared unfavourably in this respect with certain other similar institutions in the province it was in great measure because "thanks to the enlightened views of the Founders ... the generally willing though sometimes reluctant acquiescence of [the members of Corporation] ... and the resistance, the pertinacity, the obstinacy if you will so call it, of the principal and the professors."[35] The temptation to resort to low standards of admission for the sake of procuring a larger attendance of students had been resisted.

The second matter for concern was the effect on university-level teaching of the increased responsibilities for faculty in instruction in the school. Miles explained that under the new dispensation what had been the first year of university work would now be virtually accomplished in the school, so that the university course could be reduced in length from four years to three. He felt that all Canadian universities would profit from the establishment of a "common and proper" standard of examination for the province—an examination which, he implied, would confirm his claim with respect to the academic standards at Bishop's. He hoped to have demonstrated "the absence of a real foundation for those apprehensions about sacrificing more or less the interests of higher education in order to further purely elementary school work"[36]— apprehensions which he confessed to have shared for a time. Nevertheless, several passages in his address revealed the strain to which he and his colleagues had been subjected by the new regime.

In the event, the apprehensions turned out to be well founded. The recently introduced three-year degree program required a higher level of preparation from matriculants, which only the very small number matriculating from the school could in general be expected to meet. The extra tutorial work required for weak first-year undergraduates was therefore greatly increased. Until 1863 two of the assistant masters in the school had been employed for this purpose. One of the first signs of financial pressure was the elimination of this support in October. Another was the appointment of an undergraduate as an assistant master in the school while he was still pursuing his degree program.

During the next three years the number of matriculants increased, raising the undergraduate enrolment above 20 for the first time. Overcoming his natural diffidence Nicolls continued his personal efforts to restore the college's finances, but repeated refusals must have severely tested his morale. In 1863 he wrote to his wife from Quebec: "I have been in town all day ... begging in the Lower Town ... on my way up, I looked in here [Legislative Library] to see some of the members, but those I want are not here"; again in 1864 he wrote: "I have been rather unsuccessful today ... amongst other things, having waited more than an hour in the office of the Finance Minister [Galt], without seeing him after all."[37]

In contrast behold Frances (Feo) Monck, niece of Governor-General Lord Monck, boarding the ferry in July 1864 for Levis "on the arm of Mr Galt," bound for "Lennoxville College," where the governor-general was to receive an honourary degree. The vice-regal party (which included

Galt) arrived after dark and was greeted by "more than a hundred torches blazing away, boys without end ... in rifle volunteer uniforms [the Civil War was raging in the United States] and a volunteer band played Scotch airs." The next day they drove "to the pretty red college, just like an English college, with such pretty grounds." Before lunch the students competed in swimming and diving matches and in boat and canoe races under the approving eyes of the visitors seated under the trees on the bank of the Massawippi—"The boys are more like English boys than any I have seen out here." Lunch was a formal affair, to which Frances was escorted by Jasper Nicolls, and she found the food very good. Though "the hall was crammed, and it was very hot," she also reported very favourably on the speeches at convocation. Altogether, Frances Monck, not generally given to benevolence in her judgments, found Lennoxville "a charming and civilized place ... the boys seem very gentlemanly and well-looked-after."[38]

The financial statement for 1865 revealed yet another operating deficit, and Corporation had to meet in April 1866 to take steps to respond to a desperate financial situation. During the winter, the Professor of Divinity had declared his intention of resigning at the end of the session. During the first ten years of the college's existence, the principal had been Professor of Divinity, but he had found it increasingly difficult to keep up with the necessary reading during a period when the impact of scientific studies on theological positions was increasingly significant. In 1855 he had taken over the Chair of Classics and had asked Corporation to appoint a new Professor of Divinity. Corporation now resolved to ask Nicolls to resume the Chair of Divinity, leaving the instruction in classics to be provided by whatever temporary help could be obtained. The principal did not refuse the assignment, but felt that his knowledge of the field was no longer up to the standard which he considered necessary, so he offered to resign if the Visitors could find a better qualified candidate. Being apprised of the financial situation of the institution, H.H. Miles also offered to resign, effective 1 July 1867. His offer was accepted.

Without Miles the college could no longer offer the minimum breadth of curriculum necessary to attract undergraduates who were not prospective ordinands. His loss was the most serious immediate consequence of the trustees' misdirection of the institution's patrimony. A man of many parts, he had a wide-ranging concern for the development of a better system of education in Canada, which object he pursued energetically through public lectures, books, and tracts. In 1862 he had been appointed one of the commissioners for Canada at the International Exhibition in London, in the company of Sir William Logan. His account of the Exhibition, to which he appended a succinct description of the Eastern Townships, was published in London and brought him to the attention of a wider public. Aberdeen had conferred an LL.D., upon him in 1863, McGill a second in 1866.

In 1867 Miles moved to Montreal and became secretary to the Protestant section of the Council of Public Instruction. From this vantage point he agitated continuously for professional training and better pay for teachers in the Protestant schools. Observing that English-speaking Quebeckers were sadly ignorant of the history of their country, he wrote a history of the French regime in Canada, and two histories of Canada for children, one of which was adopted for use in both Protestant and Catholic schools. In the course of writing these histories he discovered that Canadian public records were "unorganized, badly preserved, widely scattered and uninventoried."[39] By 1871, with the help of several of the leading men in the Canadian government, he was able to present a petition to the House of Commons which resulted in the establishment of a preliminary records commission. The following year, Douglas Brymner was appointed the first Dominion Archivist.

In August 1866 G.C. Irving, the rector of the school, drowned while holidaying at Cacouna, one of the villages on the Gulf of St Lawrence to which well-to-do Montrealers and Quebeckers resorted during the hot weather. It was eight months before a replacement could be found, so the principal was appointed acting rector. During the 1866–67 academic year, therefore, Nicolls carried the entire administrative responsibility for the institution.

To meet the emergency he pressed into service the parish priest of Lennoxville, A.C. Scarth, and together they provided the full time of one master to the school. Under these circumstances it was manifestly impossible that Nicolls at the same time assume responsibility for divinity. A member of the College Council, the Reverend Charles Hamilton, volunteered to assume Henry Roe's parish duties in Quebec gratuitously, and Roe was appointed interim unpaid Professor of Divinity. The principal retained primary responsibility for classics in the college, with some help from the senior assistant master, C.P. Mulvaney.

Charles Hamilton, later Bishop of Niagara and Bishop of Ottawa, was the first member of the Hamilton family, wealthy timber merchants of Quebec, to take an active role in the affairs of the university. He was followed by his brother Robert, who served as a trustee from 1871 to 1898, and by Robert's son John, who was chancellor from 1900 to 1925. The Hamiltons had been timber merchants active in the Baltic trade to Liverpool at the beginning of the nineteenth century. Charles' father had opened a branch of the firm in Quebec in 1807 when Napoleon cut off timber supplies from Scandinavia to Great Britain. Over the next hundred years the firm established itself as one of the most important among those exploiting the forest resources of the Ottawa river and its tributaries. The Quebec Hamiltons were staunch supporters of the moderate churchmanship of which Bishop's, was a fount; and their munificent benefactions over a period of 60 years were of inestimable value to the Faculty of Divinity, and indeed to the whole college, in withstanding the assaults of the evangelical party in the church.

Though the winter had been a difficult one Nicolls reported to the council in the spring of 1867 that it had not been without beneficial results in some respects. He had gained a better understanding of the intrinsic difficulty of operating the college and the school on the same campus. As a first step in establishing comity he had persuaded the trustees to appoint Mrs Irving, widow of the late rector, matron in charge of the domestic establishment of both college and school.

The arrival of the new rector, the Reverend Robert Walker, in May 1867 relieved the principal of some of his administrative responsibilities. Walker had been Professor of Mathematics at the Royal Military College, Sandhurst, and he was appointed Professor of Mathematics at the college in the hope that he would be able to find time to carry part of the lecture load at university level.

However, the new rector turned out to be ambitious to raise the academic standards of the school to match those of the better "public schools" in England, and he could only spare three lectures a week for the undergraduates. He greatly increased the academic workload of the schoolboys, reinforcing the prestige of the classical part of the curriculum. He proposed to raise the requirements for admission and to limit the enrolment to the number of scholars which in his opinion could be adequately supervised by the teaching staff. His wish to limit the enrolment alarmed the trustees, but in any case the classical bent of the new regime did not find favour among parents, and enrolment decreased rapidly from year to year. Finding it impossible to maintain the school with the reduced number of scholars, Walker resigned in March 1870.

In May 1868 after another year of improvisation, the principal observed to the council that "Classical and English Literature and Composition, History, Logic, Rhetoric, Moral Philosophy and Divinity form a wide range of subjects for one mind to deal with successfully. The same mind is expected at the same time to carry on the instruction of candidates for the Ministry in a complete theological course, the one large and important subject, Ecclesiastical History, excepted (it had been taught by A.C. Scarth) ... the continuance of such a state of things is impossible."[40]

THE BRITISH NORTH AMERICA ACT

While Bishop's was thus struggling to overcome the consequences of the misdirection of its patrimony, the provinces of British North America were struggling to develop a new relationship with one another. Political instability, serious economic problems, the need to connect the provinces by rail, and the threat of annexation by a belligerent American government all argued in favour of mutual reinforcement, but the population's diversity in language and religion could only be accommodated by a federal union.

Negotiations to this end began in Charlottetown in 1864 and they finally ended in success with the passing of the British North America Act by the British Parliament in 1867. One of the most difficult parts of the act to negotiate had been section 93, which assigned responsibility for education to the provincial legislatures. The Protestant community in Lower Canada feared that their schools and universities would not receive equitable treatment from the government of the newly created Province of Quebec, and Alexander Galt made himself their spokesman at the negotiating table. He strongly influenced the final form of section 93. Unfortunately, Parliament abandoned the responsibility for the protection of the educational rights of minorities conferred on it in the section to the courts, and successive judicial interpretations have over the past century imposed enormous strain on the political fabric of the country.

The immediate result of the Confederation settlement in Quebec was the establishment of a Department of Public Instruction, the first such department in a Canadian province. This innovation was due to P.-J.-O. Chauveau, the first Premier of Quebec, who had been deputy superintendent of Public Instruction for Canada East from 1855 to 1867. During his tenure he had travelled extensively in Europe to study other school systems, and the new department, of which he was the first minister, was intended to provide him with the means to put what he had learned into practice. However, neither the Roman Catholic hierarchy nor the Protestant minority took kindly to the control of education by politicians. In 1875, the Conservative administration of de Boucherville abolished the department and replaced it with a superintendent appointed for a long term. The Council of Public Instruction (CPI), an advisory body which had existed since 1859, was strengthened and divided into Catholic and Protestant committees, and these committees established the policies for their respective schools which the superintendent was to carry out. The Protestant school system was thus provided with the autonomy Galt had sought for it, and the English-language universities, which were not under the control of the CPI, benefited from a coherent school curriculum leading to matriculation.

Louis-Philippe Audet, historian of the CPI, attaches considerable importance to the influence exerted by Bishop Williams throughout this period—as adviser to Galt during the pre-Confederation negotiations, as participant in the drafting of the act of 1869 which established separate confessional committees of the CPI, and as member of the Protestant Committee throughout his episcopacy.[41] If Audet is correct, this may explain why the bishop kept his distance from the conflict which was about to erupt between Principal Nicolls and the strongly evangelical Anglican community in Montreal.

THE SURRENDER TO THE SYNODS

Though Corporation devoted much time at meetings in June 1868 to debating various strategies for decreasing expenditure and increasing revenue, it had now become clear that, having lost the endowment, the college must find new financial backing if it was to survive. Bishop's had been responsible for training nearly all the younger Anglican clergy in Quebec and eastern Ontario, including Montreal, the commercial and industrial metropolis of Canada, and Ottawa, its capital city. Why then had the college been chronically underfunded? The answer to this question was to be found in the nature of the corporation by which it was governed and the dissensions that racked the Anglican communion in Canada at the time.

The death of Bishop Mountain in January 1863 had marked a turning point in the relations of the institution with the Anglican community in Lower Canada. Bishop's had been established as the bishop's college. While he lived, his seniority and the respect in which he was held had prevented those Anglicans who for various reasons would have preferred a more representative corporation from making any headway. The most powerful and vocal of these were the members of the evangelical party, strongly entrenched in Montreal.

The evangelical strain of Anglican churchmanship had developed as a reaction to the nominal conformity and indifference of so many of the church's leaders in the eighteenth century. The early evangelicals had much in common with the Wesleyan Methodists. They laid great emphasis on the individual Christian's acceptance of Christ as a personal saviour as an essential condition for salvation. They held that such Christians had unconditional and direct access to Grace, that is, to the working of the Holy Spirit within them. Evangelicals tended to regard the role of the sacraments of the church as a channel for Grace as one of useful reinforcement rather than a fundamental one. In particular, "an historic episcopate traceable to apostolic direction" was felt to be "conducive to the *well-being* but not necessary to the *being* of the Church."[42]

These principles generated vigorous and free-wheeling action by evangelical churchmen towards social and religious reform. The long and ultimately successful campaign against slavery in British dominions owed a great deal to their efforts. Their emphasis on the responsibility of the individual Christian led them to favour representative government, in the Church as well as in the secular domain. Until the advent of the Tractarian movement in the 1840s the evangelical contribution to Anglican theory and practice had been almost entirely positive, but the insistence of Newman and his followers on the primacy of the sacramental life of the church generated a counter-current of opposition among evangelicals. When Newman transferred his allegiance to the Roman Catholic Church, followed by a significant number of Anglicans of the upper class, and when the Roman Catholic episcopacy was re-established in England, this opposition hardened into a rigid and fear-driven anti-Romanism. Perhaps not surprisingly given the overwhelming Roman Catholic majority, this strain of evangelical churchmanship was prevalent in Lower Canada.

Bishop Mountain had a high regard for the work of evangelical clergy in his diocese, and he had been instrumental in obtaining legal authority to establish synodical government in the colonial dioceses, thus freeing Canadian Anglicans from intervention by the British Parliament. However, he held that motions of synod must be agreed to by the bishop as well as by the clergy and the laity, and he fought hard to retain the episcopal veto when the first synod was convened in Quebec in 1859.

Since the foundation of the college the bishop had made continued efforts to involve the Diocese of Montreal, which owed its existence and its episcopal endowment to his lobbying, in the promotion of the interests of the institution. These efforts had ranged from the amendment of the act of incorporation to give the Bishop of Montreal equal authority in Corporation with the Bishop of Quebec to discouraging the principal from holding a choral service of celebration to mark the consecration of the chapel, lest this be perceived by the evangelical party as a papistical innovation.[43] He had enjoyed very little success. The evangelicals knew that Nicolls had been an undergraduate at Oriel when Newman was a tutor of that college, and they were deeply suspicious of his intentions. Though the principal would have regarded himself as a moderate churchman and there is no evidence that any of the clergy he trained adhered to the Tractarian party, Montreal remained cold to appeals from Bishop's even during Mountain's episcopacy.

After the bishop's death, the evangelical party seized upon the financial difficulties of the college and school to demand that Nicolls be placed under tutelage. The animus with which they pursued their goal was in part due to the ferment generated in the Montreal diocese during the election to replace Francis Fulford, first Bishop of Montreal, who died in September 1868. His successor would be Metropolitan, or senior bishop, of the Anglican communion in Canada, and the election was bitterly contested. The bishops did not wish a clergyman newly elected from the diocese to be their chief. The evangelicals were determined to elect one of their own. At meetings of synod held in November and the following May, a total of six days of balloting failed to resolve the deadlock. Compromise was finally achieved in the person of the Reverend Ashton Oxenden.[44]

The new bishop was 60 years old, well educated, of the evangelical persuasion, and an easygoing disposition. He had spent almost the whole of his career as rector of a village in Kent, and he had no administrative experience. He owed his nomination to the success of a series of tracts he had written, which set out the claims of Christianity in simple language and had enjoyed wide circulation in working-class parishes in England. He found Canada very strange.

It was in this highly charged, not to say unstable, environment that Corporation had to deal with the financial crisis and the mistrust of the Montrealers. In June 1868 the newly formed Alumni Association had forwarded two resolutions to the annual meeting. The first of these pledged the alumni to provide $400 in order that an alumnus, the Reverend R.C. Tambs, might be appointed Mathematical Tutor in the college for the coming academic year. Since the alumni were in majority clergymen of very modest means, this was a generous expression of their loyalty. Tambs had been General Nicolls Mathematical Scholar in 1863, so Corporation gratefully accepted the association's timely offer. In the second resolution, the alumni, "sensible of the great dissatisfaction which exists among members of the Church at large regarding the management of the Institution," urged that confidence in Corporation's management would be materially reinforced if the synods of Montreal and Quebec were to participate in the election of trustees and to receive annual reports from Corporation.[45] Reform of the Corporation was thus being urged on both religious and financial grounds.

Negotiations with the synods were begun in 1868. By June 1870 agreement had been obtained on the following terms:

1 That Corporation should consist of the Bishops, the Chancellor, the Principal, the Professors of Divinity, Mathematics and Classics, and the Rector, together with six other governors to be appointed by the Bishops jointly and ten to be appointed, one-half by the Synod of Montreal and one-half by the Synod of Quebec.
2 That the term of appointment, other than for office-holders, should be three years, or for such duration as the Synods might direct for their appointees.
3 That the principal and vice-principal should be appointed in the manner provided for the appointment of ordinary professors and not as at present by the bishops—the appointment of Professors of Divinity to be vested in the bishops.
4 That the Corporation should report annually to the synods.[46]

Corporation decided at the annual meeting in 1870 that a bill incorporating these amendments should be submitted to the legislature.

In his first address to the synod of the Diocese of Montreal, Bishop Oxenden had expressed a desire to found a theological college in Montreal, where he could gather his ordinands around him, "watch their characters and superintend their preparation for the Ministry."[47] Learning during the following winter that he was actively promoting this project, Corporation addressed a memorial to him in March 1871, the terms of which made clear the extent to which they were demoralized. Noting that Oxenden's initiative would fatally divide the financial support available for theological training in Lower Canada, they urged that he await the maturing of "the great experiment for the setting of Bishop's College on a footing more satisfactory to the Church at large." The goal of the experiment was stated to be "that the entire control of the college" should be placed in the hands of the synods, which could then "mould the Institution to their mind and provide for the safe husbanding of all funds committed to their keeping."[48] Under these circumstances, the writers were confident that "funds for the resuscitation of the Professorships will not be withheld."[49]

This offer of an abject surrender of the college's autonomy seems to have persuaded a majority of the Montreal clergy to vote against Oxenden's proposal. However, he was not deterred, and by 1873 had obtained enough financial support from the evangelical laity to establish the Montreal Diocesan Theological College (MDTC) by episcopal fiat. It is interesting to note that the founders of the MDTC did not believe that *its* development needed to be supervised by synod. It was not until 1907 that a representative of synod was appointed to its board of governors.[50]

Richard William Heneker, 1900

THE ATTACK ON THE PRINCIPAL

Meanwhile, Jasper Nicolls had been soldiering on under the same conditions which he had correctly described two years earlier as impossible. Tambs had given invaluable support in mathematics, but in early 1870 the alumni had found that they would not be able to raise the full sum required for his stipend in the 1870–71 session. The principal drew the attention of the annual meeting to this situation. He also informed those present that Mrs Irving, the matron, "having received no encouragement from the trustees to stay," had accepted a post at Trinity College in Toronto.[51] Neither problem elicited any response from the members. Instead they devoted their attention to a scheme proposed by the ever-busy Mr Heneker. His plan revealed that he still believed that the school, under efficient administration, could provide an adequate flow of matriculants to the college, and he laid out in some detail the conditions under which this could be achieved. The first of these was that the principal should resign.

His motion read: "That in view of the absolute necessity of a change in management of the College in order to meet if possible the views of the majority of Churchmen in the Dioceses of Montreal and Quebec, the Rev. J.H. Nicolls, D.D., who has for so many years filled the important position of Principal of the College with untiring zeal and assiduity be requested to resign, holding office until his successor be appointed."[52] Nicolls was to be offered the post of Professor of Classics.

After considerable discussion the members of Corporation present decided that "as the present government of the Institution would be greatly changed in a few months, the scheme and the motions should lie on the table for further consideration."[53]

The legislature passed an act modifying the composition of Corporation in December 1870. Provision for synod representation was made according to the terms of the agreement reached in June, but the *ex officio* membership of the officers of the college had been eliminated, leaving the representatives of the synods with a clear majority. All the members of Corporation had resigned before the meetings of Synods were held in June 1871. The first annual meeting of the new Corporation was convened on the twenty-eight of the same month.

The Bishop and the Synod of Montreal had appointed, among others, the Venerable Archdeacon Bond and Mr C.J. Brydges. William Bennett Bond, a prime mover in the initiative to found the Diocesan College in Montreal, is described by the historian of that institution as "not a scholar—of simple faith and religious sincerity, he held fast to traditional views of scripture and to the evangelical doctrines of the Church.

Today he would be called a fundamentalist."[54] C.J. Brydges, at that time a resident of Montreal, was a major player in the development of the railway system in eastern Canada and, after 1879, Chief Commissioner of the Hudson's Bay Company during the rapid development of the Province of Manitoba. When Bond, as Bishop of Montreal, sought an act of incorporation for the MDTC in 1879, Brydges was named as one of the chief petitioners.

At the meeting of Corporation, a new committee was appointed, chaired by Heneker and including Brydges, with a mandate to "report on the finances with a special view for making the Institution self-sustaining."[55] Consideration of two requests by the principal for modest reinforcement of the teaching resources at the college level was deferred, on a motion by Brydges, until this committee should have reported.

On the eighteenth of January Corporation met in Montreal to receive this report. The committee had established that a small profit had been realized on operations in 1871. It noted a steady increase in the numbers attending the school (due to the appointment of a new rector, the Reverend C.H. Badgley) and, in spite of the view strongly held by a minority that the operation of the college should be completely separated from that of the school, recommended that the current system of management be continued for another year.[56]

The comparatively optimistic tone of this report did not mollify Brydges. A man overflowing with energy and self-confidence, his headstrong temperament and wilfully authoritarian behaviour had provoked controversy throughout his career.[57] "Looking at the small number of students who have attended Bishop's College during the past few years and the absence of any appearance of increase," he moved that a special committee of five members be appointed "to consider the whole question of the present organization and to report at four o'clock this afternoon."[58] A committee was duly appointed under his chairmanship. The other members were Bond, H.S. Scott (an evangelical layman from the Quebec Synod), Heneker, and Charles Hamilton. Not unexpectedly, the committee returned at four o'clock with a verbal report recommending that a new Professor of Divinity be appointed by the two bishops, and that he replace Nicolls as principal. Such was the demoralization of the erstwhile leaders of Corporation that this proposal to demote Jasper Nicolls was summarily approved.

The principal forthwith requested that he be discharged at once from all further connection with the college or, failing that, he be "relieved from the extra amount of work which at present lay upon his shoulders and which he felt himself the more incompetent to discharge from the failure of his general health and especially of his eyesight." Brydges moved in reply "that the *President* be requested to inform the Reverend Dr Nicolls that this meeting trusts that he will not press his proposal for being at once relieved of all his duties, and that the Bishops ... be authorized, pending the reorganization of the College, to provide such temporary assistance as they may consider necessary."[60] On this note of gross discourtesy the meeting ended.

When Corporation met in May to approve the reports to be made to the synods, one of the new members, Mr Justice T.K. Ramsay, was present for the first time. Ramsay was about to be promoted from the Superior Court to the Court of Queen's Bench. He enjoyed an excellent professional reputation as "one of the Bench's most able lawyers and its most irascible judges."[61] He had been appointed by the Synod of Montreal. When the minutes of the meeting of 18 January were read, Ramsay moved that Brydges' motion to demote Jasper Nicolls be struck from the record, apparently on the grounds that proper notice of it had not been given. Ramsay's motion was defeated. He requested that the vote be recorded. The nays included most of the long-serving members of Corporation. Undeterred, he moved reconsideration of the report of the Brydges committee. The principal was asked to withdraw. After some discussion the report was referred to an enlarged committee for further consideration, a report to be submitted to the annual meeting in June. The meeting closed with a vote of thanks to Brydges for arranging for a Pullman car for the convenience of Montreal members attending meetings of Corporation and convocation.

Neither Brydges nor Bond attended the annual meeting. The report of the enlarged committee was read by Edward Hale. Though the report apologized for the discourtesy shown the principal in January and dwelt at some length on his long and valuable services, the recommendation was unchanged, "suggesting" that the principal should relinquish his office and accept appointment as Professor of Classics. At this point Bishop Williams read a letter he had received from the principal. Jasper Nicolls had offered his resignation to the bishop or to Corporation several times during his 27 years of service on occasions when he felt that he had not met the standards of performance he had set for himself. However, he was fully aware of the source of his present unpopularity, and he was not going to resign now until he had had an opportunity to defend publicly the training which ordinands had received at Bishop's under his direction. Finding himself "forced to be my own champion, against my will and contrary to the whole tenor of my life," he had written to the president that he would resign the principalship if a majority of all the members of Corporation called upon him to do so "upon condition that the grounds on which they call upon me to resign, formally communicated to me, be recorded, together with such answers and explanations as I may wish to make to them, in the minutes." His final paragraph was a trumpet call to his successors:

> I venture to hope that the Corporation will see that, in thus defending myself, I am doing even them a service. If the Principal of the College is a mere thing that can be blown away by a blast of unmerited unpopularity with the Corporation, no man of standing, no man who has any self-respect, or who looks for the respect of those placed under his care, will condescend to accept the office or can continue in it.[62]

Corporation proved unwilling to face him. Only a recommendation that the bishops appoint a Professor of Divinity was approved.

CALAMITIES

Throughout this period no reinforcement of the teaching resources at university level had been provided. The advent of C.H. Badgley as rector in 1870 had relieved the principal of worry about the school, and he had had some support in the teaching of classics from one of the schoolmasters, F.C. Emberson. He had continued to carry entire responsibility for divinity. From the beginning of the 1870–71 session the alumni had been unable to meet fully the stipend of $400 allotted to R.C. Tambs as Mathematical Tutor, but Tambs had loyally carried on, counting on the trustees to make up the deficit at the end of each financial year. In spite of its makeshift character the undergraduates seem to have thrived under this regime. Canon R.W. Norman of Montreal, appointed examiner in classics for the 1871–72 session, submitted a very favourable report on their attainments. Norman was an Englishman, a retired headmaster of Radley College who had come out to Canada to recover his health, and was highly regarded in Montreal as a clergyman and a private tutor. He had been appointed to Corporation by the Synod of Montreal, and when the attack on the principal developed he had rallied with T.K. Ramsay to Nicolls' defence. He was elected vice-chancellor in 1878, and he subsequently removed to the diocese of Quebec, where he became Dean of the Cathedral.[63] H.H. Miles, as examiner in mathematics, also expressed satisfaction with the results, in particular with the level attained by George Thorneloe, the General Nicolls Mathematical Scholar of the time. Thorneloe went on to become Bishop of Algoma and Metropolitan of Ontario.

The financial results for 1872 and the prospects for 1873 were so encouraging that in June 1873 the trustees restored the principal's salary to its pre-crisis level of $1,500 and appointed Tambs Professor of Mathematics, raising his stipend to $700 (plus board and room). It was also possible at last for the bishops to give effect to Corporation's resolution of June 1872 by appointing Canon Gilson, formerly of Montreal, as the new Professor of Divinity, at a salary of $1,600.

During the 1872–73 session, the principal's health had continued to deteriorate under the stress of his many responsibilities, and he now felt able to ask for a year's leave of absence to go to England for medical consultation. This was granted. The deterioration in his eyes proved to be extremely serious, and after a period of intense suffering, one of his eyes had to be removed to save the other.

Though Gilson had been appointed it was Henry Roe who took up the responsibilities of the Professor of Divinity in September 1873. No mention of his appointment is found in the minutes of the meetings of Corporation. Since he had been one of Nicolls' first students and was emphatically not evangelical, his arrival marked a significant shift, and it is regrettable that no explanation has survived. It may be that it signified a decision to abandon hope of appeasing the evangelical party in Montreal. In May Robert Hamilton had offered the Church Society of the Diocese of Quebec a contribution of $400 a year for five years toward the salary of a Professor of Divinity on condition that the Diocese of Montreal raise a like sum. Montreal had shown little interest, and in September Bishop Oxenden's college opened its doors. At any rate, Roe was a major acquisition. Badgley had been appointed vice-principal in Nicolls' absence; but as he did not live in college Roe was appointed dean, with responsibility for regulating life in residence.

In the early morning of the 25 January 1874 the school building with all its contents was destroyed by fire. Fortunately there was no loss of life, and the valiant efforts of the Sherbrooke fire brigade and a number of men from the village prevented the fire from spreading to the college building. However, the building was insured for only $15 thousand, and it would cost twice that amount to replace it. When Corporation was called to deal with this crisis, lively debate developed over the wisdom of rebuilding on the same site.

The community which supported the college had begun to realize why it had thus far failed to realize fully the hopes of its founders. In his charge to the 1871 Quebec Synod, at which representatives to Corporation were first elected, Bishop Williams had reminded the diocese that the college had had, and still needed to have, an endowment sufficient to maintain its faculties without depending on the fees of the students. This endowment had been appropriated in the interest of maintaining the school, for which he felt that the provision of a building rent-free ought to be sufficient endowment. The college's endowment must be replaced, and means must be taken to guard against any future encroachment upon college capital in the interests of the school.

At the February 1874 meeting of the Corporation, a letter was read from Professor Tambs urging that the school be removed to a different site. Norman and Ramsay moved that Corporation should seize the opportunity offered by the destruction of the school buildings to separate the school from the college and establish it in a separate locality. At the request of Robert Hamilton, Vice-Chancellor Heneker estimated that if this were done, an endowment to provide the college with at least $750 per annum would have to be raised—in addition, of course, to the sum required to rebuild the school. An amendment that the Corporation should cease to carry on the school (in which case the forthcoming financial campaign would have been devoted to restoring the college endowment) was defeated, and Corporation decided to rebuild on the same site. Over the next 18 months a successful financial campaign raised the full sum required to rebuild the school. The new building was occupied following the Easter vacation in 1875.

Early in January 1876, before the students had returned from their vacation, the college suffered a second calamity. Fire broke out in the college building shortly after midnight. One of the staff ran to the railway station to telegraph for the Sherbrooke fire engine, and faculty and servants organized bucket brigades to try to contain the flames. Professor Scarth rushed up from the village and managed with some help to remove about a quarter of the books from the library before the collapse of the floor above into the adjacent corridor drove him out of the building. With the help of the Sherbrooke firemen and, again, volunteers from the village, the fire was confined to the central block, and Old Lodge and the dining room and kitchen wing suffered only water damage. However, the undergraduates and Professor Tambs had lost all their possessions, including Tambs' valuable personal library, and the college library had been gutted.[64]

This time the damage to the building was fully covered by insurance. Nevertheless, when Corporation met to consider what action should be taken, Ramsay and Norman again moved that the college and the school should be severed "locally and financially." After a prolonged discussion, Chancellor Heneker managed to have the question referred to a committee which would report at the annual meeting in June. In the interval, Henry Roe wrote a long letter to Bishop Williams, which was printed and circulated in the Bishop's community. His intimate contact with the life

Richard W. Norman, 1872   Thomas Kennedy Ramsay, 1870

of the college since 1873 had convinced him that "the existing union of the College and School is calamitous for many and deeper reasons" than he had previously understood. "The College" he claimed, "has utterly failed as an institution for the higher education of the people of the country in which it is situated." Its endowment had been given to provide a university education for the clergy of the province and for men aspiring to the professions. It had indeed provided a number of well-trained clergy, but the goal of developing a strong Faculty of Arts had been abandoned in favour of the provision of a grammar school for the education of the sons of well-to-do persons drawn from all parts of Canada and the United States. Though most of his letter was devoted to a detailed attack on the financial management of the institution, Roe's most trenchant criticism dealt with the expectation, still cherished by Heneker and many other members of Corporation against the experience of 20 years, that the school would generate matriculants for the college. As the faculty and principal had always maintained, the priorities of the student populations of the two departments, junior and senior, were incompatible. Furthermore, "The Junior institution ... independent of the Senior in its internal management, and yet possessing nothing of its own, but indebted to the Senior for whatever it uses ... must always feel some humiliation, irritation and resentment at this position. And these feelings must ever be intensified by its sense of its greater importance as the larger institution in point of numbers, and as the educator of the sons of the wealthy and ruling classes of the country ... and this produces naturally, in all connected with the School a feeling of alienation from the College ... the College is looked down upon, rather than looked up to, by the boys of the Upper School."[65]

The June report of the committee included a thorough evaluation of the education being offered by the college and the school, but its recommendations were exclusively determined by financial considerations. Three alternatives were offered:

1 The removal of the college from its site, leaving all the buildings for the use of the school. This would require the establishment of a Corporation for the school, with capital sufficient to buy out the interest of the college.
2 The removal of the school from its site, leaving all the buildings for the use of the college. This would require the college to pay to the school the amount contributed by the public for the new school building, which was "altogether unfitted for the use of the College."
3 The retaining of the college and school on their present sites "with such guarantees against loss and securities for efficient government as will satisfy the Corporation and the Public."

A committee was appointed to "ascertain the amount contributed by the Public and by the College, since the creation of the School, for which each party should receive its share of credit in the New Building,"[66] and the decision about rebuilding was postponed for a year.

Amid all this uncertainty the committee of management had one concrete development to report. Henry Roe had had enough of life in residence, and he had been unable to rent accommodation in the village. He therefore made it a condition of his continuing as Professor of Divinity that a house be provided for him on campus. The trustees obtained subscriptions of $2,500 for the purpose, as a loan to be amortized by the rent to be paid by the incumbents. Harrold Lodge was build during the 1875–76 academic year and occupied by Professors of Divinity for the next 95 years, after which it became the residence of the principal.

Though he had not entirely recovered his health, Jasper Nicolls returned to his duties in 1874. He was present during the debates in Corporation which followed the fire in the college building, but he does not seem to have made any significant interventions. He was, however, able to report progress on a cherished project for which he had been collecting funds for a number of years. The original chapel had not been big enough to seat comfortably the greatly increased enrolment in the school. He reported that enough money had been raised to permit the building of an addition, including an apse, which had been completed, but furnishings would have to await further contributions.

In 1877 C.H. Badgley, who had just married Kate Nicolls, the principal's daughter, resigned as rector because of the financial loss he had sustained in running the boarding establishment during the dislocation caused by the two fires and by epidemics of scarlatina and measles among the schoolboys. It proved to be difficult to find a replacement, and once again Corporation requested the principal to take charge of the school in the interim. This time Nicolls could, in good conscience, decline. Shortly after convocation his condition suddenly deteriorated and he took to his bed. He died on 8 August.

The minutes of Corporation recorded its "sense of great loss" in a long and laudatory resolution. The Bishop of Quebec spoke to synod of the principal's noble character and his "upright, clear, guileless, gentle, self-sacrificing life."[67] In a letter to Nicolls' widow, Bishop Oxenden acknowledged that the principal's position "had latterly been one of difficulty and trial ... but he always acted the part of an earnest Christian man ... I do trust that his chequered life has been a blessing to many."[68]

Nicolls had indeed little material progress to show for his 32 years of unremitting toil. The endowment on which the hopes of the founders had rested had been misdirected, the college building was in ruins, the college was still harnessed to the school. But it is by the influence of its teaching in the lives of its graduates that the work of a university is most justly evaluated. In an extensive obituary printed in the *Dominion Churchman*, Henry Roe wrote: "Of the clergy trained by (Dr Nicolls) the country is full ... wherever they are found there will ... be found more or less distinctly the impress of (his) character ... the absence of all extremes or extravagances in principles and character; simple unselfish devotion to duty; true fidelity to the Church of England, and a reverent sense of the infinite importance of every soul made in the image of God."[69] A graduate of 1869 wrote to Harriet Nicolls: "Often and again I have mused on the kind, wise, foreseeing training and instruction bestowed upon us thoughtless youths by him."[70] At their first meeting in October, the undergraduates resolved unanimously "that since it has pleased Almighty God to take from among us our beloved Principal, we ... wish to place on record our sense of the great loss we have sustained. He was a most able, kind and patient teacher, an example of everything a Christian gentleman ought to be, and a sympathetic personal friend to each of us."[71]

Jasper Nicolls had not laboured in vain.

CHAPTER FOUR

THE SMALLEST DIMENSIONS

During the 25 years since Bishop's had received its royal charter, the economy of the Eastern Townships had undergone remarkable development, and the character of the population had been transformed.

THE CHANGING ENVIRONMENT

The establishment under the Act of Union of an English-speaking majority in the new province of Canada had reduced the pressure to develop an English bastion in the Townships. Moreover, once the region was linked by rail to Portland, Quebec and Montreal, there was little economic reason for the BALC to promote further colonization of the St Francis tract. The company abandoned any vision it might once have had of a British-populated Eastern Townships, and Galt and his associates focused their energies on the development of industries, particularly in Sherbrooke, and on the exploitation of the region's timber and mineral resources made possible by the advent of the railway. The British-born population of the region actually diminished from 12,500 in 1861 to 11,500 in 1871.[1]

On the other hand, colonization of the region by French-speaking Roman Catholics had by the 1860s become a major enterprise. It was the era of the Great Hemorrhage. Overpopulation in the lands under seigneurial tenure in the valley of the St Lawrence had led tens of thousands of young *canadiens* to emigrate to the mill towns of New England, where American homogenizing pressures had placed both their language and their religion at risk. Seeking to offer an alternative, the Roman Catholic Church, with the support of nationalist politicians, mounted a vigorous campaign to persuade the *habitants* to settle on the untilled lands on the frontiers of the Eastern Townships. A further inducement to French-speaking immigration was the need for workers in the burgeoning industries of the region. Development was particularly rapid in the labour-intensive textile and shoe industries, which could take advantage of the skills acquired by French-speaking Canadians in the mills of New England.

By 1860 47 percent of the population in the Townships was French speaking. At Confederation, the British North America Act transferred responsibility for colonization to the provinces, and this provided a further stimulus to *canadien* immigration. By 1870, 100 thousand of the population of 160 thousand in the region were French speaking. In the five counties constituting the district of St Francis, of which Sherbrooke was the administrative centre, the relative strength of the French-speaking population was also increasing, but less rapidly. In 1871 French-speakers comprised 40 percent of the total population of the district and 50 percent of the population of Sherbrooke.[2]

The establishment and growth of French-language institutions consolidated this "peaceable conquest." In 1874 Monseigneur Antoine Racine was consecrated Roman Catholic Bishop of Sherbrooke. He wrote to a fellow prelate: "Je suis dans un pays hérétique, infidèle et *Yankee!*" and he set vigorously about the task of transforming it. Yet comparatively liberal in churchmanship, a skilled and affable diplomat and a pragmatic if authoritarian administrator, he managed nevertheless to retain the respect of many of the English-speaking and Protestant inhabitants.[3]

There had to this time been relatively little out-migration, and the English-speaking population had managed to retain much of its natural increase. In the countryside English-speakers retained most of the best arable land, though as Monseigneur Racine quickly discovered, three-quarters of the land in the best townships in Stanstead and Compton was for sale at moderate prices. In Sherbrooke and other urban centres, English-speaking capitalists had consolidated their hold on industry and finance. Political power in some areas was passing into the hands of the French-speaking majority, but the economy was still controlled by the "English."

Very little of this transformation was reflected in the life of the academic community at the confluence of the St Francis and the

Massawippi. The failure of Corporation to protect, let alone increase, the college endowment had made impossible the normal growth in the faculty which would have enabled it to broaden the curriculum, either in the direction of the humanities, as Jasper Nicolls would have wished, or in that of the more "practical" subjects which would have recommended the institution to the wealthy bourgeois of the region. Of the men responsible for the industrial development of the Townships, only Edward Hale and Richard Heneker had taken an interest in the college; and Hale died in 1875, having been replaced after a short interregnum by Heneker as chancellor. Jasper Nicolls was not at ease with Mammon, and the fact that nearly all the most active entrepreneurs were Congregational, Methodist or Presbyterian did not facilitate mutual understanding. The transfer of nominating authority for members of Corporation to the synods of Montreal and Quebec introduced a further barrier to integration with the community at large, since churchmanship and willingness to participate in the synods became the criteria for appointment. In 1871, the Synod of Quebec did appoint one active Townshipper, Matthew Cochrane, notable for his superb stock-breeding farm in Compton. In 1872, he was appointed a senator of the Dominion of Canada, but he did not attend the meetings of Corporation, and he was not renominated in 1873.

In his polemic addressed to the bishop in 1876, Henry Roe wrote: "[Bishop's] has hitherto stood before the people of the country as a sectarian institution, full of narrow prejudice, foreign in its tastes and feelings, animated by no generous sympathy with the great body of the people in their struggles, and feeling no desire to come down among them, adapt itself to their wants and win them."[4] If one makes allowances for the heat of the moment, this judgment of one of the college's most loyal and hard-working alumni was probably not far from the mark.

THE NEW PRINCIPAL

In September 1877 Corporation appointed as principal the Reverend Joseph A. Lobley, M.A., Scholar and Fellow of Trinity College, Cambridge.

Lobley had been appointed the first principal of the Montreal Diocesan Theological College in 1873 by Bishop Oxenden. When his name was proposed for the post at Bishop's, Oxenden informed Corporation that Lobley had been engaged for a term of five years, and would thus not be available before May 1878. Undeterred, Corporation appointed a committee to confer with the bishop "to ascertain if any arrangement can be effected by which the Reverend Mr. Lobley may be en-

Joseph Albert Lobley

abled to assume at once the duties of Principal of Bishop's College."[5] The negotiations succeeded, and Lobley took up his duties as principal in December 1877.

Joseph Lobley had had a distinguished career as an undergraduate at Cambridge, excelling in both mathematics and classics, and it was indeed fortunate for Bishop's that he proved willing to leave Montreal and go to Lennoxville. That he should agree to go at short notice was, given the history of the two institutions, interesting. In his memoir of his years in Montreal, Oxenden observed that Lobley, though "a good and able man," had been "a little too much of a Churchman for some of my friends at Montreal,"[6] and the fact that he was proposed to Corporation by R.W. Norman, one of Jasper Nicolls' staunchest defenders, confirms that he was considerably closer to middle-of-the-road churchmanship than the founders of the Montreal college. Since the constitution of that institution gave final authority to a board of governors of whom a majority were lay subscribers, Lobley's position cannot have been entirely comfortable. At any rate, he was ideally situated to achieve rapprochement with Montreal. As a first step in this direction, the Rev. J.P. DuMoulin was appointed as one of the external examiners in the Bishop's Faculty of Divinity. DuMoulin, lecturer in ecclesiastical history at the Montreal college, had been recruited in Ireland by Bishop Cronyn. A very able man and a powerful preacher, he went on to become rector of the cathedral in Toronto and, in 1896, Bishop of Niagara.

Though appointed to the Chair of Classics, Lobley found himself obliged to carry as well the full load of lectures in mathematics, since Tambs had been granted a year's leave of absence in which to recover his health. An undergraduate of the time recalls that the principal also lectured in English literature, logic, and rhetoric, and that his lectures "were models of perspicacity and exhibited not only a thorough mastery of the subject, but the most careful and conscientious daily preparation for each lecture."[7] The Reverend P.C. Read, the new rector of the school, provided some help in classics, rhetoric, and logic, in return for which Lobley took the senior form of the school in algebra. Tambs' health did not improve, and he resigned in 1878. Since he was not replaced, the principal continued to teach university-level mathematics. He also introduced a requirement that every undergraduate had to write three essays each term on subjects chosen by the principal. These essays he found time to correct, "ruthlessly exposing a false metaphor, a flimsy argument or an ungrammatical phrase."[8] It is remarkable that under these conditions he nevertheless retained enough faith and interest in the future of Bishop's to decline the offer, in 1880, of the provostship of Trinity College, Toronto.

THE BISHOP'S COLLEGE SCHOOL ASSOCIATION

During the 1876–77 session Corporation had continued to debate the relationship between the college and the school. A committee was established with a mandate to establish a basis for the division of the equity of the institution in the event that the college and the school should be made financially separate. In May 1877 Henry Roe proposed that in future none of the college capital should be spent on buildings and furniture or upon the school and that the financial management of the school should be the responsibility of a separate standing committee of Corporation, which should pay rent for the use of the school building and grounds. This proposal was referred to a committee which developed a series of detailed recommendations embodying the principles Roe had advocated, and these were adopted by Corporation in June. At the same meeting it was decided to rebuild the college on the same site, at a cost not to exceed the insurance money and the accrued interest thereon. This work was undertaken during the 1877–78 academic year and completed, under budget, in April 1878.

Meanwhile, because of the prevailing financial depression and the uncertainty created by the resignation of Badgley and the long-serving matron, Mrs Irving, numbers in the school had again declined. In June 1878, faced with an enrolment of only 43 boys for the Trinity term, Richard Heneker concluded that the school must have an independent financial base. He proposed to Corporation that an association be formed to carry on the school separately from the Corporation as to its financial management. The association would be formed by 30 shareholders, each holding a share of $100 and would be incorporated by an act of the provincial legislature, with the stated object of taking charge of Bishop's College School educationally and financially in connection with Bishop's College. This new corporation would replace the informal group which had for some years underwritten deficits in the school's operation. As a carrot, Heneker suggested that the college might be willing to accept a reduced rent until the enrolment in the school should reach 60. Corporation agreed to this proposal, and the principles which should govern negotiations with such an association were laid down. One of these, that the association should board the undergraduates in a manner satisfactory to the principal, was intended as a temporary measure. It in fact lasted for 30 years and was to prove a continual source of friction.

The Bishop's College School Association was duly formed in 1879, and its membership gave a clear indication of the support which Bishop's College might have enjoyed in the community if the penury of the 1860s had not stunted its growth and forced its submission to the narrow concerns of the synods. Prominent in its membership were the major entrepreneurs and the principal politicians of the English-speaking community: the Honourable Matthew H. Cochrane, Andrew Paton, managing director of the Paton woollen mill; the Honourable John Henry Pope, MP, minister of agriculture in the MacDonald cabinet and influential in the promotion of both local and national railroads; Evan John Price, one of the owners of Price Brothers, the most important lumber merchants in the Province; Colonel William Rhodes of Quebec City, sometime MLA and minister of agriculture and active in banking, railway development, and mining; and the Honourable J.G. Robertson, long-serving MLA for Sherbrooke and several times provincial treasurer. The chairman of the association proved to be none other than R.W. Heneker, who reported on its behalf to Corporation.

SANITATION

It was indeed fortunate that the Association was solidly buttressed financially, since calamity awaited it. After the undergraduates and schoolboys had gone home at the end of Trinity term, 1880, several of them came down with typhoid fever, and one died. The committee of management commissioned a report on the institution's drainage facilities by a local engineer and submitted samples of the water from the college well to a public analyst for testing. Corporation, meeting exceptionally in August, was told that the water had been found pure, but it decided nevertheless to authorize the improved drainage system recommended by the consultant.

Unfortunately, the source of infection had not been identified. In December there occurred another, more serious, outbreak of typhoid, leading to another death. The college had been comparatively little affected, but it was decided that the school must be removed to Magog for the Lent and Trinity terms. The undergraduates were billeted in the village, so that all the buildings could be thoroughly inspected. The faculty lectured in two rooms in the town hall.

This time, a medical commission was appointed, composed of James Cameron and Thomas Simpson, members of the Bishop's Faculty of Medicine, and the young William Osler, who was at that time Professor of Pathology and Histology at McGill. They quickly discovered that the latrines, cesspool and cesspool drainage pipe were not watertight and had contaminated the soil around them. An undergraduate of the class of 1883 has left a description of the sanitary facilities in question:

> There never was a single bathroom. [Bathing in the river was]
> the only means of getting a wash all over. In winter this was

impossible, so although we were not "sewn up" [in our underwear], we might just as well have been. There was only one [indoor] closet, which was never open until after 10 P.M. At other times we had to make the trip across the quad to a series of three wooden old-fashioned closets, no matter what the weather.[9]

Since these facilities were dangerously close to the college well in the quadrangle, the commission believed that they were a likely source of infection. On their recommendation, further extensive improvements were made in the sanitary facilities, and a new well was drilled much further from the buildings. The report of the works undertaken was widely circulated in the English-speaking community, and in order that parents might inspect the new facilities, members of the association persuaded the Grand Trunk and Quebec Central railways to offer reduced fares to persons attending convocation in 1881. The principal and the rector were instructed to keep a record of medical attendance on all undergraduates and schoolboys, which was to be laid on the table at annual meetings of Corporation.

The problem did not recur. Enrolment at the college was little affected, and by 1883 enrolment at the school had again reached a viable level. However, the whole of the original capital of the association had been required to cover the deficit incurred in 1880–81.

THE PROFESSIONAL FACULTIES

The primary purpose of nearly all Canadian universities founded in the nineteenth century had been to educate clergy for Christian churches, but these universities did not in general initiate proposals to provide university-level training for other professions. Training in these professions had traditionally been carried out by attaching one or more students to a practitioner, and the quality of the training achieved had varied widely. In the nineteenth century, a general move developed toward the establishment of professional schools, where aspirants were given systematic instruction by members of the profession. Professional corporations were organized in order to restrict access to the professions to those who could meet criteria established by the corporation. Where these criteria dealt with education and the need to demonstrate competence, they were in the public interest. Where they sought to impose restrictions on the number of men and women entering the profession and to establish monopolies, government had sometimes to intervene.

Because the professions needed help in teaching the basic sciences and humanities, and also because university-controlled matriculation offered a guarantee of the standard of instruction, the better professional schools sought affiliation with universities. In Montreal, for example, the Montreal Medical Institution, which had been formally organized in 1823 as the teaching arm of the Montreal General Hospital, applied in 1832 to become affiliated with McGill University. The McGill governors accepted it as a Faculty of Medicine and submitted appropriate statutes, rules, and ordinances to the governor-general for approval by the Colonial Office. Thus the McGill Faculty of Medicine had been functioning for 11 years when the Faculty of Arts admitted its first three matriculants in 1843.[10]

The other professional faculties at Bishop's were similarly generated. In 1871 a group of Montreal doctors resolved to open a second medical school for English-speaking students in Montreal. In February, Dr Aaron Hart David travelled to Lennoxville to lay before the trustees a proposal for the affiliation of the new school with Bishop's, and in March, Corporation approved, as "a step of the highest importance," the establishment of a medical faculty in Montreal. The Faculty of Medicine survived for 35 years, and its achievements merit their own history.

In 1880 several members of the St Francis bar decided that it was desirable to establish a law faculty at Bishop's University. Though they were aware that the prospects were not very encouraging, since the teaching would have to be done by busy practitioners and the reservoir of potential students was not large, they were willing to make the experiment. Corporation welcomed the proposal. The first dean of the Faculty of Law was Robert Newton Hall, Bâtonnier of the Quebec Bar, MP for Sherbrooke 1882–91, and a director of several railroads. The members of the faculty were L.C. Bélanger, E.T. Brooks, H.B. Brown, H.C. Cabana, and L.E. Morris Lectures were also given by D.W.R. Hodge, L.E. Panneton and S.B. Sanborn. Morris was joint prothonotary for the District. The others were all members of the St Francis bar practising in Sherbrooke. There were in fact 20 advocates already established in Sherbrooke to serve a population of 8 thousand, and a total of 35 to serve the population of 55 thousand in the district. Unless the Townshippers were exceptionally litigious, the local prospects for graduates of the new Faculty would seem to have been slim.

Nevertheless, a three-year course of lectures was established. To be admitted to the Faculty, students had to present a certificate of good character and pass an examination in French, Latin, and English. They were examined at the end of each of the first two years on the subjects appointed for those years, and at the end of the third year in the subjects appointed together with such portions of the course of the earlier years as convocation in conjunction with the faculty should decide.

Four students matriculated in 1880 and seven in 1881; of these, three graduated LL.B. in 1883, four in 1884. However, the initial misgivings proved to be well founded. The reservoir of potential students from the region was small, and increasingly French-speaking. Graduates of Bishop's in Arts who intended to go into Law went to McGill or Harvard. By 1888 the enrolment in the Faculty had fallen to four, and the last LL.B. in course was granted in that year. In all, 15 degrees in course were granted by the Faculty during its short life.

Corporation's enthusiasm for affiliating (financially autonomous) professional faculties was undoubtedly due to the continuing desire of its lay members (and at least one of the clerics) that "steps might be taken to promote an enlarged sphere of *usefulness* to the public in the operation of the college."[11] Since this tendency to disparage liberal education as being of little practical value has persisted in Canada until very recent times, it is instructive to consider the careers of two Bishop's Arts men who graduated during Principal Lobley's tenure.

Frederick George Scott took his B.A. in 1881. That he should have attended Bishop's at all was evidence that Lobley had enjoyed some success in his efforts to mollify Montreal, since Scott's father, W.E. Scott, an influential Montreal doctor, had been one of the founding subscribers and first governors of the MDTC. In fact, Fred had begun to reject the austerity of evangelical worship as a boy; three years of moderate churchmanship and collegiate worship at Bishop's, followed by preparation for ordination in England, confirmed him in a moderately Anglo-Catholic practice which proved unacceptable to the Bishop of Montreal. Fortunately, the Bishop of Quebec knew him as a friend of his son Lennox Williams, and was willing to cope with Scott's eccentricities. For the next 25 years, he enjoyed a somewhat controversial career as a parish priest in Drummondville and Quebec, known for his concern for the poor and his ecumenical ministry. In 1887 he had the good fortune to marry Amy Brooks, who provided him with the ballast essential to one of his combative and imaginative temperament. Of their six sons, five survived the diseases of childhood to graduate from Bishop's University. Scott greatly enjoyed writing poetry, much of which appeared in *The Mitre*, and several of his hymns have been included in Anglican hymnals. In 1902 he was appointed to the College Council, of which he was an active and at times turbulent member until the end of his life.

On the outbreak of war in 1914 the 53-year-old Scott announced to his astonished church wardens that he had volunteered as a chaplain and intended to go overseas with the first Canadian contingent. During the next four years he became widely known and universally loved as a padre in the First Canadian Division, ministering fearlessly to "his boys," including three of his sons, in the thick of the heaviest fighting. Returning to Canada a hero in 1919, he was disgusted by the shabby treatment accorded the returning veterans, and when a number of them participated in the Winnipeg General Strike later that year, he went out to support them, sharing the speakers' platform with J.S. Woodsworth. He continued to speak out against social injustice for the rest of his long life, and when he died in 1944 hundreds of "his" veterans followed his bier up the hill to Mount Royal cemetery. He was of course the product of heredity and of other influences besides that of Bishop's, but it is not unreasonable to claim that he owed to a liberal education at least some of the understanding of and concern for the human condition which he so conspicuously displayed during his life.

The career of another of Lobley's undergraduates, Grant Hall (B.A., 1883), would surely have been recognized as useful by even the most pragmatic member of Corporation. After some training in mechanical engineering, in the shops of Canadian Pacific Railway (CPR) in Montreal, he began to work his way upward through the CPR's operating divisions. Much of his early career was spent nursing the company's rolling stock in the horrendous operating conditions of the mountain passes. In 1901 he was master mechanic of the Pacific division, and by 1908 he had been appointed superintendent of motive power for the entire network. After a stint as general manager of the western division he was appointed vice-president of the company, under the redoubtable Edward Beatty, in 1918. In spite of the heavy responsibilities which this last promotion entailed, he found time to demonstrate his attachment to Bishop's, both as chairman of the executive committee of Corporation and as president of the Bishop's College School Association. His career provided striking evidence of the usefulness of an education in the humanities for a career which involved the management of men.

REBUILDING THE ENDOWMENT

The 1870s, which had brought so much calamity and crisis to the University of Bishop's College, had also been a period of severe financial depression in North America following the bank failures and the financial panic in the United States in 1873. However, by the end of the decade, the Canadian economy had sufficiently improved that Corporation felt encouraged to mount a campaign to restore the college endowment. In 1880 the institution was free of debt, but interest on investments met only the principal's salary of $1,500.

The initial impetus came from the Reverend C.P. Reid, rector of Sherbrooke and one of the original trustees, who donated $1,000 in

1880 to be applied toward the endowment of the Chair of Divinity. In the same year R.W. Heneker reported to the annual meeting that Charles Hamilton had proposed a campaign to establish the "Harrold Fund" for the endowment of the Chair, and that his brother Robert had offered an initial subscription of $2 thousand. At the same meeting, "certain gentlemen, Alumni and other friends of Bishop's College" offered to contribute a total of $500 per annum for five years to augment the salary of Principal Lobley[12]—in recognition of his having agreed in 1878 to come to Bishop's at an initial salary much less than he had been receiving in Montreal, and of his refusal of the more lucrative post of Provost of Trinity College.

In 1881 C.P. Reid made another donation of $1,000 and the SPG offered £250 if the Harrold Fund should reach $15 thousand. Robert Hamilton offered a further $6 thousand if the balance could be raised, and Henry Roe was appointed to lead the campaign. By 1884, both conditional offers had been claimed, and in 1885, with the aid of a further $3,500 from Robert Hamilton, the Fund was fully subscribed to an amount of $25 thousand.

In 1884 Robert Hamilton again challenged the Bishop's community. Expressing his opinion that the principal's salary ought to be not less than $3 thousand, he offered $5 thousand toward the endowment of the Office of Principal, provided that friends of the college raised a like sum within 3 years. Again the friends of the institution responded. By the end of 1886 the principal's salary endowment fund had reached over $10 thousand.

In the same year Mrs Jemima Davies and Miss Sarah Davidson, sisters resident in Quebec City, bequeathed to Bishop's the sum of $29,322 for the endowment of a Chair and for scholarships. Corporation decided to assign $20 thousand to endow the Davidson-Davies Chair in Mathematics, and the balance to endow scholarships. The operating revenue thus liberated was applied to the salary of a Professor of Pastoral Theology, whose principal responsibility would be to prepare the students of theology for the cure of souls in the context of parish life, but one third of his time would be applied to lecturing in the Faculty of Arts.

THOMAS ADAMS, PRINCIPAL AND RECTOR

Unhappily, Joseph Lobley was not to benefit from the restoration of the endowment which his skill and devotion had stimulated. Though Corporation had, at long last, protected the college endowment from encroachment by hiving off the BCS Association, it had not been willing to recognize that harnessing the college to the school drained the intel-

Thomas Adams, 1901

lectual resources of the faculty and depressed the morale of the undergraduates. By 1882 P.C. Read's teaching load in the Faculty of Arts had increased to the point where he felt obliged to resign from the rectorship of the school, though he remained classical master. His place was taken by the Reverend Isaac Brock, also a graduate of Oxford, who lasted six months. In extremis, the Association turned to Principal Lobley in the hope that he would assume the responsibilities of rector, in addition to those he was already carrying.

It is difficult to forgive Chancellor Heneker's obtuseness in this matter. An undergraduate of the time recalled that the principal "was up every morning in summer before five o'clock, and would work at his dearly-loved garden and lawn until about seven, when he generally had a lecture. His whole morning was occupied with lectures, and very often the afternoon hours also, from four o'clock until Chapel time." Lobley also "took the greatest possible interest in the choir, conducting all the practices himself and training the men to sing in parts,"[13] and he organized concerts and plays. Withal, his force of character, tempered by catholicity of views and a keen sense of humour, enabled him to rule effectively and with humanity. That Corporation should have even contemplated increasing the load he was carrying passes comprehension.

Nevertheless, Lobley's conscience drove him to agree to try to carry the rectorship as a temporary measure. No effort seems to have been made to recruit another rector. Inevitably, his health gave way under the stress, and he had to submit his resignation, to take effect in June 1885. At the end of the academic year he returned to England to recover his health, but it continued to deteriorate, and he died in 1889. He had been a worthy successor to Jasper Nicolls, and it was a tragedy for the college that his tenure had been untimely terminated.

The first two principals of the college had been fellows of their colleges in the ancient English universities. They had striven under the most difficult conditions, to maintain academic standards worthy of a university. Faced with evidence that this task let to the breakdown of the incumbent, Corporation seems to have decided that concern for the instruction in Arts must take second place to the need to build up the school. J.H. Thompson, who had been Professor of Divinity, but was at that time vicar of Datchet in England, was pressed into service to act as referee for applications to replace Lobley. The position advertised was Principal of the College *and* Rector of the School. The man chosen, the Reverend Thomas Adams, came from a family of some academic distinction—one of his uncles, a fellow of the Royal Society, had been offered the post of Astronomer Royal, and another, also F.R.S., was a professor at King's College, London. Adams himself had taken a first class in the mathematical tripos at Cambridge, but his most recent appointment had been as headmaster of the high school at Gateshead-on-Tyne, and he seems to have had no experience of teaching at university level.

The consequences were not long delayed. In June 1886 a letter from the undergraduates to the Visitor was read to the Corporation. In it the students complained that the new principal had failed to maintain discipline, that he had paid little attention to the needs of the undergraduates, and that little benefit was to be derived from his lectures. The bishop, assisted by the chancellor and the vice-chancellor (Canon Norman), thoroughly investigated these complaints, and reported to Corporation that the first two were substantially justified—routine had been lax, and the undergraduates had been taught with the schoolboys—but that, in their opinion, the students had become too accustomed to being spoon-fed. Adams had therefore been guilty only of assuming that they were capable of doing some of the intellectual work themselves using the basic principles of analysis demonstrated to them by the lecturer. One of the spokesmen for the students had been George Abbott-Smith, a graduate in Arts and student of Divinity, who later developed into a renowned classical scholar and became Professor of Greek at McGill and principal of the MDTC. Possibly his difficulty with Adams arose out of a clash of classical with mathematical culture! However, it also seems likely that Adams' problems derived in some measure from a failure to take into account the poor preparation of most matriculants, which had forced his predecessors to establish a tradition of detailed exposition to which the undergraduates had become accustomed.

As rector of the school Adams was a success, and aided by continuing prosperity in the country, enrolment grew to 108 boys in 1889-90, of whom 90 were boarders and 23 were nominees or sons of clergymen benefitting from reduced fees. Gross profit on the operation of the school during the previous year had amounted to over $3,700. Of this sum, $1,320 was applied to the cost of providing heating, ventilating, and sanitary facilities for the new Bishop Williams wing of the school, to which old boys, alumni and members of the association had subscribed to mark the twenty-fifth anniversary of the bishop's consecration. The new wing, which ran at right angles to the north end of the school building, was handed over to Corporation, free of debt, at convocation in 1889. In addition to classrooms and a laboratory for experimental science, it contained a common room and a large hall which the college used for meetings of convocation.

Adams also proved to be an energetic and successful fundraiser. With the aid of yet another conditional offer of $5 thousand from Robert

Hamilton, a building extension fund of over $10 thousand was generated. In 1891 the SPCK agreed to provide $11,931 (£2,450) of the $15,600 required to build Divinity House. The house, completed in 1892, provided accommodation for up to 16 Divinity students and for the Professor of Pastoral Theology who would have them under his wing. Income from a sum contributed by the Reverend J.J.S. Mountain, rector of Cornwall, was assigned to meet the operating and maintenance costs of the new building. In 1907, through the generosity of Margaret Stewart McKenzie, a grand-niece of Bishop Charles Stewart and friend of the Professor of Pastoral Theology at the time, E.A. Dunn, an oratory contiguous with the house was constructed and fitted out for the devotions of the residents.

ACADEMIC DEVELOPMENT

In his last report to the synod Principal Lobley had noted that Bishop's still stood sorely in need of a practical recognition on the part of the public generally, or at least of churchmen, of its position as the one Anglican university in the Province of Quebec. For want of such recognition, its work and influence were narrowed down to the smallest dimensions. In this context the restoration of the college endowment was a welcome indication that the tide might be turning. Relieved of concern about operating deficits, Corporation began to respond to the need for increased teaching resources for the degree programs. Unfortunately, under the Adams regime this led to further blurring of the academic boundaries between the college and the school. Masters from the school were pressed into service to relieve the professors of mathematics and classics of part of their teaching load, particularly at the preparatory level. In an effort to broaden the curriculum, lectures in physics and chemistry and a course in political economy were offered as optional subjects for the Pass degree—again taught by the masters from the school for minimal additional stipends. The curriculum for Honours in Mathematics was strengthened by the addition of hydrostatics and optics. In 1890 another full-time lecturer was added to the college staff, the Rev. N.P. Yates. Nominally, he was Lecturer in logic, rhetoric, and political economy. In practice he was employed mostly to teach the preparatory class and relieve the principal of his teaching load in the school. For several years, convocation was combined with the school prizegiving ceremonies, and the conferring of degrees was accompanied by a shrill obbligato of schoolboy voices.

During this period, the need to respond to government intervention in post-secondary education drew Bishop's into closer relations with

McGill. The Quebec legislature wished to set up a regulating council which would determine the standard of general education required of aspirants to the professions and would control their professional training. The general council of the bar proposed that this standard include examinations in subjects required for the B.ès.Arts in the French-language classical colleges, but not for the B.A. in English-language universities. Faced with this threat to their autonomy the universities sought, by means of a private bill, to establish the degree of Bachelor of Arts as sufficient preparation for professional training in Law and Medicine. During the debate on this bill the bâtonnier and the secretary of the provincial bar council alleged in a memoir that, in contrast to the classical colleges affiliated with Laval University, McGill (and by inference, Bishop's) gave degrees (without examination) to all undergraduates who followed the programs in Arts. Both universities submitted detailed reports to the Legislative Assembly refuting this charge, and in 1890 this particular battle was won. Another instance of co-operation between the two universities was the institution of admission with advanced standing for teachers holding the Academy Diploma (the qualification for teaching at the secondary level) who wished to proceed to a degree in Arts.

However, it was in the Faculty of Divinity that the new-found prosperity of the institution made the greatest difference. Since the founding of the university, the standard training in Divinity had been a two-year course in theology leading to a Licence in Sacred Theology and to ordination. All students in Divinity had to have been accepted as potential ordinands by the bishop of a diocese, but not all of them were graduates of a university. Convocation had also established regulations for the degree of Bachelor of Divinity in course, and for Doctor of Divinity, which required submission of an original thesis. However, until 1886 only five Bishop's graduates had taken a B.D. in course. Nearly all Divinity students depended for financial support on bursaries from the SPG or other benefactors, and these were granted only for preparation for ordination. Two graduates, Henry Roe and Francis Allnatt, had taken doctorates in Divinity.

In 1886 Bishop's became aware that the MDTC was contemplating application to the legislature for degree-granting powers in Divinity. Principal Lobley's overtures to Montreal had met with only very limited success. In 1879 William Bennett Bond had succeeded Ashton Oxenden as Bishop of Montreal. Though he thereby became vice-president of Corporation, he did not attend meetings, and he seems to have recognized no responsibility for the well-being of Bishop's College. Corporation recognized that it was natural for the Montreal college to wish its students to be able to earn degrees, but they wished to avoid an increase in the number of degree-granting institutions. To this end, convocation in 1886 approved new regulations for degrees in Divinity under which the selected works and subjects for the several examinations would be chosen by the bishops of Montreal and Quebec jointly every five years, and the Board of Examiners would also be nominated jointly by the bishops. When this attempt to put the students of the two institutions on an equal footing was spurned, and the Bishop of Montreal, as president of the Montreal college, petitioned the legislature, Corporation mustered their political influence, and with the aid of petitions from many parishes in the diocese managed to defeat the Montreal petition in the (appointed) Legislative Council on the grounds that only a university could grant degrees. The problem was then taken up by the provincial synod, where it was hotly debated for a further three years. The final outcome was control over degrees in course in Divinity within the Ecclesiastical Province of Canada (Ontario, Quebec, and the Maritimes) by a Joint Board of Examiners. The board was composed of six members elected respectively by King's College (Windsor), Bishop's College, Trinity College, the MDTC, Huron College, and Wycliffe College, and it was presided over by the Metropolitan of the Ecclesiastical Province of Canada, who had been constituted by the legislature "Corporation Sole" for the purpose of granting Anglican degrees in Divinity. The board was to choose the works to be studied, but each participating college had the right to veto any textbook; when that was the case, the board would specify alternatives. In the event candidates for ordination turned out to be much less interested in these degrees than were the protagonists. It was not until 1899 that the first alumnus of the MDTC took a Divinity degree under the provincial scheme, and only two Bishop's graduates took Divinity degrees during the first 20 years of the scheme's operation.

Meanwhile the appointment of F.J.B. Allnatt to the Chair of Pastoral Theology had made it possible for Henry Roe to propose a Theological Honours program leading to the degree of Bachelor of Arts. This was approved by convocation in 1887, and the first graduate from the program, B.G. Wilkinson, took first-class Theological Honours in 1890. That there was ample matter for consideration at the Honours level is made clear by the subjects prescribed for the Long essay prize: in 1890, "The Origin of Species as consistent with the Christian doctrine of Creation and Providence," and in 1891, "The geological evidence for the Antiquity of Man, considered in relation to the scripture account of Creation, the unity of the human race, and the Incarnation."[14]

The establishment of endowments for the Harrold and Davidson-Davies chairs and for the principalship led to the first serious consideration of academic tenure in the history of the institution. In September 1886 Chancellor Heneker pointed out to the College Council that these funds were trusts. In consequence Corporation had no control over the revenues, and could not for example cease to pay the salary of an incumbent of one of the chairs. Heneker urged that it was therefore desirable that a statute be framed to deal with "The Removal of Professors." After considerable discussion, extending over several meetings, a statute was agreed upon and submitted to Corporation, which approved it in June 1887. Under its provisions, the principal and professors, except those in Divinity, were removable by Corporation on six months notice terminable on June 30 in any year.[15] However, the proposal for removal had to be in writing, addressed to the president, and it had to be submitted by him to a meeting of Corporation at which at least one third of the members were present. The motion for removal required a two-thirds majority of those present.

The academic programs of the college were thus strengthened in several respects during the first five years of Principal Adams' tenure. Offsetting this, the death of Mr Justice Ramsay in 1887 deprived Corporation of one of the few members who had consistently given priority to the needs of the undergraduates and sought to liberate the college from the confines of doctrinal orthodoxy. In the words of Bishop Williams, unanimously if belatedly adopted by Corporation, "The breadth of his cultivated intelligence placed him always on the side of those who look in Education for something higher and deeper than the sharpening of the trader's knack or the forestalling of professional accomplishment; and he placed always at the disposal of the University, in all deliberations involving questions of right and honour, that keenness of intellectual vision and that unrelenting hold on right for right's sake which made him so distinguished an ornament of the great profession to which he belonged."[16]

THE STIGMA AFFAIR

On 29 October 1890 the students of Divinity and all but six of the undergraduates, 29 in all, signed a petition to the College Council, a document "of so grave a nature, and drawn up in such disrespectful and offensive terms"[17] that the council deemed it necessary to consult the president of Corporation. Thus began the (in)famous Stigma Affair, so called because Principal Adams deemed it a stigma on the escutcheon of the university.

In the petition, the students complained of the poor quality of the food and housekeeping in college, which they compared unfavourably with those enjoyed by students who boarded in the village and at other

The Stigma Group, 1890

colleges, which they listed. Under these conditions, they claimed that the charge made for board and room was "excessive and extortionate." The petition was largely factual in its contents, and none of the facts appears to have been refuted by the college authorities. However, in contrast with the 1886 petition to the Visitor, it was couched in terms which were rather more direct than the protocol of the time required of students who were addressing their preceptors. This was a serious tactical error. In one paragraph, the petitioners also speculated that the "enormous profits," which they were convinced had been made, might have been devoted to the bonuses paid to the masters and matron of the school. To the persistent failure of the administration to respect their dignity as graduate students and undergraduates had thus been added unjustified material hardship.[18]

Their speculation was well founded. The BCS Association was responsible for providing board and room for both college and school. During the 1888–89 academic year, it had made a profit on operations of $3,700, not entirely of course on board and room. Of this sum, $1,369 had been paid to the staff of the school in the form of bonuses. Chancellor Heneker, reporting to Corporation in his capacity as president of the association, confidently predicted an even larger profit for 1889–90.

Nevertheless, the College Council, led by Archdeacon Roe, demanded retraction and apology. In a judgment which began "The Council could not have believed it possible that a document composed in such offensive language and in so undutiful spirit could have emanated from students of this university,"[19] the four senior students of Divinity were to be rusticated for the remainder of the academic year, and the four junior Divinity students were to lose their term. All the signers of the petition were to be required to sign a formal retraction and apology within 24 hours. It must be remembered that a majority of the students were receiving bursaries from the SPG and other benefactors, and that the bishop had absolute control over these bursaries.

Having delivered itself of this Draconian judgment the council appointed one of its external members, Canon (later Bishop) Thorneloe, Nicolls Scholar and Prince of Wales Prizeman of 1872, to act as intermediary with the students. In the course of the next two weeks he managed to calm matters to a certain extent, conveying a second petition from the students, this one "respectfully requesting" a lesser sentence for one of the senior Divinity students who had strongly opposed the wording of the first petition. By the 7 November some members of council were beginning to have second thoughts; but when the principal suggested that the penalty for the senior Divinity students might be reduced to the loss of a term, Henry Roe accused him of systematically undermining discipline and declared that in the circumstances he felt obliged to resign his Chair (though not from Corporation).

This decision, which went into effect in June 1891, was the most lasting and unfortunate result of the affair. Roe had been an effective member of faculty and a valiant defender of the college's interests for over 20 years. In particular, he had striven to persuade the Corporation to recognize that its prime duty was to the college and that the interests of the college and school were fundamentally incompatible, at least in the context of shared facilities. His excessive regard for the niceties of protocol could perhaps be ascribed to his 61 years, but it is clear that his explosion on 7 November was but the culmination of five years of conflict with Principal Adams, whose policies he believed to be detrimental to the college students.

The College Council finally decided to reduce the penalty imposed on the student mentioned in the second petition, but the other penalties were confirmed by the bishop and by Corporation. All the students concerned appear to have made the required kowtow to established authority, but they were unrepentant, and they went downtown in a body to have their picture taken for posterity, defiant in their academic caps and gowns. Among them was a future chancellor of the university.[20]

Fortunately, both the principal and the Corporation learned from his early difficulties. In 1891 H.J.H. Petry was appointed full-time headmaster of the school. An old boy of the school and a Bishop's graduate (Prince of Wales Prizeman, 1882), Petry had been a master in the school since his graduation, and under his leadership the institution flourished, for a time. Relieved of direct responsibility for the school, Adams set about developing a more secure intellectual and social space for the college men. Corporation was urged to provide a separate dining hall for the graduates and undergraduates, and convocation became again an exclusively university function. In an address on college discipline, read to the Ontario Educational Association in 1895,[21] the principal gave his opinion that a system of self-government—to be employed with caution and within certain limitations—was best suited to a residential college. He had come to appreciate the wisdom of showing "that deference, even to a student, which preserves his self-respect and wins his affection."[22]

THE FIRE OF 1891

On 5 February 1891 Bishop's again suffered ordeal by fire. Fortunately it broke out during the afternoon, when the dormitories were empty, but the system of heating by furnaces through hot air ducts ensured that it would spread rapidly from the attic of the school building where it was first detected. In spite of the efforts of the professors, masters, students, and villagers, it was soon evident that the school building was doomed, including the Bishop Williams Wing which had been completed only the year before. The arrival of the Sherbrooke fire brigade with its steam fire engine provided welcome reinforcement to the firefighters, who now concentrated their efforts on the college building. The flames leaped to the chapel, and the college was saved only by the steady streams of water from the fire engines and the heroic efforts of firemen and members of the college who clambered about on the roof, extinguishing fires started by flying embers. Some of the personal effects of the boys were saved, but the school was a total loss, and only the walls of the chapel remained.[23]

The community rallied to provide housing for the 110 schoolboys. Principal Adams placed the Lodge at the disposal of the School Association, and the infirmary (Morris House) was pressed into service. Many friends of the school in Lennoxville and Sherbrooke opened their homes to the boys. Dr Allnatt, who had been living in the house built for the rector at the south end of the school building, moved into the partly finished Divinity House. Corporation appointed a committee to oversee the rebuilding of the school. In June this committee reported that the total cost would be little short of $60 thousand. Insurance would provide $33 thousand and the government of Honoré Mercier had consented to a grant of $10 thousand, payable in five equal annual instalments, toward the cost of the new building. This was the first capital grant Bishop's had ever received from the government; it is remarkable that it came from a premier who is remembered as the first to claim that his government was the "national government" of the people of Quebec. A campaign was mounted to raise the balance of $17 thousand, and, with some misgivings, bonds from the college endowment were pledged as collateral for a loan against the promised government grant. In the event, one of the contractors for the new building went bankrupt, and the ensuing legal battle with his creditors gave the trustees some anxious moments. However, the new and improved building was completed on the old site by the beginning of Lent term, 1892.

Rebuilding the chapel proved to be a more controversial project. Some members of Corporation wanted to rebuild on the same site, arguing that the chapel was a memorial to Jasper Nicolls, who had raised the funds required to enlarge and embellish it, and that it was in harmony with the other buildings. Others coveted the site for college facilities including a separate dining hall. A compromise was finally achieved, by which the chapel was rebuilt on the same site and some of the needed facilities were provided in new floors added above the ante-chapel. Much of this work was completed by the end of 1892, but the superb interior woodwork was not completed until 1898. In 1894 the cloister passage from the school to the college was built at the expense of the School Association, completing the northeast corner of what has become the Quadrangle.

The financial campaigns for the building of Divinity House and the rebuilding of the school and the chapel had drained the financial resources of the Bishop's community. In consequence, when economic recession produced its usual effect on the school and the enrolment declined below the break-even level, Corporation decided in June 1894 that expenses must be reduced. The college enrolment had been slowly increasing for several years, but the committee appointed to consider the matter recommended the termination of the appointment of N.P. Yates as lecturer and a reduction in the salary of the Mountain Professor of Pastoral Theology. J.J.S. Mountain had partially endowed this chair, on condition that the incumbent should devote his time exclusively to Divinity students, so the committee had to ask him to allow amendment of his trust deed to enable the Mountain Professor to pick up the resultant slack in instruction in Arts. A reorganization in the teaching of classics in the school had already enabled the school authorities to dispense with the services of the Professor of Classics for the coming session. The committee decided that the college could not pay his whole salary, so Corporation gave him the required year's notice of termination. The incumbent, the Rev. Benjamin Watkins, seems to have been highly regarded by the undergraduates, both as a teacher and as an active participant in the extra-curricular life of the college, and when in the course of the next academic year they learned that, as they understood, he had resigned, they drew up and unanimously signed a petition requesting Corporation to persuade him to reconsider. However, by this time the matriculation of a large class of freshmen in September 1894 had persuaded the committee to take a less gloomy view of the prospects, and they had recommended that the position be restored. It was advertised, a number of applications were received, and the Rev. R.A. Parrock was appointed. Parrock was an excellent classical scholar who ultimately became principal, but it is nevertheless clear that Corporation had again given priority to the needs of the school, whose full-time staff had not been reduced. Watkins moved to Western University in London, Ontario, of which he became provost and dean of the Faculty of Theology.

In 1891 Edward Chapman, citing ill health, resigned as bursar. In recognition of his services to Bishop's over 46 years, Corporation decided to continue his salary until the end of his life. His health continued to deteriorate, and he died in May 1895. Thus Bishop's lost the last of the original members of faculty, "the very type and model of a Christian gentleman,"[24] an exemplar for successive generations of undergraduates and schoolboys of the value of a sound and liberal education.

JUBILEE

Bishop's was rapidly approaching the fiftieth anniversary of its founding. What was its standing in the spectrum of Canadian university education?

With the completion of the CPR, Montreal had been confirmed as the commercial and financial capital of Canada, and its wealthy men vied with one another for the honour of financing the growth of McGill University. Thanks to major benefactions totalling well over $2 million, not including the gifts of Donald Smith and George Stephen for the construction and maintenance of Royal Victoria Hospital, McGill had made great strides toward being seen as useful by its benefactors. Under Principal Sir William Dawson's leadership, distinguished scholars had been appointed to endowed chairs in the natural sciences, and the Faculty of Applied Science had been established. The faculties of Law and Medicine had been reinforced, and for a time a Faculty of Veterinary Science flourished. The variety of career-oriented degrees and diplomas proved attractive to students, and by 1893, when Dawson retired, enrolment had grown to over a thousand. Of these students, the majority were undergoing professional training. Enrolment in Arts, including natural sciences, was only 350, of whom one third were women.[25] In his history of McGill, S.B. Frost describes Dawson's reign as the period in which McGill College matured into McGill University. Though the definition of a university implicit in this claim was perhaps not (as Frost remarked) what James McGill had had in mind when he endowed the institution, it was certainly a definition which appealed to Canadians. To train young men and women for a career in one of the professions has been, and still is, regarded as the essential function of a Canadian university. For this role, McGill was by 1895 superbly equipped.

The development of Queen's University since 1845 was perhaps a more pertinent standard of comparison for Bishop's. In the 1890s Queen's was still governed by a board of trustees, the great majority of whom were Presbyterians, and the principal was an ordained minister of that communion. As a result of its denominational adherence and of the monopolizing pressures of the University of Toronto, Queen's received no grants from the provincial government. On the other hand, its trustees had jealously preserved for the benefit of the faculties of Arts and

Theology the income from the endowment and the financial resources of the community which supported the university. While the training of students in medicine and surgery had been carried on continuously since 1855 by an institution which after several metamorphoses became in 1892 the Queen's Faculty of Medicine, it had received no financial support from the Queen's trustees.

Whereas Bishop's had been forced to submit its governance to the restricted vision of the synods, Queen's had seized the opportunity offered by the 1874 negotiations toward the union of the several Presbyterian churches in Canada to establish the principle that the united Church should not be required to elect the trustees of the Arts department of any college. Henceforward the board would itself decide on the term of appointment of all trustees and elect all new members of the board. In 1877 the newly liberated board appointed George Monro Grant as principal. A man of great breadth of vision, who had strongly supported both the Confederation of the Canadian provinces and Presbyterian Union, Grant was determined that Queen's should be recognized as a university catholic in its intellectual pursuits and devoid of parochialism. As a result of his success in promoting this philosophy, and of his apparently boundless energy, the endowment campaign he launched in 1878 realized $150 thousand, much of it from Canadians who owed no allegiance to the Kirk. Ten years later, a jubilee campaign raised another $250 thousand.

The careful husbandry of the trustees and Grant's success as a fund-raiser had made it possible to expand the university's classical curriculum to include physics, chemistry, natural history, English literature, and modern languages, all taught by full-time professors. He had also managed to persuade the Ontario government (led by Oliver Mowat, a native of Kingston and a brother of a member of the Queen's faculty) to establish a School of Mining and Agriculture in Kingston, over strenuous objections from the University of Toronto. During the 1890s Grant manoeuvred to obtain through this school money to strengthen the Queen's science departments and extend its buildings—this from a government which still maintained a formal policy of refusing grants to denominational institutions. When Queen's relinquished its denominational status in 1912, the School of Mines was formally absorbed into the Faculty of Science. In the 1890s there were some 600 students on campus, of whom about 40 percent were enrolled in professional programs.

By 1891, though Corporation had authorized the establishment of a Bishop's Faculty of Music, there was no immediate prospect of funding for full-time instructors, and the university's activity in this field had been limited to the drawing up of examination syllabi and the appointment of an examiner, a Doctor of Music of the University of Cambridge. Bishop's could therefore boast only two professional schools, the faculties of Medicine and Divinity. The Faculty of Medicine had its seat in Montreal, and in the Jubilee year, 60 students were enrolled, including eight women. Relations with the Lennoxville campus were cordial but not significant, though the medical professors did follow the Bishop's tradition of individual instruction and the precept of the founders that instruction should be provided at as little expense to the students as possible. Corporation made no financial contribution in support of medical instruction, and the medical convocation was held in Montreal.

Insofar as the academic community was concerned then, Bishop's in the Jubilee year consisted of some forty students, 35 of them fully matriculated, in the faculties of Arts and Divinity. Seven of the nine students in Divinity were Bachelors of Arts. Of the 27 fully matriculated undergraduates in Arts, 13 were destined for ordination, but only four of them took Theological Honours. Of the other prospective ordinands, three took Classical Honours, two Mathematical Honours, and four pass degrees. Small as these numbers were, they did constitute a residential *community* of learning. In this respect Bishop's was a better approximation to, for example, John Henry Newman's idea of a university than were its larger rivals.

The misdirection of its endowment had seriously restricted the college's curriculum, but within the subject matter which Newman held to be the staple of the mental exercises proper to a university—classical literature, rhetoric, logic, mathematics, music, and in particular theology, which in his view ceased to be a liberal study only when made *use* of for the specific practical purposes of the catechism and the pulpit—within this scope, the junior members of the university were "living among those and under those who represent the whole circle [of knowledge]." Newman wrote, "This I conceive to be the advantage of a seat of universal learning considered as a place of education. An assemblage of learned men, zealous for their own sciences and rivals of each other, are brought by familiar intercourse and for the sake of intellectual peace to adjust together the claims and relations of their respective subjects of investigation. They learn to respect, to consult, to aid each other. Thus is created a pure and clear atmosphere of thought which the student also breathes, though in his own case he pursues only a few sciences out of the multitude. He profits from an intellectual tradition."[26] The end of liberal education then, was (and is) to produce what Newman called a "philosophical" habit of mind—an ability to think which is independent of the particular subject matter and so is the instrument of all, and a

Bishop's College and Bishop's College School, 1895

mind that seeks "a comprehensive view of truth in all its branches, of the relations of science to science, of their mutual bearings and their respective values."[27]

Those who have had intimate experience of universities may question whether intellectual peace is commonly regarded as a goal by their members, and by no means all of the matriculants at Bishop's were mentally equipped or motivated to strive for a comprehensive view of truth. Nevertheless, Bishop's undergraduates were led to form their opinions and were required to defend them in a *community* of learning, and the more able among them amply demonstrated in their careers the usefulness of their education.

The jubilee was celebrated with great pomp and circumstance at convocation in June 1895. The degree of Doctor of Civil Law, *honoris causa*, was conferred upon the Governor-General of Canada, Lord Aberdeen, and upon the Lieutenant-Governor of Quebec, the Honourable Joseph-Adolph Chapleau, to whom illuminated addresses were presented. In his opening address, the chancellor dealt faithfully with the founders and with the other servants of the University of Bishop's College upon whose shoulders the graduating class were standing, and he made a timely appeal for the confidence and the financial support of his audience.[28] The day closed with a conversazione, which was brilliantly illuminated, thanks to the Sherbrooke Gas, Water and Electric Light Company, (president, R.W. Heneker), by a lavish display of electric lamps—harbinger of the triumph of technology to come.

RETROSPECT

Bishop's had been founded to "provide the country at large with the blessing of a sound and liberal education on reasonable terms." In particular, the founders wished to produce an educated clergy for the Anglican communion in Lower Canada. Looking to the time when "our country has gone on, as in all human probability it will in a few generations, to independence," Jasper Nicolls hoped that graduates of the college might improve the quality of the government.[29] To what extent had these goals been realized during the first 50 years?

In 1895 the college was still almost unknown to the general public outside Lower Canada. For the last ten years three quarters of the graduates in Arts had come from "mainland" Quebec.* Nearly all those who had

---

* Mainland Quebec refers to that part of the province which lies off the island of Montreal.

come from outside the province had been sent by the bishops who were sponsoring them for ordination. No systematic record has been preserved of the origins of students who matriculated before 1885, but what records there are indicate that most came from rural Lower Canada.

The loss of the endowment had made it impossible to broaden the curriculum and thus to extend the range of the college's influence. A complete record of the numbers enrolled during the period 1875–87 appears in Appendix D. It will be seen that the average number of students admitted had barely increased, from a little less than six during the period 1845–57, to seven per annum. On the other hand, whereas only 21 of the 72 students admitted during the earlier period achieved the standing of Bachelors of Arts, 60 of the 83 students admitted from 1875 to 1887 were graduated B.A. The latter rate of success compares favourably with current proportions. The improvement seems to have been largely due to increased financial support for candidates for ordination, which enabled them to complete their studies in Arts before undertaking theological work. During this period, more than half the undergraduates were receiving exhibitions or bursaries.

Of the 170 graduates in Arts during the first 50 years, 104 became clergymen. Of these, 50 served at one time or another in Quebec. Since more than 30 men had studied at Bishop's during the period and been ordained without proceeding to a degree in Arts, the college could fairly claim to have fulfilled the founders' hopes. Bishop's graduates were also to be found in most of the other Anglican dioceses in Canada, and some 15 had been welcomed in episcopalian dioceses in the United States.

Of the other graduates in Arts during the period, 10 were reported to have practised law, 15 medicine, 6 to have taught at college level, and 6 in secondary schools. Only two had become legislators: George H. Baker (B.A., 1855), MP for Missisquoi, appointed a senator in 1896, and Thomas Donnelly (B.A., 1894, M.D.C.M., 1904), MP for Wood Mountain, Saskatchewan.

THE JUBILEE AND HAMILTON MEMORIAL FUNDS

Enrolment in the college continued to increase, to 43 in 1895 and 60 in 1896. In these favourable circumstances, Adams lost no time mounting a financial campaign to raise a Jubilee Fund to meet needs totalling $85 thousand. In order to reduce the financial effects of fluctuations in enrolment, emphasis was placed on establishing endowments of $20 thousand for the Chair of Classics and the headmastership of the school, and on raising the endowments for the Office of Principal, the Chair of Pastoral Theology, and a Chair of Natural Science to like sums. A new

Robert Hamilton

gymnasium and the finishing of the interior of the chapel completed the list. Robert Hamilton was again first into the breach, with an offer of $20 thousand if bona fide subscription from other sources of $20 thousand could be raised by 1 July 1896. By June 1897 with the help of donations of $5 thousand each from Senator Evan Price and J.H.R. Molson and of £1 thousand from the SPCK, the Hamilton offer had been claimed, and the fund had reached $42 thousand, well on the way to the principal's immediate goal of $50 thousand.

Endowment of the essential core of the university's teaching resources was thus within sight. But Bishop's had always, in the tradition of the ancient universities of England, regarded residence as an essential qualification for a degree. Sharing the common life of the academic community was fundamental to the founders' idea of a university. In spite of the completion of Divinity House, the buildings could no longer accommodate the increased enrolment, and a number of students had to live in the village. Increased residential accommodation for undergraduates was added to the list of projects to be realized with the aid of the Jubilee Fund.

There seemed in 1897 to be little prospect of raising the required sum. However, Robert Hamilton died in 1898, and it was found that he had bequeathed another $25 thousand to the general endowment of the college. In recognition of the vital role of his perceptive munificence in the survival and subsequent growth of the college, the Bishop of Quebec (Andrew Hunter Dunn) and Senator Evan Price each offered $2 thousand toward the establishment of a Hamilton Memorial Fund, which would be devoted to the renovation and enlargement of the Arts building. The fund proved attractive to English-speaking Quebeckers, and it finally reached $20 thousand. More than $1 thousand had been raised by the students and schoolboys. With this sum it proved possible to extend the third floor over the whole length of the building, from the Lodge to the ante-chapel, and to renovate much of the interior. The kitchen facilities were enlarged and improved, and at long last a separate dining hall was provided for the faculty, graduate students, and undergraduates. A number of new student rooms, with improved sanitary facilities, were added along the third floor, the Lodge was renovated, and a room of some dignity and more adequate proportions was provided for the deliberations of Corporation, its committees, and the College Council. In 1903 the central tower was raised to balance the greater dimensions of the building, and a new entrance and stone balustrade were installed. Together with the new gymnasium, completed in 1898, the college now possessed a very adequate physical plant for its increased enrolment.

FURTHER ACADEMIC DEVELOPMENT

The need to increase the number of secondary school teachers who were university graduates had already led Bishop's and McGill to offer admission with advanced standing to holders of academy diplomas. However, only the normal school, under the direction of McGill, offered the required training in pedagogy and the lectures on the laws governing education and the legal position of the teacher. To enable Bishop's graduates in Arts to qualify for certification, Dr S.P. Robins, principal of the McGill Normal School, generously agreed to give a course of lectures on the Art of Teaching at Bishop's during the Lent term, 1897. Twelve undergraduates attended the lectures and passed the examination on the subjects treated[30], and the department of public instruction approved four schools in the neighbourhood for practice teaching. Encouraged by student interest, Corporation requested the principal to meet with the College Council and a committee of trustees to develop permanent means for the training of prospective teachers at Bishop's. A scheme consisting of a course of 52 lectures was drawn up and submitted to the Protestant Committee of the Council of Public Instruction for its approval, together with a proposal to secure opportunities for supervised teaching in local schools. Approval was duly granted, and the lectures were delivered for the first time during the 1898–99 session by the secretary of the Protestant Committee, G.W. Parmalee, by members of the college teaching staff, and by the headmaster of BCS and the principals of the Sherbrooke and Lennoxville Academies. The committee's central board of examiners participated in examining the seven students who took the course, which marked the beginning of the long and fruitful engagement of the college in the battle to raise the standard of teaching in the schools of the province.[31]

Corporation also took steps to reinforce the college's involvement in the teaching of music by entering into an affiliation agreement with the Dominion College of Music in Montreal. The Dominion College had been incorporated in 1895, initially to establish examination standards for training in music in Ontario and Quebec. By 1898 a teaching faculty had been developed, and under the affiliation agreement the Associate and Licentiate diplomas of the college admitted holders to advanced standing with respect to the examinations for the Mus.B. degree at Bishop's. Unlike the members of the Medical Faculty, the instructors in music did not hold university appointments. The direct involvement of convocation was limited to the drawing up of curricula and the appointment of examiners for the theoretical part of the program, the standards of performance being set by the Dominion College. Miss J.E. Howard and W.H. Jackson received the first Mus.B. degrees conferred under this program in 1899.[32]

Parallel with the growth in enrolment and the expansion of the physical plant had been enrichment of the curriculum and reinforcement of academic standards during the latter half of the 1890s. The Mathematical Honours program was reorganized to cover the full three years of residence, and the requirements in applied mathematics were considerably increased. New options for the pass degree were developed, and full-time lecturers in mathematics (W.J. Rusk) and political economy and logic (L.R. Holme) were appointed. In 1899 convocation took a great and long overdue step by authorizing the establishment of an honours program in English subjects, comprising logic, psychology, political economy, moral philosophy, history, and English literature. To facilitate matriculation, convocation agreed to drop Greek as a requirement for matriculation and a compulsory subject for students in Arts for all but prospective ordinands. Inevitably, this prompted suggestions that the undergraduates would henceforward be divided into Greeks and barbarians!

This potentially seminal development had been stimulated by the arrival of L.R. Holme, who had been Hulsean Prizeman at Cambridge University in 1895. Holme's initial appointment had been as lecturer in political economy and philosophical subjects in 1897, with some additional teaching responsibilities in the school. During the 1897–98 session, he persuaded the College Council to agree to a revision and strengthening of the pass options in his field, providing the college could secure the whole of his time. To this Corporation agreed. At the end of the following session Holme proposed an honours program in English. Again the College Council endorsed his proposal and transmitted it to Corporation, with a recommendation that a Professor of English be appointed together with another lecturer who would assist in classics and English. Moving with unusual celerity, Corporation approved the new program in June 1899, appointed Holme Professor of English (his salary to be a charge on Robert Hamilton's bequest), and authorized a salary of $750 for the requested assistant. Holme went to England during the summer and took back with him in September G. Oswald Smith, newly graduated from Oxford with a double first in classics and philosophy. Holme's academic standing was sufficient guarantee that the new honours program would not become an easier alternative to Classical or Mathematical Honours. Nevertheless, half the graduating class in 1899 had taken degrees in the pass option, embracing political science, constitutional history, and philosophy, all of which Holme had developed and taught. To launch the option, Sir John Bourinot, secretary of the

Royal Society of Canada, had been invited in November 1898 to receive the D.C.L. and to give a lecture in which he urged the importance of teaching political science to undergraduates and congratulated the college on Holme's initiative. The new honours program was thus launched on a very favourable tide.

THE MITRE

Another important development during the latter half of Principal Adams' tenure was the founding of *The Mitre*, an undergraduate initiative. The declared object of the magazine was to create a spirit of unity and fellow feeling among the various members of the collegiate body and to make *The Mitre* a link for the institution, its alumni, and the old boys of BCS. The masthead of the first issue in June 1893 included representatives of the three Arts years, Divinity, Medicine, and the school, and contributions were solicited from alumni.

From the beginning, the magazine included articles of high quality on a variety of subjects which give some insight into the literary and intellectual interests, both official and unofficial, of the students and the faculty. The annual volumes usually consisted of seven issues, so the notes from correspondents in the several faculties provided a continuous record of undergraduate life and opinion, not unduly coloured by filial piety. Reminiscences from alumni provided information on the earlier days of the college which has been invaluable to historians.

Editorials, usually moderate in tone, typically dealt with the need for honours programs in English and science, the desirability of establishing a uniform examination standard for Arts degrees in Canada, the importance of advertising the high quality of a Bishop's education and the possibility of opening the Arts program to women. Editorial opinion was generally in favour of British but opposed to American imperialism.

UNDERGRADUATE LIFE

In September 1894 the eldest son of L.C. Wurtele, the diarist of 1857, matriculated at Bishop's. His younger brother followed three years later. "High thinking" still prevailed, and both Wurteles graduated with good honours degrees, but living on campus could no longer be described as "plain." Compton Ladies College (CLC) had been established at Compton in 1874, and it was patronized by many of the same families who sent their sons to BCS. On Wednesday afternoons the young women at Compton received visitors, and *The Mitre* reported that the number of "cousins" at the institution claimed by each undergraduate had had to be limited in the interests of fairness. It may also be assumed that CLC increased the number of partners available for the dances held on campus or in the larger private homes in the neighbourhood. Some of these were formal affairs, requiring the undergraduates to be equipped with evening dress. Public speaking now took place within the forum of a mock parliament, which met regularly to debate the burning political issues of the day. Plays and concerts produced on campus had to stand comparison with the professional entertainment now available in Sherbrooke.

Increased enrolment had made it possible for team sports to flourish. The issue of *The Mitre* for December 1898 listed the officers of the seven clubs of the Bishop's College Athletic Association. Football and hockey games were played against local clubs and occasionally against teams from Quebec and McGill. The "clear, sparkling waters" of the rivers were used a great deal for swimming, boating, and picnics, particularly during Trinity term. A newspaper account of 1887 describes the result of this regime: "The most striking thing to a visitor from Montreal attending a Convocation of Bishop's College, Lennoxville was the manly, healthy, hardy sunburnt faces of students and boys, coupled with the evident signs of their having the very best of tailors."[33]

During the 1890s the students were forced to defend their water rights. The International Paper Company was in the habit of installing an illegal log boom on the Massawippi which made it useless as a waterway during much of the year. Annual protests to the company went unheeded, so during the spring of 1895 a party of undergraduates led by Armine Nicolls, the bursar, rowed up the river and began to dismantle the boom. They were finally driven off by the lumberjacks, but they did succeed in stirring the municipal and Township authorities to consider taking legal action.[34] (Nicolls, the younger son of Principal Nicolls, had been forced by ill health to give up a promising legal career in Montreal. As well as being a competent bursar and secretary to the Corporation, he took an active part in alumni affairs and in the extracurricular life on campus; he was greatly missed when he died in 1897 at the young age of 42.)

Unfortunately, the rivers could also be dangerous. In June 1899 a Divinity student, Henry Richmond, was drowned in the Massawippi in the course of rescuing a boy from the school who had been trapped in an undertow above the CPR bridge. Three students had participated in the rescue, and so powerful were the currents that a second student escaped drowning only because two other schoolboys managed to guide a log within his reach. Richmond's body was eventually found upstream of the scene of the rescue. The students and schoolboys subscribed for the bronze plaque in the chapel which commemorates his heroism.[35]

A REVERSAL OF FORTUNE

During the summer of 1898, just as the full effect of the Jubilee Fund was becoming evident, Thomas Adams suffered a paralytic stroke. By the end of September his condition had improved sufficiently that his physician held out hope of a full recovery. Corporation, in tribute to his indomitable energy and his devotion to the interests of the college, decided to grant him a year's leave of absence with pay and to appoint temporary lecturer to take over his teaching responsibilities in mathematics. Dr Allnatt was to assume the administrative responsibilities of the principal as well as those of the Dean of Divinity. The principal did not recover during the winter, and Corporation extended his leave for a further year in June 1899. By October it was clear that he was not going to be able to resume his duties, and a committee was appointed to recruit a new principal.

In September 1899 the college suffered a second heavy blow. Without warning the grant of $2,250 which the institution had been receiving annually from the Quebec government was cut in half for the year 1899–1900. The grant had been taken out of the fees charged by the government for Protestant marriage licenses, and the part of the proceeds granted to McGill and Bishop's recognized their contribution to English-language education, in particular as a source of teachers for the secondary schools. However, the government of the day found it more profitable politically to use the money to subsidize the school boards in "poor" municipalities, and it seemed likely that the whole of the universities' portion would be used for this purpose in future. The Protestant Committee of the CPI found no particular fault with this new policy, only resolving, on division, to request that the grants be not reduced until the following year. The government ignored this request, and in protest Chancellor Heneker, who had been chairman of the committee, resigned. As he noted, the Arts course was an essential preparation for secondary school teachers and for those who supervised their training, and "while technical and strictly professional training was easily provided for by other means, the practice is universal [in other countries] of aiding the universities [with state funds] in this important part of their work."[36]

The university's operating expenditures were now seriously in excess of revenues, in spite of the burgeoning enrolment. The extra expense of a lecturer to replace Principal Adams had continued for a second year, and the declining rate of interest on bonds had partly offset the recent increase in endowment. The loss of $1,125 from the government grant had been announced after all the financial commitments had been made for the session. The committee appointed to consider the situation reported that, exercising the strictest economy, the institution faced a deficit of $1,750 on the year's operations.

Faced with the possibility that the remaining half of the government grant would be cut for the 1900–01 session, Corporation lost its nerve. At a meeting in January 1900 it was decided to accept the resignation of L.R. Holme and to terminate the appointments of Smith and Rusk as lecturers, effective June 1900. (Several other professors placed their resignations in the hands of Corporation in case the qualifications of the incoming principal should make it necessary to redistribute the teaching responsibilities at university level. These offers Corporation gratefully declined.)

The minutes of the meeting record Corporation's deep regret that these decisions had had to be taken; and, recalling the effects which the debt incurred to build the school had imposed on the college for fifteen years, it is difficult to criticize their refusal to consider going into debt again. Nevertheless, the loss of Holme and the consequent shipwreck of the honours program in English were among the two or three most serious setbacks in the entire history of the academic development of the university. An exceptional scholar and an energetic and stimulating lecturer, he had also adapted quickly to his new country and had participated fully in the extra-curricular life of the college. Expansion of the rigidly classical curriculum of the Faculty of Arts had been long overdue, and it would almost certainly have led to a further increase in enrolment. There was indeed "a tide in the affairs of men" to be taken at the flood, and it must have been profoundly disheartening for Thomas Adams, confined to his sick-bed in England, to learn that the opportunity had been missed.

Chancellor Heneker's resignation from the Protestant Committee, though understandable, proved to be a serious tactical error. Principal Peterson of McGill did not resign. In 1899 the government managed to find another $3 thousand a year for the normal school at McGill. Encouraged by this mark of official favour, McGill decided during the 1899–1900 session that they would prefer to no longer share with Bishop's the responsibility of conducting the Associate in Arts (A.A.) examinations. In May 1900 McGill proposed that its the newly constituted matriculation board be given complete control over these examinations. The course of study for what was in effect the graduation diploma for the Protestant secondary schools of the province was to be determined by the Corporation of McGill University, in consultation with the Protestant Committee.

According to the minutes of the relevant meeting of the committee, its members were informed that Bishop's had agreed to these proceedings. This was not the case, but in the absence of Heneker this information was not challenged, and the McGill proposal was adopted.[37] As a result of this further demonstration of McGill's increasingly imperial ambitions, the headmasters of the academies and other secondary schools quite naturally made a study of the McGill requirements and the McGill courses in order that their graduating students might not find themselves at a disadvantage either in writing their A.A. examinations or in their early years at college. From the Sherbrooke Academy, in consequence, only three students matriculated at Bishop's during the next four years.

This development must have caused further distress to Principal Adams. The news that he had had to resign was greeted with dismay by every constituency in the institution. His successful campaigns to raise money for buildings and the endowment, his energetic and, latterly, skilful administration, and the development of the curriculum which had been achieved at his perceptive prompting had completely erased his early difficulties from the collective memory. It is sad that, like Lobley, he was not spared to enjoy the fruits of his labours. One also feels that, had his health not given way (in which case of course the deficit of 1899 would have been less unmanageable) he would have found a way to nerve Corporation to maintain the English honours.

CHAPTER FIVE

THE END OF THE BEGINNING

PRINCIPAL WHITNEY

Corporation appointed James Pounder Whitney to replace Thomas Adams as principal in May 1900. Whitney had been a Foundation Scholar of King's College, Cambridge, from which he graduated with a double first in mathematics and history in 1881. Priested in 1885, he combined lecturing in history at Owens College, Manchester, with pastoral duties in various parishes before then returning in 1895 to a college living at Milton (near Cambridge), tutorial work for his college, and the opportunity to pursue his interest in ecclesiastical history. When he came to Canada, Whitney's scholarship had already been recognized by Lord Acton, Regius Professor of History and chief designer of the Cambridge Modern History, who had commissioned an article from him on the Reformation in Switzerland. He proved to be a competent teacher and a sound judge of the needs of the university.

At a special convocation in December 1900 John Hamilton was installed as chancellor in place of Richard Heneker, who had resigned after 22 years in the post. Heneker had exercised a determining influence over the development of the university for 42 years. The institution had benefited greatly from his sound business sense, his meticulous attention to its finances, and his influence, particularly on the Protestant

James Pounder Whitney

Waiting for the governor general. Jubilee Convocation, 1903

Committee of the Council of Public Instruction. On the other hand, although he had been a powerful public advocate of the value of liberal education, he had little understanding of the nature of academic communities. His failure to defend Jasper Nicolls against the evangelicals and his acquiescence in the fatal overloading of Joseph Lobley had had serious and lasting effects on morale in the college. Moreover, he had continued to believe against all the evidence that the school ought to be a natural source of matriculants for the college and that the school and the college could profitably share one campus. In fact, during the period from 1860 to 1900, fewer than 50 of the 207 graduates of Bishop's in Arts had studied at BCS,[1] and the consequences of harnessing the college to the school have been abundantly described in this history.

Whitney inherited a situation which required prompt remedial action. On the one hand, thanks to the success of the Jubilee and Hamilton Memorial campaigns the buildings were more nearly adequate to the needs of the campus community than they had been since the foundation of the college—though the new principal and his wife had to spend their first winter in temporary quarters on the top flat of Divinity House, awaiting completion of the renovation of the Lodge. On the other hand, due to the uncertainties of the previous two years enrolment in 1900 had fallen to 30 full-time, fully matriculated students—far below the capacity of the newly expanded residential accommodation—and the full-time faculty had been reduced to the occupants of the endowed chairs. Oswald Smith had agreed to return in September at a reduced salary, to be augmented if finances permitted. During the summer of 1900 the government had been persuaded to maintain the grant at the new reduced level, and Smith's salary was restored to its original value, but in December he was offered the Chair of Classics at Trinity College, Toronto, and Corporation released him from his contract. He was replaced by C.W. Mitchell, Prince of Wales Prizeman at Bishop's in 1896 and 1897. Mitchell filled the gap in Classics until 1902, when he left to study theology at Cambridge. His place was taken by H.F. Hamilton, a graduate of Christ Church, Oxford, who had enrolled in Divinity at Bishop's.

Charles Mitchell, who had grown up on a farm near Huntingville, was successful in both the Theological Tripos and the Oriental Languages Tripos at Cambridge. He was then appointed Hebrew master at the Merchant Taylors' School in London, and he profited from his easy access to the British Museum to perfect his knowledge of Middle Eastern languages and to become known for his translation of ancient manuscripts in the Syriac languages. He also prepared himself for ordination at the hands of the Bishop of London. When World War I broke out he volunteered as a chaplain. He was for a year attached to headquarters staff, where his skill with languages made him invaluable, but in 1916 he managed to obtain an appointment to a battalion of the East Yorkshire Regiment in the line. He survived the battles on the Somme in 1916 but was killed the following May while tending the wounded under fire—in the words of the battalion's C.O. (also a Canadian), "Always up near the men—beloved by all."

With the arrival of Hamilton, classics was adequately provided for. However, it was obvious that the principal could not carry the responsibility of honours programs in both Mathematics and English, and that the curriculum developed by Holme and Smith would have to be modified. Fortunately, the incoming Professor of Pastoral Theology, E.A. Dunn, was also qualified in mathematics, and he was pressed into service in support of that program. The English Honours program was replaced by Honours in History, which became the principal's special charge. By the time he prepared his annual report for 1901–02, moreover, he had become convinced that the poor grounding of the majority of matriculants made it impossible to use classical texts in the original languages as vehicles for educating undergraduates. In his opinion, "a good English course would probably give as good an education as these students could receive."[3]

WOMEN ADMITTED TO LECTURES

The universities of Quebec were for many years comparatively unresponsive to the movement in favour of the higher education of women which had developed in the western world during the nineteenth century. A very large number of the influential men of the province seem to have considered that there was no need to educate women for the professions, and that to do so would disturb the division of responsibilities in the family on which domestic harmony was founded at the time. Many recognized that women were quite as well intellectually endowed as men, and that much talent was being wasted, but even they feared the effect of mixing the sexes (at the age of undergraduates) upon those finer qualities which they believed to be peculiarly feminine—to say nothing of the risk of unsuitable marriages! The result was that consideration of professional education for women almost inevitably involved the setting up of separate classes for them, and the universities were desperately short of money with which to cope with the classes they already had.

Since McGill enjoyed the generous support of the Montreal business community, it was in the McGill Faculty of Arts that the first women undergraduates matriculated in Quebec. The groundwork had been laid

John Hamilton, 1925

by the establishment of the Montreal High School for Girls in 1874 at the urging of the Montreal Ladies Education Association (founded by Mrs John Molson) and of Principal Dawson of McGill. Several graduates of the school wished to proceed to a Bachelor of Arts degree, and in 1884 a deputation waited on the principal seeking admission to the Faculty of Arts. By this time the question was being hotly debated in the faculty. A majority favoured university education for women; some of these, led by Dawson, advocated separate but equal instruction for the ladies, while others, led by John Clark Murray, Professor of Moral Philosophy, advocated admission of women to the regular lectures of the Faculty. This aspect of the question was decided by the president of the CPR, Donald Smith, who informed Dawson in 1884 that he would immediately make available $50 thousand to establish a university course for women on condition that the classes were entirely separate from those for men. The first women graduates in Arts took their degrees in 1888; Donald Smith subsequently provided, through his magnificent gift of Royal Victoria College, the residential and common facilities required for the women (dubbed "Donaldas") to become full, if separate, members of the academic community.

Lacking a benefactor of Smith's stature, Bishop's could only declare its willingness to accept women if money could be found to provide instruction for them. In 1883, Mabel Aldrich became the first woman Townshipper to pass at Lennoxville the examination for the Associate in Arts Certificate.[4] In 1885, Bishop's and McGill agreed to admit holders of academy diplomas to advanced standing in the faculties of arts, but only McGill could in fact offer places to the large majority of these aspirants who were women. In his convocation address in 1890 Chancellor Heneker spoke of the need to provide opportunity for women to cultivate their mental powers, and cited the "noble gift of Sir Donald Smith" to McGill as an example to be emulated. The following year he had the great pleasure of conferring the degrees of M.D.C.M. upon Octavia Grace Ritchie, the first woman medical graduate in the province of Quebec. Though the dean of the Bishop's Faculty of Medicine reported that it had been necessary to separate the sexes in only a few lectures and in the dissecting room, and that men and women had worked harmoniously together, the Faculty of Arts seems to have favoured the McGill model. At convocation in 1892 the chancellor again lamented that the university's means were too slender to enable it to follow McGill's example, but he said, "If any enthusiast in the cause—a most worthy cause as it seems to me—will send our bursar a cheque for $50 thousand, the Corporation will without hesitation make the experiment."[5] No one did, and for a further ten years the subject remained matter for debate by the undergraduates and comment, generally favourable, by members of the faculty and the editor of *The Mitre*. During the spring of 1903 applications from four women to the Faculty of Arts brought matters to a head. In June the College Council, on a motion by two of the external members, F.G. Scott and R.W.E. Wright, decided to request Corporation to rule on the applications. Corporation, meeting later the same day, appointed the chancellor, the faculty, and three external members as a committee, to be chaired by the principal and given power to act. At the October meeting of Corporation, this committee reported that the women had been admitted to lectures, and no dissenting voice appears to have been raised. *The Mitre* was "delighted to welcome among us, in the lecture room, the ladies," and further reported that the women had been cheered by their fellows when, duly gowned, they first entered the room. The women all boarded in Lennoxville, and went to campus only for lectures.

However, the matter was not quite settled. In October 1905 the question of continuing to admit women students was raised in Corporation by the chancellor. The new principal, T.B. Waitt, reported in May 1906 that the faculty were in favour, "more especially as the education of the province is so largely in the hands of women."[6] However, when a trustee, William Farwell, moved to confirm the policy, F.G. Scott intervened to have the decision postponed until the next meeting of Corporation, to be held on 7 June. An unusually large number of external members attended a meeting of the College Council that morning, and Scott succeeded in outvoting the faculty on a motion that no more women be admitted. This recommendation was read to Corporation later in the day. After considerable discussion, Scott moved that the council's recommendation be adopted, with the addition of the words "at present." The vote on this motion was a tie. Due to the absence of the president and the recent death of the principal, the vice-principal, Dr Allnatt, was in the chair, and he of course had been present at the earlier council meeting. He gave his casting vote in favour of admitting women, and the Farwell motion was then passed by a similar division.[7]

The first woman to take a Bishop's degree in Arts was Anna Bryant. A teacher at the Lennoxville Academy who had studied at McGill and been admitted to Bishop's with advanced standing in 1904, she took her B.A. in 1905. In 1906 Maria Claribel Taylor, one of the first class who entered in 1903, was graduated B.A. with a first class in Honours Mathematics.[8]

THE A.A. EXAMINATIONS

By 1904 the full effect on enrolment of McGill's takeover of the A.A. examinations had become evident, and Bishop's decided to counterattack. Since McGill had been unwilling to work with Bishop's in supervising the exams, Corporation suggested to the Protestant Committee that it would be in the interests of education in the province if they were placed under the direct control of the committee. Alarmed by this threat to university control of matriculation standards, McGill offered to eliminate all mention of the university from the examinations and certificates and declared its willingness to discuss the problem with the committee. Following its meeting in November, at which Principal Whitney represented Bishop's, a sub-committee was appointed, with a mandate to develop a compromise satisfactory to both institutions and the committee. After three months of negotiations, the sub-committee proposed a solution, of which the essential features were:

1 That the course of study and the texts to be used for the Associate in Arts examination would be determined by the Protestant Committee after consultation with the McGill Matriculation Board.
2 That to the McGill Matriculation Board would be added two members of the faculty of Bishop's University, three members representing the Protestant Committee, and two assessors representing the teachers.
3 That the examinations would be set and conducted in Montreal, Quebec, and Lennoxville by the McGill Matriculation Board, but that the name of McGill would not appear on the examinations or documents connected with them.
4 That a detailed annual report on the examinations would be made to the committee.[9]

This proposal, with minor modifications, was agreed to by the two universities. Unfortunately, it gave the public authority a foothold in the setting of matriculation standards. In the long run university education in the province might have been better served if McGill had been willing to continue to work with Bishop's, so that the two universities might have presented a united front against intervention by the state.[10]

PUBLIC RELATIONS

Several other steps were taken during Whitney's tenure to increase the number of matriculants. Largely as a result of continued pressure from *The Mitre*, the university calendar was revised and printed much earlier in the year and circulated, with a brochure containing pictures of the campus, to all the secondary schools in the province. The joint Alma Mater Society was dissolved in 1901 and an Alumni Society for the college organized by A.H. Moore and F.G. Scott, with enthusiastic support from Principal Whitney and (from England) Principal Adams.

The alumni adopted recruitment as their most important task. The principal gave a series of public lectures in Sherbrooke during the winter of 1903–04. Attendance was encouraging, so he lectured again in 1904–05.

In 1903 a young graduate of Peterhouse, Cambridge, H.V. Routh, was appointed Lecturer in Modern Languages. As well as providing reinforcement for the modern languages option for the pass degree, he proved to be a valuable contributor to *The Mitre*, and a vigorous participant in college athletics. During the summer of 1904, largely at his own expense, he undertook a thorough canvass of the Townships in the interest of the university, and in the October issue of *The Mitre* he presented a penetrating and perceptive analysis of the public image of the institution.

In reply to the question "What impression does the college make?" Routh answered, "No impression at all!"[11] He heavily discounted the received view, garnered from those who had tried to raise money for the institution, that Bishop's suffered from being "too High Church" and "too English." The only serious objection against the university which he had encountered was that the degree at McGill was regarded as more valuable than the degree at Bishop's—"not by those who had conscientiously compared the two courses, nor by those who had tested the examination papers of the two universities, nor yet by those who know how to value the comparative merits of 25 months of residence at Montreal and 27 months of residence at Lennoxville," but simply because "one is always hearing about McGill and never about Bishop's." He concluded that "there are some thirty citizens of the Townships who should be kept personally informed of all our new developments, should become regular receivers of our calendars and pamphlets, and should be invited to our public functions."[12]

Nevertheless, Routh had found that there was a more fundamental reason for the small enrolment at Bishop's—the lack of desire for university education in the region. From St Andrew's to Scotstown he had found only 12 boys and girls who planned to matriculate in Arts in September. He concluded that "besides giving a thorough education, Bishop's has another and greater work to perform, that of *creating a desire for college education,*" particularly among the often highly gifted young people who were growing up in what he described as "arcadian simplicity" on farms and in small settlements. He believed that the most effective emissaries for the purpose were the undergraduates and the alumni, and that education in a residential college would prove to be the most attractive option for those who were thus persuaded of the value of higher education. He believed that in the long run the opening of the

A.F. Cecil Whalley's study, ca. 1905

universities to women would prove to be a turning point in the history of the college, since most of them would go out into the secondary schools of the province to demonstrate the value of a university degree.[13]

Routh's work was typical of the stimulation young graduates from England had provided during the difficult years since 1898. It was therefore a severe blow when he left in 1905 to take up a post as lecturer at Trinity College. Trinity had just entered into federation with the University of Toronto and was anticipating further growth in enrolment. Observing this, the irrepressible F.G. Scott wrote to the *Montreal Star* to propose federation of Bishop's with McGill. Whitney was furious. When he learned that *The Mitre* had been requested to print Scott's proposal, he appended a note in which he emphasized that the proposal had no official support. The principal was aware of the not very successful British experience with federation, and he also had reason to be fully aware of McGill's attitude toward Bishop's. "Irresponsibility," he wrote, "has many advantages, but maturity of thought is not always one of them; and I fear I must regard the letter as one of the least successful of my gifted friend in the realms of imagination and fancy."[14]

MUCH CHOPPING AND CHANGING

In January 1905 Principal Whitney called an assembly of the undergraduates to announce that he had submitted his resignation to Corporation—not, he assured them, because of any difference of opinion or strained relations with the governing body, but because his mother's state of health required his presence in England. *The Mitre* cited the manner of his going as an example of the close relations Whitney had established with the students. The editor went on to praise the zest with which he and his wife had participated in collegiate life and the beneficial effect of his diligence as a scholar on the scholarship of the undergraduates. With considerable prescience, *The Mitre* observed that, freed from the onerous and trying duties of a principal, Whitney would be able to devote more time to historical research. In 1906 he was appointed Hulsean Lecturer at Cambridge, and in 1907 joint editor of the *Cambridge Medieval History*. After ten years as a professor at King's College, London, he was elected in 1919 to the Dixie Chair in Ecclesiastical History at Cambridge, which he occupied until his death in 1939.[15]

The choice of a new principal generated unusual interest and discussion in the Bishop's community. The participation of a distinct Canadian contingent in the Boer War had marked a stage in Canada's progress toward political independence, and the opening of the Northwest Territories (now Saskatchewan & Alberta) to settlement had stimulated a burgeoning self-confidence. Acknowledging the Bishop's debt to the ancient English colleges on which it had been modelled, *The Mitre* nevertheless felt that the time had come to appoint a Canadian-born principal or at least one who had some experience of Canadian life and thought.[16] In a speech to the Allied Colonial Universities Conference in 1903 Principal Whitney had expressed the same opinion.

The short list presented to Corporation contained three names: R.A. Parrock (who although born and educated in England was reckoned by his supporters to be Canadian) and two men from England; T.B. Waitt, who had been runner-up to Whitney in 1900, and H. deB. Gibbins. Corporation met for the election on 9 May, amid great undergraduate excitement. Parrock led on the first two ballots, but he was one short of a majority. After two more ballots, Waitt obtained 10 of the 19 votes cast, and he was declared elected.[17] Many of the undergraduates proclaimed their disappointment by sallying forth to the village in a torchlight procession.

The new principal had the necessary academic qualifications. He had been offered the Chair of History at Trinity College, Toronto, in 1891, and he came very highly recommended as a stimulating lecturer and tutor. However, his career in England suggests that he regarded his task in Lennoxville primarily as a mission rather than as the leadership of an academic community. He was genuinely interested in Canada—three of his brothers had settled in Manitoba—and he worked hard during his first winter to adapt to his new environment. Unhappily, he did not succeed. Unaccustomed to the Canadian climate, he contracted pneumonia after a long swim in the Massawippi river in May and died five days later.

The committee appointed to look for his successor included only one member of the faculty. In June, "after very carefully considering what will be best in the interest of the University,"[18] it recommended the appointment of Dr Gibbins, who was duly elected.

Though the new principal had taken Classical Honours at Oxford, his scholarly publications, recognized by a D.Litt. from Trinity College, Dublin, had been in the field of economic and industrial history. He too came highly recommended as a teacher and "a kindly man, possessing to a marked degree the saving quality of humour."[19] Unfortunately his health did not prove equal to new responsibilities in a harsh climate, and in June 1907 he submitted his resignation to Corporation. He died in England later in the year.

Richard Arthur Parrock

For the third time in as many years a new principal had to be elected. Richard Parrock was again a candidate, and the minutes of the meeting of Corporation called for the election reveal the serious rift which had hitherto prevented his election. At that time the trustees, backed by several legal opinions as to the correct interpretation of the statutes, maintained that they alone could authorize expenditures. Parrock had early shown himself to be an energetic and imaginative administrator and fundraiser. He had persuaded Corporation to build a house for him to rent adjacent to Harrold Lodge, and had raised part of the cost by private subscription. He had played an active role on Corporation while the Hamilton Memorial Fund was being raised and spent, but in so doing he seems to have incurred the displeasure of the trustees. Undaunted, during the meeting at which the election was to be held he persuaded Corporation (i.e., the bishop and the College Council as well as the trustees) to reimburse E.A. Dunn, Mountain Professor 1901–07, for repairs to his apartment in Divinity House to the amount of $60—which the trustees had not authorized and had for five years refused to pay.

Dunn had just been instrumental in persuading friends of his to contribute $2,000 for the construction and equipping of the Bishop Stewart Memorial Oratory at Divinity House. Nevertheless, the trustees felt that their authority was being challenged. When the appointments committee proposed a short list of two names, R.A. Parrock and G.W. Abbott-Smith, the chairman of the trustees, William Morris, moved adjournment of the meeting for a month to await further deliberation by the committee. Led by Francis Allnatt and Edward Dunn, Corporation defeated this motion nine to seven. Morris then proposed Allnatt as a candidate. Allnatt declined to stand. Noting the vote on his previous motion, Morris moved that a two-thirds majority be required for election. This was agreed to. After 4 ballots, Parrock's support remained steady at nine of the 17 votes cast. After a further attempt to postpone the election had been defeated, it was decided by the casting vote of the president to accept a simple majority; Parrock was elected on the next ballot.[20]

It was thus with the staunch support of the faculty and students, but in the teeth of determined opposition from the trustees, that the new principal took office. He inherited a recently renovated physical plant which provided accommodation for nearly all the undergraduates who did not live at home, but the faculty had been sorely buffeted by the frequent changes in administration. The calendar advertised honours courses in six subjects and a pass course with optional concentrations in the same subjects plus natural science. Since the principal also held a chair, and the full-time faculty numbered 6, the College Council had to meet immediately after each election to redistribute teaching responsibilities to take account of the qualifications of the new principal. In spite of remarkable versatility of competence among the staff, only theology, classics, and history had been continuously provided for at honours level since 1904, and history had been taught by three different professors, each of whom also carried the responsibilities of the office of principal. Parrock's first task, therefore was to attempt to restore continuity in the college teaching.

Enrolment in Arts had held up remarkably well in the interim. The new principal had to find teaching resources for 43 fully matriculated undergraduates in Arts as well as another dozen part-time and preparatory students. Enrolment in the Faculty of Divinity had nearly doubled during the previous two years, due to the availability of a number of new bursaries provided from the diocese and from overseas to enable clergy to be trained for the missions in the rapidly developing Northwest Territories. The total college enrolment of 77 included 15 from England or Ireland and 9 women.

Theology was well provided for. Allnatt was a respected and experienced teacher, and H.F. Hamilton, the incoming Professor of Pastoral Theology, had profited from study for the B.D. at Oxford and a year at the General Theological Seminary in New York since he had resigned his lectureship in 1905. Arts proved to be more difficult. Parrock continued to occupy the Chair of Classics, but it was not until 1908 that C.F. Gummer, who had taken a first class in Mathematical Honours and another in Theological Honours at Christ Church, Oxford, filled the Chair of Mathematics. The English subjects were taught by two new lecturers, E.E. Boothroyd, a graduate of Trinity College, Cambridge, and F.G. Vial, a Bishop's graduate, who also helped Parrock in classics and Allnatt in divinity. Boothroyd was the first of the young lecturers from England to put down roots. An excellent teacher, his course in history and English literature became an essential element of a Bishop's education for the next 35 years. Vial had taken a first class Bishop's degree in Classics in 1895 and gone on to ordination and parish work in the diocese, continuing to study for the synod B.D., which he obtained in 1905. Two more lecturers were appointed in Arts in 1908, H.C. Burt from Trinity College, Toronto, and F.O. Call, a Bishop's graduate of 1905. The full-time faculty establishment was thus raised to seven, but natural science was still taught by R.N. Hudspeth, the senior mathematical and science master of the school.

On the professional side, the faculties of Medicine and Dentistry had been absorbed by McGill, and the embryo Faculty of Music was about to expire. The raison d'être of the Dominion College of Music had been to develop a Canadian system of examinations in music. However, the college had failed to attract the necessary financial support. When Charles Harriss, an energetic Montreal musician with imperial ambitions and the independent means with which to promote them, moved with the support of McGill to establish a system of examination centres across Canada in association with the (London) Royal Academy of Music and Royal College of Music, the Dominion College was unable to compete. By 1904 the McGill Conservatorium, backed by Donald Smith, who was by then Lord Strathcona, had been established near Royal Victoria College. In 1908 McGill hired a full-time Professor of Music at a salary of $4 thousand guaranteed for three years by a wealthy graduate, and the university terminated its association with the English institutions. Unable to compete with this, Bishop's ended the affiliation with the Dominion College, and very few candidates presented themselves for the Bishop's Mus.B. examinations after 1908.

The training of teachers, however, had prospered. In 1904 the editor of *The Mitre* noted that of the 20 men with university degrees who held positions as principals in the Protestant superior schools of the Province, eight were Bishop's graduates,[21] and in 1905 Principal Whitney reported that Bishop's graduates held more posts in the academies and schools under the Protestant Committee than those of any other university. Since members of the faculty and the principal attached a high priority to the need to improve the academic standards of the schools, and so to increase the pool of potential matriculants, they directed many of their public lectures primarily to audiences of teachers.

THE COMMON LIFE

Willingness to participate in the extra-curricular life of the college continued to characterize younger members of the faculty, who were usually given some responsibility for overseeing life in residence. H.V. Routh was a notable harrier during his two years at Bishop's. Boothroyd and Gummer had both rowed in their college eights at Cambridge, but Bishop's could not afford eight-oared shells, so Boothroyd turned out to practise with the football team. He also founded and took an active part in the affairs of the Churchwarden Club, a select society of members of faculty and students which met periodically "for the colouring of Churchwardens [clay pipes] and the mutual amusement and instruction of its members."[22] Gummer became a valued member of the Dramatic Club, which had been formed in 1906 to produce *She Stoops to Conquer* in the Clement Theatre in Sherbrooke. Encouraged by the reception accorded this first venture, the club went on to produce annually one of the classics of English drama, and Gummer's performance in Pinero's *The Magistrate* in 1909 was highly praised. He also founded, possibly to compete with the Churchwardens, the Parergon Society, which met from time to time to discuss topics "other than those included in the curriculum."[23] During its first year these included "Elements of Polytheism" and "The Origin of Religion," this latter stimulated by a brilliant freshman, R.J. Meekren, whose paper provoked much controversy. For some reason, Meekren regrettably did not continue his career at the university, but he continued to participate in campus life from time to time—as a part-time librarian and a stimulating and welcome voice in academic discourse. Another popular form of entertainment was the mock trial. These were conducted on Gilbertian lines by the best speakers among the faculty and students, and with the meetings of the Debating Society they provided opportunities for fledgling orators to cut their teeth.

The women undergraduates were excluded from this rich common life of the collegiate society. They seem to have been regarded by most of the men as a sub-species of womanhood, to be respected for their academic ability, but otherwise incomprehensible within the canon of normal social relations. In the April 1908 issue of *The Mitre*, one of the ladies responded eloquently to the editor's annual sermon to the freshmen on the importance of loyal participation in the extra-curricular life of the college. "What chance do we have to be loyal?" she asked. "To be sure, we can study, there is no bar to that pleasure; but how little a man is thought of who is efficient only in his studies. Why should a woman be judged by a standard so entirely different?"[24] Why indeed? Nevertheless, "Women admitted to lectures" remained the rule in the Faculty of Arts for another 40 years, and it was not until the construction of Pollack Hall in 1950 that women were able to participate fully in the common life of the university.

The men of the college felt much more at ease with the daughters of Sherbrooke and Lennoxville and the girls of Compton Ladies College. *They* were co-opted for the female parts in plays, and invited to dances, both formal and informal, which faculty wives were usually willing to chaperon. Invitations to dances at Compton were prized, even though in winter that often involved waiting on the Compton station platform at two o'clock in the morning in sub-zero temperatures until the northbound train could be flagged down. In a light-hearted but perceptive article in *The Mitre*, "The Ethics of Flirting,"[25] the author (Boothroyd? Meekren?) provided some insight into the nature of the difficulty. Flirting, he maintained, was a fundamental instinct, and indulging it had been since Adam and Eve a normal social relationship between men and women. He went on to make a clear distinction between "flirting" and "love-making" and to emphasize the role of a well-developed sense of humour in both parties in preserving the distinction. In his view, females who had no inclination for such frivolity were "usually of the bluestocking variety, earnest, unsentimental young creatures bent on the universal betterment of mankind or, more important work still, the emancipation of their own sex." To this humourless category the men of the college seem to have assigned, presumably without trial, the early women students!

Since the foundation of the university, successive principals, chancellors, and convocation speakers had urged undergraduates to learn to speak French so that they might communicate with their French-speaking compatriots, who were by now very much in the majority in the region as well as the province. Very few had responded. Inspired by the success of Sir Wilfrid Laurier, relations between the leaders and potential leaders of the English- and French-speaking societies were cordial during the early years of the century, and several exchanges developed between Bishop's and Laval. When the Dramatic Club took *The Rivals* to Quebec, the lieutenant-governor attended the performance and Laval students turned out in force, enlivening the intervals with their glees. Bishop's participated in receptions in the region for groups of Laval students from Quebec and from Montreal. The principal greeted them in French, but the undergraduates do not appear to have followed suit. In 1905 Laval invited a Bishop's student to the annual banquet of the Law Faculty in Quebec. By great good fortune, an undergraduate from France was available. Otherwise, the apparently invincible insularity of young English-speaking Quebeckers would again have been a source of embarrassment.

THE ALUMNI ASSOCIATION

Starting in 1905 the three members of the College Council appointed by the bishops from a larger number elected by convocation had been specified as representatives of the graduates of the university. In the royal charter, a fee for membership in convocation had been specified which most of the clerical graduates had found to be beyond their means. Wishing to stimulate the interest of graduates in their Alma Mater, Corporation began in the same year to seek legal opinion as to the advisability of seeking an amendment to this provision of the charter.

In contrast to McGill, nearly half of the graduates of the university were clergy on very modest stipends, and although the refounded Alumni Association participated vigorously in financial campaigns, it was not at that time able to make very much difference to the total subscribed. On the other hand, a great many of the graduates were parish clergy and teachers who were strategically situated to influence the decisions of the young concerning higher education. Under the prompting of *The Mitre* and of members of faculty, Corporation had begun to recognize the need to keep these people informed of developments at the university.

During Parrock's tenure the Alumni Association began to exert appreciable influence on university development. In the course of the winter of 1909–10 the council had mandated a committee headed by G.W. Abbott-Smith to examine the advantages and disadvantages of introducing the degree program of four shorter academic sessions which had been adopted by nearly all other Canadian universities. After a full discussion of the committee's extensive report by a largely attended meeting, the council recommended the adoption of a four-year program in Arts and a three-year program in Divinity. Corporation and Convocation approved these programs for implementation in September 1910. Though the committee's report has not survived, the strongest argument in favour of the change would have been the difficulty of establishing equivalence between the Bishop's curriculum and the programs of other Canadian and American universities. The duration and the number of courses in the Bishop's three-year program were similar to those in the four-short-year program of the other universities, but these institutions were not disposed to recognize that, in a residential college community, the Bachelor level could be attained in three long sessions. The argument that Oxford and Cambridge granted the B.A. after three years' study was held to be irrelevant because of the much better preparation of English matriculants. The Canadian matriculation standard also played a role in the council's decision. Under the four-year scheme the work required of freshmen would be considerably reduced, and it was hoped that it would no longer be necessary to accept weak students in a preparatory year. Finally, the short academic year would allow the undergraduate a better opportunity to earn money at summer jobs. Bishop's students finishing their examinations late in June found that the best jobs had been taken by students whose academic year ended during the first week in May.

In February 1912 a deputation from the Alumni Association reported to Corporation that the alumni were strongly opposed to the new programs. Graduates in Arts proceeding to studies in Medicine, Law, and other professional programs would be forced to finance an extra year, and prospective ordinands an additional two years, of residence in college, and the Divinity students in particular would find this very difficult.

In view of the great disparity in the quality of the secondary schools of the province, especially in the rural areas, the alumni also held that the university must continue to provide instruction at the preparatory level. The principal responded with a detailed explanation of the reasons in favour of the new programs and an estimate of the cost of re-establishing the preparatory year. Nevertheless, after considerable discussion Corporation resolved, on motions by F.G. Scott, to return to three long years and to re-introduce the preparatory year.

The convocation issue of *The Mitre* for 1912 contained a letter which gave notice that another generation of Scotts was about to enter the fray. The canon's eldest son, William (B.A., 1908), had graduated at the top of his class in Law at McGill and begun a practice which would lead him to become Associate Chief Justice of Quebec. In his opinion, Bishop's was slowly but surely dying of dry rot. As a remedy he proposed that Corporation be composed of a much smaller number of men who were able and willing to promote the growth of the university. They should elect a president and a vice-president from among the members, and they should be free to appoint the best man available as principal, whether or not he was in holy orders. This blast produced no echoes at the time, but W.B. Scott would live to see all his proposals carried out and to participate as chairman of the Executive Committee in the secularization of the government of the university.

DEVELOPMENT UNDER PARROCK

In order to provide accommodation for the increased enrolment, and also perhaps because the Parrock family wanted a little more privacy, the College Council recommended in October 1907 that the Lodge be converted into lecture rooms and rooms for undergraduates and that a new detached Lodge be built for the principal. Corporation appointed a strong committee to raise the necessary $10 thousand. In spite of difficult economic conditions, and largely due to the efforts of the principal, the project was completed during the following summer.

This was in striking contrast to the lack of progress in the matter of a library. In celebration of the fiftieth anniversary of the granting of the royal charter which made of Bishop's a university, a fund had been established in 1903 to build a library and to endow scholarships. Having just made a very generous grant to Laval University, the government was persuaded to contribute $5 thousand, and A.H. Moore, appointed to canvass the two dioceses, obtained promises of a further $3,500. However, the committee mandated to obtain plans and estimates was unable to agree on a plan that could be realized with the funds available, and during the next four years Corporation had been too busy recruiting principals and negotiating with the School Association to give the question of the library its full attention. Stimulated by the rapid conclusion of Parrock's project, it reactivated the Library Committee and in May 1909 authorized the construction of the library wing behind McGreer Hall, at a cost of $9,700. Two rooms on the ground floor of the wing were to be fitted out as a laboratory for experimental science.

In 1908 C.F. Gummer had been appointed Professor of Mathematics, but the other three honours programs advertised in the calendar were unsupported by senior members of faculty. The next year Parrock resorted to the dubious expedient of appointing Boothroyd to the Chair of History, though Corporation could not pay him the salary of a professor. Boothroyd was fully qualified to take charge of an honours program, but the precedent was a bad one, and within four years two other lecturers had achieved professorial rank by the same route. As well as depreciating the standing of the Chairs, this effectively closed the possibility of recruiting fully qualified men for the other honours programs. The principal was more fortunate when Gummer resigned in 1911 to take up a Chair in Mathematics at Queen's, where the needs of undergraduates in pure and applied science gave the subject a much higher priority. Gummer's replacement, A.V. Richardson, from Queens' College, Cambridge, proved equally competent and took root, retaining responsibility for Honours in Mathematics until 1951.

In 1909 the Reverend E.J. Bidwell, headmaster of the school since 1903, resigned to become dean of the Diocese of Ontario. It proved difficult to find a successor, and by March 1910 the school was again in financial trouble. Two years of difficult negotiation over the terms of the school lease followed. F.G. Scott urged Corporation to buy out the school. The directors of the school, on the other hand, wished to buy the school building and grounds from Corporation. They were convinced that if they owned the building, they could raise enough capital to greatly improve the facilities. They also believed that it would be much easier to recruit a competent headmaster if he did not have to be a clergyman. By April 1912, under the pressure of 30 days notice by the school's creditors, a compromise had been hammered out. The school would no longer be under the control of Corporation, but the bishops would continue to be the Visitors. The headmaster would be appointed by the School Association, but he must be an Anglican communicant. The rent charged the school for the next 10 years would be greatly reduced, in order that the association might renovate the facilities and raise the masters' salaries. Finally, the college would feed its own students. This new dispensation removed many of the sources of friction between the college and the school. Under its terms the financial condition of the association was rapidly restored to health, and the affairs of the school disappeared for a time from the minutes of the meetings of Corporation. On the other hand, the reduction in the rent received from the school led to a deficit in the university's operations for the 1911–12 session.

WAR

In December 1909 *The Mitre* printed a poem by a member of faculty, F.O. Call, entitled "The Voices," which had been inspired by the observation that "today all Europe is divided into two armed camps, waiting breathlessly for the morrow."[26] Though general hostilities did not break out until 1914, the fear of war cast long shadows. In 1913 the bishops of Quebec and Montreal launched a Diamond Jubilee Appeal for $100 thousand for the university endowment fund. Though the Hamilton family and other members of the Bishop's community were quick to respond with traditional generosity, it was soon evident that the province's English-speaking community had other priorities. With the help of a government grant of $12,500, the fund had with difficulty reached $37,500 by May 1913. It was decided to apply the revenue from the fund to increase the salaries of the Professors of History, Philosophy, and Modern Languages, and to appoint a full-time Lecturer in Natural Science. Since his arrival in 1911 A.V. Richardson had lectured in natural science as well as in mathematics. Though the promised laboratory in the library wing had not yet materialized, he had managed to have the school laboratory partitioned off from the playroom so that simple experiments could be carried out. The new lecturer was N.C. Qua, a graduate of the University of Toronto who had been a demonstrator in their laboratories, but he did not arrive until September 1914.

The spring of 1914 was memorable for several events. In May the newly organized Alumnae Society sponsored a first annual lecture, addressed to an audience which included the president of the Alumni Society. The speaker was Carrie Derick, an early Donalda who had been appointed Professor of Comparative Botany at McGill in 1912. She was the first woman to be appointed a full Professor at a Canadian university, and the Bishop's alumnae obviously took great pride in the warm reception given her lecture.

In June the governor-general, HRH the Duke of Connaught, received a D.C.L. *honoris causa*. He, the Duchess, and their popular daughter the Princess Patricia were the sixth vice-regal party to grace a Bishop's convocation. The weather was brilliant, the audience large and distin-

Frederick George Scott, Belgium, 1915

guished, the principal's Latin sonorous, the speeches short and lighthearted, and the women undergraduates carried off nine of the 16 prizes awarded.

But the lights were indeed about to go out over Europe, and with them would be extinguished the imperial certainties of which the afternoon's principal ceremony had been a symbol. Over the next four years the rich fount of cultural resources which had nurtured Bishop's since its foundation would be exhausted in the mud of Flanders.

The principal had reported an unusually large number of freshmen matriculating in 1913, and he anticipated an even larger number in September 1914. His hopes were realized, but two of the undergraduates volunteered for service in the first Canadian contingent which went overseas in October 1914. In March 1915 N.C. Qua and eight more men enlisted in the fifth Canadian Mounted Rifles, a battalion which was largely recruited from the Eastern Townships. The following year 21 more undergraduates enlisted, reducing the university enrolment to five in the Divinity Faculty and 16 men and 10 women in Arts. Six of the Arts men who were prospective ordinands had enlisted in the Field Ambulance. By May 1916 over 80 alumni were serving, including 12 as military chaplains. In February 1915 the bursar, J.C. Stewart, had also left to take up a commission in the Forty-Second Highlanders.

Once again, hard-won stability in enrolment and revenue was threatened. Corporation nevertheless resolved to pay Qua half his salary while he was on active service. A.V. Richardson again undertook the lecturing in science, for which he was given a supplement of $300. Parrock also managed to introduce a course of lectures in accounting, commercial law, and banking, taught by a public accountant from Sherbrooke, and these proved popular. The series of public lectures given by the faculty was extended to other centres in the Townships with the aid of a more adequate and portable projection lantern.

Pressure for infantry reinforcements for the Western Front continued, and by 1917 nearly all male undergraduates of military age and fitness had volunteered for service. On the other hand, the faculty's persevering efforts to encourage students from the Townships to enter the Faculty of Arts were beginning to bear fruit, and matriculations of 27 undergraduates in 1916 and 30 in 1917 maintained the total registration at a viable level. However, these undergraduates were markedly less mature—some were only 16—and morale suffered the effects of war casualties and a lack of leadership on the part of the remaining senior students. By 1917 the women students in Arts outnumbered the men, but this potentially epochal event seems to have been regarded with greater alarm by alumni than by the undergraduates.[27] The female roles in the annual plays were now taken by college women, and the editor of *The Mitre* made valiant efforts to stimulate—even to provoke—the women to write for the magazine.

The pages of *The Mitre* gave abundant evidence of the profoundly unsettling effects of the war on the undergraduates. These ranged from the cry of the editor, "Into what insignificance does our little life sink when compared with the great death-struggle into which our brethren are passing?" to the numerous excerpts from letters from alumni at the Front—many of them familiar faces to those who were still at college—letters full of meetings with other Bishop's men, leaves in Paris, London, and Rome, the comradeship of battalion and battery, the earning of commissions in the field, and the winning of awards for gallantry, but saying nothing of the desperate daily struggle for survival.[28] An exception was a letter from several companions of R.J. Meekren to his mother reporting that he, who had been regarded as the father of the platoon, had gone missing after a five-hour shelling had destroyed the trench in which they were sheltering. Incredibly, he turned up again as a prisoner of war in a military hospital in Aachen, where he was being treated for shell-shock and loss of hearing. Happily the Lutheran chaplain of the hospital had supplied him with books, and he was able to speed his recovery by sending off pages of trenchant literary criticism to his friends.

THE SCHOOL MOVES

The terrible conflict which was stripping the university of its undergraduates had generated an industrial prosperity in Canada, and especially in Montreal, which greatly increased the potential parent pool for the school. Enrolment grew rapidly. In January 1915 the building near the corner of College and Reid which had housed the preparatory department was destroyed by fire. Anticipating a large enrolment for 1915–16 the new chairman of the board, J.K.L. Ross, cheerfully proposed that the five remaining Divinity students and the Professor of Pastoral Theology move out of Divinity House, which would then be occupied by the preparatory department. Corporation expressed a desire to be helpful, but regretted that Divinity House could not be converted from the purpose for which it had been built. In June 1916 Ross returned to the charge. He was a very wealthy industrialist from Montreal, given to such impulsive acts as writing a cheque to cover the school's deficit for the year. He now proposed to Corporation that the School Association be granted a 99-year lease on all the university's land north of the CPR tracks and east of the centre of the quad. The school would have exclusive use of the gymnasium, as well as the school building of course, and options to purchase Harrold Lodge and the house adjacent to it, occupied at the time by Professor Boothroyd. In return for this takeover of nearly all of the university's property, Ross proposed that the rent paid should conform to the provisions of the 1911 lease! Led by Principal Parrock and Chancellor Hamilton, Corporation replied that the proposal was incompatible with the interests of the university. Several amendments seeking alternative solutions were also rejected, but the association was granted an extension of six months, to the first of January 1917 to decide whether to renew the 1911 lease.

According to the school's historian, Ross then "in a two-hour chauffeured business trip secured ownership of or options on some four hundred acres"[29] at the other end of the St Francis River bridge, on the opposite bank from the university. There he set about building his own school—The Lennoxville School. While it was being built, the Boothroyds moved to a partially restored Old Lodge, so that the headmaster could occupy the "Classics" house and the Prep could be installed in the headmaster's house at the south end of the school building. Corporation began to consider what might be done with the school buildings when the school moved. One possibility was that they could be used to accommodate the growing number of women students whose homes were not within commuting distance.

In June 1918 the governor-general, the Duke of Devonshire, opened the magnificent new Preparatory School buildings across the St Francis; but unfortunately, Commander Ross incurred heavy financial losses at the end of the war, and he was unable to complete his project, on which he had already spent $750 thousand. He transferred the grounds and the new buildings to the Association and resigned from the Board, leaving Grant Hall, the incoming chairman, with a mortgage of $250 thousand to carry. In 1922 the Upper School moved across the river to occupy the buildings which had been constructed for the Prep, and the Prep was installed in the ample residence which had been built for its headmaster. The university remitted the final year's rent on the old buildings, and since the school was again to be known as Bishop's College School, the Association laid claim to the income from the Hamilton Jubilee Endowment designated for the office of headmaster. The two most distinguished lawyers among the alumni delivered contrary opinions as to whether the school was still being operated in connection with Bishop's University, as the terms of the gift had specified, but Corporation finally decided, in the interest of preserving comity in the English-speaking community, to recognize the Association's claim. On this comparatively amicable note, Corporation's 80 years of responsibility for the school came to an end.

Grant Hall

THE RESIGNATION OF PRINCIPAL PARROCK

Though Parrock had been a forceful and sound administrator, he was by this time no longer popular with the undergraduates. This was no doubt partly due to the increasingly evident bias against the appointment of clergymen from England as principals. However, he also seems to have held uncompromisingly classical views on the educational process. In an article, "The True Bases of Education," in *The Mitre*, he claimed that "education must give adequate training in two important particulars, accuracy of thought and expression, and voluntary attention. We believe that Greek, Latin, and Mathematics provide both these essentials."[30] He went on: "The second point in favour of the old training is the practice of voluntary, as distinct from spontaneous, attention. In order to train this faculty, the basis of education must be uninteresting in itself. And the *elements* of Mathematics and of Latin and Greek grammar are certainly uninteresting, they certainly do not arouse spontaneous attention." This philosophy was likely to appeal neither to wartime undergraduates nor to the evangelists of "socializing" education who were beginning to exert a powerful influence on the curricula of the public school system.

Toward the end of 1918, as it became evident that the war was at last going to end, Canadian soldiers began to be shipped home from Europe. With them they brought a pride forged in the victories the Canadian Corps had won in France and a sense that colonial status was incommensurate with Canada's contribution toward the winning of the war. Many soldiers also returned disillusioned with the quality of English political and military leadership. This reinforcement of already nascent nationalism agitated even the profoundly conservative and Anglophile constituency which supported Bishop's University. Under the influence of that nationalism, the Alumni Association and the Students' Association submitted to Corporation in the spring of 1919 a joint resolution which strongly criticized the government and administration of the university. The text of the resolution has not been preserved. However, it appears to have combined the complaints of the undergraduates, concerning what they perceived to be slack administration and undue importance attached to religious observance, with the proposals of several activist alumni who wished Bishop's to be freed from church control and to become more like other Canadian universities.

The resolution did not call for Principal Parrock's resignation. However, he seems to have felt that Corporation's willingness to receive it placed him in an impossible situation, and though he had no job to go to, he resigned on the spot. Fortunately, a former pupil was aware of a vacancy in classics at Colgate University, to which he was appointed in

September. In spite of the unhappy circumstances of his departure, he and his family retained their connection with Sherbrooke and the English-speaking summer colonies on the lower St Lawrence. He even made a financial contribution to the campaign of 1924, writing to the principal to express his pleasure that Bishop's had survived and was thriving. Parrock could in all fairness have claimed to have made a significant contribution to that survival, and wishing him well, Corporation had granted him a year's salary when he resigned. However, his rigidly classical philosophy of education was out of tune with the times, and during his tenure the university had drifted into a backwater. It may be that the realization that he was not equipped to deal with post-war undergraduates played a part in his decision to resign.

THE CONSTRUCTIVE REPORT

At the October 1919 meeting of Corporation the Alumni Association presented a "constructive report," which proposed sweeping changes. "First and foremost," the report began, "being a Canadian university, and a leader in Canadian thought and educational life, [Bishop's] must not forget the duty she owes to the general public of Canada in setting forth to the best of her ability those ideals and aims which should dominate the Canadian people. With all her English university system, she must be governed by a Canadian spirit and a Canadian policy designed to meet the present and future needs of our own country." The report went on to propose the re-establishment of the faculties of Law and Medicine, the institution of degree programs in Agriculture and Commerce, and a change in title to "The Eastern Townships University." The Faculty of Divinity was to become "the premier theological college of Canada", and programs leading to the Ph.D. and D.Litt. were to be developed.[31]

In urging that Bishop's adopt a frankly utilitarian approach to university education, the authors of the report were breaking with the intent of the founders and running counter to a tradition of liberal education which had been defended by every principal since Jasper Nicolls. In their detailed proposals, emphasis was (rightly) placed on the need to broaden the constituency from which the Corporation was drawn, to rally support from the Townships, and to appoint energetic and influential trustees. However, the rest of the report was unrealistic. At a time when most of the instruction in faculties of Law and Medicine was given by practitioners, the resources for such instruction were not to be found in the Townships. Moreover, thanks to the princely benefactions of W.C. MacDonald and other Montreal patrons, McGill was already firmly established in agriculture and pure and applied science. Expansion would require major injections of capital, not only for buildings but also to increase the endowment, the interest from which would have to meet the larger part of the salaries of new teaching staff. Yet no attempt seems to have been made by the authors either to estimate the cost of their proposals or to suggest where the money might be obtained—nor had they considered whether the probable growth in the English-language population of Quebec was likely to justify doubling the number of professional programs offered in English at the university level.

As it was constituted in 1919 Corporation had not the resources to deal with proposals of this scope. Reflecting religious controversy which had passed from the forefront of the community's concerns, the procedures for the appointment of trustees and members of the College Council were designed to ensure that the level of Anglican churchmanship should be an overriding concern in the government of the institution. In consequence, though the trustees of the time were men of recognized probity, who could be counted on to invest the endowment conservatively and to scrutinize the smallest expenditure with critical eye, they were, with one or two exceptions, not men with either the resources or influence to enable them to lead a successful financial campaign. Almost all the members of the College Council were clergymen without experience in university teaching or administration.

Nevertheless, Corporation set resolutely to work. The 15-member Committee on New Methods was appointed and subdivided into five smaller committees who were to consider the desirability of revision in the areas of statutes and constitution, curriculum, internal economy and management, finance, and scholarship and trust funds. Only two of these sub-committees have left any trace. The sub-committee on curriculum produced a report which was adopted for submission to Corporation, but only the report of the sub-committee on statutes and constitution was acted upon. This report proposed some broadening of the constituency from which members of Corporation were appointed and the institution of a board of governors (in effect an executive committee), drawn from the trustees and the College Council, which would meet frequently during the academic year and exercise operational control over the university.[32] Though Corporation formally adopted this report on 21 April 1920, the amendments to the statutes which were finally passed more than a year later provided only for a board of governors. No change in the method of appointing members of Corporation was instituted.

Chancellor Hamilton was fully aware of the financial implications of the "constructive report," and he urged the need to undertake a financial campaign with a target of at least $500,000. In June 1921, Corporation appointed an organizing committee with a mandate to investigate the potential for a campaign and, if the times were thought propitious, to recruit a campaign committee. However, lacking energetic leadership and, to be fair, an attractive list of projects on which the money would be spent, this committee made little progress. In June 1922 it reported that, in its judgment, the time was not ripe for a campaign. There was therefore very little to show for the three years of committee work which had been stimulated by the reforming zeal of the alumni. Evidently a more coherent and energetic campaign would be required to overcome inertia and generate fruitful change.

Meanwhile, male enrolment was recovering. An influx of returning veterans had added a much needed complement of maturity to the student body, and a grand rally of alumni veterans was organized at the college immediately before convocation in June 1919. The editor of *The Mitre* observed with amusement the "ponderous gambolling of middle-aged barristers and doctors of medicine," but he welcomed their encouragement of a progressive policy in university affairs. Canon Scott had returned to his family and his parish in Quebec in May, and he made a triumphal entrance and a memorable impromptu speech at the alumni dinner.[33] Those present could look back with pride to the Alumni Roll of Service. From a Faculty of Arts which had admitted 150 male students during the sixteen years from 1899 to 1914, 70 men had enlisted for active service, and the Faculty of Divinity had provided 18 chaplains. Three alumnae had served as nurses with the Canadian Army Medical Corps (CAMC). Twenty-four alumni had been killed in action or had died of wounds. *The Mitre* for Lent 1919 listed 16 decorations, including a Distinguished Conduct Medal awarded to L.A. Robertson (matriculated 1913) and eight Military Crosses, two of them to chaplains.

One of Canon Scott's sons, Francis Reginald (Frank), was a Rhodes Scholar and the valedictorian of the class of 1919. As senior man, he had been the channel through which undergraduate complaints about the administration of the university had reached the alumni. However, since he had been a familiar of the Parrock household since his freshman year and had frequently escorted one or other of the Parrock daughters, it seems unlikely that he was a prime mover in the campaign to unseat the principal.

Nevertheless, in his valedictory, he dwelt on the opportunity for change the return of peace offered. "If education is to be the guiding principle of the future," he said, "the Armistice must mark a turning point in the history of each university. Bishop's like all other universities, stands at the parting of the ways. Her future depends upon the policies

Francis Reginald Scott, B.A., 1919

adopted in the next few years. Inertia and indifference will spell inevitable failure. Success can only be obtained by energy and cooperation on the part of the governing bodies." He urged that a campaign to make the university better known be undertaken, that women students be provided with a residence on campus so that they could participate fully in collegiate life, and that Corporation continue its efforts to maintain a high standard of education in the college.

Scott's peroration gave evidence that Bishop's can claim to have sown at least some of the seeds which bore fruit in the career of one of its most distinguished graduates:

> I said before that the Armistice placed the College at the parting of the ways. But it does far more than that. It lays an additional burden of responsibility on the University. It puts an entirely new aim before all her educational work. Bishop's has always been a centre of scholastic education. Bishop's has always aroused in her students a patriotic love for their nation and empire. But now there is a higher duty for her to discharge: she must instil into those who study within her walls that love of humanity as a whole, that feeling of the brotherhood of man—that universal spirit which alone can make the League of Nations possible.[34]

PRINCIPAL BEDFORD JONES

When Principal Parrock tendered his resignation, it was too late in the year for a replacement to be found for the coming session. Dr Allnatt was the senior member of the faculty, the vice-principal, and dean of the Faculty of Divinity. Corporation appointed him acting principal. Allnatt, a much venerated figure, was nevertheless 78 years old and in failing health. During his interregnum of two terms, nothing was done to remedy the slack administration of which the undergraduates had complained, and student morale and discipline continued to deteriorate.

In April 1920 the new principal, Canon H.H. Bedford Jones, took office. He was a graduate of Trinity College School and of Trinity College in the University of Toronto, of which he had been a fellow, lecturer in Divinity and member of Corporation. He was a great-grandson of Richard Cartwright, perhaps the foremost member of the Legislative Council of Upper Canada from 1792 to 1815. In his undergraduate days, he had been an outstanding athlete. He seemed well equipped to stop the drift.

During his first year in office Bedford Jones made a favourable impression. He enjoyed the company of undergraduates, and was keenly interested in their activities and sympathetic to their problems. He established friendly relations with the off-campus community—an innovation at Bishop's—and during his tenure the government of Quebec was persuaded to include Bishop's among the universities to which it was beginning to give financial support.

However, by the beginning of the 1921–22 session it was becoming clear that the new principal was not much interested in administration and that the new principal lacked the firmness of purpose needed to give direction to the university. Undergraduate discipline had not improved, and the faculty began to lose confidence in him. In February 1922 the finance committee considered a report, probably from the bursar, which cited unruly behaviour of undergraduates in the Arts building as the cause of extra expense. Though the cases cited were not earth-shaking, it seems likely that members of the Board of Governors (which had just begun to function) were aware of other instances of slack administration. At any rate, the board requested a formal report from the faculty on the state of undergraduate discipline. This report and the principal's reply to it were considered at a well-attended meeting of the board on 22 March. Neither the report nor the reply has been preserved, but after adjourning the meeting for further consideration, the president asked for and received Bedford Jones' resignation, which he then presented to the board.

This action was reported to a special meeting of Corporation held on April 16. A motion to open a full inquiry into the matter was defeated. Another was passed, regretting the necessity of accepting the resignation and granting Bedford Jones a further six months' salary. Rocksborough Smith, the new dean of Divinity, was appointed acting principal for the remainder of the academic year.

It was widely believed that the faculty had initiated the complaint, and both the undergraduates and the off-campus community rallied to the support of the principal. A deputation of students went to Montreal to present the undergraduates' case to the president of Corporation and to ask for an explanation of the decision. At the April meeting of Corporation petitions were presented from the Lennoxville Board of Trade, the Montreal branch of the Alumni Association, a group of Lennoxville citizens, and the undergraduates. One enraged partisan from Lennoxville threw a rock through the window of a member of faculty who was believed to have led the attack on the principal.

The bishops wrote a letter to the undergraduates which laid out the sequence of events and made clear that the faculty had not taken the initiative. However, the bishops steadfastly refused to discuss the details of the case against Bedford Jones. The students remained convinced that the principal had been unjustly condemned, and several members of Corporation from Montreal let it be known that they were seriously considering resigning over the affair.

In the absence of the primary documents, it is not possible to judge the merits of the case. However, at subsequent meetings of the faculty, both under Rocksborough Smith and under the new principal, much time was devoted to drawing up new regulations governing undergraduate behaviour and to establishing responsibility for enforcing them. It seems likely that the Corporation had again been caught napping by a situation which had been developing for many months and which made even more clear the need for a thorough revision of the machinery for governing the university.

There was general agreement among members of Corporation that the next principal should be a Canadian, and a strong minority lobbied for the appointment of a layman. However, the selection committee finally presented two clerical candidates to Corporation, the Reverend Canon G.W. Abbott-Smith and Honourary Lieutenant-Colonel the Reverend A.H. McGreer.

Abbott-Smith was a member of the faculty of the MDTC and would later be Professor of Greek at McGill. He was a graduate of Bishop's who had been an examiner in classics since 1896, and more recently an active member of the College Council. He had been nominated for the office of principal in 1907 and again in 1919. There seems moreover to have been some dissatisfaction in the Diocese of Montreal concerning the action of Corporation in accepting the resignation of Principal Bedford Jones. At any rate, Corporation now offered Abbott-Smith the post; but he was 58 years of age and comfortably established in Montreal. He was fully aware of the lack of cohesion and leadership in the government of the university. The institution's buildings were badly run down, and no money was available for renovation. The most recent (pre-war) financial campaign had met with very limited success, and the courageous decision of the trustees in 1919 to raise the minimum salary for professors from $1,500 to $2 thousand (plus room and board or a $300 allowance) had imposed a heavy stress on the endowment. Finally, Rocksborough Smith was High Church, with which Abbott-Smith would have had very little sympathy. He declined the appointment. McGreer was appointed, and took office during the summer of 1922.

CHAPTER SIX

THE REIGN OF PRINCIPAL McGREER

Arthur Huffman McGreer was born in Napanee, Ontario, on the 11th of August 1883. After graduating from the local high school, he matriculated at the University of Toronto. Though of Ulster stock the family preferred the churchmanship of Trinity College to that of Wycliffe, and it was from Trinity that he emerged in 1909 with a B.A., several academic prizes, and in priest's orders. His first parish was the military establishment at Barriefield, near Kingston. He then went in 1911 to Montreal as assistant at Christ Church Cathedral. During the next three years he no doubt became acquainted with several of the members of Corporation who later appointed him principal of Bishop's University.

When war broke out in Europe in 1914, he volunteered and served as a chaplain with the First Canadian Division in France. During the heavy fighting on the Somme in 1916 he was attached to the Third Canadian Field Ambulance. He was mentioned in dispatches, and on the 14th of November awarded the Military Cross for "tending the wounded and organizing stretcher parties under very heavy fire with great courage and determination."[1] He went on to become assistant director of the chaplain service of the Canadian Corps, to be made an Officer of the Order of the British Empire, and to develop his talent for mixing easily with influential members of the Establishment—in particular with General Sir Julian Byng, Commander of the Canadian Corps and subsequently Governor-General of Canada.

Arthur Huffman McGreer, 1935

At the war's end, McGreer married a young Englishwoman, Kathleen Lee, in Oxford, and matriculated with advanced standing at Queen's College, of which Jasper Nicolls had been a fellow in 1845. After completing work for a B.A. in Honours Theology, he undertook postgraduate studies in Comparative Religion and Christian Doctrine. In the spring of 1922 he was a candidate for the vacancy created by Bedford Jones' resignation.[2]

The new principal was a man of many parts. His wartime experiences had reinforced what was probably a naturally autocratic bent, and his public presence was that of a commanding officer and a gentleman. From the beginning he seems to have felt that in order to gain the confidence of the community in the future of the university, he must himself radiate confidence. He is remembered by undergraduates of the 1920s as a formidable figure, "the embodiment of his Office."[3] If some members of faculty were unwilling to concede omniscience to him, they kept their own counsel, and were content to find a firm hand on the reins after wartime decay and post-war turbulence.

The principal was keenly interested in the personal development of the undergraduates. Behind the public façade, they found a warm-hearted and generous paterfamilias, skilled in counselling the men "man-to-man" and unsparing in his efforts to find money to support their studies, and frequently (in those days before universal medical insurance, to pay their medical bills. His wife was an accomplished hostess, and the hospitality of the Lodge was much appreciated by the Visitors and other senior members of Corporation who stayed there when visiting Lennoxville.

Yet another facet of McGreer's personality was the ease with which he gained the confidence of the leaders of the English-speaking community in the province and stimulated their interest in the university—a skill singularly lacking in his more academically gifted predecessors. Though well-educated, he was not a scholar, and he had little interest in or patience with academic debate, but he had a lively and wide-ranging interest in the way the world worked, which served him (and the university) well in his contacts with industrialists and businessmen. He was also an unabashed imperialist, determined to educate Canadian youth to take up their responsibilities to the British Empire's family of peoples. In a letter describing a lecture given at the university, he wrote: "I know that the students who heard Mr Pilcher will never think of Imperialism except in terms of service to mankind."[4] In this respect, the first Canadian-born principal proved to be "more English than the English," who became less and less enamoured of their imperial obligations during his tenure.

The campus, 1923

McGreer quickly made it clear that he intended to rule. The previous two principals had been unseated by turbulence generated from within the academic community, and Corporation had failed to deal effectively with the causes for complaint. During this period, the undergraduates had become accustomed to the idea that their voice should be heard in the government of the university. McGreer made plain his opinion of this state of affairs in his first report to Corporation in October 1922. He said:

> I was pleased to find that the type of Canadian represented in the student body was on the whole a good one. I soon discovered however that they inherited as a legacy from the past an attitude towards College authority which I had never experienced before. I do not mean that it was one of unmitigated hostility. It was rather one in which the idea prevailed that the students possessed prerogatives which can be, and are, vested only in the governing bodies and administrative officers of the College. That idea was very firmly established; and while we must not expect that it will disappear completely within a few weeks or a few months, I think I may say that it is gradually but unmistakeably giving way to the idea that students possess authority and prerogatives only to the extent that these are conferred upon them by superior authority.[5]

Under McGreer these prerogatives were limited to responsibility for extra-curricular activities—within the parameters he established for life in residence and with considerable help and guidance from members of faculty. Nevertheless, he enjoyed the company of high-spirited youth. As he wrote to the father of an undergraduate who had been 'sent down' for a week, "Exuberance of youthful spirits and an Irishman's propensity for challenging authority are not things to be deplored—on the other hand, they have to be kept under control!"[6]

McGreer had also a very clear vision of the mission proper to the university. For him the bounds of truth had been very thoroughly explored by classical and Christian authors, and the task of the university was to inculcate the corpus of truth in the undergraduates and thus to generate informed, temperate, and responsible graduates. In a letter to Premier Taschereau, seeking financial support, he wrote:

> (i) The University aims at giving an education in Arts and Pure Science which will provide a mental training, a range of knowledge and a development of character which will be a firm foundation for whatever career the student may adopt.

(ii) It is a residential university, with regulations designed to foster a sense of individual responsibility and a sense of social duty in its students. Being in a district of great natural beauty, its surroundings are wholesome and free from many of the temptations which assail the adolescent in the city.
(iii) It is definitely committed to the ideal that the study and practice of religion should form part of every student's education.[7]

In his more optimistic moments he dreamed of a university of several residential colleges on the banks of the St Francis, as closely modelled after Oxford as finances would permit.

THE RENEWAL OF CORPORATION

The new principal rapidly perceived that his most urgent task was to strengthen the Corporation. As he wrote to G.H. Montgomery, "The history of this place, and the history of the other Church universities in this country, justify a merciless indictment of the methods by which they have been governed."[8] McGreer was fully convinced of the value of sound and liberal education and of its potential attractiveness to possible undergraduates and their parents, but growth in enrolment would necessitate a building fund and a major increase in the endowment. In order to achieve this, the constituency from which Corporation was appointed would have to be greatly enlarged. In particular, more men respected in business and financial circles would have to be recruited.

It was evident from the ease with which the proposals of the constructive report had been smothered that McGreer would have to tread carefully. Not until December 1925 did he feel strong enough to give notice of a motion "advocating a change in the numerical strength of Corporation, and in the method of securing it."[9] The ground had been carefully prepared, and a majority voted in favour of revision. After considerable debate it was decided that the simplest revision which respected the royal charter, on which the university's degree-granting powers depended, would be to repeal all acts of the legislature subsequent to the date of the charter. This would eliminate appointments by the synods and leave a corporation consisting of the two bishops with such persons as they might select as trustees and members of the College Council. All other details could then be regulated by such statutes as the new corporation might see fit to establish.

The synods were persuaded to give their blessing to this revision, and it was effected by a private bill presented to and passed by the Legislative Assembly. Under the provisions of this act, all members of Corporation in office prior to the date of sanction of the act ceased to be members as of 1 July 1927. The number of trustees was raised from 16 to 20. Nine of the outgoing trustees were reappointed. Of the 11 new trustees, eight were major figures in business and industry in the province. All but one of these new men were Anglicans—a clear indication that the synods could have preserved the essential character of the institution without adopting such narrow criteria in making their appointments. The principal was also appointed a trustee—an innovation—and over the next 20 years he succeeded in obtaining the total and fruitful collaboration of the new board in promoting the interests of the university. The College Council remained firmly under clerical control, but the new Executive Committee (replacing the Board of Governors) was chaired by a trustee, and nine of its 14 members were laymen. It rapidly became a body upon which McGreer could rely for advice and practical support.

THE FINANCIAL CAMPAIGN OF 1924

However, enrolment was rapidly increasing under the principal's energetic promotion, and the needs of the students could not wait for this rather ponderous procedure to reach fruition. McGreer had quickly discovered that Bishop's was little known outside the Townships, and that its prospects were considered poor. When he was applying to the provincial government for a grant, the provincial treasurer and MLA for Sherbrooke, Jacob Nicol, told him that opponents of the proposal had argued with considerable vehemence that Bishop's had lost its Medical Faculty, its Dental Faculty, and its Faculty of Law.[10] It was only a question of time before its Arts Faculty would disappear too. Promotion of the university in English-speaking Quebec had obviously to be given top priority.

At his first meeting with Corporation McGreer asked for an annual entertainment allowance of $1,000 (25 percent of his salary). The request was referred to the finance committee, but Chancellor Hamilton countered with an offer of $500 from his own pocket if the other $500 could be found within 5 weeks.[11] The principal got his allowance. Thus armed, he laid siege to Quebec's English-speaking Establishment, inviting its members to lunch to discuss the problems of education in the province. Many of these men had adolescent children or relatives who were being affected by the general relaxation of social norms during the post-war period. McGreer made an excellent impression, with his military bearing, his easy cordiality, and his message of the value of residential college life in training the youth of the country to be responsible citizens. This message he carried into every corner of Quebec society. He organized a conference for the principals of high schools, and persuaded the Protestant secretary of the Council of Public Instruction to come and speak to them at dinner. He invited the Rotary Club of Sherbrooke to a reception on campus—this prompted a worried letter from the chairman of the Corporation's publicity committee, inquiring whether he had obtained prior permission from the trustees! Another weapon in McGreer's armoury was the honourary degree. Shortly after he took office, he had made his presence known to Lord Byng of Vimy, and had been invited to spend a weekend at Rideau Hall. In December 1923, the governor-general visited Bishop's and received a D.C.L. at the hands of Chancellor Hamilton—an event which of course received appropriate notice in the press!

By the fall of 1923 McGreer had identified the three men whom he wanted to lead his first financial campaign. They were Grant Hall, vice-president of the CPR, and two leading members of the Montreal bar, F.E. Meredith and G.H. Montgomery. Hall we have already met. Meredith, son of Chief Justice Sir William Meredith, was a director of the Bank of Montreal and of the CPR. G.H. Montgomery also held a number of directorships in the electric power and the pulp and paper industries. He was later to become the historian of the Missisquoi Bay settlement of United Empire Loyalists from which Gilbert Hyatt had come to settle Ascot Township, in which Bishop's would subsequently be founded. All three men were graduates of Bishop's University. Not one of them had been invited by the bishops or the synods to become trustees. Enlisted by McGreer's eloquence, they agreed to head the campaign, and the principal persuaded Corporation to give them the support of an experienced campaign secretary. The goal was set at $500 thousand—a sum which would have enabled the accumulated deficit of $46,000 to be eliminated, the endowment to be increased to meet the need for more and better-paid faculty, and a beginning on the most urgent needs for physical facilities.

In the event, $214 thousand was raised, to which could be added a grant of $20 thousand per annum for five years, which was wrung out of the provincial government. Though no money would be available for building, the sum raised was nevertheless equal to the total increase in the endowment over the previous 25 years. The subscription list made it clear that the campaign had aroused the interest of a wide constituency, including a number of industrial and commercial enterprises. Generous subscriptions from alumni and the community which had sustained Bishop's for generations confirmed that McGreer had restored that community's faith in the future of the university. Given the state of the economy and the relatively short time McGreer had had in which to make the university better known, the campaign had been a notable success. The principal redoubled his efforts to broaden the base of Corporation and set about achieving consensus on the priorities to govern the planned expansion in the physical facilities.

ACADEMIC DEVELOPMENT

In 1922 there were seven male candidates enrolled for the M.A., six for the Licentiate in Sacred Theology, and 33 male and 24 female candidates for the B.A. There were in addition some dozen unmatriculated students who had to be coached to entrance level in several subjects, particularly Latin, which was not taught to the required standard in several of the small high schools in the region. Undergraduates at that time were admitted from grade 11, usually at the age of 17. The Arts program involved seven courses in the first and six courses in each of the second and third years. Because of the long academic year (September to June), the personal contact between members of faculty and undergraduates, and the heavy course load, Bishop's continued until the end of McGreer's tenure to claim that its three-year B.A. was the equivalent of the four-year program for the B.A. adopted by nearly all other Canadian universities. There is ample evidence that this was true for the stronger students, and the three-year program gained a year for the considerable percentage of the graduates who proceeded to post-graduate professional training. The claim was further buttressed by the decision of the Oxford Hebdomadal Council in 1931 to recognize the Bishop's B.A. for purposes of admission to senior standing in Oxford University. However, it involved the administration in much correspondence with the admission committees of graduate programs in Canadian and American universities.

Average students followed the ordinary program, in which Divinity, Latin, and English were compulsory for the first two years. Throughout the 25 years of his reign, McGreer insisted on two years of university level Latin for the B.A. During the depression of the thirties, fewer and fewer high schools offered Latin to matriculation level, and more and more remedial work had to be provided for the freshman class in spite of the principal's vigorous promotion of the classics at the meetings of the Protestant Committee of the Council of Public Instruction. His enthusiasm occasionally led to embarrassment. In 1929 the governor-general, Lord Willingdon, was to receive the D.C.L. at convocation. On these occasions, the students were marshalled with quasi-military precision, and McGreer thought it would make a good impression if they lined the driveway leading up to the arches into the Quad and greeted His Excellency with shouts of "Vivat Legatus!" The senior man was co-opted to organize the line-up and cheers, to which Lord Willingdon, looking a little puzzled, responded nevertheless with the customary vice-regal signs of appreciation. However, before the official party moved on to convocation, the principal introduced the senior man to Willingdon, who expressed his pleasure at the warmth of the welcome but confessed that he had had to ask the principal what "Vivat Legatus!" meant![12]

Students achieving at least a second class standing at the end of their first year were allowed, if they wished, to follow a more specialized honours course in classics, mathematics, history, modern languages, philosophy, or theology. These students were usually taught in tutorials, which encouraged the undergraduate to expand the scope and quality of his or her work.

To cope with this range of subjects and a wide variation in the preparation and competence of the undergraduates, there was one professor in each of the honours disciplines. The principal and the Professor of Pastoral Theology helped with the teaching of the compulsory courses in Divinity and Latin. For the period, the faculty were well-qualified for their responsibilities, and several had a breadth of knowledge and interest less common among the faculty after the expansion of the sixties. However, the lecturing and tutorial load was very heavy, and it was difficult for them to find time during term for reading and other scholarly pursuits. Moreover, the decay in discipline during and immediately after the war had adversely affected academic standards. While keen students found a ready and effective response in their professors, little pressure was exerted on the less academically inclined, of whom a number were ill-prepared for university-level study.

The growth of enrolment to a total of 145 in September 1926 rapidly brought staffing to the forefront of McGreer's concerns. For the principal, fostering the development of character in the undergraduate was just as important as maintaining a high standard of scholarship. In his address to convocation in 1928 he quoted with approval a dictum of Daniel Coit Gilman, former president of John Hopkins University, who said: "Physical strength is most desirable, intellectual power is invaluable, but moral greatness reigns supreme over both!"[13] McGreer's remark to a trustee concerning Evelyn Waugh's conversion to Roman Catholicism is also worth quoting: "The group of authors who have recently seceded undoubtedly have unusual intellectual gifts; but such qualities are frequently found in people who are not very well balanced."[14]

Since newly appointed junior members of faculty were automatically appointed sub-deans of residence, candidates for teaching posts were required to meet moral as well as academic criteria. Specifically, the principal maintained that Bishop's was obliged by its constitution to support the Christian religion. He was determined that Bishop's graduates would not be among the majority of university men and women in Canada who, he believed, were graduating with "little or no appreciation of those moral sanctions which are at once the cement and the only sure foundation for the stability and well-being of Canadian society."[15]

Nevertheless, McGreer did manage to recruit well-qualified men for the faculty. The most urgent need was in science. When he arrived, the 38 students opting for science in the ordinary (pass) degree program were taught by a junior lecturer. By 1924–25 this number had increased greatly, due largely to the requirements for admission into Medicine and the High School Teaching Diploma course. To cope with this development, Corporation was persuaded in 1923 to establish a new Chair in Science. The first incumbent, A.G. Hatcher, left after two years; but his replacement, Albert Kuehner, took root, lecturing for 40 years and retiring as vice-principal in 1965.

This was a seminal appointment. Kuehner perceived no fundamental conflict between his Christian faith and his scientific vocation. He was moreover an exceptionally able teacher, who brought with him from Queen's exacting standards for undergraduate experimental work in chemistry. He was joined a year later by Maurice Home from McGill in physics, and together they established the Bishop's tradition of direct faculty supervision of undergraduate experimental work. In 1929 an honours program in chemistry was approved, and Kuehner was promoted to Professor, at the age of 26. Within a very few years, his honours graduates were in demand in the industrial laboratories of the province, and Bishop's graduates going on to Medicine found themselves well prepared for their pre-clinical laboratory work. Three of his early students went on to doctorates and distinguished careers in chemical research.

Another concern was the teaching of English. In keeping with Oxbridge practice, English composition was supposed to have been mastered by matriculants, and English literature was considered to be a part of the general background, rather than a subject for serious study by honours candidates. E.E. Boothroyd, known to the undergraduates affectionately as "Boots," was responsible for both history and English literature, and many alumni of the period testify to the breadth of his scholarship and the stimulation of his teaching.

However (*plus ça change!*) by no means all of the first-year men and women had in fact mastered the art of composition in English. By the late 1920s, with the growth of enrolment, the burden of correcting essays had become intolerable. In 1928 McGreer persuaded Corporation to establish a Chair in English, and recruited W.O. Raymond to occupy it. Raymond, who had been Associate Professor of English at the University of Michigan, was a Canadian, an Anglican clergyman, and a recognized authority on the poetry of Robert Browning. He thought the ambience at Bishop's would be more to his liking, which proved to be true. His scholarship and his gentle—in some respects saintly—character contributed much to a Bishop's education over the next 22 years.

To lecture in classics, McGreer appointed Eivion Owen, sometime scholar of New College, Oxford, "one of the best scholars who ever taught at Bishop's."[16] Owen left in 1928 to study for his doctorate in English at Harvard, and then obtained an appointment at the University of British Columbia. Unfortunately that university's grant was severely cut in the early thirties, and Owen found himself out of a job. In 1934 McGreer was able to offer him a post as a lecturer in English at Bishop's, but Raymond occupied the Chair, and ten years later Owen was still only an assistant professor. He left the University in 1945 to join the staff of the Director of Protestant Education in Quebec.

Appointments to the Faculty of Divinity were complicated by the need to satisfy the Visitors that the churchmanship of candidates lay within the episcopally established norms. In 1925 Rocksborough Smith, the dean of Divinity, was elected Bishop of Algoma. McGreer, who during his tenure spent almost every peacetime summer in England, conducted a vigorous and fruitful search there for a successor. However, despite the principal's eloquent advocacy, certain aspects of his candidate's private devotional practice rendered him suspect to the Bishop of Montreal. The candidate had other offers, and he opted for a more congenial institution. The refusal of the first choice again proved providential. The position finally went to Philip Carrington, under whose energetic and scholarly leadership the faculty became much more widely and favourably known.

Yet another area which benefited from McGreer's energy during the early years of his tenure was the training of teachers. (As Table 3 in Appendix Four demonstrates, teaching had replaced the Christian ministry as the professional goal of a majority of the undergraduates in Arts.) When he arrived the Protestant Committee had just raised the standard of training for high school teachers. Henceforward, an expanded course of lectures on the theory of education, a course of physical education, and 50 half-days of supervised practice teaching were to be required of all candidates. Bishop's had responded by appointing Dr W.O. Rothney, the school inspector for the region, to supervise this professional training, which candidates were to undertake in addition to their work in Arts.

By 1925 it was evident to the faculty that this laid too great a burden on the students. Satisfactory results could be obtained neither in Arts nor in Education. At Rothney's urging McGreer agreed that a graduate year in Education must be established, and a full-time professor appointed to supervise it. The principal made a strong case to the Director of Protestant Education for an increase in the annual grant sufficient to pay the professor's salary. As he pointed out:

(i) There were between sixty and seventy graduates of Bishop's University teaching in forty of the high schools and intermediate schools in the province.
(ii) There were 53 undergraduates in the three years of Arts who had declared their intention to take the High School Diploma course, and they came from 26 cities, towns and villages of the province, outside the city of Montreal.

He also undertook to establish a summer school for teachers, which would include courses for experienced teachers who aspired to positions as principals or inspectors.[17]

McGreer obtained an increased grant, and he persuaded Rothney to leave his secure and pensionable position with the government in 1928 to become the first Professor of Education. The graduate year was a fruitful innovation in the training of teachers for the high schools of the province. It laid the foundation for the remarkable influence Bishop's graduates have exercised in the Protestant school system, particularly in mainland Quebec. Unknown to McGreer, it also accentuated the decline in the number of students offering Latin at matriculation. Rothney believed that the primary task of the high schools was to adapt students to the society in which they would have to earn their living, and he exerted continual pressure to replace Latin in the curriculum both more "useful" subjects.

THE PROTESTANT COMMITTEE AND PUBLIC EDUCATION

McGreer was acutely aware of the vital importance of both defending the matriculation standard in the province and increasing the proportion of the population of high school age which achieved it. Bishop's continued to invite the principals of high schools to an annual conference during the Christmas break, when accommodation in residence was available. By 1927 this conference was submitting resolutions to the Council of Public Instruction which, embodying the experience of teachers of long standing, constituted a valuable input to the development of educational policy. In 1930 the principal was appointed to the Protestant Committee of the council, the body which controlled publicly financed education of

English-speaking children whose parents were not Roman Catholic. Though he kept a close eye on curriculum, resisting the thrust of the teachers to liberate the high school leaving certificate from the requirements the universities had established for matriculation, his activity on the committee was chiefly concerned with the consolidation of school districts.

At that time, a large number of the schools of mainland Quebec, particularly those within the geographical boundaries of the Anglican Diocese of Quebec, served small rural school districts whose population justified schools of only one or two rooms, in which one teacher taught a number of grades. Even when the local school board took its responsibilities seriously, this led to high schools in which teachers were not qualified to cope with the full matriculation curriculum. At worst, the structure produced schools such as one Dr Rothney encountered in his inspectorate. The equipment of the school was so dilapidated that when his protests proved unavailing, he informed the chairman of the board that if nothing had been done by the time of his next inspection, he would destroy the schoolroom furniture. On his next visit, he took along an axe. Finding the situation unchanged, he reduced the furniture to kindling—then called on the secretary-treasurer of the board to inform him that he had done so.[18]

Though the solution to the problem was obvious, consolidation was politically sensitive. The technique of the consolidation sub-committee, which McGreer chaired, was to induce one or more boards in a region to invite the members of the committee to address an open meeting on the advantages of consolidation. Teachers and others interested in improving the schools would try to generate as big an audience of parents as possible at the meeting. If the parents were convinced, they would exert the necessary pressure on the boards. However, it was a slow and painful process, particularly when the economic situation deteriorated and the fear of increased school taxes loomed large in the eyes of the ratepayers. Nevertheless, his speaking at a number of these meetings made McGreer (and Bishop's) better known in the rural areas.

COLLEGIATE LIFE

McGreer believed that residence in a community of learning was essential to a liberal education. New residences were given high priority in all his plans for expansion. He also believed that there was an upper limit to the size of community in which a true collegial spirit could develop. If the capital had been available, he would have added a second residential college to the university when the enrolment exceeded 150. It is a measure of the constraints under which he laboured that in spite of the importance he attached to life in residence, he was able to increase the accommodation Bishop's offered only once during his 25-year tenure. In 1922 BCS had at last vacated the school building. During the summer of 1923 it was converted to college use. The dormitories were partitioned off into rooms, raising the total number available to 79. Several lecture rooms large enough for the compulsory courses were equipped, and women undergraduates were assigned a small common room and cloak room.

Life in residence was very strongly stamped with the University's English and Anglican heritage. For the undergraduates, many of whom came from small towns in mainland Quebec and had little idea of what a university was all about, Bishop's represented an immersion in a mode of living which left an indelible impression on them long after they had forgotten the details of academic instruction.

All undergraduates wore gowns to chapel (at least seven times per week), at meals, and at classes and tutorials. In the dining hall students sat at long tables arranged by class year. At the end of the dining room, on a low platform, was the faculty table, at which the staff living in residence and the occasional visitor were seated. Grace was said in Latin partway through the meal, and permission to leave before this ceremony had to be obtained by rising and standing until the request was acknowledged by one of the members of the faculty.

Alumni recollections of the university at this period are strongly imprinted with the character of James Dewhurst, who served Bishop's as waiter and head steward for 47 years. Dewhurst, remembered affectionately by one alumnus as "an engaging scoundrel," was a college servant cast in a peculiarly English mould, never at a loss for a riposte and always in full charge even when he had had one pint too many. Another alumnus recalls that "he took full advantage of, but never abused, the perquisites of his position. A judicious scattering of his favours, in the form of a second dessert or some special sample of the bill of fare assured his supply of cigarettes, to which he was passionately addicted. Furthermore, a long-practised technique of turning a blind eye to quantities of food being carried out of the dining room for midnight snacks virtually guaranteed a reasonable ration of beer at the Georgian."[19] Since the purloined food fuelled the bull sessions which contributed a great deal to the education of the young men in residence, Dewhurst might have claimed to be an essential cog in the educational machinery. An undergraduate, sick in bed, could usually depend on Jim to appear at the door of his room with dinner on a tray. Withal, he succeeded in convincing the student body that he had their interests at heart; and the decision in 1968 to christen the new dining facility Dewhurst Hall in his honour was a popular one—though he would never have consented to preside over a cafeteria![20]

During the latter years of the 1914–18 war the only male undergraduates on campus had been either medically unfit for military service or under the age of 18, and women had outnumbered men in the Arts lectures. By the time Principal McGreer arrived in 1922, however, the men again outnumbered the women, and the surge in enrolment which resulted from his effective promotion of the university was almost entirely male. During his tenure as principal, Bishop's remained, in the eyes of the Corporation and administration, essentially a university for male undergraduates. Several influential members of Corporation would have preferred to exclude women altogether, believing that university education for women served no useful purpose and tended to distract the male undergraduates from the business at hand. McGreer seems to have had no objection in principle to higher education for women, and he was instrumental in setting up the first post-graduate course for the training of high school teachers in Quebec, a great many of whom were women. However, he set great store by the intellectual and social maturing process of residential collegiate life, to which women could make, in his opinion, only a marginal contribution. As public pressure developed to make university education available to women, a [small] residence for women reached the top of his list of building priorities. If women were to become full members of the university they must have the facilities necessary to developing a collegiate life of their own.

In practice, the women undergraduates of the 1920s and 1930s were, in the words of Marion Burt Bourne (B.A., 1928), "tolerated with a kind of whimsical indulgence."[21] Most of the faculty favoured their presence. However, the daily routine excluded them from the corporate life of the community. Most boarded in private homes in the village. Their small common room in New Arts was only open to them on weekday mornings, so they rented a small apartment on the village square as a "home away from home" where they could spend their spare time. They formed their own student association and elected a senior lady to represent them. However, when Professor Boothroyd, as the representative of the faculty, invited a senior lady to a meeting of the Students' Executive Council (SEC), she was not made welcome. Extra-curricular activities, particularly the Dramatic Society and *The Mitre*, provided opportunities for men and women to work together which did a good deal to soften the effects of the official regime for those who participated.

Little opportunity was provided for informal contact between the sexes on campus. Informal conversation between lectures was discour-

The Bishop's Candlesticks, 1926

aged, and the dining room was not open to women. There was, however, a considerable organized social life. Several faculty wives generously acted as chaperons for Saturday afternoon tea dances and invited undergraduates of both sexes to their homes. Parents of women students whose homes were in Lennoxville or Sherbrooke often opened their homes to undergraduates. Several formal dances were held each year, at which the principal, the faculty, and their wives received the guests. Saints' days were usually holidays, and these were celebrated by climbing excursions in the warm weather and by skating, snowshoeing, and tobogganing parties in the winter.

Difficult though it must be for a later generation to believe, most of the women were not unhappy with their lot. To quote Mrs Bourne again, "We were not ambitious to become doctors, lawyers, engineers or members of Parliament—we took everything in our stride, and did not realize what mighty changes would evolve in the years to follow."[22] Another alumna of the 30s recalled her years at Bishop's as among the happiest of her life.[23]

Before the advent of experimental science, all instruction took place before lunch. Both Corporation and principal strongly encouraged participation by male undergraduates in team sports, in particular football and hockey, during the afternoons. Most students agreed. In an appeal to the alumni for financial support, the editor of *The Mitre* opined: "Without athletics, a university is dead. Without money, athletics rapidly approaches its end."[24] Several members of Corporation also supported the teams out of their own pockets.

Intercollegiate competition had been interrupted by the war, and the post-war enrolment at Bishop's was for several years so low that it was difficult to field a football team. By 1921, however, home and away games were played with McGill Juniors and Loyola. Though Bishop's lost these games, the scores were close enough to encourage greater participation by the rapidly increasing student body. In the absence of a coaching staff the teams depended entirely on the skills the students brought with them. One of McGreer's first initiatives was to write to the great "Shag" Shaughnessy at McGill in search of a football coach. Shaughnessy recommended S.J. McDonald, a Loyola Arts graduate, who had played on McGill's senior intercollegiate team and had been Shanghnessy's assistant in coaching the McGill team. McDonald completely won the loyalty of the Bishop's men. He was plagued, as all his successors have been, by a shortage of reserves.[25] On the other hand, the distance of Lennoxville from the urban flesh-pots made it comparatively easy to produce a well-conditioned team, most of whose members could and did play the full 60 minutes. In 1924, Bishop's defeated both the McGill Juniors and

Loyola—to universal rejoicing, since beating Loyola was then and for the next forty years the criterion of a successful football season.

In the absence of artificial ice, hockey tended to be a variable feast. When weather permitted, games were played in the Eastern Townships Hockey League against teams from Lennoxville, Sherbrooke, Coaticook, and other towns in the region. Not to be outdone, the women undergraduates, practising in an unheated gymnasium, and deprived of any possibility of a bath or shower on campus, organized a basketball team which competed against local teams. Since most of them, as candidates for the High School Teaching Diploma, were subjected to regular physical training by a sergeant-major from the local militia, they were fit, and were frequently successful. An annual fixture was the ice hockey game against the "divines," under rules which heavily penalised any bodily contact as "immoral conduct"! Again, the women often won.

The spring term (which lasted until late June) was less highly organized. Much tennis was played, and in the days before upstream pig factories, the rivers were much used for excursions by canoe. Other extra-curricular activities at various times during the year included debating, producing plays (in which members of the faculty and their wives often took part), editing *The Mitre*, and of course numerous bull and bridge sessions in the undergraduates' rooms.

Yet another enterprise for occupying the spare time of the male students was the Canadian Officers' Training Corps (COTC). In November 1922 the principal invited a wartime friend, General MacBrien, to speak to the undergraduates about the government's plans for the armed services in peacetime. These plans laid heavy emphasis on part-time training, and foresaw the development of OTCs in Canada's universities. McGreer convened a meeting of the student body at which he explained the conditions under which a contingent would be authorized by the military authorities, and called for volunteers. A large percentage of the men signed up. Not the least incentive was the need of the university's teams for financial support, to which purpose the officer-candidates' honoraria were devoted. Under the approving eye of the principal, the corps continued to flourish on a "voluntary" basis through the pacifist reaction of the 1930s up to the outbreak of the 1939–45 war, when membership became compulsory for any undergraduates eligible for call-up under the National Resources Mobilization Act.

A NEW CHANCELLOR

John Hamilton had been chancellor of the university since 1900. He had been persuaded to withdraw his resignation several times since the end

Frederick Edmund Meredith

of the 1914–18 war, but in 1925 he made it clear that he intended to resign. He had been active in the affairs of the Corporation over a period of 40 years. He was a generous contributor to the financial campaigns of 1913 and 1924, and capital sums from his estate were still accruing to Bishop's in 1979. The liberal traditions of the university owe much to the support of such distinguished families as the Hamiltons, whose significant contributions to the development of Quebec's English-speaking community extended over more than a century.

To replace Chancellor Hamilton, McGreer recruited F.E. Meredith, one of the leaders of the successful financial campaign of 1924. The new chancellor was also a scion of one of Quebec's leading families. His success as an advocate for several of the province's largest corporations and the strength of character strikingly evident in the Torrance Newton portrait had given him very considerable influence. This he used effectively for the benefit of the university. Writing his obituary in 1942, McGreer recalled that all the substantial financial gifts from 1924 onward had in some cases been entirely, and in most cases largely, due to him. From 1924 onward until the end of the Union Nationale regime in 1960, Bishop's could also count on recognition by the government of the province as a university representative of a politically significant element of Quebec's population.

Education in Quebec was still above, or at any rate outside, secular politics, but the financial difficulties of the Université de Montréal following disastrous fires in 1919 and 1922, had forced the government to give it large grants. The other universities of the province naturally laid claim to their share of the manna. As the government became used to the idea that universities must be subsidized, it sought additional sources of revenue from which to meet these demands. The most important such source proved to be a tax on wood pulp. Since the pulp and paper industry was largely controlled by English-speaking capitalists, the English-language universities could hardly be ignored. The perception that Bishop's was well represented in the corridors of power contributed a great deal to the morale of the faculty over the next 35 years. On the other hand, it also helped to establish in French-language universities a (false) impression that the Bishop's coffers were filled and running over.

Though the new trustees had generated unprecedented financial security for the university, by no means all Bishop's supporters agreed with the new complexion of Corporation. The Bishop of Montreal objected to the appointment of men as trustees "simply because they are in high finance."[26] He feared that they would not regularly attend meetings. In a letter to the next chancellor, Mr Justice Greenshields (1932–42), McGreer observed that the bishops had for many years appointed men to the College Council simply because they were members of the clergy, and that they too had been frequently absent from meetings. He was unrepentant. "We have done the right thing; and we shall always do the right thing. And no one will rejoice more in the good results which will some day be evident than the Bishop of Montreal."[27]

CRUISING SPEED

By 1930 Bishop's had reached what could be considered cruising speed. The residential facilities were over-full—96 men occupied 79 rooms, 40 men were living out of college, and it was difficult to find approved lodgings in the village for the 24 women "admitted to lectures" who were not living at home. After a particularly successful performance by the Dramatic Society in Ottawa, McGreer wrote to Chancellor Meredith: "The patronizing attitude of six years ago has completely vanished, and people have approached me with considerable anxiety lest they should be unable to secure admission to Bishop's University for their sons."[28] A majority of the students still came from mainland Quebec, most from families of very modest means.

The principal's persistent importuning of the provincial government had at last produced a capital grant of $250,000, but the whole of it had had to be added to the endowment in order to eliminate the accumulated deficit and provide for an increase in faculty. The stock market crash of 1929 and the ensuing severe economic depression had ended any prospect of mounting a second financial campaign. Further growth of Bishop's as a residential university would have to wait for better economic times.

The early thirties were the apogee of McGreer's tenure. It is therefore pertinent to take stock of the society which had developed under his leadership. On the academic side, A.W. Preston, arriving from Edinburgh and Oxford in 1928 to replace Owen in classics, found the education offered to be very solid and basic but rather old-fashioned. At McGreer's insistence Latin and Divinity were still compulsory subjects. Freshman Divinity, a study of several of the Old Testament prophets, he taught himself; he was inevitably referred to by some of the less respectful Frosh as "Jahweh." Since library holdings were sparse and laboratory facilities rudimentary, the quality of education depended entirely on the quality of lectures and tutorials. The program offered was well integrated, but the lack of time for reading, due to the heavy teaching loads, and the classical background of the faculty prevented much attention being given to the economic problems and the rise of the various "isms" which were the burning issues of the day. By no means all the undergrad-

Students' Executive Council, 1934–35

uates were academically inclined, but Rhodes Scholars in three successive years, and the Divinity class of 1932, which produced four bishops, bore witness to the faculty's ability to cope with the needs of strong students. In spite of the heavy teaching loads, aggravated in Preston's case by the abysmal preparation of many of the matriculants in Latin, he found Bishop's sufficiently attractive that he encouraged his Oxford friend Christopher Lloyd to apply for the vacant lectureship in English in 1930. Lloyd stayed for four years before leaving to join the staff of the Royal Naval College (RNC), Dartmouth, where he could pursue his interest in the history of the Royal Navy. He went on to become a distinguished naval historian and professor of history at the RNC, Greenwich.

As a junior lecturer Preston was appointed a sub-dean responsible for enforcing residence regulations, which he found strict and based on an out-of-date interpretation of regulations at Oxford. Doors were locked at 10 P.M. and only two late leaves were allowed to midnight each week. The record of leaves was kept by the porter, the unbribable Mr Pryde, retired from the navy and an adherent of the Salvation Army, who was inclined to worry about the less-than-pious attitudes of the students, especially of those in Divinity. Alumni reminiscences provide details of several alternative means of entering the residences which, it would appear, were much used—though not always with impunity. On one memorable occasion the captain of the football team and valedictorian fell from the fire escape while returning from an eve-of-graduation celebration and broke his arm. He was then faced with the task of addressing the assembled relatives and friends with his arm in a sling.

That alcoholic beverages were strictly forbidden in residence offered an irresistible challenge to many undergraduates. Smoking on the other hand was accorded official patronage. The principal, informally called the "Prin," met the freshmen at the beginning of term at a smoker, for which cigarettes seem to have been provided without charge by a tobacco company.

Nevertheless, Anthony Preston found Bishop's a very friendly, family sort of place. Bachelor members of faculty were frequently rescued from meals in college by their married colleagues, and undergraduates invited to lunch with the Prin and to tea with their professors. That portion of local society which was in touch with the university Preston found to be very hospitable, if a bit Victorian. Newly arrived wives were taken in hand by the wives of senior colleagues, and a great deal of practical help was dispensed.[29]

And what of the moral enterprise? As defined by McGreer, the outward and visible signs were the discipline of daily attendance at chapel, compulsory lectures in Divinity, and staunch support for "British institu-

Philip Carrington, 1935

tions," including the duty of preparing oneself to defend them by enrolling in the COTC. Compulsory chapel was increasingly a sore point with both faculty and undergraduates, and much ingenuity was devoted to circumventing the rules for attendance. Admission records (Appendix Four, Table 4) show that barely half the undergraduates declared themselves to be Anglicans, but the parents of most of the others presumably approved of McGreer's regime. At any rate, compulsory chapel was still the rule when he retired in 1947. Though the Divinity students lived in Divinity House, their dean encouraged them to mix with the other undergraduates. This was good for them, and it probably helped to make religion at least a subject for intelligent discussion in the student body. Individual contacts with members of faculty were frequent, and several of these men exercised a maturing influence.

However, the community remained isolated from the events of the times. Respect for "British institutions" led the principal to characterize the not infrequent mass demonstrations of unemployed men in Canada as "Communist inspired." Though he was personally both kind and generous in coping with the needs of undergraduates and others who were in financial difficulties, he was simply unable to conceive of socialism as other than profoundly disloyal to the British way of life. J.G. McCausland, a member of the Divinity class of 1932 who became Superior of the Cowley Fathers at Bracebridge, remembered that Bishop's under McGreer did not always defend the Anglican principles of freedom of expression in the external forum and freedom of conscience in the individual's mind and heart. As he remarked, that had to await the secularization of the Corporation![30]

DEAN CARRINGTON

During the early years McGreer had rallied a number of the leaders of Quebec's English-speaking society to the support of the university. Secure in their favour, he brooked no opposition on campus. However, with the advent of Philip Carrington in 1927 from New Zealand as dean of Divinity, it became evident that a fresh wind was blowing. Carrington was an outstanding scholar and teacher—an odd but effective mixture of intellectual brilliance and emotional susceptibility. He and his wife rapidly made their presence felt on campus. During the 1928–29 academic year he undertook a thorough revision of the Divinity program, which would require the Divinity class of 1930 to remain at the university until 1932. When he preached, the chapel was full. His performance of the New Zealand rugby team's Maori war cries became a star turn at the annual football dinner, and he was conspicuously successful in his direction of undergraduate plays. Mrs Carrington appointed herself "whipper-in" of the women students, encouraging them to develop their own community and seeing to it that they were trained in the social graces. Harrold Lodge, which was then the residence of the dean of Divinity, became a major attraction on campus.

Carrington was soon perceived to be challenging the moral authority of the principal. His own faith rested securely on the analyses that had won him widespread recognition as a New Testament scholar, and he was open to new ideas and fearless in debate. He was also possessed of an impish delight in challenging authority. St Mark's Chapel became the field of battle. McGreer's Christianity owed much to his study of the Old Testament. Carrington preached the liberation implicit in the New. McGreer continued to enforce compulsory attendance at chapel. Carrington "openly stated his conviction that this had ceased to be of service to the Christian apologetic." The conflict reached a climax when the principal attempted to prevent the dean of Divinity from preaching in chapel. The two men finally established an uneasy truce, which lasted until Carrington was elected Bishop of Quebec in 1935.[31]

Though it is part of the Bishop's oral tradition that McGreer aspired to bishopric, and that Carrington's election was therefore a defeat for the principal, there appears to be no evidence that McGreer wished to leave Bishop's. His respect for hierarchy led him to attach great importance to bishopric, but Bishop's had become his family and his life's work. The retiring bishop, Lennox Williams, lobbied vigorously for McGreer, but several lay members of synod believed he could not be spared from the university. Carrington was elected by a small majority, and McGreer wrote to Chancellor Greenshields that he was glad he had not had to decide whether to leave the university.[32] Carrington's election meant that he would eventually become president of Corporation, but it also removed him as a source of dissent on campus. Nevertheless, McGreer would never recover the complete ascendancy of his earlier years.

To replace Carrington at short notice as dean of Divinity and Harrold Professor, McGreer had temporarily appointed the Reverend Sydney Childs, a graduate of the University of Toronto in philosophy. Finding him congenial, the principal proposed to make the appointment permanent. However, Carrington ("Philip Quebec") was not satisfied with Childs' qualifications for the post. In March 1936 the bishop sailed for England to look for a new dean. In May he appointed the Reverend Basil Jones, another brilliant scholar and an exceptional preacher, neglecting however to inform McGreer of his action before the principal had learned of it via the grapevine. Relations between the new dean and the

Robert Ernest Alfred Greenshields

principal were never cordial. Jones' understandable perception that final authority over the Faculty of Divinity was vested in the bishops rather than in the Corporation and its chief executive officer[33] was ultimately to lead to a clash with the newly secularized Corporation and to his dismissal.

A SECOND FINANCIAL CAMPAIGN

In 1936 economic conditions had begun to recover in eastern Canada. The principal persuaded Corporation that a second financial campaign would be feasible to increase the endowment so that the costs of increased faculty could be met without increasing tuition fees. D.C. Coleman, president of the CPR, was persuaded to lead the campaign, and S. Stalford, Jr, was again appointed campaign secretary. In spite of the barely convalescent state of the economy (McGill's governors had decided that their campaign should be postponed and had undertaken to cover the university's annual deficit out of their own pockets), the campaign was successful, exceeding the goal of $300,000 by 15 percent. Stalford reported that one third of the 2,500 prospects had contributed, including 90 percent of Montreal alumni, but the parishes of the Montreal diocese had shown little interest. McGreer took further advantage of the upturn in the economy to work with the faculty and a consultant to establish an actuarily sound pension plan for the salaried employees of the university.

THE EVOLUTION OF THE B.SC. PROGRAM[34]

McGreer's attitude to the natural sciences seems to have been a product of his exposure to Oxford prejudice, which tended at that time to regard the humanities as representing the broad culture of the governing class, and science the skills of the technicians who served it. The principal had no religious problems with the evolutionary theory of creation, believing simply that, whatever the details, the creative activity had been the work of a personal Being. He would not, however, admit that this and other products of the scientific method were to be considered equal to classical philosophy or the plays of Shakespeare as evidences of civilization. He dealt with the admission of matriculants himself, and he not infrequently registered strong scientific aspirants as candidates for the B.A. rather than the B.Sc. That the only difference between the two programs in the first year was that compulsory Latin was replaced by French or German in the B.Sc. curriculum suggests that he still hoped they might see the error of their ways!

Albert Kuehner and Maurice Home had been appointed to meet the scientific needs of undergraduate candidates for admission to Medicine or to the High School Teaching Diploma course at Bishop's. It is doubtful that the principal contemplated the introduction of scientific method as a serious alternative to the study of the classics as a basis for a liberal education. At any rate, he was dismayed to find that Kuehner insisted on regularly scheduled experimental laboratory periods in the afternoons, which perturbed the long-established rhythms of collegiate life, and in particular limited the availability of science students for practice with the university teams. However, Kuehner held his ground, and this innovation marked the beginning of the serious study of natural science at Bishop's.

Kuehner and Home personally supervised the laboratory work of the undergraduates. Home, "by general consent the most brilliant of the science instructors,"[35] was particularly skilful and ingenious in designing and constructing experimental apparatus which the university could not otherwise afford. This activity and the recognition and nurture of the brilliant among his students satisfied his professional aspirations during a career of 38 years at Bishop's. Kuehner on the other hand was a builder with a strong desire to develop a successful educational enterprise. McGreer recognized a kindred spirit. Since Kuehner could be found all day every day in his tiny office in the chemistry laboratory underneath the library, the principal came to depend on him in administrative matters beyond the purview of his discipline. This rapport and the interest of several of the industrialists whom McGreer had recruited to Corporation, notably A.S. Johnson, led in 1935 to the establishment of a Bachelor of Science program (at first "in Arts"!) for which matriculation in Latin was not required.

The tensions between the humanities and sciences were not peculiar to Bishop's University. It is interesting to note the parallel development in the classical colleges which at that time furnished the education available in the French language to students in the same age group as undergraduates at Bishop's. Until the 1930s the program leading to the "classical B.A." was based on an idea of the purpose of higher education which was remarkably similar to McGreer's, though cast in the more restricted mould dictated by the canons of the Roman Catholic church. The curriculum was based on the *cursus studiorum*, a study plan which had not changed in its essentials since the sixteenth century and had its roots in classical antiquity and in Roman Catholic philosophy and theology. It was designed to produce "l'homme bien pensant et bien parlant"—a male élite trained in classical modes of thought and able to express themselves, orally as well as in writing, in French of the highest quality. Great importance was attached to residential life in college, which enabled academic instruction to be supplemented by a routine of living which developed civility ["*les bienséances*"] and sound physical health—all important attributes of "l'honnête homme." In this ambiance, the rise of science was regarded with alarm—as leading to materialism and atheism.

In 1929 the tranquillity of this venerable regime was rudely shaken by a series of ten articles by Adrien Pouliot in *l'enseignment secondaire*, the organ of the classical colleges. Pouliot was a graduate of l'Ecole Polytechnique in Montreal who had undertaken study for his Licence in France, and was teaching mathematics at l'Université Laval. He maintained that, far from causing "the spirit to be puffed up, the heart to wither and religious impulses to be extinguished," as the Establishment feared, the study of the natural sciences, in a context which guaranteed its speculative and disinterested character, was an essential element of a liberal education—"une école de sincérité, de solidarité et de modestie, qui cultive l'intelligence par la précision, la rigueur et la clarté, tout en développant l'imagination."[36]

Pouliot's articles stimulated a debate among French-Canadian educators which lasted for 30 years and was not finally settled until the advent of the Quebec Ministry of Education in 1962 and the subsequent dissolution of the classical college system. Change came more slowly in French Canada because of the identification of the classical B.A. with the cultural heritage of the French-Canadian people.

The decision to establish a B.Sc. program at Bishop's called forth truly heroic efforts from both faculty and undergraduates. Before Arthur Langford arrived in 1937 to take over Biology, three instructors, Kuehner, Home, and A.V. Richardson, offered over 40 hours of lectures per week in biology, chemistry, mathematics, and physics as well as supervising laboratories in the afternoons. The attempts to accomplish in three "long" years what other Canadian universities took four years to complete proved much more difficult in the experimental sciences than in the humanities. Since each instructor wanted his courses to be equivalent to those given in other Canadian universities, the courses in science each called for three hours of lectures per week plus a three-hour laboratory, as compared with two hours of lectures in the Arts subjects. The seven-course load (including compulsory Divinity and English) imposed on freshmen was in these circumstances extremely heavy. However, in A.L. Langford's recollection, "There were fewer distractions for students in those early days. They were not called upon to participate in the administration of the university. In general, the undergraduates faced up to the program."[37]

Langford was yet another "second choice" who became one of the builders of the academic traditions of the university. When Kuehner succeeded in persuading the principal that he must have a fully qualified biologist to complete the B.Sc. program, two candidates were considered for appointment, Honeyman, an Anglican zoologist, and Langford, a Presbyterian botanist. Kuehner leaned to the botanist, probably because he was a graduate of Queen's, but certainly also because of the materials he would need for his work. McGreer offered the position to Honeyman. Fortunately for Bishop's the decision had been delayed, and Honeyman had already signed a contract with another institution. Langford was appointed, the principal having first ascertained that he had no objection to attending at least two services at week in St Mark's.

The experimental laboratories occupied the ground floor of the library wing of Old Arts and the basement of the Convocation Hall wing of New Arts. Kuehner, as the senior member, had the whole 1700 square feet in Old Arts to himself—though chemistry would in any case have been an uncomfortable bedfellow! During Langford's first year, he and his students shared the two thousand square feet of floor space in New Arts with Home's students in physics but during the summer of 1938 the laboratory was partitioned, Langford retaining 400 square feet for biology. The exiguous space assigned to him made it extremely difficult for the biology program to catch up with the stable and well-organized programs in physics and chemistry. The advent of war, which drastically reduced undergraduate enrolment and superimposed three half-days of COTC instruction on an already overloaded academic schedule, further hampered its growth. It was not until the post-war period that Langford's boundless energy and enthusiasm reaped the harvest they merited.

In spite of the cramped conditions, the lack of technical support, and the home-made equipment, the pioneers turned out a number of "Natural Science" graduates who had successful careers. George H. Tomlinson, Jr (B.A., 1931), took a Ph.D. at McGill and became vice-president (research and environmental technology) of Domtar and the inventor of a number of processes in the pulp and paper industry. Roger Boothroyd, who graduated in 1938 as the first Bachelor of Science in the history of the university, also went on to graduate work at McGill, where he ultimately became Professor of Genetics. Interestingly, it was their skill in experiment which seems to have recommended many of the early graduates in science to their employers!

THE HEPBURN COMMITTEE

McGreer attached great importance to his seat on the Protestant Committee. It enabled him to counter the pressure from advocates of "socializing" education to introduce a more "practical" curriculum in the high schools, and in particular to eliminate Latin from the subjects taught to matriculation level. It also enabled him to keep the members of the committee aware of the work of the Graduate School of Education, with a view to discouraging any move towards the centralization of teacher training in Montreal. In 1937 the committee became involved in a first-class row over the control of Protestant education in the province.

The incoming Union Nationale government had been made aware of widespread criticism directed against the policy and administration of the committee, several members of which had themselves been of the opinion that their powers and duties were ill-defined and that reform was necessary. However, the report of a sub-committee appointed in 1935 to study the situation had failed to propose changes which were acceptable to all committee members.

Maurice Duplessis entrusted provincial treasurer Martin Fisher with the task of recommending reforms. Encouraged by W.P. Percival, the Director of Protestant Education, Fisher and the other four Protestant members of the Assembly concluded that radical surgery was necessary. Without consulting Duplessis, they authorized Percival to request the resignation of seven of the 19 members of the committee, including McGreer and the recently retired Bishop of Quebec, Lennox Williams. Percival's letter to McGreer, dated 2 September 1937, offered no explanation for the request, and was couched in the most summary terms.[38] On 10 September Percival's action was reported in the press. McGreer was furious. He refused to resign, urged his fellow scapegoats to follow suit, and mounted a vigorous counter-attack, demanding Percival's resignation. Fisher and his party defended themselves in a statement in which they suggested that all members of the Protestant Committee should resign. The statement made it clear that the politicians were constituting themselves a committee to reform Protestant education in Quebec.

On 24 September the committee formally rejected Percival's request for resignations, reminding the public in a statement of the long-standing tradition in Quebec that there should be no political interference in the administration of publicly financed education. Within three weeks Duplessis had become alarmed by the backlash. He announced that the demand for resignations had not had the approval of the government, that the autonomy of the Protestant community in education would be safeguarded, and that the Protestant Committee remained the authority competent to deal with Protestant education.

The members of the committee had been forced nevertheless to recognize the strength of the dissatisfaction with the Protestant system of education. To deal with it they appointed an independent survey committee with a mandate to inquire into and report on all matters affecting Protestant education in the Province of Quebec. To guarantee the autonomy of the survey, and to renew the connection with the Scottish system of public education on which the Quebec public schools had been modelled, the committee appointed W.F. Hepburn, the director of education of Ayrshire, to chair the survey committee. He was supported by nine able members who were widely representative of the Protestant community. Written memoranda from over 100 interested bodies and persons were submitted and committee members conferred with a comparable number of organizations, including representatives of 38 rural school boards. In October 1938 the Hepburn Committee published an extremely thorough and comprehensive report, including 188 recommendations for the reform of the system, beginning with one for the dissolution of the Protestant Committee and its reconstitution on a broader base.[39]

Reaction to this report made it clear that several members of the Protestant Committee intended to treat these recommendations as advice they were free to accept or reject. One of the key recommendations gave the reconstituted Protestant Committee full power to appoint officials for the discharge of its business, in particular the Director of Protestant Education, and to receive and disburse all moneys available for Protestant education. This pleased neither the politicians nor Percival. A majority of the committee was persuaded to appoint a sub-committee to consider the report, and the report of this sub-committee was then considered clause by clause in committee of the whole, where information provided by Percival and his officials was used to contest the Hepburn recommendations.

McGreer considered this procedure a breach of faith with the public. The committee should have been dissolved and reconstituted before any further consideration was given to the recommendations. He had his own reservations about some of the Hepburn proposals, but the report had in general been well received by the universities, school principals, and teachers. However, it soon became evident that the political battle was lost. In February 1939 he and Professor Rothney offered their resignations to the premier in the hope that Duplessis would act, but he had more urgent problems, and with the advent of war the whole question became secondary. Nevertheless, McGreer had identified himself as a leader of the reform party. In October he was elected an honourary member of the Provincial Association of Protestant Teachers in appreciation of his efforts to have the recommendations of the survey report implemented.

THE SYLLABUS FOR ORDINANDS

Since Philip Carrington had been elected bishop, communications between him and McGreer had been, if not cordial, at least frequent and correct. The bishop was a member of the Hepburn Committee and he provided both ammunition and encouragement to the principal in his battle to have the recommendations of the survey report implemented.

In 1939 the truce abruptly terminated. The source of contention was a proposal by the Faculty of Divinity to make a three-year Arts course a prerequisite for all Divinity students. In McGreer's opinion, the House of Bishops had not established a sufficiently high standard of education for ordinands, with the result that the clergy had not developed the habit of reading which would enable them to keep their minds active amid the pressure of their pastoral responsibilities. During the 1938–39 session, the Divinity professors worked with the Faculty of Arts to develop a syllabus of pre-theological Arts courses leading to the B.A., which would become a prerequisite for admission to the Faculty of Divinity. This syllabus, followed by a two-year program in Theology, would replace the four-year B.A. in Theology program, in which only the first year was devoted to general Arts subjects. Carrington had already informed Basil Jones that he was not interested in the project. He believed that the syllabus of the B.A. in Theology program offered as good training for the mind as that of the general B.A. He was already having enough difficulty finding funds to support the studies of prospective ordinands following the four-year program, and he also believed that five years was too long to spend at one institution. He sent a memorandum to the members of the Faculty of Divinity which made it clear that, as Visitor, he expected to be consulted if any major revision of the Divinity course was under consideration.

Nevertheless, the faculty unanimously recommended the syllabus drawn up by the dean of Divinity to the academic committee. The bishop warned of a serious conflict in convocation if they persisted in their project and threatened to withdraw his candidates for ordination if the revision were authorized. McGreer wrote to him urging that the Faculty of Divinity should be allowed all the freedom possible within the limits fixed by the statutes, rules, and ordinances of the university. Carrington replied that in his view the statutes required the Divinity Faculty to "loyally accept some measure of direction from the Visitors."[40] The issue had become one of academic freedom.

The "academic" committee to which the proposed revision had been recommended consisted of the bishops of Quebec and Montreal, the chancellor, the vice-chancellor, Canon Abbott-Smith, Professor Boothroyd, and Dean Jones. On 13 June on a motion by the chancellor seconded by Canon Abbott-Smith, the committee decided to postpone further consideration of the matter until the next meeting, which was scheduled for June 1940.[41] Nothing more was heard of the proposal, and the issue of the responsibility of the Faculty of Divinity to the Visitors was left unresolved. It was to surface again in more acute form after the Corporation had been secularized.

THE 1939-45 WAR

At the time of the Munich crisis in 1938 McGreer wrote to D.C. Coleman, the chairman of the Executive Committee, of his "indescribable relief" that Bishop's men would not again be asked to volunteer for service overseas. However, by 1939 he had come to accept the inevitability of war. He was invited to become director of non-Roman Catholic chaplain services in the Canadian Army, but when he learned that if he accepted he would have to take leave of absence from Bishop's, he declined the appointment.

When the regulations governing National Service were first established, they recognized the value of higher education to the war effort, and exempted undergraduates in good academic standing from call-up. From the first days of the war there was a renaissance in the COTC. *The Mitre* reported that "inflamed with patriotic enthusiasm—and with the prospect of dropping a Divinity course—eighty students enlisted."[42] The corps was taken much more seriously at Bishop's than at some other Canadian universities, and the three three-hour parades a week cut heavily into the extra-curricular life of the undergraduates. In October 1940 the corps activities received further impetus from the appointment of Major Howard Church (B.A., 1929) as commanding officer. He organized the more athletically inclined cadets as ski troops, making full use of the rolling terrain of the Townships for winter "schemes." Morale was greatly reinforced by the discovery, at the annual summer camps, that the Bishop's contingent could more than hold its own in competition with those from the larger universities.

Many undergraduates again left their studies to volunteer for active service, and by 1941-42 enrolment in Arts and Science had fallen to 116, only 17 men remaining for their final year. The battalion of the Royal Rifles sent to defend Hong Kong in 1941 was largely recruited from the Townships. Ten of them, including eight of their officers, were Bishop's men; and when the Japanese attacked Hong Kong on 18 December, McGreer cabled the BBC to ask that a message of pride and confidence be broadcast to them from the university. The message was broadcast on the Far Eastern service of the BBC on Boxing Day. Unhappily the garrison had been overrun the previous day.

During the six long years of the war the Prin corresponded with as many of the alumni overseas as possible, and he invariably wrote to the parents of casualties. He and his wife were also active in organizing the reception in the Townships of British children evacuated early in the war, two of whom were invited to spend their holidays at the Lodge. The McGreers had no children of their own, and it is evident from the Prin's letters how much they enjoyed introducing the visitors to Canadian winter and summer recreations. During the last year of the war, inspired by the example set for Canadian troops by British universities, the principal organized a series of week-long courses at Bishop's for the personnel of the RAF Ferry Command in Montreal. The visitors were housed on campus and entertained by the undergraduates, both male and female. The RAF commanding officer reported that far more airmen wished to follow the course than he could spare!

Intercollegiate athletic competition under the aegis of the Canadian Intercollegiate Athletic Union (CIAU) had been terminated for the duration, but scratch games were arranged with a number of local teams. The students knitted socks and gathered magazines for the men and women in the services, and contributed generously of their scanty means to the Victory Loan campaigns. However, the highlight of the undergraduate war effort, apart from the COTC, was the harvest excursion of 1942. That September the Canadian government appealed to university students to help in the harvest of the crops in western Canada, where the reserve of labour for stooking and threshing had been seriously depleted by enlistment in the services. The Bishop's students persuaded the Prin and the faculty to cancel lectures for four weeks, and 75 men set out for Alberta in the colonist cars of the CPR under the care of a faculty member, Eric Yarrill. Though few of them had had much experience with a pitchfork, the farmers gave them high marks for enthusiasm and they and their fellow students from other Canadian universities made a useful contribution before snow put a premature end to the harvest. Most seem to have used their earnings to further explore the beauties of Alberta and British Columbia before returning to Lennoxville and the battle to make up lost study time.

Academically it was again a question of holding the line until the end of the war. Fortunately, nearly all the faculty were past military age, and only Eric Yarrill took leave, to join naval intelligence. In 1942, in order to cope with the continuing decline in the number of potential undergraduates offering Latin at admission, the Faculty of Arts asked convocation to authorize a course of study leading to a B.Sc. (Economics), for which French would be substituted for Latin as a compulsory subject at matriculation. Otherwise, the syllabus did not greatly differ from the several options of the Arts program, and the instruction in economics continued to be given by the Reverend H.C. Burt. Though he had officially retired in 1942 after serving the university for 34 years, Burt was persuaded to go on teaching for another seven years. The new program was in fact only a device to circumvent McGreer's cherished principle that Latin was essential to a liberal education in Arts. (In 1949 a fully qualified economist joined the faculty, H. Michell [yet another graduate of Queen's College, Oxford], who had just retired from the Faculty of Arts of McMaster University. In the course of the extensive revision of academic programs undertaken that year by the new principal, Latin was eliminated as a compulsory subject for admission to the Faculty of Arts, and the B.Sc. [Economics] vanished from the calendar.)

In 1942 "Boots" Boothroyd became ill and was ordered by his physician to take a leave of absence. The other members of faculty rallied to take on his teaching responsibilities, but the teaching resources of the university were stretched very thin. The teaching overload and the stress of the losses of Bishop's men and of relatives in the U.K. made some of the faculty less and less willing to put up with McGreer's autocratic ways. Relations became particularly tense between the principal and Basil Jones, who had been appointed vice-principal in 1942.

Boots returned to his lecturing duties in 1942, though he had to curtail his extra-curricular activities. However, his health continued to deteriorate, and in 1944 he retired. The death of his eldest son, killed in action in France in August of that year, was a stunning blow, bravely borne; but his strength continued to fail, and he died in April 1945. Though Dicky Richardson continued to teach mathematics for a further six years, and Jeff Jefferis had arrived in Education to establish a link with the Bishop's of the twenties, Boothroyd's influence on the teaching of English and history, at the heart of the university's cultural heritage, had been such that his passing marked the end of an era—an era in which the Professor of History could be counted on for an entertaining and illuminating lecture on Molière, and the Professor of Pastoral Theology was qualified to teach university-level mathematics. The development of academic research had enormously increased the volume of material to be mastered in most disciplines, and few post-war recruits to the faculty would have been able to spare time and energy to broaden their horizons.

Edward Boothroyd, ca.1941   William Rothney, ca.1938

CRISES, ACADEMIC AND DOMESTIC

The session of 1943–44 brought a crisis in the Graduate School of Education. Dr Rothney fell critically ill, and the three students following the High School Diploma course had to be transferred to McGill. When Rothney died, Cyril James, Principal of McGill, saw an opportunity. He proposed to the Protestant Committee that all training for high school teachers be confided to McGill, citing the very small enrolment at Bishop's and no doubt counting on the difficulty of replacing Rothney in wartime. However, McGreer was convinced of the value of the Bishop's graduate year in Education and confident that enrolment would recover after the war. Fortunately, he had remained in touch with J.D. Jefferis, an alumnus and an experienced high school teacher who had completed his doctorate in classics at the University of Toronto and was teaching at Waterloo Lutheran College. "Dr Jeff" was ideally equipped for the job, and he was able to liberate himself at short notice to replace Rothney in September 1944. With that problem solved, McGreer marshalled his by now formidable lobbying resources to repel boarders and, with the help of an editorial in John Bassett's *Gazette*, he was able to persuade James to withdraw his proposal.

In 1943 Mrs McGreer was found to be suffering from cancer. In October specialists in Montreal diagnosed the tumour as inoperable and sent her home. The principal had depended heavily on her support, and she had always been able to exert a calming influence on him in his more excitable moments. The strain of comforting her in her pain took further toll of his energy and his patience.

Kathleen McGreer died on D-Day, 6 June 1944, in the middle of the principal's battle with Cyril James over the Graduate School of Education. His sister-in-law, Miss Lee, who had been living with the McGreers since the beginning of the war, took over the management of the Lodge, but the Prin was spiritually and physically exhausted. At the annual meeting of Corporation in October he was granted leave of absence "for whatever period of time would be necessary to restore him to health."[43] He and Miss Lee went off to Victoria, leaving Basil Jones to enjoy interim authority as acting principal. The climate and society of Victoria proved beneficial, and McGreer returned to duty in February, apparently restored to more normal health and spirits. However, though he continued to promote and to plan the expansion of the university which he knew to be necessary for its survival, he had come to recognize that, like Moses, he would not have the joy of leading his people into the Promised Land.

Basil Jones, 1947

In the spring of 1945 the simmering conflict with the faculty boiled over. The war had greatly reduced the male undergraduate population. When the faculty came to consider the award of the Howard Ferguson Cup, for which the criteria were academic standing and qualities of character and leadership, they found that the strongest candidate had an academic average of only 76 percent and had displayed no particular leadership in student affairs and athletics. McGreer had suggested to the donor in 1933 that the faculty should nominate the recipient. At a meeting of the faculty at which McGreer was present, it was decided that the cup should not be awarded in 1945. However, the governor-general, the Earl of Athlone, was to receive a D.C.L. at convocation. On further reflection, the principal apparently decided that it could not be admitted on such an occasion that no member of the graduating class had merited a prize which so nearly epitomized the goal of a Bishop's education. He therefore notified the Montreal papers that it had been won by the candidate whom the faculty had rejected.

Basil Jones was on the point of departure to attend a meeting in Montreal, but he made formal complaint on behalf of the faculty, and requested that discussion of the matter be deferred until he returned to the campus. However, the principal chose to convene a meeting of the faculty in Jones' absence, at which he invited them one by one to express their opinion of his administration. Dissatisfaction had been general, but only three members of faculty voiced their objections. One of them, Eivion Owen, had already decided to leave at the end of the session, and had obtained a position with the government. The other two, Arthur Langford and Anthony Preston, felt sure that they were risking termination of their appointments, but they were determined to uphold the principle of the autonomy of the faculty in academic matters.[44]

THE SECULARIZATION OF CORPORATION

In October 1945 the principal submitted his resignation at the annual meeting of Corporation. The chancellor and the president were appointed to consider the situation, and in May 1946 they reported that the principal, in a letter dated 22 March, had asked permission to withdraw his resignation. The vote of Corporation to accept the withdrawal was unanimous.[45]

Though no correspondence on this question has survived, it seems probable that McGreer was persuaded to carry on by several of the able and active leaders of the English-speaking Quebec whom he had recruited to Corporation. These men were planning a financial campaign to raise capital for the renovation and expansion of the physical plant and an increase in faculty positions. If contributions were to be obtained from major corporations, the university must be freed from denominational control—the outward and visible sign of which was the provision that the Anglican bishops of Quebec and Montreal were ex-officio presidents or vice-presidents of Corporation. The leaders of this party were also determined that the next principal should be a layman. The growth in enrolment under McGreer had taken place in the Faculty of Arts, and the theological students were now a small fraction of the student body. However, if the bishops should prove recalcitrant, the case for the amendment of the charter might have to be made before a legislature controlled by the conservative and Gallican Maurice Duplessis. This case would therefore be greatly strengthened by the support of McGreer, whose determination to preserve the university's Anglican heritage was widely recognized. The reform party was nevertheless confident that, in spite of ecclesiastical pressure, the principal would give priority to the need for new capital.

The final battle of the campaign for autonomy—a campaign which, in the case of W.B. Scott, dated from as long ago as 1912[46]—began on 8 October. The reform party wished to avoid troubling the waters if at all possible. On the other hand, they were informed that it was likely that the Excess Profits Tax, imposed as a wartime measure, would probably be eliminated within the year, and this would have a very significant bearing on appeals to corporations.[47] The campaigners therefore asked McGreer to propose to Carrington that he move at the Annual Meeting on October 31st that henceforward the president and vice-president of Corporation be appointed by the senior bishop on the recommendation of a nominating committee composed of the president, vice-president, chancellor and vice-chancellor.

This attempt to achieve a face-saving resolution was not well received by the archbishop. He declined to abdicate. At the annual meeting he noted that there had been no discussion of the proposal by the Executive Committee. "The principal," he said, "has apparently been sent to me by a group of 23 members of Corporation, whose names are not given, to ask me to lay down within 23 days, on behalf of myself and the Church of England, the responsibilities which have belonged to the Anglican episcopate for over 100 years. The action seems to me to have been hastily and unfortunately conceived, and I ought not, in the interests of constituted procedure, and indeed of the Corporation itself, to accept it."[48] Nevertheless the chancellor then gave notice of motion to amend the statutes.

It is difficult to understand how men who had been close to the university for many years and were well acquainted with the history of the relations between Carrington and McGreer could have supposed that the choice of the principal to bear the bad tidings would have produced any other result. Carrington's opposition to the proposal was entirely consistent with his contention that the overriding responsibility of the university was to promote Christian values in the education it offered. He also judged that neither McGreer nor the members of Corporation he had recruited would, if faced with the choice between God and Mammon, keep faith with the founders of the university. However, his antipathy toward the principal led him to misunderstand the scope of the chancellor's motion.

Whatever may have been the ultimate goals of some of its members, the reform party's initial proposal dealt only with the method of appointment of the president and vice-president, which had been established as a by-law by decision of Corporation when the university was founded. In his address to the 31 October meeting the principal made clear his position: "Let me say with all the emphasis at my command that I hope the connection of the university with the Church of England at present maintained through the bishops of Montreal and Quebec, with all the powers they enjoy by virtue of the act of incorporation and the royal charter, will never be severed. That connection is a guarantee of a specifically Christian tradition as a normal and necessary part of the life and work of the university."[49]

At this stage the episcopal veto provided for by the act of incorporation was not threatened. The reform party was concerned only with the administrative practice of the university, and was content to leave the veto power intact, to be used if "the specifically Christian tradition" of the university were to be threatened. However, Carrington believed that his ability to fulfil his duties would be fatally weakened. He wrote to the chancellor: "At present the balance of the constitution is maintained by the extraordinary powers of the president. If your proposals go through, there will be no balance to the constitution at all: the church will have no effective voice; the academic people will have no effective voice; 20 persons representative of nobody and answerable to nobody will perpetuate themselves almost as owners of the university."[50]

In a highly emotional meeting with the chancellor on November eighteenth, Carrington made it clear that he believed that McGreer was orchestrating the attack, and declared that he would not relinquish any of his powers "until a suitable successor [to the principal] is duly installed."[51] When informed of this, the principal responded in kind. From this point on, no compromise was possible. The chancellor, at considerable risk to his failing health, continued to strive to persuade the bishop to accept the amendment in the spirit in which it had been proposed, but McGreer was now determined to eliminate the episcopal veto.[52]

Carrington had declined to call a special meeting of Corporation in December to deal with the chancellor's motion. McGreer therefore set about organizing a formal request signed by all the trustees that a "Special Meeting be called for the purpose of considering and, if deemed advisable, adopting" the proposed amendment. Carrington's response was to convene a meeting of Corporation on 7 February 1947 "for the purpose of a full consideration and discussion from every point of view, but not to pass upon the same at the said meeting, of certain proposed amendments."[53] In the interval he had appointed as replacements a new trustee and three new members of the College Council without consulting the chancellor and the principal as required by the rules, orders, and regulations. This demonstration of his understanding of the powers conferred on him by the act of incorporation and the charter did nothing to improve the climate at the meeting. After a long discussion, during which the conflicting positions of the president and the chancellor were clearly stated but no progress was made toward a compromise, the chancellor moved his motion, and the president declared it out of order. The trustees demanded that an expression of opinion be recorded. Sixteen votes were recorded in favour of the motion, 10 in favour of reconsideration.[54]

The trustees then turned to the Legislative Assembly for relief. They submitted a private bill in which they petitioned that the episcopal veto be deleted from the act of incorporation, that henceforward the trustees and members of the College Council be appointed by the bishops on the recommendation of a nominating committee appointed by the Corporation, and that the president and vice-president of Corporation be elected by the Corporation from among its members. Provision was also made that in future any five members of Corporation could themselves convene a meeting of Corporation if the president refused to do so.[55]

The archbishop prepared to contest the bill. However, the Bishop of Montreal would not support him. According to Carrington's biographer, Duplessis—who decided the fate of all private bills—intervened to ask Carrington not to precipitate an open conflict.[56] Since the French-language universities all had clerical chancellors and rectors at that time and several of the trustees were pillars of the Union Nationale, the premier's concern is understandable. Finding himself in total isolation except for the clergy, the archbishop desisted. The bill was passed, and John Molson was elected president at a meeting held in Montreal on 9 May.

In the short term the transfer of ultimate authority made very little difference in the domestic economy of the university. The lay principal who followed McGreer, Arthur Jewitt, hastened to reassure the bishops of the dioceses from which Divinity students came that Corporation was determined to maintain an Anglican Faculty of Divinity. He also strove to mend the breach with the archbishop, and Carrington rapidly became reconciled to the new order. The archbishop visited England nearly every year, and Jewitt was happy to make use of his connections and his judgment to recruit and to interview British candidates for teaching vacancies in the Faculty of Arts as well as in Divinity. Jewitt was also at pains to appoint to the faculty candidates whose religious opinions were not in open conflict with the Christian traditions of the university. It was not until the rapid, in some respects reckless, expansion of the 1960s, made possible by large grants from the provincial government, that the mould was finally broken. However when at the end of that decade the executive of the Anglican Church of Canada began to exert pressure to reduce the number of Anglican theological colleges in Canada, there was no one in authority to fight for Divinity as Arthur McGreer had fought for Education, and the university's venerable and fruitful tradition of theological training was abandoned.

McGREER'S LEGACY

The struggle over secularization left McGreer once more exhausted—he was 64—and the faculty even more bitterly divided. Several clerics reproached him for the betrayal of his cloth. To recover his spirits and renew his faith, he sailed for England in June 1947, but England he found in the hands of a socialist government. Britannia no longer believed herself called to offer guidance to Commonwealth and Empire. The ancient universities he had so admired no longer functioned primarily as schools for the education of enlightened governors of society. The moral consensus on which that role depended had not in fact long survived the 1914–18 war. Oxford and Cambridge were completing their transformation into academic communities devoted almost exclusively to the nurturing of the intellectual resources of the country. McGreer found himself *dépaysé*.

Bereft and confused, he returned to Lennoxville in August. He feared that dissension in the faculty would place at risk the moral enterprise he had worked so hard to establish. He had already encouraged Arthur Langford to seek a post at Cornell. He now abruptly informed Anthony Preston that his appointment would be terminated (after 19 years of service!), but that arrangements had been made for Preston to take over the post at Lower Canada College which had just been vacated by Hugh McLennan. However, the chancellor and the chairman of the Executive Committee were in touch with the university and they intervened to dissuade the principal from carrying out his plan.[57]

McGreer was clearly not well. A few weeks before Christmas, he fell while walking on an icy path, and suffered a severe blow on the head. Two days later he failed to return from his customary walk after tea. Alerted by Miss Lee, faculty and students quickly organized a thorough search of the ice-bound river and the surrounding country. His cap was found at the Lennoxville end of the railway bridge over the Massawippi, but no further trace of him was found until spring, when his body was recovered from the St Francis near Pierreville.

Basil Jones conducted the funeral service in St Mark's Chapel. The principal was buried in Malvern Cemetery. The faculty and the entire student body, in their academicals, formed the funeral cortege, which wound its way over the bridge across the St Francis. Neither the Bishop of Montreal nor the Archbishop of Quebec was present.[58]

When Arthur McGreer arrived at Bishop's, the program in Arts was moribund. The university was known chiefly as a seminary for the training of clergy, and its Corporation was controlled by the synods of the dioceses of Quebec and Montreal. Over the next 25 years, McGreer succeeded in reviving the Corporation and establishing the university's reputation on a much broader basis, becoming in the process, as he remarked, "the very symbol of deficits."[59] Deficits, he believed, were inevitable in a university that aspired to growth, and he persuaded the able and energetic men whom he had recruited to Corporation to allow him to incur total operating deficits of $262 thousand over the period 1925–45. During the same period, two successful financial campaigns and his continual solicitation had increased the endowment from $400 thousand in 1922 to $1.3 million in 1945.

Throughout McGreer's reign, the university's buildings remained, in the words of W.B. Scott, "totally unsuited to the university's needs and, heated as they were by 17 furnaces, a serious fire hazard."[60] Nevertheless, enrolment had been maintained at a level well above the capacity of the residences, despite a long and severe economic depression and six years of war. It is sad that the principal did not live to see the remarkable post-war expansion for which he had laid so solid a foundation.

Arthur McGreer's legacy was an autonomous university solidly established in the English-speaking community of Quebec and buttressed by a considerable endowment and an active and influential Corporation. In speaking of that legacy to convocation in June 1948 Chancellor

George Hugh Alexander Montgomery

Montgomery revealed the extent to which the members of corporation were in harmony with the principal's goals. He recalled the first line of the charter of UNESCO, which declares: "Since wars begin in the minds of men, it is in the minds of men that the defence of peace must be constructed." Quoting Sir Richard Livingstone, he drew on the wisdom of ancient Greece to define the role of education in that difficult process:

> For Plato saw, what we ignore, not only that education is the basis of the state, but that the ultimate aim and essence of education is the training of *character*, to be achieved by the discipline of the body, the will and the intelligence."[61]

This was Arthur McGreer's creed, and although his idea of the university as a moral enterprise would ultimately become untenable, his influence on the personal development of a great many alumni bore witness to its virtues.

CHAPTER SEVEN

TRANSITION

Basil Jones was appointed acting principal for the remainder of the 1947–48 session. In the wake of the traumatic events of 1947, the leaders of Corporation were anxious to reassure the bishops that the university remained an Anglican institution of which the Faculty of Divinity was an essential component. In this context, Jones' scholarly reputation and the relations of mutual confidence he had established with many members of faculty and students might well have recommended him for permanent appointment. However, the great majority of the undergraduates were now registered in the Faculty of Arts and most trustees were determined that the next principal should be a layman. After widespread consultation, their choice fell upon Arthur Russell Jewitt, head of the Department of English at the University of Western Ontario.

THE NEW PRINCIPAL

Jewitt was a Maritimer, a graduate of Dalhousie, Oxford, and Cornell. As well as possessing impeccable academic credentials and over 20 years of university-level teaching experience, he was a staunch and uncomplicated Anglican layman, well known to and favourably regarded by the principals of the Anglican theological colleges in Eastern Canada and by

Arthur Russell Jewitt

the Bishop of Huron. He was a humanist, believing that "the proper subject matter of a liberal education is human values as poets, artists, musicians, philosophers, and historians have found and expressed them."[1] He believed wholeheartedly in the importance of a small residential university with a liberal curriculum, similar to that of Amherst or Swarthmore in the United States, in the post-secondary education of young Canadians. Most of his professional career had been spent at Dalhousie and Western, so he was thoroughly at home in small academic communities. He seemed well equipped to oversee the transition of the university to a more broadly based curriculum and secular government.

THE TRIUMVIRATE

When the new principal arrived, 40 percent of the university's revenue came from interest on investments, and almost all the rest from undergraduate fees. The endowment was one of the largest per capita in Canada, and it gave the university an unusual degree of financial autonomy. By 1959, when grants from the provincial government had risen to 25 percent of income, the endowment still furnished 20 percent of total revenue. Nevertheless, without the energetic and successful efforts of the trustees to raise money for a larger and better-paid faculty, new buildings, and scholarships, the unprecedented growth Bishop's was to experience during the next 12 years would not have been possible. In addition, since the administrative echelon consisted of the principal (who also carried a considerable teaching load) and the bursar, several of the trustees had during this period to take an active part in the management of the institution. Three men in particular exerted wide-ranging influence on the university's development during the whole of Jewitt's tenure.

John Bassett was appointed chancellor in 1950. A strong and active Tory, he had served as a staff officer to General Sir Sam Hughes during the 1914–18 war. A career in parliamentary journalism led him into publishing and he became president of the Gazette Printing Company. His political convictions made him a natural ally of the Union Nationale government of Maurice Duplessis, and as a trustee he had been instrumental in obtaining that government's munificent contribution of $1 million to the 1948 financial campaign. Throughout his tenure as chancellor he was the university's primary adviser in financial matters and in relations with the government of Quebec. He also enjoyed assembling every year a procession of remarkably distinguished honorands to receive the degree of Doctor of Civil Law (D.C.L.). Shortly after his appointment he obtained a grant of $25 thousand from an anonymous

John Bassett, 1950

benefactor to establish the Chancellor's Special Aid Fund, the income from which he used with great discernment to alleviate distress among members of faculty and undergraduates in the days before universal medical insurance. With several other influential trustees he attached great importance to maintaining competitive salary scales for the faculty. His concern for their welfare even ran to using his influence to arrange ship passage to Europe for them and for Bishop's graduates proceeding overseas on fellowships at periods of the year when reservations were hard to obtain.

The president of Corporation in Jewitt's time was John Henry Molson, vice-president of Molson's Brewery. A scion of a family which had taken a leading role in the affairs of the province since the eighteenth century, he had seen active service in both wars. Principal McGreer had enlisted his support for the university, and throughout Jewitt's tenure he took detailed interest in its affairs, corresponding frequently (in times of crisis, daily) with the principal. In 1948 he had instituted the Annual Gathering, for which the members of the faculty were transported to Montreal and lodged at the Ritz-Carlton at his expense so that they might meet the members of Corporation at dinner, first at his house, later on at the Field and Stream Club in Dorval. This did much to reinforce the faith of the more senior members of faculty in the benevolent concern of the Corporation for the university's welfare. It also enabled John Molson to become acquainted with the faculty on informal terms, and so to establish alternative lines of communication with the university community. In his correspondence with the principal Molson most often appears as Jewitt's spokesman and advocate to the trustees, and as mediator when differing opinions were strongly held. The principal was very frank in his letters to the president, sharing with him not only his troubles and difficulties but also "nice letters" which he received from graduates and parents of undergraduates attesting to the value of a Bishop's education.

The third member of the triumvirate was William B. Scott, eldest son of Archdeacon F.G. Scott, appointed chairman of the Executive Committee in 1949. After losing an eye in action during the 1914–18 war, "W.B." had studied law at McGill and become a distinguished member of the Montreal bar. In 1952 he would be appointed Associate Chief Justice of the Superior Court of Quebec by Louis St Laurent. He had been an active trustee since 1941, and had prepared the legal ground for the amendment of the charter in 1947. Unlike Bassett and Molson he was a graduate of the university, and the son of a graduate; and unlike his more famous brother Frank, poet, socialist, authority on the constitution, and thorn in the side of the Duplessis government, he was viscer-

John Henry Molson, 1949

ally and vigorously conservative. He looked with disfavour on the steadily increasing enrolment of women, whom he suspected of undermining the essentially male traditions of the university and distracting the attention of the male undergraduates from the business in hand. At a period when nearly all formal instruction took place before lunch, he believed strongly in the necessary role of team sports, preferably involving bodily contact, in counteracting any tendency to waste the afternoon. Over a period of 12 years he agitated continuously for the construction of a covered rink with artificial ice so that hockey could be played on campus in every season of the academic year. Jewitt was fully aware of the importance of extra-curricular activities to a Bishop's education. Nevertheless, he felt bound to defend the endowment and to plead that the money for the rink be raised in a separate and specific campaign. His stand did not improve his relations with the chairman.

Though coping with the enthusiasm of these three powerful and active men often required diplomacy and drew heavily on Jewitt's limited store of patience, he fully recognized how fortunate Bishop's was to have merited their interest.

THE CONFLICT WITH THE DEAN OF DIVINITY

Shortly after the new principal took office during the summer of 1948, it became evident that his political skills were to be severely tested. Though Basil Jones professed to be satisfied with the Corporation's choice of McGreer's successor, he had not digested the transfer of ultimate authority from the church to the trustees. A man of strong character, and not devoid of ambition, he soon made clear his opinion that under the new dispensation, he and his colleagues in the Faculty of Divinity should be regarded as the true inheritors and guardians of the university's traditions. Jewitt strongly resented the implication that the Bishop's ethos was not safe in the hands of a lay principal. Since he was of a somewhat choleric disposition he was soon at odds with the dean.

After a winter of sniping the conflict came to a head in the spring of 1949, when the principal failed to make the still customary report to the synod of the diocese of Montreal. Unfavourable comment on this was reported in the Montreal press,[2] whereupon Basil Jones wrote a letter to the Montreal *Gazette* regretting the absence of a report, which he attributed to the pressure of the new principal's multifarious responsibilities. He went on to observe that "the appointment of a lay Principal to this Institution necessarily involves some devolution of responsibilities in respect of its ecclesiastical activities and relationships, and as Dean of Divinity and administrator of the religious establishment of the University, I may actually be in a better position than the Principal to

William Bridges Scott, 1954

provide the information which the Montreal Diocesan Synod is likely to require."[3] Though Jewitt was aware that several trustees were still smarting from criticisms emanating from both synods concerning the secularization of Corporation, it is possible that his failure to report was simply an oversight. However, the dean's letter had made an amicable resolution impossible. The conflict became one of principle. Jewitt maintained that the Faculty of Divinity was responsible to him, as the chief executive officer of Corporation, while Jones insisted that, unless the status of the Faculty of Divinity were to be altered, he was, as its dean, responsible not to Corporation and its officers but only to the Visitors—that is, to the bishops of Quebec and Montreal.[4]

Neither man would yield, and it became necessary for the Corporation to act. The trustees decided that they must establish their authority once for all and that domestic tranquillity necessitated replacing the dean. Two distinguished lawyers, G.H. Montgomery and W.B. Scott, prepared the ground with great care—there had been no precedent in the history of the institution—and Dean Jones' appointment was terminated, with a generous financial settlement, at a meeting convened for the purpose in August 1949.[5]

Since the dean had a considerable following among the faculty and students, many of whom believed that he had been treated with unnecessary harshness, his dismissal opened a rift in the university community. The class graduating in 1950 dedicated their year-book to him; and in his message to them, printed as a foreword, he quoted a passage from Horace which, he explained (for the benefit of the scientists among them), meant roughly "Stick to your guns, in spite of the clamour of the mob or your employer's [in the original the word was *tyranni*!] displeasure. Stick to your guns, even if the fragments of a bomb-shattered world tumble about your head in ruins!"[6]

Jewitt was unfortunately inclined to be somewhat irascible in his contacts with faculty and students—particularly if he thought his authority was being challenged—and he lacked the diplomatic skills with which to restore comity. For the rest of his tenure he seems often to have been unable to consider faculty initiatives on their merits. This lack of trust reinforced what was perhaps an inherent tendency to try to solve every problem himself. Inevitably he was not always successful, and in a community of academics grievances accumulate at compound interest. Jewitt recognized how important it was to achieve consensus, but like Robert Hutchins, the famous president of the University of Chicago, whom he cited rather ruefully in a letter to John Molson, he admitted that "lack of patience is one of my principal disqualifications as an administrator."[7]

Corporation had thus confirmed its authority over and responsibility for the Faculty of Divinity. However, Jewitt fully realized that its continuing health depended on the goodwill of the bishops who sent their prospective ordinands to the university for their education and theological training. He set to work at once to restore their confidence in the Faculty. Archbishop Carrington rapidly became reconciled to the new order, was regularly consulted about academic appointments, and was instrumental in recruiting excellent faculty reinforcements in Divinity.

THE FINANCIAL CAMPAIGN OF 1948

Though spectacular, this conflict and its resolution were in fact peripheral. In the words of W.B. Scott, the new principal had come to an institution in which "the loyal teaching staff were grossly underpaid" and where "the buildings were totally unsuited to the students."[8] Having established the autonomy and authority of the Corporation, the trustees lost no time mounting the financial campaign which would be necessary to remedy these deficiencies. The Extension Fund Campaign was launched in June 1948 under the joint chairmanship of John Bassett and John Molson.

The campaign executive established a goal of $2.5 million of which $1 million was destined for the endowment, to support increased salaries and an increase in the number of faculty, and the balance was to make possible a major expansion and renovation of the physical facilities. The campaign brochure urged that "the trained mind, the disciplined spirit, the balanced judgment are essential to the preservation of our society," and it underlined the importance of residence in an academic community in achieving that goal.[9] In the aftermath of the war, it was deemed wise to include a picture of Principal McGreer in uniform.

The total sum raised was $2.35 million. Generous subscriptions from banks and other major corporations in Montreal and mainland Quebec confirmed the opinion of the trustees that secularization of the Corporation would loosen the purse-strings of the English-speaking community. Individual supporters of the university donated many equally generous gifts, but the most noteworthy contribution to the fund was certainly the one million dollar grant from the government of Quebec. Though Bishop's represented an educational tradition of which Maurice Duplessis approved, the exceptional generosity of his response must be credited to the influence of John Bassett.

NEW BUILDINGS

Jewitt was thus faced at the beginning of his tenure with the heavy responsibility, and the opportunity, of transforming the Corporation's

Harry Norton

Breaking ground for the Norton residence, 1949

building fund of $1.35 million into more adequate physical facilities and of using the income from the increased endowment to establish more competitive salary scales and to recruit new members of faculty.

Building on a scale which was now possible was unprecedented in the history of the institution. There was a general consensus that facilities to reinforce the residential character of the university should be given overall priority. In particular, women undergraduates had to be installed on campus and made full members of the undergraduate community (though support for this was not quite unanimous). It was immediately evident that the skeletal administrative echelon had neither the time nor the experience to make detailed plans and obtain reliable estimates of costs. Fortunately two members of the Executive Committee, George Tomlinson and Philip Scowen, had extensive experience in these matters and were willing to devote themselves to the task. Under their critical eyes priorities were established and the university's wish list was whittled down to conform to the funds available.

As a foundation for this and future expansion, a central heating plant was given first priority, and other services were also to be centralized, including primary treatment for sewage—an innovation in the region at that time. A new residence complex, consisting of one residence for 85 men, another for 32 women, and a dining hall, came next on the list. In recognition of a very generous contribution by Harry Norton and his sister, of Coaticook, followed by an even more generous bequest a year later, Corporation named the men's residence Norton Hall. The women's residence was named Pollack Hall in recognition of a generous gift from Maurice Pollack of Quebec City, a friend of Senator Jacob Nicol. These residences were sited to form the third side of the quadrangle which had been implicit in the siting of the school ("New Arts") building 70 years earlier. Finally, a new and much larger gymnasium-auditorium was to be built, including a stage for the production of plays and concerts.

The scientific members of faculty had been pressing for a new building at long last to provide adequate laboratories. Jewitt also lobbied for a new building for them. Though Tomlinson was sympathetic to their needs, he was convinced that the residential space to be vacated on the upper floors of New Arts could be converted into good laboratories at comparatively small expense. This, together with renovations to "Old Arts" (McGreer Hall) and Divinity House which the newly centralized services made possible, completed the building program.

Architects and engineers were engaged and deadlines established, but only the principal was available to ensure that deadlines were respected and to provide the necessary liaison between Executive Committee, ar-

Norton Dining Room, ca. 1951

chitects, engineers, contractors, and the construction site. Jewitt threw himself energetically into the task. He travelled to Amherst, Dartmouth, Middlebury, and several Canadian universities to seek advice on the design of residences. He consulted a friend who was director of dining services at Cornell on the design of kitchens and dining halls. Tomlinson had urged upon him the need to supervise closely the work of the architects, and in the event their work was at first unsatisfactory in several respects. In particular, Jacob Nicol rejected the architect's first proposal for Pollack Hall as being "more suited to a private house than to a university residence" and much too expensive for the accommodation provided.[10]

Aided by Albert Kuehner, Jewitt continued to do battle with the architects, to pursue the engineers, to look for a clerk of works to represent the owner at the construction site, and to try to keep everyone informed throughout the spring and summer of 1949. However, by the opening of Michaelmas term it was evident that they must have help. In November John Molson instituted regular meetings of the architects and engineers with a building committee composed of himself, the principal, Kuehner, Tomlinson, Scowen, and Scott, and regular conferences at the construction site of the architects, engineers, and contractors. Thus stimulated, the contractors delivered first the new residence complex for occupation in September 1950, and then, after serious problems due to the underdesign of the steel framework, the new gymnasium in the late autumn of the same year.

ACADEMIC APPOINTMENTS

When the new principal arrived there were just over 200 undergraduates in the university and 12 professors in the Faculty of Arts and Science. Only English and chemistry were taught by more than one man, in both cases because the professor had administrative responsibilities. The excellent George Whalley, alumnus and Rhodes Scholar, who had returned to teach English at Bishop's after distinguished wartime service in the RCNVR, was about to leave to study for his Ph.D. at the University of London, and the saintly W.O. Raymond, also in English, was about to retire. Sidney Childs, who had taken over in Philosophy when H.C. Burt retired during the war, was made acting dean of Divinity in 1949, and A.V. Richardson, vice-dean of Arts and Science and Professor of Mathematics, was ailing. The principal set to work to avail himself of his extensive acquaintance in the academic world to find replacements.

As he wrote to a candidate, Jewitt believed that "for an education in the old-fashioned sense, the subject matters little and the teacher is almost everything."[11] He sought competent scholars who enjoyed teaching and whose personal beliefs were compatible with the Christian heritage of the university. Aided by the retrenchment in American and Canadian universities following the post-war boom, he was remarkably successful. He brought in James Gray, graduate of Aberdeen and Oxford and veteran of the Burma campaign, and Arthur Motyer, a Mount Allison graduate who had gone to Oxford as a Rhodes Scholar, to teach English. Gray stayed for 24 years, carrying a heavy teaching load and increasingly heavy academic and extra-curricular administrative responsibilities. Withal, he retained enough enthusiasm for his subject to complete the requirements for his Ph.D. in 1970. Motyer also took root, and was responsible for the rapid growth of interest in theatre arts which led to the creation of the department of Drama and ultimately to the construction of Centennial Theatre, which he designed. In Philosophy, Jewitt brought in Dallas Laskey, another veteran, who left after two years to complete his doctorate at Harvard, returning a few years later as professor.

When he was able to persuade Corporation to provide additional teaching resources in Classics and History, Jewitt recruited another Harvard graduate, Roderick Thaler, who taught in both disciplines for nine years until the increasing faculty establishment allowed him to devote all his energies to History. The principal was particularly proud of this last appointment since, as he wrote to W.B. Scott, again quoting Robert Hutchins, "'The most striking change in Liberal Arts colleges over the last fifty years is the multiplication of courses and departments and the decline in the intellectual scope of the individual teacher.'"[12]

In most cases, Corporation was content to leave academic appoints to the judgment of the principal. Early in his tenure, he agreed to appoint two women as part-time lecturers in Zoology: Marie Laskey (wife of Dallas Laskey) in 1949, and Louise MacIntosh (wife of the newly appointed lecturer in Economics, R.M. MacIntosh) in 1951. However, when J.D. Jefferis in 1953 urged the appointment of Frances Crook, governor-general's medallist of the class of 1939, M.A. (Bryn Mawr), Ph.D. (Columbia), as lecturer in Mathematics and Education, Jewitt had to reply that he saw no hope of persuading the Executive Committee, chaired by W.B. Scott, to agree to the appointment of a woman to the tenure-stream faculty. It is a measure of the progress made in this respect during Jewitt's tenure that in 1957, by which time the chief justice had retired from the Chair, no objection was raised to the appointment of Sylvia Burt Smith, governor-general's medallist of 1955, as lecturer in Chemistry. She was followed by Marion Fry, a graduate of Dalhousie and Oxford who was appointed lecturer in Classics and Philosophy in 1958.

Though some of Jewitt's appointees later left Bishop's for posts which allowed them more time for scholarly activity, his high standards in faculty recruitment bore fruit in the steady improvement in the academic results of undergraduates during his tenure. At convocation in 1952, three graduands were awarded first-class degrees and 23 were awarded second-class degrees, out of a total of 50. At convocation in 1959 there were 9 first-class and 39 second-class degrees out of a total of 70. In the interval the degree course had been lengthened from three to four years, and the requirements for the degree had been considerably increased. In 1956 Murray Greenwood became the eighth Bishop's undergraduate to be awarded a Rhodes Scholarship. He was followed in 1958 by Peter Blaikie.

Jewitt had also to find a replacement for Basil Jones as dean of Divinity. The history of conflict between Divinity and the governors of the university made this a sensitive appointment, and Archbishop Carrington was not disposed at the time to be helpful. However, Jewitt had excellent church connections in Ontario. One of those to whom he wrote was Derwyn Owen, then Associate Professor of Ethics and the Philosophy of Religion at Trinity College. Owen, son of the late archbishop, had distinguished himself in post-graduate studies and served as a chaplain with the Fifth Canadian Armoured Division in Italy and northwest Europe. Though only 36 years old he was obviously very well equipped for the post. However, Owen replied that he feared that the responsibilities of dean of Divinity at Bishop's would fatally blight his career as a scholar. In any case, he believed that only the resources of a large university could provide the training future ordinands would require if they were to cope with the rapid changes in society. Presaging the policy decisions which led to the abandonment of theological education at Bishop's 20 years later, he suggested that the "divines" would be better off in the newly founded interdenominational Faculty of Religious Studies at McGill.

Jewitt disagreed. He believed that Bishop's had demonstrated that a residential university with a liberal curriculum, in comparatively tranquil surroundings, provided good ground for the growth of solid and sound religion,[13] and he could point to Carrington as an example of a dean who had been able to combine inspired teaching with scholarly development. He continued his search.

After wide-ranging consultation, he was able to recommend the appointment of W.R. Coleman, a Wycliffe graduate whose churchmanship might not be entirely sympathetic to the Bishop's tradition, but who was an established scholar. Coleman arrived in September 1950. His excellent teaching and conciliatory manner rapidly raised morale within the

Faculty of Divinity and established more harmonious relationships with the rest of the university.

It was therefore with consternation that Jewitt learned that Coleman had contributed a series of articles on "Some Spiritual Aspects of Classical Marxism" to the *Anglican Outlook*,[14] a leftish journal of which he was an editor. Copies of the article had been sent (it is interesting, if perhaps unfruitful, to speculate on the source) to the chancellor, John Bassett, who was not amused. Conservative Montreal had not yet recovered from the shock of discovering that scholars of McGill, in at least one case of impeccable Westmount antecedents, had been subverted to the cause of communism and had transmitted classified information to Soviet Russia.

The principal was able to convince Coleman that the Dean of Divinity of Bishop's University could not serve as an editor of *Anglican Outlook* and the Executive Committee that the articles in question were examples of scholarly analysis rather than of advocacy. Philip Carrington intervened to reassure the Bishop of Ottawa that Coleman was sound. Nevertheless, when Coleman's appointment came up for confirmation in January 1952 the chancellor opposed his reappointment and carried the Executive Committee.[15]

Coleman was popular with his Divinity students and highly regarded by many members of faculty. A.L. Kuehner (who was not an Anglican) described him as far and away the best dean of Divinity he had known in his 27 years at Bishop's. Jewitt feared that unless the decision could be reversed the university would be split and the Faculty of Divinity, so recently convalescent, would not survive. He therefore enlisted the aid of John Molson to talk the chancellor round and energetically lobbied the other members of the Executive Committee. He managed to turn the tide, and the decision was reversed at the next meeting.

Unhappily, John Bassett was not the only resident of Montreal who was offended by Coleman's interest in classical Marxism. Shortly after his appointment as principal Jewitt had succeeded in convincing a wealthy Montreal woman of the value of liberal education in a Christian environment, and she had willed more than $200 thousand to found a Chair of Philosophy at Bishop's. In September 1951 she wrote to the principal to tell him that, having read the offending articles in *Anglican Outlook*, she felt that Coleman should not be permitted to teach at Bishop's. Since the articles had not been deemed sufficient cause for his dismissal, she had revoked her will.

It is not untypical of the fate of university administrators that the principal's labours on behalf of Dean Coleman finally came to naught. In June 1952 Coleman was invited to become principal of Huron College and he accepted the appointment, leaving Jewitt to find yet another dean.

It was very late in the year to begin the search. Fortunately, Archbishop Carrington had become reconciled to the new order and he was in England. When the principal appealed to him for help, he conducted an energetic search which led to two excellent appointments, Sidney Jellicoe as dean of Divinity and Lewis Clarke as Lecturer in New Testament and Christian Ethics. With these reinforcements, Jewitt was able to persuade the bishops who controlled the entry into Divinity that the Faculty was fully restored to health, and he had no more trouble from that quarter.

THE LIBRARY

Another academic resource that needed attention was the library. A.W. Preston, arriving in 1928, had found that the quality of education depended entirely on the teachers themselves, because the library and laboratory facilities were so rudimentary. Responsibility for the library was added to the regular teaching load of a member of the faculty, who was rewarded with the title of Honourary University Librarian. Each professor had a key, but access by the students was limited to the working hours of a part-time assistant.

In the 1930s the Carnegie Foundation began to make grants to enable Canadian universities to strengthen their libraries. Bishop's applied for a grant and was visited by an emissary from the foundation, who reported that the collections were uncatalogued and that not much interest appeared to be taken in the library. In rebuttal, Professor Raymond, the Honourary Librarian at the time, wrote at length to the head of the Canadian Library Commission of the foundation, giving statistics of the use of the library by undergraduates and, in the context of a small and close-knit academic community, arguing against the emissary's view that the absence of a standard system of classification condemned the Library as hopelessly inefficient.

After further correspondence, the foundation consented to a grant of $1,500 per annum for three years on two conditions: that the university hire a graduate of a recognized school of library science to catalogue the collections, and that the library be open to undergraduates throughout the day and for at least two hours in the evening. The new assistant librarian was Grace Jackson, a Bishop's graduate who had just completed a B.L.S. at McGill. She began work in January 1933. According to Raymond's report to the Carnegie Commission later that year, the total amount available for the operation of the library, including cataloguing

Albert Lincoln Kuehner, 1960   Arthur Nicol Langford, ca.1965

and the acquisition of new books (but excluding Miss Jackson's salary) was $2,526.95, of which $1,518 came from the Carnegie grant. Each member of Faculty was allowed to order books to the value of $135. For supervising the use of the library and, in her spare time, beginning to catalogue the 20,500 volumes in the university's collections, the new assistant librarian was paid $70 per month. In September the Executive Committee recognized that she must have help, and a full-time assistant was engaged.

Miss Jackson continued in office until her marriage in 1943, by which time she had been appointed librarian, her stipend had risen to $100 per month, and she had been included in the Corporation's pension plan. She was replaced by Viola Johnston. However, salaries offered to trained librarians in Canada were rapidly increasing, and Miss Johnston left in January 1944 for a more attractive and better-paid job in Vancouver. Her successor, Constance Oakley (B.A., 1936, B.L.S.), lasted until 1950, when she too left for greener pastures. At this point, Arthur Jewitt recognized that his ambitions for the university required him to give top priority to a search for a fully-qualified University Librarian. However, the salary he could offer, $1,800 a year, was by that time unattractive to a new Bachelor of Library Science and totally inadequate for anyone with family responsibilities. His first appointment, a Miss Morrison, left after one year, finding the task too heavy. A second appointee, daughter of a member of the faculty, withdrew late in the year after accepting an appointment, writing that "on reflection, I could not endure Lennoxville for very long." *In extremis*, manna fell from heaven in the form of Arnold Drew Banfill. A native of East Angus and a graduate of Bishop's, he had taken a B.C.L. at McGill and, in 1947, a B.L.S. Since then he had worked as an assistant to the director of the Law Library at Harvard, but he welcomed the opportunity to return to the Townships. Jewitt managed to scrape a salary of $2 thousand, which, since Banfill was unmarried, could be supplemented by rooms and meals on campus. He was appointed Librarian in 1951, and welcomed as a member of the faculty.

He found a library of some 20 thousand catalogued volumes and a further 5 thousand which were uncatalogued. To cope with the demands of honours tutorials, the faculty frequently supplemented the library's resources from their own books. The annual budget for acquisitions and journal subscriptions was $2 thousand. The total cost of the library operation was thus less than 3 percent of the university's revenue.

Banfill set to work to persuade the Corporation to provide his Alma Mater with a library worthy of the university. The principal was sympathetic, and among other trustees Philip Scowen was active in support on the Executive Committee and generous with his donations. He and another trustee, Judge C.G. Mackinnon, were keen collectors of Canadiana, and they laid the foundations of the university's extensive collection of documents relating to the settlement and development of the Eastern Townships.

Both the number of volumes and the undergraduates' use of them increased rapidly during the next decade, and it became evident that the library wing behind Old Arts (McGreer Hall) was no longer adequate. A new building to house the collections and to provide study space for a much larger undergraduate population was given top priority in the assignment of funds from the 1957 financial campaign. In 1959 the John Bassett Memorial Library (the central portion of the present building) was completed. The Corporation had at last been able to authorize the appointment of an assistant to Banfill, but Jewitt, in an intensely competitive market, had not been able to find one. Consequently, the librarian could be seen during the summer months supervising the transfer of books to the new building on a child's wagon, pulled by a boy from the local high school.

THE FOUR-YEAR DEGREE PROGRAMS

The principal's major source of concern on the teaching front was the steady decline in the ability of matriculating students to read and write. Thanks to McGreer, Bishop's was one of the last universities in Canada to retain three-year pass and honours degree programs. These included the same number of courses as the four-year programs in other universities, and in theory the longer terms at Bishop's and the close contact between professor and student compensated for the shorter calendar time. This was true for the stronger students. However, these were forming a smaller and smaller proportion of the matriculants from the high schools, and Jewitt was seriously concerned about the high academic failure rate—especially among male freshmen. There had been as well a strengthening of honours programs at some of the better Canadian universities which Bishop's, with its exiguous library, was ill-equipped to match. Finally, there was an increasing tendency in Canada to admit to graduate programs only students who had followed four-year honours programs as undergraduates. Sometimes this was due to rules established by external accrediting bodies, such as the American Library Association. More often it was associated with the larger number of applications for entry into graduate studies, which made it difficult for graduate admissions committees to use other than administrative criteria in their decision-making.

Another tradition that placed Bishop's at a serious disadvantage in recruiting good students was the requirement that freshmen in the B.A. program must have matriculated in Latin or must make up the deficiency in their first year of study. In 1949, 46 out of 69 matriculants registered in the B.Sc. program, but as Jewitt reported to a member of the Executive Committee, many of these had told him that their chief interest lay in the humanities, but they had not studied Latin in high school.[16]

There had already been considerable ventilation of these matters in meetings of the faculty. The science professors were finding it extremely difficult to compress an honours program into the compass of three "long" years. Another difficulty was the problem of the university credit to be given to graduates of the grade 12 classes which were beginning to appear in mainland Quebec high schools. Albert Kuehner had proposed in 1946 that all honours programs should be of four years, but the faculty finally decided in favour of providing for both three- and four-year programs.

Jewitt was readily persuaded of the soundness of the Faculty's proposals. In the form in which they were finally presented to the Executive Committee in 1949, these comprised recommendations:

1 That all Honours programs be of four years' duration.
2 That the B.Sc. (Economics) program be abolished.
3 That matriculation in Latin be no longer required for admission into the B.A. program.
4 That Latin be no longer a compulsory subject for undergraduates.[17]

Latin was to be replaced by first- and second-year courses in Greek and Roman Civilization, to be taught by Anthony Preston. Preston's courses rapidly became an essential ingredient of a Bishop's education, providing undergraduates with the appreciation of the virtues of classical antiquity which McGreer had so ardently wished for them.

The Executive Committee approved the last three of these recommendations. However, initially, there was some resistance to lengthening degree programs. Since approximately one third of the cost of an undergraduate education was met at that period by income from the endowment, an increase in the length of the programs would require a considerable increase in the endowment. Several trustees were also concerned that graduands who intended to proceed to professional training in Law and Medicine would have their already long period of formal education and training further extended, and W.B. Scott reminded Jewitt that Latin was still useful for the study of Law in Quebec. But the academic case was strong, and the committee finally authorized the new dispensation, to take effect with the class matriculating in September 1949.

The principal was less convinced of the merit of a four-year pass degree. In 1951 the faculty proposed such a program, which convocation endorsed. The Executive Committee refused to authorize it. However, the continuing decay in the standards of preparation of matriculating students exerted increasing pressure on the three-year course, and in 1956 the trustees agreed to extend it to four years providing that it remained possible for first-class students to obtain a pass B.A. in three years. In theory this was an admirable example of the Bishop's concern for the individual student. In practice it raised almost insuperable scheduling problems for the small faculty, and by 1958 all undergraduates were enrolled in four-year programs.

FURTHER DEVELOPMENTS IN SCIENCE

At the end of the war it had proved possible to increase the space available in the New Arts basement for laboratories, and for the first time biology obtained facilities adequate for undergraduate instruction and experiment. Though there was a surge in enrolment in the B.Sc. program (artificially stimulated by the requirement that B.A. candidates offer Latin at matriculation), first-year students were generally poorly prepared for biological studies. This was due to the fact that requirements for admission to Applied Science at McGill were the major factor determining matriculation level offerings in science in the high schools of the province.* Biology was taught in only a few schools.

Partly for purposes of propaganda to remedy this situation, and partly for its pedagogical value, Arthur Langford decided to institute a series of Biological Exhibitions, inspired by the "conversaziones" in which he had participated as a graduate student in botany at the University of Toronto. The first of these, in April 1946, was so successful that they became an annual fixture. The undergraduates were wholly in charge of dealing with the public, and the experience increased their confidence in their grasp of their subject. Students were bussed in from nearly all the high schools of the region. Their enthusiasm increased the pressure on school boards to offer biology at matriculation level. The success of the exhibitions also helped to establish the study of natural science as

---

* A Bachelor's degree was at that time required for entrance to Law and Medicine.

fully in keeping with the university's tradition of liberal and humanistic education. In reply to a congratulatory letter from John Molson, Principal Jewitt wrote, "Like yourself, I was pleased with the natural and easygoing manner with which the students expounded various methods of reproduction. It indicated a very healthy state of mind, and shows that biology may in its results be considered as one of the humanities as well as a science."[18]

In 1948 the three scientific members of the faculty were able to persuade Basil Jones, the interim principal, that teaching in natural science had reached a level which merited the establishment of separate departments of Biology, Chemistry, and Physics. The conversion of the upper floors of New Arts to laboratories in 1951 at last provided the space for properly designed laboratories, and the departments managed, with the help of equipment recovered from the closing of the Hendry Connell Research Foundation in Kingston and gifts from local industrialists, notably A.S. Johnson, to provide undergraduates with a more satisfactory level of instrumentation.

The absence of technicians and the increasingly heavy task of developing and supervising undergraduate laboratories continued to be a problem. Biology benefitted for several years from the presence of faculty wives who were trained biologists. An experience of one of these, Mrs MacIntosh, part-time lecturer in Comparative Anatomy, gives a striking illustration of the relations between teacher and student at Bishop's. She and her husband were living in the faculty apartment immediately adjacent to the south end of New Arts, where the biology lab was located. At the time in question, she was pregnant, suffering from phlebitis, and able to give only distant supervision to the experimental work. During her illness a male student, exasperated by the difficulties of a particular dissection and finding no assistance at hand, crossed the nine feet from the lab to the MacIntosh residence, entered the house unceremoniously, strode upstairs and into Mrs MacIntosh's bedroom, displaying the partly dissected animal on its wax-bottomed tray, and, pointing to the perplexing portion of the animal, asked, "What's that?"

A further and more serious impediment to the development of strong programs in the natural sciences at Bishop's was the failure of the administration to recognize the need for a sabbatical leave policy. The heavy teaching loads made it impossible for the staff to pursue research during term, and in the absence of such stimulus it was inevitable that most would fail to keep up with developments in their fields. Langford managed to obtain permission for a year's leave of absence in 1959–60, at no expense to the university, but it was 1968 before the first university-financed sabbatical was obtained.

COLLEGIATE LIFE

In 1948 most of the undergraduates entered university from grade 11 at the age of 17. The post-war ballast of veterans had nearly all graduated. Roughly half the students came from the Townships, and another third from the Montreal area. Though many were offspring of well-do-do families, there were also many of very modest means. Corporation attached great importance to increasing the amount of financial assistance available to undergraduates. A committee formed in 1954 under the chairmanship of Alfred Penhale raised $13,000 of new money for scholarships from industries in the Townships. As Jewitt remarked in his report to Corporation in 1955, "Bishop's is not a rich man's college but rather a college where rich men in the past have made, and in the present are making, it possible for poor men's sons to gain a university education."[19] The men and women undergraduates on scholarships provided a useful counterweight against some of the wealthier students who were inclined to exert social pressure on those who took their academic work seriously. The principal was gravely concerned by this latter "tradition", and worked hard to overcome it.

The steadily increasing enrolment provided reinforcement for the Bishop's intercollegiate teams. Football flourished in competition with the Royal Military College, St Patrick's College, and MacDonald College, and the Bishop's teams were league champions in 1954, 1955, and 1956. The long association of the Smith family with Bishop's basketball began with Garth Smith's appointment as coach of the men's team in 1956, while his wife, Sylvia Burt Smith (B.A., 1955), coached the women's team. The hockey team, hampered by lack of a covered rink with artificial ice on campus, competed robustly but with only moderate success in the Ottawa-St Lawrence League. Don Stringer (B.Sc., 1957), outstanding in football and basketball as an undergraduate, represented Canada in singles paddling in the 1956 Olympic Games at Melbourne and again at Rome in 1960.

Undergraduate life during Jewitt's tenure was marked by a gradual increase in the responsibilities given to student government and by unspectacular but steady improvement in the status of women. The principal was still considered to be "in loco parentis" and ultimately responsible for discipline, but this responsibility he delegated as far as possible to members of faculty, and as the number of students in residence increased to joint faculty-student committees. A significant landmark was the recommendation of the Student's Executive Council to the principal in April 1955 that two undergraduates be excluded from residence in 1955–56. With support from Archbishop Carrington, Jewitt also managed to persuade the more conservative members of the Executive Committee to approve a policy of voluntary attendance at chapel.

With the building of Pollack Hall in 1950 women could for the first time be present continuously in collegiate life. How this was to be accomplished was a principal topic of debate on campus and in the governing bodies of the university for the next ten years. When the new dining room was opened in the Norton-Pollack residence complex, the principal's proposal that women who wished to should be allowed to lunch with the men was initially turned down by the Executive Committee. One disgusted undergraduate wrote to *The Campus*: "It is quite beyond my ken/Why women cannot sit with men/We can only meet in line/ Before sitting down to dine!"

In February 1951 the committee relented, also authorizing the use of the dining room as a "common Common Room" for snacks from 8:15 to 10:45 in the evenings. Actually, neither the women nor the men were unanimous in support of increased informal contact between the sexes. A correspondent complained to *The Campus* that women were now frequently seen "roaming about" on the second floor of McGreer Hall— hitherto a male preserve. A poll conducted by *The Campus* revealed that 75 percent of women undergraduates preferred separate dining halls. However, the decision whether to socialize or not was increasingly left to the individual.

The men's and women's student associations had amalgamated in 1950 under a new constitution which assigned fewer positions to women than to men on the executive. Nevertheless, two of the five newly established Golden Mitre honour awards went to women in 1951. In 1953, an amendment to the constitution which would have given equal rights to women in student government was vetoed by the Executive Committee.[20] However, three years later, under the chairmanship of A.S. Johnson, the complexion of the committee had changed, and it authorized the expenditure of $9 thousand to renovate and furnish a large common room in the basement of McGreer Hall for both sexes. By this time, debating, dramatics, *The Campus*, and the Glee Club all benefited from full participation of women in their activities, and it is doubtful that the residual misgivings of Corporation had any significant influence on relations between male and female undergraduates.

Alcohol continued to be forbidden in residence, and a certain amount of activity inevitably developed off campus. Undergraduates turned up fairly regularly in Lennoxville and Sherbrooke drinking establishments (as they had since the founding of the university) and occasionally caused disturbances. By 1948 several drinking clubs had been formed, which rented premises off campus for their partying activities. These were to be formally disbanded several times during the next 20 years, but they proved very difficult to eradicate.

In 1944 Phil Beaudry and Fred Kaufman had founded an undergraduate newspaper, *The Campus*, which rapidly replaced the venerable *Mitre* as a record of collegiate life and an outlet for student opinion. J.D. Jefferis was appointed faculty adviser, and he proved to be the ideal godfather, protecting the fledgling journalists from petty censorship but counselling moderation and discouraging polemic. Though the paper was financed by the SEC, the editor was elected by the members of *The Campus* staff and was thus able from time to time to function as an effective and necessary critic of student government. Undergraduate opinion developed both provincial and national voices during the 1950s, particularly on the question of participation in international student organizations and on the need for federal grants to Canadian universities. The latter question was a particularly delicate one in Quebec. The contributions of Bishop's student officers and of successive editors of *The Campus* to the debate was characterized by a maturity and an independence of thought that spoke well of their education. A number of them were students of theology—a dwindling band, but still exerting a significant influence on extra-curricular life on campus.

However, the student body remained largely isolated from its environment, particularly from the French-speaking population. There had been spasmodic efforts to close the gap. In 1949 John Dunn and Ray Setlakwe organized home and away debates with l'Université Laval, in English at Lennoxville and in French at Quebec. Though these were successful, they were not followed up. The founding of the French-language Université de Sherbrooke five years later provided another incentive for Bishop's to develop a French channel of communication. In 1958 the success of an exchange of student visits and a joint, bilingual carnival seemed to offer promise, but the experiment was not repeated. In 1960 a bilingual University Naval Training Division would be established at l'Université de Sherbrooke, with participation by members of faculty and undergraduates from both universities. Again the initiative would not last.

In fact fruitful contact would never be achieved until a significant number of Bishop's undergraduates were willing to make the effort to become fluent in French. Jasper Nicolls had emphasized the need to do so in 1860. In 1952 the principal had still to acknowledge the tradition of teaching French at Bishop's as a means of access to the literature of France, rather than as a means of communication with French-speaking Canadians. This disdain for oral communication skills as a goal in university-level teaching was deeply rooted in Canadian university culture. Though the external pressure of the French culture on the university is much greater today than it was then, and the mother tongue of 20 percent of the full-time undergraduates at Bishop's is French, the problem has still not been entirely solved.

Nevertheless, in October 1953 the principal could in good conscience, write to John Bassett, "We are succeeding in giving our students a good sound basic education, without fads or frills. We require them to be considerate and courteous in their daily living, and they know we are uncompromising on issues involving the dignity of man, loyalty to country and reverence towards God."[21]

Jewitt's claim was supported by enrolment figures. Against the trend in Canada, enrolment had grown steadily from 210 in 1948 to 285 in 1955. However, the principal was aware that this welcome recognition of the high quality of a Bishop's education was not without problems. In a university where the great majority of the faculty and students lived on campus, and where in nearly all cases one person was responsible for the instruction in a discipline, this rapid growth produced serious stress levels, which Jewitt did his best to alleviate.

His own priorities were firmly academic. He kept before the Executive Committee both the difficulty of providing adequate instruction with one-person departments and the importance of reducing teaching loads so that members of faculty might have time free to renew their scholarly resources. From the beginning of the post-war period, the trustees had attached a high priority to achieving competitive salary scales for the faculty, but it was not until 1955 that they were able to authorize an increase in the full-time faculty establishment. From 17 that year it grew to 24 by the end of Jewitt's tenure in 1960, by which time nearly all disciplines had been given at least half-time reinforcement.

THE PROGRAM IN BUSINESS ADMINISTRATION

The principal continued to worry about the unsatisfactory quality of many of the male freshman. In 1954 academic and psychological testing of candidates for admission was introduced, a step he had opposed in 1951. In 1956 minimum standards for admission were raised to 65 percent in Arts and 70 percent in Science. Nevertheless, Jewitt perceived that the low "market value" at that time of an Arts degree in the eyes of many parents was a serious impediment in recruiting good students. The University of Western Ontario, from which he had come to Bishop's in 1948, had established a successful undergraduate program in Business Administration, initially within the Faculty of Arts and Science. He believed that a similar program could be developed at Bishop's. Another factor that influenced him to take this step was the staff training program for the employees of the Canadian National Railways, which had been instituted as a summer program at Bishop's in 1954 and had proved very popular with those who attended it.

The majority of faculty and students opposed the idea, holding that professional training should be undertaken at a post-graduate level, following a degree which guaranteed a sound and liberal education. When made aware of this by A.L. Kuehner, John Molson commented: "Surely if Corporation decides for very good reasons to include a course of any nature in the next year's activities, it is not a great deal of concern of the members of the faculty."[22] This remark sheds an interesting light on the conception of the university held by the president of Corporation and many of the able and influential trustees recruited by McGreer. In their eyes, the university was a ship, of which they were the owners. The principal was the captain and the faculty were the crew. The principal was expected to hire the best crew available, to know their capabilities, and to manage day-to-day operations so as to obtain the best possible performance. However, the destination of the ship and its passengers, the undergraduates, was to be determined by the owners!

Jewitt persevered, and the proposal proved attractive to the chancellor and to other trustees who were trying to raise money from industry for scholarships and for the endowment. The principal was authorized to appoint a Professor of Business Administration with effect from 1 July 1958. There were comparatively few men qualified to teach in the field at the time, and competition for them was intense. A young graduate of Bishop's, Errol Duval, who had obtained an M.B.A. at Western, was teaching at Assumption College in Windsor. When consulted, Dean Walter Thompson of the School of Business Administration at Western spoke highly of Duval's teaching ability, though he recommended the appointment of someone more senior to head the new department. However, Bishop's did not have the financial resources to attract such a man, and Duval was appointed (Full) Professor and given responsibility for developing the new program.

The faculty remained unconvinced. The old Academic Committee had recently been replaced by a committee which included all members of the faculty. This committee passed a resolution that the new program should be the responsibility of a separate faculty and should lead to Bachelor of Business Administration.[23] However, Jewitt was opposed to the introduction of a professional first degree, and his opinion prevailed. The first undergraduates to complete the new program received the degree B.A. (Business Administration). Principal McGreer would not have approved!

The following year D.C. Patridge, an M.B.A. from Harvard, was appointed to assist Duval, and together they instituted extension training courses for executives of the region. These were very successful and greatly increased awareness in business and industrial circles of the Bishop's contribution to post-secondary education in Quebec. The new undergraduate program did in time prove attractive to matriculants, and the enrolment thus generated was of crucial importance during the struggle for survival in the 1970s.

A POLICY FOR EXPANSION

As increasing enrolment exerted heavier pressure on academic resources and physical facilities, the Executive Committee, stimulated by Philip Scowen, appointed a sub-committee in March 1954 to consider whether the university should continue to expand or whether the enrolment should be limited to approximately 300 undergraduates. If the sub-committee recommended a cap on enrolment, it was also to suggest criteria for the selection of freshmen. This committee recommended that enrolment should not exceed 300 before 1957, that higher academic admission standards should be established, and that a study should be made of the new physical facilities which would be required to accommodate another 50 undergraduates on campus.[24]

However, as the number of young Canadians of university age increased, as more and more voters were persuaded that the solution to all Canada's problems lay in universal higher education, and as competition among employers for graduands became more and more intense, it became evident that holding the line was not a tenable policy. Late in 1955 another sub-committee on future policy was struck.

Both faculty and Corporation believed that *residence* in an academic community was essential to a Bishop's education, and in any case there was little accommodation to be had in Lennoxville. Expansion was therefore a much more expensive matter for Bishop's than it was for urban universities, most of whose students lived at home, and governments had not yet got around to providing capital grants. The new committee had therefore to canvass the possible sources of funds and to consider whether a financial campaign would be feasible. Though there were some misgivings on this score, the committee recommended in February 1956 an increase in enrolment to 400 undergraduates, with a ratio of two men to each woman.

The principal estimated that an increase of eight faculty would enable the university to provide core instruction for a further 150 students and would permit some enrichment of the curriculum as well. He believed that this was an upper limit beyond which Bishop's could not grow without placing at risk the unique character of the university. He was also convinced that the real crisis in the expansion of Canada's university system would be encountered in the shortage of adequately educated teachers.

From the debate over building priorities in the Executive Committee and among the members of faculty and undergraduates, there emerged a list for the reconstituted building committee to consider: a new residence to accommodate 115 women, additional faculty offices and housing, a new library building, a student centre to provide facilities for extra-curricular activities, and a covered rink with artificial ice. To provide these facilities, and to fund the increase in faculty, an objective of $3 million was set for the financial campaign.

Though the campaign was vigorously pursued, several major contributors, in particular the government of Quebec, failed to respond with the hoped-for generosity. The final amount raised was $2,253,613. At the annual meeting of 23 October 1958 the Corporation endorsed action by the Executive Committee to raise faculty salaries to match the rapidly rising salary scales for university graduates in business, industry and government. The Executive Committee reconsidered the needs for facilities and decided to give priority to the new library, the new residence for women, and the covered rink.

Chancellor Bassett died in 1958, and the new library was named in his memory. The residence for women became Mackinnon Hall, after Mr Justice C.G. Mackinnon, a long-serving trustee and generous benefactor of the university. When it was finally completed in 1960, the rink was christened the W.B. Scott rink, in the presence of the associate chief justice himself. To mark the occasion, the university gave him an engraved hockey puck, which remained one of his most treasured possessions. As well as removing from the agenda of the Executive Committee an item which had generated debate, at times heated, over a period of 12 years, the construction of the rink permitted the auditors to eliminate from the university's liabilities a rink reserve fund derived from fire insurance on the old rink, which Scott had tenaciously maintained against all comers since 1944!

FEDERAL FINANCING FOR UNIVERSITIES

Though Bishop's had managed to raise funds to pay for this expansion (which was of course modest in absolute terms) it had been evident for some time that private and corporate benefactions would not be sufficient to enable Canada's universities to meet the demands of the rapidly growing population of university age and that governments must contribute.

The British North America Act gave the right to legislate with respect to education exclusively to the provinces, and until 1945 public funds devoted to university education came almost entirely from the provincial governments. In 1945 the federal government established a liberal program of assistance for veterans of World War II who wished to attend university, a program which included a subsidy to the universities of $150 per veteran per year and some funds for emergency facilities. In the 1946–47 session veterans accounted for almost half the total number of Canadian undergraduates, and the universities had had to considerably increase their facilities and especially their teaching staffs. When the peak of the veteran enrolment had passed, undergraduate numbers began to decline, revenues declined, and the universities soon experienced serious financial problems.

In 1949 the National Conference of Canadian Universities (NCCU) presented a strong brief to the Massey Commission stating the case for federal grants to the universities on the grounds that they were national institutions. By a happy coincidence, the members of the commission were all graduates, and four of the five were officers of universities. The commission recommended unrestricted annual federal grants to the universities.

Early in 1951 Principal James of McGill, anticipating this recommendation, urged upon the NCCU the desirability of mounting a vigorous public relations campaign in support of federal aid to universities. This was to be run by professional public relations consultants and buttressed by statistics culled from university financial statements and presidents' reports. Bishop's had enjoyed excellent relations with the Union Nationale government of Maurice Duplessis, and had received from that government a munificent contribution to the 1948 financial campaign. With the support of the Executive Committee, Jewitt therefore declined to participate in the NCCU initiative. In the event, when the report of the Massey Commission was tabled in the House of Commons in June 1951, Parliament immediately appropriated $7 million for university grants in the fiscal year 1951–52. Duplessis accepted this grant very reluctantly, arguing that it would be much more in keeping with the terms of Confederation for the federal government to return to the provinces the taxing powers which it had "rented" from them during the war. In order to give formal recognition to provincial autonomy in the field of education, he also insisted that the grants paid to Quebec's universities should be in the name of a joint federal-provincial commission created for the purpose.

However, when the federal-provincial tax-sharing agreements were renewed in 1952 they did not satisfy Duplessis, and he "advised" the universities of Quebec to refuse the federal grants. They did so, and after a somewhat painful interlude, the Province of Quebec provided compensatory grants. This situation continued for four years while the financial condition of most Canadian universities continued to deteriorate and the post-war surge in population made its way through the high schools. Finally, after further stimulation from the NCCU, the federal government proposed in 1956 to double its appropriation for university grants and to hand over the responsibility of distributing the money to the NCCU (which would establish a foundation for the purpose). It also established the Canada Council, with two $50 million funds, one to endow support of the arts, humanities, and social sciences, the other to form a university capital grants fund. Neither of these initiatives found favour with Duplessis, and for the remainder of Jewitt's tenure he and his fellow principals and rectors had to watch funds finally totalling $25 million accumulate in the Canadian Universities Foundation to the credit of Quebec's universities—while university salaries in Quebec lagged further and further behind those in the rest of Canada and university deficits increased. Nevertheless, annual grants to Bishop's from the government of Quebec had increased from $40 thousand in 1952–53 to $100 thousand in 1957–58, and amounted in that year to 25 percent of the university's revenue.

JEWITT'S ILLNESS

On at least two occasions during his tenure, the principal's health had given way under the stress of his responsibilities, and he had been forced to vacate them for a period of several weeks. In August 1957 he was stricken by a severe brain haemorrhage. By means of a very recently developed technique, the celebrated Dr Elvidge of the Montreal Neurological Institute managed to tie off the damaged blood vessel and save Jewitt's life, for which act a grateful university conferred upon Dr Elvidge a D.C.L. *honoris causa* at the following convocation. However, there had been extensive flooding of the brain. The principal was told that his convalescence would last at least a year, and that he would not be allowed to teach when he returned to his post. In his absence A.L. Kuehner, with some help from the bursar, Lyman Tompkins, took over the duties of the principal. A.W. Preston became acting dean of Arts and Science and James Gray acting head of the Department of English.

Kuehner had become increasingly valuable to the administration during the rapid expansion of the physical facilities. As an active member of the building committee he had supervised many of the details of construction and had had considerable influence on the choice of the equipment and the interior decoration of the buildings. Though he was not a comfortable man in committee, being disinclined to compromise, the Executive Committee fully appreciated his ability and industry. In 1956 he had been honoured with the D.C.L. for his services to the university. Preston welcomed the opportunity to expand his horizons and to spend more of his time with the undergraduates outside the classroom. Though both men were exemplars of their profession, they were men of very different training and temperament. James Gray, on whom the main burden of undergraduate discipline fell during Jewitt's illness, was yet another man of definite views, and the troika did not always run comfortably. However, rather to the surprise of some members of faculty, it was remarkably successful in coping with the administration of the university during the next three difficult years.

In the event, though he made a valiant attempt to take up the reins for the 1958–59 session, the principal never fully recovered his powers. During the following winter it became evident that he would have to be replaced. He still hoped for a complete recovery and wished to continue. It fell to the lot of A.S. Johnson, who had succeeded W.B. Scott as chairman of the Executive Committee in 1956, to break the news to him. The kindly chairman, who had been counsellor and friend to Jewitt throughout the whole of his tenure at Bishop's, found the whole episode so painful that he had subsequently to be dissuaded from resigning.

Though his regime ended unhappily, the principal had every right to look back with satisfaction on the university's growth under his direction. He had wished Bishop's to become equal to the best small American residential liberal arts colleges. During his 12 years as principal the physical plant had been renewed and greatly expanded, and the undergraduate enrolment and faculty establishment had doubled, but he never lost sight of his goal or allowed academic priorities to be lost in the excitement of expansion. The academic scope of the curriculum had been broadened to include economics, psychology, and geography, and he had persuaded Corporation to allow the experiment of teaching business administration in an environment of liberal education. By energetic recruiting for faculty who had to meet exacting standards, he had managed to preserve much of the Bishop's ethos during the transition to secular government and a more broadly based curriculum. He accurately foresaw that in the context of the rapid expansion of the Canadian university system which federal funding would make possible, the recruitment of faculty of this quality would become much more difficult and that in consequence further expansion would place the university's traditions at risk.

During most of his career at Bishop's, Jewitt carried a considerable teaching load, adding freshman German to several courses in English. He loved teaching, finding in it refreshment and relief from the stress of administration and relishing to the full the joy of finding kindred spirits among his students. He worried a great deal over and tried to combat the decline in the ability of matriculants to write respectable English. He was continually grateful for the strong and active group of trustees he had inherited, and he was remarkably successful in channelling their enthusiasms into productive paths. Under his regime Corporation was gently but effectively persuaded that women undergraduates were not fatally weakening the fabric of undergraduate society and that a liberal education could only benefit from a reasonable amount of social and intellectual intercourse between the sexes.

Nevertheless, Jewitt was not a popular principal. Of the faculty, only Kuehner sat on the Executive Committee and the undergraduates were not represented. The university community had therefore no means of appreciating his staunch defence of liberal education and academic priorities. Many of its members, on the other hand, resented his lack of urbanity in personal relations. It was singularly unfortunate that he was faced, during the first few months of his tenure, with intense divisions among the faculty and students because of the Corporation's dismissal of Basil Jones. The rift thus created seems never to have healed, and in consequence Jewitt's regime did not enjoy as much support from the academic community as its achievements merited. Nevertheless, he left a strong faculty and academic standards which served the university well in the turmoil of the 1960s.

CHAPTER EIGHT

THE WINDS OF CHANGE: 1960-70

From 1944 to 1959, under the Union Nationale government of Maurice Duplessis, the Roman Catholic Church had continued to control higher education in the French language in Quebec. The education of young men and some young women of the age of Bishop's undergraduates was confided to the collèges classiques, which had cultivated the minds and formed the philosophy of the leaders of French Canada for over two hundred years. The Baccalauréat ès Arts[1] conferred by these colleges was required for admission to the professional faculties in the universities—Law, Medicine, and Theology—and to the *Grands Séminaires* in which the clergy were trained. The English-language universities were also governed by private corporations which derived only a small portion of their revenues from the government.

The sudden death of Duplessis in September 1959, followed four months later by the equally sudden death of his designated political heir, Paul Sauvé, led to the disintegration of the Union Nationale and exposed this venerable and venerated system to the winds of change. In June 1960 a Liberal government was elected under the leadership of Jean Lesage. During the election campaign Lesage had been at pains to underline the clerical connections of each of the Liberal candidates, but after the election it soon became evident that the goal of his government was to make the state dominant in economic, educational, and social af-

Charles Lapslie Ogden Glass

fairs in Quebec. During his short time in office Sauvé had admitted that he would have to provide more adequate financial support for the universities. If he had lived, the necessary reform of the system of education in Quebec might have been accomplished without direct state intervention, but Lesage and his ministers wanted transformation and were willing to pay for it. Bishop's University was thus, under its newly appointed principal, sailing into uncharted waters.

THE NEW PRINCIPAL

Charles Lapslie Ogden Glass was the first graduate of Bishop's University to be appointed principal. His career as an undergraduate had been brilliant: a popular and active man-about-campus, captain of the championship football team, winner of the Howard Ferguson Cup for all-round achievement. He graduated with first-class standing in English Honours in 1935, and was selected as a Rhodes Scholar from Quebec in that year. After taking his B.A. at Oxford in 1938 he spent a year as a reporter on the *Montreal Gazette* before settling into a career of teaching and administration in independent boys' schools, broken only by service on the Atlantic in the Royal Canadian Naval Volunteer Reserve (RCNVR) from 1941 to 1945. When appointed principal in 1960 at the age of 47, he had for ten years been headmaster of Bishop's College School.

The appointment was greeted with enthusiasm mixed with relief by many of those senior members of Corporation whom McGreer had recruited. Several of them had never been comfortable with Jewitt's style. Glass was a scion of a family respected in the Montreal business community, and he was obviously a most satisfactory exemplar of McGreer's idea of an educated man. As head of BCS he had raised the academic standards of the school and made valiant efforts to persuade the boys that it would be useful to be able to speak French. He also appreciated the importance of building character. The confidence of these trustees was reinforced when the new principal devoted much of his installation address to the need for Canadian education to respond to the menace represented by the Communism being instilled in the children of Russia.

The academic community for which he was now responsible had survived the interregnum during Jewitt's illness in good heart. John Rayner, a graduand in 1960, had been awarded a Rhodes Scholarship, and from a strong class of 1961, Elma Beall would win a Woodrow Wilson Fellowship and Jonathan Wiesenthal a Commonwealth Foundation Fellowship to Oxford. Among extra-curricular activities, the university debating team would win the Canadian intercollegiate championship in March 1961, the intercollegiate football, basketball and hockey teams

Intercollegiate Football Team, 1964

were competitive at the intermediate level, and Donald Masters had marshalled a very strong contingent of speakers for the conference on Canadian studies he was planning. Against this, the editors of *Le Devoir*, organ of the French-language intelligentsia, declared that "because a mistake was made in granting university charters to [Bishop's and Sir George Williams universities], institutions of barely secondary degree, there is no justification for consecrating the error" by building a second French-language university (l'Université Ste Marie, being promoted by the Jesuits) in Montreal. *Le Devoir* predicted that, in any case, Bishop's was destined to disappear with the decline of the English-speaking population of the Townships.[2]

In answer to an enquiring reporter from *The Campus* the principal declared that his basic goal was to preserve and where possible strengthen the university's position as a traditional liberal arts institution. He foresaw no need for further growth, emphasizing the value of the close faculty-student relationships which were usual in a small institution. Unhappily, the looming rapid increase in the population of university age, a consequence of the post-war "baby boom," and the impact of the generally higher standard of living in the sixties would produce very strong political pressure on all Canadian universities to provide instruction for much higher enrolments. In this environment, preservation of the Bishop's ethos would prove to be more difficult than he could have imagined.

Nevertheless, several of Glass' early appointments did provide strong reinforcement for sound and liberal education. The growth of enrolment and revenue had made it possible to consider the introduction of new disciplines for systematic study, and political science had a high priority. During the winter of 1960–61 Dr James Quintin, a consultant to the university, was a member of the Canadian Medical Association delegation to an international conference in Australia. In the course of a reception given by T.W.L. MacDermot, the Canadian High Commissioner, Quintin learned that he was about to retire and was thinking of returning to teaching. Quintin suggested that he write to Glass, which he did at the end of March 1961. Moving with a speed which would have been impossible for his successors, the principal, who knew MacDermot, cabled encouragement, enlisted Chancellor D.C. Abbott[3] to negotiate with External Affairs in Ottawa to smooth the end-of-career paper work and early in April cabled an offer of a Chair in Political Science. MacDermot accepted the offer and took up his post in September. He was yet another Rhodes Scholar, and had had considerable teaching experience at both secondary and university levels before joining External Affairs in 1944 at the beginning of the rapid expansion of the Canadian foreign service. Both experience and temperament admirably qualified him to initiate the systematic study of political science at Bishop's, and from the beginning his lectures attracted many of the brightest students.

When Ogden Glass arrived, the Student's Executive Council (SEC) was in the throes of a financial crisis, due as usual to the sporadic attention which the council had been able to give to controlling its expenses. In order to stabilize one of the heaviest charges on the student budget, an athletics board with minority student representation was set up to regulate all athletic functions, and the bursar was made responsible for financial control. In order to further reinforce athletic activity on campus, the principal decided to appoint a full-time Director of Athletics. As an undergraduate, Glass had led Bishop's teams to intercollegiate championships at intermediate level when the enrolment had been less than 200. Now that it had reached 450, he felt that the university ought to be competitive at senior level, but he wanted no part of the American philosophy of intercollegiate competition which attached overriding importance to winning and had led some Canadian universities to provide financial subsidies from various sources for students of outstanding athletic ability. The leaders of intercollegiate teams exerted considerable influence on campus. He was therefore looking not only for a record of athletic performance which would attract athletically gifted undergraduates but also for personal qualities which would enable the new man to turn the athletes' love of the game to good account in influencing them to become mature members of the Bishop's community.

After a number of fruitless interviews another friend of the university suggested that the principal approach Bruce Coulter. Coulter had been an outstanding member of the Montreal Alouettes who had competed for the Grey Cup three times in the 1950s, and he had just crowned his freshman year as a football coach by driving the McGill senior team to their first football championship in 22 years. He came to the campus to talk to Glass, who was delighted to find that he was a gentleman, that their views on the proper role of sports in university life were identical, and that Coulter would enjoy the opportunity to put them into practice. Fortunately for Bishop's, Coulter and his wife Joyce were persuaded to move to Lennoxville. Few appointments in the history of the university have had as great an influence on a Bishop's education. Shortly after his arrival he made it clear to a gathering of alumni that he was not looking for bursaries with which to tempt promising athletes. Nevertheless, when he retired 30 years later several of the Bishop's teams had for many years been fully competitive at the senior intercollegiate level, and 500 members of the Bishop's community—alumni, parents of alumni, colleagues,

Bruce Coulter, 1983

members of faculty and of the Corporation and friends—gathered at dinner to pay tribute to his role in the education of a generation of undergraduates.

THE PARENT COMMISSION: I[4]

In 1959 Quebec was still the only Canadian province without a minister of education. However, as grants from the government grew to form a larger and larger portion of the revenues of the institutions offering higher education, the Roman Catholic authorities decided to disclaim responsibility for the allocation of these public funds. In 1959 the Catholic Committee of the Council of Public Instruction formally declared that, while the law required the superintendent of public instruction to conform to the instructions of the committee, the committee would henceforward distinguish between responsibility for pedagogy—which it would retain—and that for administration, in particular of government grants—which it would leave entirely to the superintendent. Legislation prepared under Sauvé and adopted under his successor Antonio Barrette in 1960 established rules for new statutory grants to post-secondary institutions, which gave the superintendent many of the powers of a minister of the Crown; but he remained subject to removal only by a joint address to the lieutenant-governor by the Legislative Council and the Legislative Assembly.

When Sauvé succeeded Duplessis, Quebec was still refusing to allow the province's universities to accept grants from the Canadian government. One of Sauvé's first initiatives was to negotiate an agreement with Donald Fleming, federal minister of finance, whereby Quebec could opt out of programs involving federal grants for educational institutions, receiving by way of compensation a corresponding increase in the amount of the equalization transfer. Thus Quebec obtained full control of its share of the federal grants for higher education, and the importance of the role of the superintendent of public instruction was greatly increased.

When the Lesage government took office, it therefore placed the department of public instruction under the authority of the Ministre de la jeunèsse, Paul Gérin-Lajoie, one of the leading members of the new cabinet. Citing the Catholic Committee's distinction between the *régie académique* and the *direction administrative* of the system, Gérin-Lajoie insisted that he was not the minister of education. But the Archbishop of Quebec, Monseigneur Roy, speaking on behalf of the Roman Catholic episcopate, thought it necessary to remind the government that in education its authority was limited by the rights of the family and the

Church. On the other hand, a considerable lobby was developing in favour of the establishment of a full-fledged ministry of education. It was becoming evident that this was the most urgent question to be decided in the course of the wide-ranging study of the province's education system which, in its pre-election manifesto, the Liberal party had promised to undertake.

This promise was fulfilled in March 1961 when the bill creating the Royal Commission on Education was given royal assent. Monseigneur Alphonse-Marie Parent, vice-recteur de l'Université Laval, was appointed chair. Six of the eight voting members had had teaching experience, mostly at university level, and both the Protestant and Catholic English-language communities were represented. The commission was given a mandate to study the organization and financing of education in the province of Quebec, to report the results of its study, and to recommend the measures to be taken to ensure *progress* in the system of education in the province.

The commission invited submissions from interested parties dealing with every aspect of the education system, and it received some 300 of them, a great many of which were presented and subjected to close examination in public sessions. Nevertheless, commission members were determined to undertake their own analyses of the problems and to propose those solutions which seemed to follow from their analyses.

Under pressure from Gérin-Lajoie the commission agreed to give priority to the question of the administrative structure which should control education in the province and to make their recommendations on this question in a first report, to be issued before their deliberations on other questions were complete. He confidently anticipated that commission members would recommend radical transformation, and the government wished to introduce legislation to give effect to their recommendations no later than the session of 1963.

These expectations were well founded. Volume one of the report was made public in April 1963, and in it the commission recommended that the department of public instruction and the ministry of youth should be united to form a ministry of education. In June 1963 the Lesage government presented a bill to the legislature which created the Quebec Ministry of Education and Youth with authority over the organization of all educational institutions in the province except universities and *centres d'apprentissage*. However, the minister was to be responsible for coordinating the programs offered at the different levels of instruction, and this would permit him to determine the conditions for admission to the universities. After a prolonged and intense debate, chiefly over safeguards for confessional influence on pedagogy in the public schools, a revised version of the bill was given royal assent in May 1964, and Paul Gérin-Lajoie took oath as first minister of education.

Bishop's University had responded to the commission's invitation and had submitted a cogent defence of the university's ethos and its curriculum and academic standards, buttressed by appendices listing the more recent academic and professional distinctions achieved by Bishop's graduates. The brief urged that "when pressures towards uniformity of organization and centralized control are everywhere apparent ... there is greater need than ever before for variety in educational institutions as the best defence against monolithic trends."[5]

Unhappily, it became evident as the debate developed that the pressures cited were indeed very strong, and that they were being exerted by men who viewed education primarily as a machine for social engineering rather than as a means for training minds and developing talents. For these men, the best system of education for a *modern* society was one which kept the largest portion of the population under instruction for the longest time. In order to achieve their social goals, they also insisted that as large a range of intellectual capability as possible be catered to in a given institution in order to eliminate social divisions based upon level of education. Since the difficulty of coping adequately with such a clientèle increased rapidly with increasing age, this philosophy led inevitably to very large and complex institutions at the secondary and especially at the post-secondary level.

In this context the classical colleges were regarded as elitist and retrogressive relics of a Quebec which needed to be transformed, and to transform them was a primary goal of the reformers. Bishop's, viewed in these circles as an English-language classical college, could therefore not anticipate sympathetic treatment under the new dispensation.

GROWTH

By 1961 the principal had revised his opinion that no further growth in enrolment was necessary. Informed by a series of studies prepared by Edward Sheffield of the Canadian Universities Foundation,[6] provincial governments were bracing themselves for an increase in university enrolment from 120 thousand in 1961–62 to 310 thousand in 1971–72. Since Bishop's was now receiving more than one third of its revenue from the government of Quebec, Glass foresaw that it would be very difficult for the university to refuse to accept its share of the increase. Moreover, expansion would be much more expensive for Bishop's, as a residential university, than it would be for McGill or l'Université de Montréal, but it was unlikely that the ministry of education would be willing to recognize this in its financial dispositions. The Future Policy Committee was therefore reconvened—five members of the Executive Committee, including A.L. Kuehner, to whom were added two senior members of faculty, James Gray and Anthony Preston, and the committee was asked to consider the financial implications of several options for development during the period 1965-70.

There was general agreement that Bishop's should remain a small, primarily residential university offering a sound and liberal education, and that no new Faculties should be introduced. However, it proved difficult to quantify "small." At one end of the range, the chair of the Executive Committee, Mr Justice William Mitchell, noted with approval that Kenyon College had achieved an international reputation while limiting its enrolment to 550 undergraduates. At the other end, speakers at a recent NCCU symposium had suggested two to three thousand as limits for a "small" university. The principal reported that for the moment the government was foreseeing an expansion of 25 percent in the rate of capital spending. In the end the committee decided to plan for a rate of growth of 11 percent from 1965 to 1970, which corresponded to Sheffield's prediction for the average across the country. The estimate for capital needs would therefore be based on the facilities required for an enrolment in 1969-70 of a thousand undergraduates, of whom at least 600 would be in residence.

These decisions determined the program of the building committee and the needs for capital for the rest of the decade. They also provided the assumptions on which the recently organized Bishop's Association of University Teachers (BAUT) prepared a plan for academic development during the period. The BAUT forecast of the growth of faculty, which proved in the event to be remarkably accurate, was based on the need to increase the number of courses offered in order to improve and consolidate existing programs, and on the need to limit teaching loads to three courses so that members of faculty should be able to pursue at least modest research projects. The association hoped that it would also be possible to reduce the ratio of students to faculty from 14.3 to 1 to something closer to 10 to 1.

Thus the basic premise was "the mixture as before." Neither the Future Policy Committee nor the BAUT seems to have faced up to the stresses rapid expansion of this magnitude would inevitably impose upon vital aspects of a Bishop's education.

Perhaps the most important stress was that on the university's teaching resources. It was already evident, as Principal Jewitt had foreseen, that there was no hope of finding the number of Canadian men and women fully qualified to teach at university level which the politically driven rate of growth of Canadian universities would require.[7] This would be a problem for almost all universities during the decade, and Bishop's would not have the facilities for research and the salaries to compete for the few fully qualified people available. Recruiting for teachers in the Bishop's tradition was particularly difficult. Much of the strength of the university's teaching in the humanities had come from senior members of faculty who had received a comparatively broadly based education and whose wide-ranging intellectual resources and enthusiasm for sharing them had enabled them to cope successfully with heavy teaching loads. The increasing specialization of graduate schools was producing men and women with a much narrower focus, yet the enormous increase in the rate of production of knowledge made it necessary for them to be active scholars and researchers if they were to maintain their standing in their disciplines. In the sciences, including the social sciences, which were attracting a larger and larger proportion of undergraduates, the rapid development of new theoretical foundations made it even more necessary for faculty to participate in symposia and to contribute to the literature.

The principal tended to believe that original research contributed little to the teaching resources of the university, and he was generally unwilling to give priority to the need to provide faculty with the free time and facilities necessary for original scholarship. In consequence, Bishop's would experience increasing difficulty attracting and retaining fully qualified faculty. In September 1961, 14 of the 32 members of faculty had earned doctoral degrees, and at least six of the remaining 18 had solid and broadly based qualifications for university teaching. In September 1965 the number of faculty had grown to 56, but only 17 had completed doctoral qualifications. Many of the newcomers aspired to a doctorate, but only six of them achieved a Ph.D. and remained at Bishop's.

The decision of the BAUT to focus on content in reinforcing the existing programs was understandable in the context. Graduate schools were typically requiring a qualifying year of candidates who had not followed courses on nearly every topic offered by their own undergraduate departments, and in several cases professional corporations were imposing requirements on curriculum for prospective members. Nevertheless, the university had declared in its brief to the Parent Commission that its prime goal was to teach undergraduates to think and to develop their skills in critical analysis and synthesis. The need to give priority to specialization (usually a popular one and therefore in short supply) over the intellectual capacity and skill in teaching of the prospective member of faculty tended to dilute the resources available for this purpose. In fairness, it has to be said that even without expansion, by no means all the undergraduates were equipped and motivated to acquire the foundation in principles and method that Bishop's sought to give them—a foundation which would enable them to embark independently on a study of any given period or particular field with only tutorial supervision.

Finally, the brief to the Parent Commission had emphasized the value of close personal contact between teacher and learner and the continual communication between professors of one discipline and those of another as advantages of a small residential academic community. Rapid growth and the increasingly specialized focus of the individual members of faculty were bound to make such communication more difficult.

CAMPUS LIFE

The first half of the decade proved to be a productive and comparatively tranquil period for Bishop's. In an effort to control growth in enrolment, admission standards were raised in 1961 to 70 percent on ten papers of the Quebec High School Leaving Examinations (grade 11), and in 1962 candidates were required for the first time to sit the American College Entrance Examination Board Scholastic Aptitude Tests. In the days before the abolition of departmental matriculation examinations, this was a very respectable standard, though Albert Kuehner was not impressed with the result. He believed that many students whose grade 11 marks fell in the 65 to 69 percent range but had other talents made a greater contribution to the university life than those who could offer nothing but 70 percent in the examinations.

At the other end of the academic spectrum, there was a steady increase in the number of graduands achieving first-class standing, in the successes of graduates enrolled in post-graduate professional schools, and in the number of external distinctions awarded to graduands, including a Rhodes Scholarship to Norman Webster in 1962. A major factor in generating this increase was the work of Alfred Penhale's committee in obtaining funds for scholarships from Townships industry and friends of the university. This period also saw the beginning of post-graduate study to the Master's level in science to complement the activity in theology, history, and English toward the M.A. degree.

By 1963–64, however, the first signs of stress were beginning to appear. Enrolment had reached 570, and in his annual report to Corporation in November 1964 the principal reported increases in the failure rate in both Arts and Science and noted with regret that it was no longer possible to get to know new members of faculty, many of whom were not staying long enough to absorb the traditions of the university.

Tartuffe, 1966

By 1964 Philip Scowen, chair of the building committee, was able to report that the facilities foreseen for an enrolment of 500 had been completed. Since 1961 the Nicolls and Hamilton buildings and Bishop Mountain House had been completed, a beginning (Abbott Hall) had been made on the new men's residences, New Arts (A.S. Johnson) had been substantially renovated for science, six new faculty houses had been constructed, and outside services had been greatly improved. To cope with the projected expansion to 1,000 undergraduates, the committee was working on plans for another stage of construction: at least one more men's residence (Kuehner Hall), a large and expensive addition to the Johnson building, a theatre-auditorium (Centennial), a new wing for the library, a new dining complex (Dewhurst Hall), and enlarged athletic facilities. Scowen reminded the Executive Committee that almost all the construction since 1961 had been financed by grants of public funds and that future construction would probably be similarly financed. Though this radical change in the university's policy was unavoidable if the current rate of growth was to be maintained, Bishop's had thereby surely forfeited some measure of its autonomy.

Undergraduate participation in several of the principal extra-curricular activities on campus was enthusiastic during this period and produced some notable achievements. In debating, the Canadian intercollegiate championship of 1961 was followed by a second in 1962, and these successes generated a revival of interest in model parliaments. In 1964 John Piper, vice-president external of the SEC, made a determined attempt to organize a bilingual parliament in collaboration with the students of the Université de Sherbrooke. This timely initiative attracted some very distinguished visiting speakers, but the Sherbrooke student government proved unable to generate enough interest in their constituency to justify their participation.

The enthusiasm of Arthur Motyer had nurtured a steady rise in undergraduate interest in drama and produced a remarkably high standard of performance. In 1963–64, for example, the Dramatic Society organized a two-day seminar in which nearly all aspects of stagecraft were examined and discussed and Motyer revealed his plans for a new university theatre. Three one-act plays and a reading play were also produced during the fall term. One of the one-act plays was chosen to represent Bishop's at the Canadian Drama League Festival the following February, earning its lead the award for best actor, while the play itself earned honourable mention for both best direction and best production. After Christmas the society produced Christopher Fry's *A Sleep of Prisoners* in St Mark's Chapel, and the season was brought to a fitting climax by a successful production of *Twelfth Night* in March. In this play alone, 15 per-

Arthur Motyer in Centennial Theatre, 1967   *The Knight of the Burning Pestle*, 1967

cent of the entire undergraduate body was involved, and over the entire season 20 percent of the students participated in the society's productions.

Another society which attracted strong undergraduate support was Dr McCubbin's Deep Purples, the university choral society, who proved to be effective ambassadors for Bishop's during their annual tours through Quebec and eastern Ontario. In the absence of a department of Music, musical performance at Bishop's depended entirely on the annual intake of musical talent, but there were still strong music programs in the secondary schools at the time. In 1964, for example, a folksinging trio of John Piper, Roma Baran, and Peter Walford won the award for best performance at the annual Macdonald Folksong Festival. Piper was to go on that year to compose the music for the legendary *Ookpik* musical revue, which benefited from the support of a 16-piece orchestra. Again, over 20 percent of the undergraduates were involved in the production.

Students were also actively participating in athletics. Bishop's intercollegiate teams in football, hockey, men's and women's basketball, golf, and soccer competed at the intermediate level, and the new Scott rink added greatly to the facilities available for intramural competition.

THE PARENT COMMISSION: II

In 1964 the Parent Commission published the second volume of its report. The structural reforms it proposed for higher education were consistent with the principles which it had enunciated: every person had *right* of *access* to all the various fields of knowledge; that, in keeping with a *child-centred* philosophy of education, the adolescent was deemed competent to decide what this right of access entailed; that the need for the social integration of the adolescent took precedence over any advantages which might accrue from streaming students according to their intellectual abilities at pre-university levels; and finally that coherence among the different career paths should be guaranteed by centralized control of programs of instruction. Naturally the proposed reforms were influenced chiefly by the perceived needs of the French-language system of education, but they were to be imposed as well on the English-language system—presumably to ensure, in the words of the report, "a cultural and spiritual unity ... a single world outlook, common attitudes, shared values."[8]

The most radical of these reforms introduced a new pre-university level of education to be dispensed by what the commission called institutes, but which subsequently became collèges d'enseignement général et professionnel, or CEGEPs. These colleges would provide for a majority of high school (grade 11) graduates a twelfth and thirteenth year of instruction, to be followed for the academically inclined by three years of instruction at university to the bachelor's degree level. The first cohort of these colleges was to be created by transforming the *collèges classiques*, which were "invited" to "become integral parts of greater and truly comprehensive entities." These entities would be open to a very wide range of intellectual abilities, and the prescribed classical curriculum would be replaced by a system of electives "sufficiently flexible and diversified for students arriving at university to have the benefit of all the courses they need, all of them of excellent quality."[9] The CEGEPs were conceived as an autonomous level of education, in which the curricula were not to be unduly influenced by the prejudices of university faculties. The *Diplôme des études collègiales* was to be the only criterion for admission to any university Faculty, and the commission deemed it essential that "a unified pedagogical authority, vested with real power" should direct the education provided by the CEGEPs.[10]

At the time, entrance to Medicine and Law in the French-language universities required completion of a classical B.A., and it was principally to ensure that none of the classical colleges attempted to ignore the reform and continue as independently financed institutions that the minister of education was to be given authority over the requirements for admission to university faculties.

The implications of these new institutions for Quebec's English-language universities were enormous. In 1964 the English-language system of publicly financed education provided secondary schooling to a twelfth year of instruction in the cities, and generally to an eleventh year elsewhere in Quebec. The universities admitted graduates of grade 11 to a four-year program leading to the degrees of Bachelor of Arts and Bachelor of Science, and they allowed up to one year of university credit for candidates achieving adequate standing in the senior high-school leaving examinations (grade 12). This corresponded in general to the systems of the other Canadian provinces and allowed graduates of the English-speaking secondary schools to gain admission on equal terms to universities in the other provinces.

The initial reaction of the English-speaking community to the proposed reform was almost entirely negative. The universities doubted that teachers could be found to provide the postulated range of elective courses of excellent quality, and they feared loss of control over academic standards. Some administrators perceived that the new institutions might provide a less traumatic transition from the close supervision and prescribed curriculum of secondary schooling to the comparative independence and freedom of choice in the university, and thus improve the preparation and orientation of prospective matriculants and reduce the high failure rate in the first year of university work. However, the English-language CEGEPs would have to be developed from scratch, since there were no institutions to serve as nuclei, and English-speaking students (and their parents), unlike their French-speaking counterparts, had the option of leaving the province for their post-secondary education. On the other hand, the government now provided most of the money for post-secondary education, and the political climate made it extremely unlikely that the minister of education would consent to exempt the English-language system from the proposed reform. Without enthusiasm, the English-language post-secondary institutions (ELPSI) formed a consultative group to work with the minister to ease the transition to the new regime.

These developments were particularly unsettling for Bishop's. As well as inserting an autonomous level of education between the high schools and the universities, the commission proposed the amalgamation of small rural high schools into large—in some cases, very large—multifaceted secondary schools which would be required to cope with a very broad spectrum of intellectual ability and interest. Bishop's feared the loss of the close liaison which, through the work of the Graduate School of Education, the university had established with a great many small high schools in the province. Since these schools often offered only Grade XI, Bishop's had a comparatively large first year (twelfth year of instruction), and over half the undergraduates were following twelfth and thirteenth years of instruction in Arts and Science. As the ministerial committees began to flesh out the curricula for the CEGEPs, it became evident that influential members of these committees considered that Bishop's, with its excellent facilities for a residential academic community, could make the most valuable contribution to the reformed system by surrendering its charter as a university and becoming the CEGEP for the English-language community in mainland Quebec.

These men maintained that Bishop's was too small to be able to offer the highly specialized first degree they believed should be the goal of undergraduate education under the new dispensation. It would take seven years of patient but determined lobbying to obtain from the Conseil des Universités the university's *lettres de noblesse* as an institution providing education to the less specialized degree which the commission had specifically recommended as an alternative in keeping with the spirit of the reform.[11] In the meantime, uncertainty as to the university's future added considerably to the stress on faculty and administration.

CHANGING MORES AND STUDENT DISCIPLINE

The character of the undergraduate society Ogden Glass inherited did not differ greatly from that of which he had been a part in the thirties. Women now made up 40 percent of the enrolment, and they were provided with a fair share of the residences on campus. They participated vigorously in many extra-curricular activities, but student government was still largely a male preserve, and some members of the Executive Committee viewed the increasing percentage of women with alarm. The maintenance of discipline was in the hands of the principal and the professors, several of whom were deans of residence, and it was still possible for members of faculty to know their students well enough to exert some influence on their behaviour. *The Campus* was new to Ogden Glass, but the content of the paper still conformed largely to the editorial policy enunciated in 1944 by its godfather, J.D. Jefferis: "*The Campus* is neither an instrument of revolution nor an organ of reaction. It proposes neither to reform nor to perpetuate abuses. It has no axe to grind—it proposes to revile no-one, from Mr Dewhurst down to the humblest of professors."[12] Moreover, a sense of humour was still thought to be a desirable attribute for its editor, in happy contrast with the policies of the student newspapers at several of the larger universities.

However, Glass was not satisfied with the tone of the undergraduate community. The bill for wanton damage in the residences had become excessive, and he took steps to reinforce residence supervision. Alcohol was still forbidden on campus, and in consequence the activities of off-campus drinking clubs in North Hatley were damaging the university's reputation in the community. In dealing with this problem and coping with much more difficult situations which developed later in the decade, the principal was consistently an apostle of moderate reform. Many of the parents of undergraduates had chosen to send their offspring to Bishop's because it was a residential university which still accepted some responsibility for students' behaviour on campus, and the senior members of Corporation still expected civility from members of the university. On the other hand, graduates were going out into a society whose moral standards were under attack, in which alcohol in particular was increasingly employed to oil the wheels of commerce and industry. Glass felt that the university must try to prepare undergraduates to respond with maturity to the pressures to which they would be exposed in their careers.

His response to the drinking problem was to allow male undergraduates who met the legal age limit to have a quiet drink in their rooms and to increase the severity of sanctions against drinking to excess. His philosophy was neatly summed up by a phrase in a memorandum prepared for the guidance of male students: "In general, any breach of common sense will be regarded as a breach of the college rules." Unfortunately, common sense would by the end of the decade be in short supply.

During the first half of the decade, general responsibility for discipline of male undergraduates was delegated to a discipline committee composed of five members of faculty and the registrar, and chaired by Arthur Motyer. The women had their own dean of residence. Motyer's work with the undergraduates in the production of plays over a period of 15 years had given him a perceptive understanding of the undergraduate psyche and a marked sympathy for the problems of undergraduates in adapting themselves to life on campus. On the other hand, he set great store by Bishop's "backbone in history," and in his contacts with reform-minded SECs he was at pains to persuade them that the reform of the "great and continuing life of the university" (which he agreed was necessary) must be guided by men who had longer terms of service to the university than had the officers of student governments. Extra-curricular life on campus was thus ultimately under the control of a benevolent hierarchy of men who were well informed about and sincerely interested in undergraduate problems. They were usually willing to discuss suggestions for change; but they felt under no obligation to justify their decisions to any student representatives.

As undergraduate enrolment increased and it became more difficult for members of faculty to know their students other than as faces in a classroom, this paternalistic regime came under increasing pressure. The problem that would finally render it untenable first appeared in administrative correspondence in 1964. Women were now able to dine with men, and the large common room in the new student union building (Bishop Mountain House) was also open to both sexes. However, the converse which a number of men and women undergraduates were now seeking on campus required a less public setting. Common rooms in some of the residences were open to "mixed companionship" during restricted hours. In October 1964 the SEC requested that all common rooms should be open to men and women throughout the day and evening. The council seems to have assumed that men and women who preferred the informal society of their own sex should be satisfied with their residence bedrooms.

A month later the house committee of Abbott Hall, a male residence with no common room, wrote to the principal to propose the "controlled admission" of women to their residence bedrooms. The argument of the students, who were all seniors, was strictly pragmatic. They pointed out that some 20 percent of the undergraduates, in search of mixed drinking and semi-privacy, were participating in the week-end activities of the drinking clubs in North Hatley. Nor were outdoor drinking parties on the golf course uncommon. Would it not be more civilized to hold, for example, sherry parties in undergraduate rooms before dances on campus, under the control of the house committee? The principal replied promptly and sympathetically, but he did not commit himself to any course of action.

As Glass remarked in his reply, this was a most difficult and delicate question. That he was willing to consider it at all placed him well to the liberal side of a great many parents and several of the most influential trustees. Undergraduates matriculated at 17, and the student body was one of the youngest in Canada. He believed that the great majority would respond to his appeal for common sense, but that the university's reputation would inevitably be governed by the behaviour of the small minority whom the community had not yet succeeded in civilizing. It was in any case becoming increasingly difficult to enforce existing residence rules, and the deans of residence were beginning to raise the fundamental issue of whether the university could continue to accept the responsibility of acting *in loco parentis*.

The SEC's request for open common rooms had to be set against the observation that the activities of the more enthusiastic couples were already making the common rooms unattractive to a majority of residents. On the other hand there was, as the Abbott house committee pointed out, no place on campus where a man and a woman could study or work on assignments alone together. The problem was to retain the necessary minimum control. By now the benevolent hierarchy would have been delighted to be able to hand over responsibility to the students—and this solution was being proposed with increasing insistency by successive student governments—but experience had shown that regimes proposed in good faith by one student government could prove unenforceable by its successor. A constituency was also developing among both faculty and students that held that the university should no longer regard itself as a moral enterprise and that the social relations of at least the older undergraduates were their own private business.

During the next three years failure to achieve a mutually satisfactory solution to the problem of mixed sexes in the residences generated increasingly severe stress on relations between the undergraduates and the administration, and pressure continued to build in support of the right of undergraduates to take full responsibility for their social behaviour. Events elsewhere were to extend this pressure to include the right of students to participate in the academic administration of the university.

COLLEGIAL GOVERNMENT

Since Canadians had come be perceive higher education as the key to realising all the country's hopes for the future, provincial politicians had vied with one another to promote the rapid growth of the universities under their jurisdiction, and the funding of both the operating expenses and capital needs of the universities had become chiefly a public responsibility.

For universities governed by private corporations, such as Bishop's, this represented a major change. Since the time of Principal McGreer the expansion of the university had been funded mainly by leaders of Quebec's English-speaking financial and industrial community, and most of the trustees had been drawn from their ranks. These men had been content to leave academic matters entirely in the hands of the principal and the faculty, but Corporation decided such matters as building programs and the authorization of new faculty positions, and many of them had strong views on the overall character of the university.

Henceforward, operating revenues and capital grants would depend chiefly on political considerations, and salary scales, which were the major items in the list of operating expenses, would be determined by negotiation with the government. It now seemed reasonable that faculty members should participate in discussion of financial matters affecting the academic life of the institution.

In response to this development, the Canadian Association of University Teachers (CAUT) collaborated with the Association of Universities and Colleges of Canada (AUCC) to establish a commission to study university governance in Canada and make recommendations for its reform. The members of the commission were Sir James Duff, formerly vice-chancellor of the University of Durham, and Dr R.A. Berdahl of San Francisco State College, and their report strongly favoured the democratization of university government.[13] They recommended that governing boards should be opened to representatives of the academic staff and of the concerned public and that departmental chairs and faculty deans should be elected by members of faculty instead of being appointed by the administration. Their recommendations were timely, since the government of universities had become a subject for general debate both within and outside the academic community. The Parent Commission had also considered the question, and had recommended that both faculty and students should participate in a collegial form of university government.

The need to assign to members of faculty primary responsibility for the academic policies at Bishop's had been recognized in 1964 by the establishment of a senate composed of eight members elected by and from the faculty, the principal, the vice-principal, the deans of the faculties, and the Bishop of Quebec. Initially it was conceived of as a co-ordinating body for the three faculties and graduate studies and as a less unwieldy replacement for convocation. However, some members of faculty strongly opposed any transfer of powers from convocation, and the extent of Senate's powers was a subject for continuing debate.

In November 1967 a committee which had been appointed by Corporation in 1964 to revise the rules, orders, and regulations (RORs) of the university obtained the approval of Corporation for its seventh draft. In this formulation Senate was to govern the academic life, work, and discipline of the university, subject to the overriding control and jurisdiction of Corporation. Its members were to be the chancellor, the principal, the vice-principal, the deans of the faculties, the head of the Graduate School of Education, the chair of the Committee on Graduate Studies, the librarian, eight members of the Faculty of Arts, and five members of the Faculty of Science. The deans and the vice-principal were still to be appointed by the Executive Committee, but academic policies were to be developed collegially. Under the new dispensation, four tenured members of faculty were to be elected to Corporation by a committee of the faculty as a whole, but no seats were reserved for such members on the Executive Committee, which retained control over expenditures, in particular of salaries. For the first time, regulations were introduced governing appointments and the award of tenure, and the need to discuss such regulations with the BAUT was recognized.

Meanwhile the undergraduates were agitating to be represented at the committee level in the faculties of Arts and Science. A good many members of faculty were unwilling to extend collegiality to include undergraduates, but in the fall term of 1967–68, students were represented on three of Senate's sub-committees. However, the Student's Executive Council noted that the principal was still the only channel of communication between the governing bodies of the university and the undergraduates, and that the channel was in consequence seriously overloaded. The council urged that minutes of the meetings of the governing bodies should be made public, and recommended student participation on the building committee and the library committee as well as on faculty committees. The administration's response was to establish yet another consultative liaison committee to "increase dialogue." The president of the SEC agreed to sit on this committee, but most of the council's members were rapidly losing patience with what they regarded as delaying tactics by the administration.

Though the diffusion of responsibility into the academic community was as yet only in its initial stages, one consequence of democratization was already evident—a rapid increase in the time devoted to committee work by faculty members and undergraduates. At the administrative level this was compounded by the need for Bishop's to defend its ethos and justify its financial needs on the ministry's numerous committees. As a result, not nearly enough energy was available for curriculum development and for facing the challenge of the CEGEPs.

NEW FACILITIES: THE BISHOP'S 70 CAMPAIGN

In 1963 Philip Scowen had warned the president of Corporation that capital expenditure of the order of $4 million would be necessary to provide facilities for the enrolment of 750 students forecast for 1967–68. In November 1966 the chair of the finance committee reported to Corporation that the university had spent or committed over $2 million on the extension to the A.S. Johnson Science Building and on Dewhurst Hall, in the expectation that the government would eventually provide grants to cover the expenditure. Now faced with the prospect of finding space for a thousand students by 1970, Corporation decided that another financial campaign was necessary. A.O. Mackay, a member of Corporation, accepted the chair of the Bishop's 70 Campaign, and he was ably seconded by R.R. McLernon as vice-chair and by J.H. Price, who had succeeded John Molson as president of Corporation in 1965. Under their stimulating leadership, some $3 million was raised by the end of 1969. With these funds and with the aid of continuing major capital grants from the government, the new wing of the A.S. Johnson building, the Dewhurst dining complex, a second and a third men's residence on the south side (Kuehner and Munster), and the Centennial Theatre were completed, and a new wing to the Bassett Library was begun.

Centennial Theatre represented the culmination of Arthur Motyer's work since 1950 to establish a tradition of excellence in dramatic performance at Bishop's. The theatre, designed to his specifications, included a 600-seat amphitheatre and a stage which could be adapted for both thrust and proscenium arch performance. It was at the time the most versatile facility on any university campus in Canada, and the architects had also succeeded in producing a modern building whose strong simple forms and vertical groining were nevertheless in harmony with the more traditional architecture of the older buildings on campus.

The theatre was opened officially in January 1967 at a special convocation at which six distinguished Canadian representatives of the arts received honourary degrees from Chancellor D.C. Abbott. Robertson

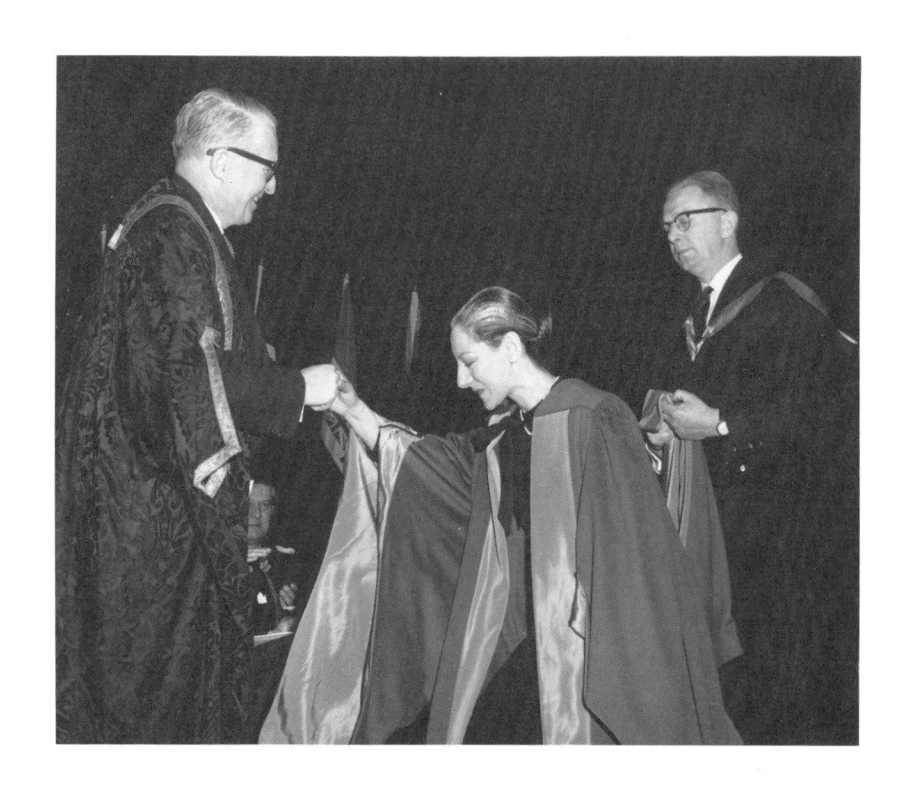

Chancellor Abbott and Celia Franca. Inauguration of Centennial Theatre, 1967

Davies chaired a symposium in the course of which the honorands discussed the value and the state of the arts in Canada in the nation's centennial year. Particularly pertinent to the occasion was the contribution of Jon Vickers, who pleaded for wider participation in artistic activity, which would he felt produce much needed confidence in artistic judgment: "We must take our art off its cold impersonal marble pedestal, we should handle it and learn to love it."[14] This had been Motyer's creed. To increase and to raise the standard of undergraduate participation in the theatre arts had been his goal, and many of his students carried their love of the theatre with them into their subsequent careers.

CONFRONTATION

Ogden Glass believed that the agitation to admit women to the men's residences was not broadly based. In particular, he suspected that the proposals emanating from the male-dominated SEC did not accurately reflect the opinion of women undergraduates. Early in 1966 the Executive Committee was persuaded to appoint a committee to examine the facilities and the rules and regulations affecting women students and to make such recommendations for change as they might consider desirable.

The three members, Marjorie Donald, who chaired the committee, Mary Chinn, and Vera Pederzoli, were all university graduates with considerable experience of undergraduate life and a lively concern for undergraduate problems. In April 1967, after a thorough study of the situation at Bishop's and at several other universities where women lived in residence, they presented a comprehensive report to the Executive Committee. Observing that the importance of common rooms in the social life of the undergraduates "could not be overemphasized," they urged the establishment of several new rooms to respond to a variety of needs—socializing, recreation, reading and discussion—and to include at least one large lounge for women only.[15] During the following summer, the administration responded by converting the former Mackinnon dining hall to a mixed common room and restricting the Mackinnon common room to women. In so doing, it gave priority to the recommendations of the Donald Committee over those of a joint faculty-student common room committee which had been established during the previous year.

This decision did not improve relations between the SEC and the administration when the students returned to the campus in September. The elections of the previous March for the officers of the SEC and the editor of *The Campus* had produced an unusually talented team of undergraduate leaders—four of them would proceed overseas on post-graduate scholarships in 1968—who were able to give eloquent expression to the discontent of their constituents.

In contrast to the situation at several of the larger Canadian universities at the time, the politically active fraction of the Bishop's undergraduate body did not support the iconoclastic philosophy and revolutionary rhetoric spawned by the civil tensions generated in the United States by the war in Viet Nam. The incoming president of the SEC, Andrew Sancton, had been in favour of the decision of the Student Association to withdraw from the militant Canadian Union of Students on the grounds that the student government had no mandate to represent its constituents on political questions which were not of direct concern to students. Even the decision of the SEC, after intense debate, to recommend that Bishop's join l'Union générale des étudiants du Québec (UGEQ) was narrowly repudiated at a meeting of the Student's Association called to ratify it. There was very little support on campus for the politically committed syndicalist philosophy of the student governments of the French-language universities, who controlled the policies of the UGEQ.

On the other hand, many Bishop's undergraduates were increasingly determined to obtain a measure of self-government in the matter of social relations on campus. As the editor of *The Campus* observed: "Students are agitated, even frustrated, not because they don't have women in their rooms—everybody knows that they do—but because the administration refuses to recognize the fact."[16] He went on to enunciate the widely held student opinion that the numerous "joint" committees had been convened not to consider the question but to delay consideration.

In October 1967 the SEC called a meeting of the Student Asociation to obtain support for a recommendation that women be admitted to the men's residences at stated hours. Restrictions were otherwise limited to maintaining unlocked room doors, but the SEC pledged to rigidly enforce both hours and restrictions. Pointing out that previous resolutions on the question had produced no visible result, James Mabbutt, a member of the university's excellent debating team, moved an amendment that the students *demand* that the administration agree to the proposal by mid-November failing which the SEC would recommend suspension of all students' responsibility for discipline in residence after the Christmas holidays. After prolonged debate the association voted nearly unanimously to include the deadline but rejected the threat to suspend student supervision. When no reply was received from the principal by 15 November, about 60 placard-waving undergraduates, including

Mabbutt, Sancton, and the editor of *The Campus*, Peter Yearwood, staged an orderly march around the campus and a five-minute sit-in in the hall outside the principal's office.

In comparison with the demonstrations that were becoming commonplace at other Canadian universities, this was a very mild challenge to constituted authority; but a challenge of this kind was unprecedented at Bishop's. The principal did not speak to the gathering, but in due course a notice appeared on the bulletin boards that residence regulations would be strictly enforced. Shortly afterward a male and a female undergraduate were punished with unusual severity for a breach of the regulations. There is little doubt that most of the Executive Committee approved of the principal's response, and the Donald Committee had also been extremely wary of permitting female visitors to the men's rooms.

In January Ogden Glass announced to the undergraduates that he had obtained the Executive Committee's approval to work out a plan whereby senior male students might receive women in their rooms "with adequate safeguards and sanctions," but he made it clear that this was to be regarded as a privilege, which the undergraduates must earn by proving themselves responsible and generating effective enforcement of the regulations. As he explained to the Executive Committee, his aim was "to guide the undergraduates as gracefully as possible into civilized social practices whereby men and women can meet in privacy and decency and in the way nothing can prevent them from meeting upon graduation. Surely this is an educational process."[17]

This olive branch was greeted with derision by *The Campus*, whose editor flatly rejected the principal's view that he must act as a guardian of undergraduate morals. For the rest of the academic year *The Campus* was a thorn in the flesh of the administration. Though the quality of the writing in the paper remained remarkably high, many of the articles were provocative, and in February Yearwood infuriated the principal by publishing a shortened version of the notorious article "The Student as Nigger," which had been written by a professor at California State College in Los Angeles and widely reprinted in student newspapers. Yearwood insisted that his goal was not to overthrow the existing administrative structure but to achieve the means to modify it by negotiation, but the principal believed that the purpose of the article was to provoke the administration into precipitate action which could then be used to raise the level of student activism. Although he did not rise to the bait, his patience was sorely tried.

Ogden Glass had observed that the rapid growth of enrolment had rendered ineffective the traditional informal co-ordination of the several bodies responsible for student discipline. During the summer of 1968 he worked with the SEC to develop a more rational system with clearly defined responsibilities. Henceforward, student dons and student house committees would be responsible for all disciplinary matters in residence, and the highest disciplinary body for students in the university would be a discipline board composed of four students elected by the Student Association and two members of faculty appointed by the principal in consultation with the SEC. The principal retained the right to intervene at any level in the disciplinary structure, but he hoped that the new student officers would shoulder their responsibilities and reduce the need to intervene to a minimum. In September he introduced new regulations under which all but first year women undergraduates were permitted to visit the rooms of male undergraduates in the evenings.

FACULTY DISCONTENT

The fall term of 1968–69 proved to be relatively tranquil on the disciplinary front, but financial exigency and the uncertain future of the university were in any case rapidly replacing the undergraduates as the principal's chief concerns. In March 1968 the government had for the first time overtly discriminated against the English-language universities in the matter of operating grants. For six years the French-language universities had benefited from much larger operating grants per student than the English-language universities, which had tacitly accepted the fact that such *rattrapage* was necessary for the French-language system to overcome the effects of years of neglect. However, since 1965 a university grants committee chaired by the excellent Germain Gauthier had been moving toward a more equitable distribution of grants per student. In 1968 the minister of finance decreed that the recommendations of the Gauthier committee were too expensive, and in the somewhat overheated political climate of the time the government found it expedient to require the English-language universities to bear over 90 percent of the reductions he imposed.

As a result, the Bishop's budget committee, meeting during the winter of 1968–69, faced an extremely bleak prospect. Enrolment had increased to 1,022 undergraduates, and the academic administration was pressing for the establishment of new academic positions. On the other hand, the faculty were asking for improved salary scales to more nearly match those at other Quebec universities. In December 1968 the Faculty Association submitted a resolution to the annual meeting of Corporation expressing its "extreme dissatisfaction" that the budget committee had not implemented the association's proposed salary scales in the budget the university had submitted to the government. In another resolution passed at a general meeting, the association recommended that no additional members of faculty be engaged until these salary scales could be fully implemented.

One of the most respected of the senior members of faculty, Dallas Laskey, posed three questions to the meeting of Corporation which provided its members with a clear indication of the causes and extent of faculty dissatisfaction.

Laskey asked first if there was any planning at any level of the university to meet "emergency situations." He noted that a number of members of faculty, disturbed by the rapid and sometimes turbulent changes in Quebec society, were entertaining grave doubts about the future of the university. They believed that the true situation was not known, and that there was no attempt to meet the recent developments. Rumours were also rife that the government might withdraw its support from the university, that Bishop's would become a CEGEP, or that pressures from outside would succeed in changing the entire pattern of education at Bishop's.[18] As a result of this general feeling of insecurity (some members of faculty were already looking for employment outside the province), Laskey urged that it would help the present state of faculty morale if some assurance could be given that the Corporation was fully aware of the situation and that some planning was in process.

Second, Laskey pointed out that it was becoming increasingly difficult to attract and keep faculty of high quality. Since it was unlikely that the Bishop's salary scales and facilities for research would become truly competitive with those of the larger universities, Corporation might consider whether other local advantages might be exploited—for example an expanded program of faculty housing, which would be particularly attractive to young scholars whose financial resources had been strained by long years of postgraduate study.

Finally, he asked: "How can we find more effective ways for faculty and Corporation to communicate? The present arrangement [the annual meeting], as pleasant as it is, does not seem to be the most effective way of bringing about an interchange of ideas."

The principal observed that the points raised by Dr Laskey were excellent. So that they would not be *overlooked* or *forgotten*, he suggested that Laskey write a letter to Corporation expanding somewhat on his three points. The principal's response provided ample confirmation that Laskey's concerns were justified. Neither the Corporation nor the administration had faced up to the imminent establishment of English-language CEGEPs under the direct control of the ministry. That Laskey's analysis of the temper of the faculty might be in danger of being overlooked or forgotten by Corporation was a striking illustration of the still-existing barriers between the governing body and the academic community.

THE PRINCIPAL RESIGNS

It had been a difficult year, and the principal's report to Corporation at the annual meeting showed evidence that the high stress level was beginning to take a toll of his reserves of patience. He had bitterly resented the damage he felt the actions of the SEC and the columns of *The Campus* had done to the reputation of his Alma Mater, and he inveighed against the "tiny minority of destructive activists" who had been harassing him, describing them as "windy nihilists" whose "poisonous and quite frightening rectitude" reminded him of the young Nazis and Communists he had met in Europe during the thirties.[19] Unhappily this was the first meeting of Corporation to which the president of the SEC and the president of women had been invited. The relevant portions of the report found their way into the columns of *The Campus* at the beginning of the winter term along with the "surprise and consternation" with which the SEC had taken note of them. However, by this time it was evident that the principal's outburst had been an indication that his health was giving way. In January his doctor advised him to take three months leave of absence. In May, finding no improvement, he resigned.

Ogden Glass had been singularly unfortunate. Appointed to maintain the university's traditional role in higher education in Quebec, he had had to defend the Bishop's ethos against a strongly interventionist ministry of education which increasingly controlled the purse strings and whose bureaucrats considered liberal education on the Bishop's model to be elitist and antisocial. He believed strongly that education must include character as well as intellect and that life in a residential academic community was an ideal milieu for developing social maturity in adolescents. He was fated to see the idea of a university as a moral enterprise become untenable. Throughout his tenure he had striven "to contain the activist movement; sort out as objectively as we could what was warrantable in their requests; deny any demands; and at all costs keep our patience."[20] As one of his flock admitted rather ruefully in *The Campus*, "We find that [Dr Glass] is, contrary to our activist opinions, indeed a very wise man. He has stalemated us into being what we really should be, temperate and slow to act. This is called The Politics of Arbitration and Reconciliation."[21] Thanks to the principal's patient negotiating, Bishop's survived the decade without the violent ruptures in the academic community of several other Canadian universities.

PRINCIPAL PRESTON

Anthony Preston was appointed to carry out Ogden Glass' duties during his leave of absence. When it became clear that the principal would not return, it was much too late in the year to begin a search for a replacement. The president of Corporation asked Dean Jellicoe to call a meeting of Senate to consider the immediate replacement of the principal and the establishment of a search committee to find a new principal for the 1970–71 academic year.

Senate recommended that Preston be appointed principal forthwith and that the search committee be composed of two persons chosen by the Corporation, two chosen by the Senate, two chosen by the faculty, one chosen by the SEC, and one chosen by the national executive of the Bishop's Alumni Association. This proposal, which represented a significant move in the direction of collegial government, was accepted by the Executive Committee.

Tony Preston was in his sixty-seventh year. He had welcomed his 1960 appointment as dean of Arts as an opportunity to meet undergraduates in a broader context than the study of classics. During his tenure he managed to have properly recorded annual interviews with nearly every undergraduate in Arts—over 550 during the 1964–65 academic year. He nevertheless retained his responsibility for the course in Greek civilization which was still compulsory for all first-year students. In 1965 he had succeeded Albert Kuehner as vice-principal and had had to give up teaching. He then seems to have assumed most of the final responsibility for academic administration as well as for much of the domestic economy of the institution. The records contain many of his lucid and concise memoranda, the more remarkable in that his eyesight, never good, had seriously deteriorated, and his handwriting had in consequence become difficult to decipher.

Preston needed almost immediately to draw on the faculty's considerable confidence in him. In December 1968 Dr Jean-Paul Plante, a popular lecturer in French, had not been offered reappointment on the grounds that he had almost totally neglected his responsibility for the evaluation of student work and had been unavailable for departmental meetings. In an interview given to *La Tribune* in Sherbrooke, Plante alleged that he had been discriminated against because he was a French-Canadian and because he refused to comply with departmental norms. *The Campus* seized upon the case as a convenient stick with which to beat the "bureaucratic" administration, and in a special edition listed Plante's quite impressive curriculum vitae with a number of enthusiastically favourable comments by undergraduates. It was not difficult for the prin-

Anthony William Preston, 1968

cipal to refute the charge of discrimination, but Plante's case became a matter of intense debate among members of faculty.

Rapid expansion had changed the character of the faculty. Half the full-time faculty in 1969 had less than four years' service, and it had become increasingly difficult to identify a Bishop's academic tradition which might have served as a unifying influence. A majority of them had not yet established themselves in their discipline, and there seemed to be little prospect of doing so under existing conditions at Bishop's— even if the institution were to escape transformation into a CEGEP by ukase of the ministry of education. As a result, the BAUT had been converted into a more militant association, the Bishop's University Faculty Association (BUFA), which from its inception sought to establish itself as the representative voice of the faculty in negotiations with the administration and the Executive Committee. In February 1969, 55 of the 80 full-time members of faculty attended a meeting of BUFA, and a bare majority of those present voted to recommend to the administration that an independent committee, whose composition must be approved by BUFA, Plante, and the administration, be appointed to examine the case. If this committee had not reported by 15 March, Plante should be reappointed for the 1969–70 year.

Another motion recognizing that Plante had given the administration cause for concern by his neglect of his duties had received unanimous support. What many members objected to was the fact that the recommendation that Plante should be let go had come from the head of the Department of Modern Languages and had been confirmed by the dean of Arts, both of whom had been appointed by administration. In the developing climate of insecurity it seemed increasingly important both that deans and heads of departments should be elected by the faculty and that decisions to terminate appointments should be subject to appeal. When the administration refused to reopen the case, BUFA referred it to the CAUT, whose investigating committee concluded that Bishop's had been justified in refusing to reappoint Plante, but urged that procedures should be established to permit appeal from decisions to terminate appointments.

At the beginning of the fall term, Preston's diplomatic skills were again called into play. The SEC had continued to press for student representation in the deliberations of the faculties. Finding that the Faculty of Arts was in favour but the Faculty of Science was opposed, Senate had temporized, but in October the issue came to a head and Senate voted down a motion to recommend student representation. In protest the SEC attempted to organize a three-day boycott of classes, during which "teach-ins" were addressed by several of the younger members of faculty, but the boycott soon petered out. The principal had refused to convene an emergency meeting of Senate in response to the threat of boycott, and during the next six weeks Senate was quietly persuaded to reconsider. In November Senate recommended student representation if the faculties agreed, and in December the Executive Committee agreed to amend the RORs accordingly.

Though these conflicts were time and energy consuming, they were peripheral to the major crisis facing the university. In September students from grade 11 were enrolled for the first time in a CEGEP-equivalent program. What effect would the insertion of the two CEGEP years have on future enrolment in the new university program, and what were the government's intentions with respect to Bishop's University?

THE CEGEP-EQUIVALENT PROGRAM

In 1967 James Whitelaw was seconded from Sir George Williams University to the ministry of education, with the responsibility of co-ordinating the development of university programs during the period of transition while English-language CEGEPs were being created. In answer to Whitelaw's invitation, Ogden Glass wrote to him in October 1967 to express the university's considered opinion that the least unsatisfactory solution would see the universities simultaneously introducing the two years of the general (non-technical) CEGEP program to replace their current first-year programs. As CEGEPs were established, the universities would phase out these collegial programs. It was assumed that the government would continue to fund the existing faculty establishment during the "temporary" decrease in enrolment following the hiving off of the CEGEP students.

At this stage the administration apparently believed that the *diplôme des études collégiales* (DEC), which was to establish the entrance standard to the new three-year B.A.-B.Sc. program, would be roughly equivalent to the senior high school leaving certificate (grade 12), so that no significant revision of the current university programs would be necessary. However, as the ministry's curriculum committees began to flesh out the CEGEP programs, it became evident that the ministry was determined to make full use of the extra year of instruction the Parent Commission had introduced. Moreover in February 1968 Nancy Brodie, another member of the remarkable 1967–68 SEC, obtained strong student support for the recommendations in her comprehensive and well thought-out report on educational policy. One of these urged the administration and the faculty to give full support to the CEGEP system, to work for the co-ordination of the English and French sides of the system, and to take advantage of the new regime to raise the requirements and standard of the Bishop's degree.

Senate had begun to discuss the prospect of CEGEPs in 1967, but it was not until May 1968 that the Senate planning committee noted that "a reassessment of the aims and purposes of Bishop's University is urgently required and should be the result of a combined effort of Corporation, administration, faculty and students."[22] Principal Glass as chair of Senate duly transmitted this recommendation to the Executive Committee, where it sank without trace. In November Senate finally requested department heads to submit their proposals for the CEGEP-equivalent program to the Senate planning committee. When the program was approved in May 1969 for implementation in September, it differed from the then-current first- and second-year programs in only one significant respect. The first-year courses in Greek civilization and on the role of Christianity in the development of western civilization were no longer compulsory, and the Bishop's ethos, already under attack from within and without, was deprived of the common nurture which had been a unifying factor since the founding of the university.

Another unifying factor which came under fire in 1969 was the wearing of academicals. Members of faculty and undergraduates had always worn gowns to lectures, tutorials, and meals as a mark of their common membership in a community of learning. For the undergraduates, gowns had the added advantage of concealing the state (and the quality) of their clothing. When the Student Association was consulted on the matter in October 1969, 61.6 percent voted in favour of retaining the gowns. However, many of those who had opposed were intransigent, and a number of recently appointed faculty declined to wear gowns. In the climate of the time it would not have been practical to enforce the rule, and so another tradition of the university was allowed to lapse.

In December 1968 the dean of Arts, Ian Campbell, had urged Senate to undertake detailed planning to prepare for the strengthening of the university's programs which the improved preparation of first-year students coming from the CEGEPs would in theory make possible. Since his appointment in 1965 he had been attempting, with only lukewarm support from the administration and most of his colleagues, to generate a serious study—and a potentially comprehensive revision—of the program in Arts. Nothing concrete had resulted, and this most recent proposal also failed. Many of his colleagues shared his doubts about the academic standards of the instruction in the newly established CEGEPs, and they were not yet ready to consider what incentive Bishop's might offer to induce young Quebeckers to stay in Quebec and undertake the extra year of study to the B.A.-B.Sc. level which the new regime imposed.

John Herbert Price

The failure of the makers of academic policy to respond more adequately to the introduction of the CEGEP was at least in part due to the uncomfortable, not to say hostile, environment in which the university was now functioning. Bishop's, with its small enrolment, its comparatively high admission requirements, its Anglo-Establishment history, and its high proportion of students in residence, was regarded by the ministry's ideologues as an elitist institution, and there were few more pejorative adjectives in their lexicon. In an effort to respond to the new climate, the governing bodies of the university had vigorously pursued the policy of expansion decided upon in 1963, and a large number of new faculty positions had been authorized. However, since government grants were now the major source of revenue, it was not possible to make firm offers of employment until the amount of the grant was known. As the cost of the great educational reform spiralled upward, the government found it more and more difficult to reach a decision on university grants. In his report to Corporation on the 1967–68 academic year, the dean of Arts noted that the administration had not been able to make firm offers until well into the spring, by which time the most promising candidates had been taken by other universities. As a result, in his opinion, "far too many completely inexperienced faculty had been engaged."[23]

In a further attempt to accept the "social responsibility" which the ministry expected of the reformed educational system—that is, to provide places for some of the several thousand English-speaking grade 11 graduates whom the ministry wished to see enrolled in CEGEPs in 1969—the minimum average for admission to CEGEP I at Bishop's had been lowered to 60 percent. In spite of this, the intake in September was 197 students, less than two thirds of the first-year class of 312 in September 1968. Since 296 of the latter were still on campus, forming the *new* first university year, total enrolment had remained steady at 1,021, but the English-language Quebec community was already making evident its mistrust of the new regime.

Another serious consequence of the advent of the CEGEP-equivalent program had been financial exigency. The ministry had decreed that the grant for a CEGEP student at Bishop's would be half that for a university-level student, considerably less than the grant per student allowed Dawson College, the first autonomous English-language CEGEP—but a Bishop's the CEGEP students were being taught by university professors in comparatively small classes. In addition, no candidates for the new first university year would be emerging from any English-language college program in 1970, and a decrease in enrolment at university level had to be anticipated. In order to try to balance the budget for 1970–71, therefore, the finance committee was forced to project an increase of 500 in the CEGEP enrolment at Bishop's in September and a corresponding increase in average class size. In February a deputation from Bishop's waited upon Germain Gauthier, chair of the newly established Conseil des universités, which had been formed to guide the policy of the ministry with respect to university development. Gauthier gave the Bishop's case for a revision of the grant criteria a full and sympathetic hearing, and the principal returned to Lennoxville guardedly optimistic that Bishop's would be treated as a special case. However, in June he was abruptly informed that an order-in-council had restricted total enrolment for 1970–71, including CEGEP students, to one thousand for the purpose of determining grants to Bishop's until its role and function should be redefined. Further, the extension to the John Bassett Library, which was under construction, would not be recognized for either capital or operating grants. Political considerations had evidently triumphed, and unless the new Minister, Guy St Pierre, could be persuaded to reconsider, the university faced an immediate large deficit on the year's operations and a very uncertain future.

THE CHANGING OF THE GUARD

During the latter years of the decade, while the university's traditions were being so sorely buffeted, the Bishop's community had by unhappy coincidence been deprived of the influence of a number of the most effective defenders of those traditions.

In 1967 Philip Scowen had resigned from Corporation. He had served on the Executive Committee since 1946, and had been an active member, then chair of the building committee throughout the years of the rapid expansion of the university's physical facilities, during which his sound judgment and wise counsel had been instrumental in controlling costs and establishing priorities. He had also been a strong supporter of the Bishop's intercollegiate teams, and had been the first chair of the athletics board which was established in 1961.

Arnold Banfill had found in Scowen an effective advocate for the library on the Executive Committee. A keen collector of Canadiana, particularly of books and pamphlets recording the history of the Eastern Townships, he had with C.G. Mackinnon laid the foundations of the library's special historical collections.

Throughout his tenure Philip Scowen had been an outspoken advocate of autonomy and self-sufficiency, and he deplored the influence of

Jeffrey Jefferis, 1960   Philip Scowen, 1956

government financing on the development of the university. In 1961 the chancellor conferred the D.C.L. on him in recognition of his services to Bishop's.

In 1968 Jeffrey Jefferis retired. Since his appointment as Professor of Education in 1944, he had built up the enrolment in the graduate year of teacher training to the largest number for which facilities for practice teaching could be found in the region's English-language schools. The program leading to the degree of Master of Education had been filled out, and in 1964 the department had been expanded into the Graduate School of Education.

The program involved much more practice teaching than was generally required by other teacher training programs at graduate level, and Jeff supervised the practice teaching himself. A classical scholar of demonstrated competence, who had also made his mark as an undergraduate debater, actor, and member of the football team, he was also a gifted teacher who was unsparing in the demands which he made on his trainees. Many of his trenchant comments on their performance have been remembered and are often gleefully recounted at alumni gatherings.

Jefferis' graduates tended to remain active in the teaching profession much longer than average. In 1964, 79 of the 87 men he had trained were still teaching. That the retention rate had been somewhat lower for woman graduates was not due to any lack of dedication, as he remarked, but rather to "marriage and motherhood."[24]

On his retirement his long and distinguished contribution to Bishop's traditions had been recognized by a D.C.L. His address to convocation, in which he dealt faithfully with the turbulent class of 1968, will long be remembered as a model of brevity and wit.

In 1969 it was decided that Bishop's would cease to offer training for Anglican orders. For several years, the authorities of the Anglican Church in Canada had been pressing for the consolidation of theological training at large urban universities, where ecumenical schools of theology could be developed and ordinands could be exposed to the full range of psychological and sociological innovations. Since all candidates for ordination were still sponsored by bishops, there was little the Faculty of Divinity could do to counter the development, and in any case the Faculty was deeply split on the issue.

Sydney Jellicoe, the dean of Divinity, was an established scholar. The distinction of his work on the Septuagint was about to be recognized by his nomination as Grinfield Lecturer at the University of Oxford, the first such nomination of a scholar who was not an Oxbridge graduate. At the request of the Senate planning committee, he had laid out his views on university education in a memorandum entitled "The

Academic and the Practical in the University." In the Bishop's tradition, he held that to teach undergraduates to think was the most *practical* education the university could offer. In his opinion the inculcation of principles must be the goal of every university-level course, and he inveighed against the superficiality of "survey" courses and the proliferation of narrowly focused and largely descriptive courses which encouraged the atomization of knowledge. Senate was unimpressed.

Jellicoe's views on theological training were equally unfashionable. In answer to a reporter from *The Campus*, who asked whether Christianity's moral demands might not have to be adapted "to a modern situation," Jellicoe replied forthrightly that "the message of the Church today is the same as the message of the Prophets in the eighth century B.C. If a thing is right, it's right!" Much more to the popular taste was the view, reported on the same page of *The Campus*, of his colleague in the Faculty of Divinity, W.A. Sadler, who "approached religion as a social scientist," without commitment to any particular doctrine. "Once we get over the notion that religion is a product which you have to sell, once we stop worrying about the religious life of the student, then we can treat religion intelligently."[25] The two points of view were irreconcilable, and in the temper of the times it was inevitable that Sadler's point of view would prevail. The Faculty of Divinity would become the Department of Religion, whose major function would be the scientific and comparative study of religions and their impact on society.

The winds of change of the 1960s had thus profoundly affected the Bishop's ethos. The university would still strive to impart principles and to teach undergraduates to think and to develop their powers of analysis and synthesis, but it would no longer aspire to produce Christian gentlemen and gentlewomen. The only institutional moral imperatives would be integrity in the search for understanding and intellectual rigour in scholarship and teaching.

In 1970 two more of the wheel-horses of the Bishop's enterprise left Bishop's. A fellow Bermudian had endowed a Chair of English at Arthur Motyer's Alma Mater, Mount Allison, and Motyer was persuaded to become the first incumbent. His departure was particularly unfortunate at a time when the policy for the utilization of Centennial Theatre was being developed. Dallas Laskey, another of Jewitt's early appointments, had been profoundly mortified by the role he believed his department had played in generating the boycott of classes earlier in the year. He had resigned forthwith as head of the department of Philosophy, and in June he left for Sir George Williams. Finally, James Gray had obtained a Canada Council fellowship to enable him to finish work on his doctoral thesis, and he would be absent during the critical 1970–71 session.

Chancellor William Mitchell

Bishop's was thus facing an uncertain future with depleted resources. However, not all the signs and portents were negative. The traditionally amicable relations between the French-speaking and English-speaking communities in the Townships had not been shaken by the antics of the radical nationalists in Montreal. In March 1969 le Mouvement pour l'intégration scolaire had mustered many thousands of supporters to march on McGill shouting "McGill français," but when the notorious Stanley Gray attempted to organize a similar march on Bishop's in January 1970 the students of l'Université de Sherbrooke declined to participate. Gray finally turned up at the head of some 85 *illuminés*, mostly from Montreal, to find that, in the words of the principal, "the town population had made preparations on a considerable scale,"[26] and the Sureté du Québec was established in force on the campus. Bishop's undergraduates refused to be drawn, and the evening ended without further incident.

THE NEW DISPENSATION

In October 1969 Alex K. Paterson, chair of the search committee for a new principal, had reported to the president of Corporation that the committee had recommended the appointment of Dr Dennis M. Healy. Healy's name had been submitted to Senate, where it had received unanimous approval. His appointment was authorized by the Executive Committee at a meeting called for the purpose on October ninth.

Dennis Healy was a graduate of the University of Alberta and of l'Université de Paris. He had served with distinction during the 1939–45 war, notably with the partisans in German-occupied territory in Italy. He had had many years of experience in academic administration, as dean of the Faculty of Arts at the University of British Columbia and as academic vice-president of York University. He spoke excellent French and was well known to and highly regarded by senior administrators in Quebec's French-language universities. The appointment was greeted with enthusiasm by *The Campus*. The general opinion was that the committee was to be congratulated on securing a candidate with such excellent qualifications for the negotiations with the ministry and at the Conference of Rectors and Principals of the Universities of Quebec which would determine the future of the university.

When Ian Campbell resigned as dean of Arts in 1969 the Executive Committee requested Senate to establish procedures for selecting a successor and to recommend a candidate. Senate in turn appointed a committee for these purposes, with an additional mandate "to consider and recommend on the nature of the appointment, its terms of reference and duties,"[27] and a representative of the undergraduates was included in the membership.

In order to ensure continuity in the functions of the office, the committee quickly recommended the appointment of D.D. Smith as dean for the 1969–70 academic year, but the larger problem of defining both the nature and responsibilities of the position and the incumbent's relations with the principal and the Senate occupied the committee for the rest of the year. In the meantime, it was decided to advertise the position nationally and abroad.

It was not until January 1970 that the committee was ready to recommend an appointment. Fifty-three candidates had presented themselves, of whom four had been interviewed. The committee had finally decided, by a vote of four to three, to recommend the appointment of Philip Deane, a graduate in classics of the University of Toronto. His referees had spoken highly of "the width and depth of his administrative experience ... his versatility, his talented literary ability, his brilliant scholastic record and ... his good relationship with students."[28] He was fluent in English, French, and Greek.

Questions from senators revealed that Deane had had no experience in academic administration and that his appointment could be regarded as a "calculated gamble"; but it was felt that "a fresh approach and an open mind" might in fact be beneficial.[29] Dennis Healy had been consulted and he approved of Deane's candidacy. Senate voted 15 to two (with two abstentions) in favour of the recommendation, and Deane was duly appointed.

Thus for the first time in the history of the university the principal and the dean of Arts had been appointed on the recommendation of committees broadly representative of the academic community and with nearly unanimous support from Senate. Another broadly representative committee chaired by Alex Paterson was revising the Rules, Orders, and Regulations of the university to bring them into line with the Duff-Berdahl recommendations. It was reasonable to hope that all the constituents of the Bishop's community would work together to cope with the crisis facing the university.

EPILOGUE

The crisis proved to be more severe and lasted much longer than anyone could have foreseen.

In July 1971 the newly constituted Champlain Regional CEGEP, whose Lennoxville Campus was to share the grounds and facilities of Bishop's University, took over the CEGEP years. Bishop's agreed to teach the non-technical college-level courses for Champlain during the 1971–72 session as an interim measure while Champlain recruited its own faculty. The hiving-off of the CEGEP enrolment left Bishop's with a projected enrolment of less than 600 in the three university years in September 1972, and the ministry notified the university that for the 1972–73 session, it would fund only 45 of the 72 authorized faculty positions. Further negotiations postponed the reduction until 1973–74, and the Executive Committee agreed to use the endowment fund to add 12 positions for that session. Nevertheless, a considerable number of faculty appointments had to be terminated. Some of those laid off were taken on by Champlain College.

These events intensified the climate of insecurity which had been developing among the faculty, and the spirit of collegial responsibility which had been the goal of the administrative reforms failed to develop. Relations between the Faculty Association and the administration became very strained, and in 1976 an adversarial relationship was formally recognized by the accreditation of the Association of Professors of Bishop's University as a faculty union under the province's labour laws.

The abrupt reduction in the authorized enrolment in 1970 and the equally abrupt reduction in faculty establishment in 1972 had made it evident that the ministry's bureaucrats were not yet persuaded of the value of liberal education on the Bishop's model. Fortunately, in 1971 the autonomous Conseil des universités had been given the responsibility of defining the mission and orientations of the several universities in the province. Bishop's vigorously defended its liberal traditions before the Conseil, and in 1973 the Conseil recommended that Bishop's be recognized as an institution offering broadly based liberal education in the Arts and Sciences to an undergraduate enrolment which, it was anticipated, would settle at about 1,200 students. The ministry accepted this recommendation, and the Bishop's community was thus relieved of the fear that radical change would be imposed.

Unhappily, enrolment was very slow to recover. English-speaking Quebeckers had not yet acquired confidence in the CEGEPs, and a great many graduates of grade 11 enrolled at universities in the Maritimes or in qualifying years at Ontario universities. In 1976, the Parti québécois led by René Lévesque was elected to form the government of Quebec, and in 1977 the notorious Bill 101, which imposed severe restrictions on access to education in the English language in Quebec, was passed by the Assemblée Nationale. As a result, a large fraction of the English-speaking population of the Montreal conurbation emigrated to Ontario or the west, taking with them their adolescent children. Full-time enrolment at Bishop's did not reach 1,200 until 1986. In the interim, it proved possible, at the expense of what remained of the endowment and with some consideration from the ministry, gradually to rebuild the teaching resources of the university with candidates of excellent attainments, to restore academic standards to pre-crisis levels, and to enrich the curriculum with degree programs in Fine Arts and Music.

During this extremely difficult period Bishop's drew great strength from the loyal support of its community. The support staff defeated two determined attempts to unionize them, and they continued to make a major contribution to the viability of the university by cheerfully and effectively doing whatever needed to be done. Animated by the same spirit, the skeletal administrative echelon coped with domestic emergencies and dealt with the inspirations of the ministry of education at an administrative expense per student far below the average for Quebec's universities. Several members of faculty carried heavy teaching loads.

Undergraduate morale was very little affected by the institution's straitened finances. Arthur Motyer's place was taken by David Rittenhouse and London Green; Ian Gaskell took the operation of Centennial Theatre in hand, and the students continued year after year to produce plays of very high quality. Undaunted by lagging numbers and exiguous budgets, the Bishop's teams, competing now in the Quebec Universities Athletic Association conferences, were increasingly successful, winning more than their share of conference championships in competition with much larger universities. The women's basketball team led the way, winning two national championships. Only hockey had to be abandoned, when the conference voted in 1982 to increase the number of games per year to a level incompatible with the academic responsibilities of full-time students.

Under the leadership of Chancellor John H. Price, funds raised by the Bishop's 70 Campaign, supplemented after many delays by grudging support from the ministry, were used in 1974 to build an athletics complex, which provided excellent facilities for athletic competition and recreation for both Bishop's and Champlain students and greatly increased participation in intramural games. In 1975 Brigadier-General Price, now president of the newly created Bishop's University Foundation, generated another financial campaign to raise funds to increase the income available for scholarships and bursaries, to improve student services, and to reclassify the library's collections to national cataloguing standards. This Opportunity Fund Campaign was equally successful, raising some $3 million. More recently, to enable Bishop's to cope with its present enrolment of 1,650, the Learning for Life Campaign has been mounted. Under the leadership of John Cleghorn, and with notable support from the faculty, the students, and other members of the Bishop's community, over $10 million has been realized.

Thus buttressed by the faith of its community, Bishop's has been gradually restored to its present (1993) robust good health. Quebeckers have come to realize that the education offered by the province's English-language CEGEPs is of excellent quality, and that the CEGEPs provide an intermediate academic regime which greatly eases the transition to study at university level. As a result of the emigration of the 1970s, Bishop's has become better known outside Quebec and enrolment from the other Canadian provinces has more than compensated for the decline in the enrolment in Quebec's English-language school system. Finally, in an employment market in which most university graduates will have to adapt themselves to the challenge of new responsibilities several times during their careers, it has become evident to more and more counsellors of the young that, as Sydney Jellicoe maintained, to teach undergraduates to think, on as broad a front as the individual student can cope with, is indeed the most *practical* education a university can offer.

APPENDIX ONE

THE ACTS RELATING TO BISHOP'S UNIVERSITY

7 VICT. CHAP. 49.
AN ACT TO INCORPORATE "BISHOP'S COLLEGE"
IN THE DIOCESE OF QUEBEC
(9th December, 1843)

Whereas it has been represented to the Legislature of this Province, that divers inhabitants of the said Province have used their efforts to establish a College, in connection with the United Church of England and Ireland, near Lennoxville, in the Township of Ascot, in the District of Saint Francis, and within the Diocese of Quebec, under the style and title of "Bishop's College", and are engaged in erecting and establishing the same; And whereas, it would tend greatly to advance and extend the usefulness of the said College, and to promote the purposes for which it was established, that it should be incorporated; Be it therefore enacted by the Queen's Most Excellent Majesty, by and with the advice and consent of the Legislative Council and of the Legislative Assembly of the Province of Canada, constituted and assembled by virtue of and under the authority of an Act passed in the Parliament of the United Kingdom of Great Britain and Ireland, and intituled: *An Act to re-unite the Provinces of Upper and Lower Canada, and for the Government of Canada:* and it is hereby enacted, by the authority of the same, that there shall be and there is hereby constituted and established, at or near Lennoxville, in the Township of Ascot, in the District of Saint Francis, in the Province, and within the Diocese of Quebec, a Body Politic and Corporate, under the name of "Bishop's College", which Corporation shall consist of— Firstly, the Lord Bishop of Quebec, or other the Superior Ecclesiastical Functionary of the United Church of England and Ireland, in the said Diocese of Quebec; Secondly, the Trustees of the said Bishop's College, not less than three in number, and Thirdly, the College Council of the said Bishop's College, not less than three in number which said Trustees and Members of the said College Council shall be named by the said Lord Bishop of Quebec, or other Superior Ecclesiastical Functionary as aforesaid and shall, in the event of their death, removal from the Province, dismissal from office, or resignation, be replaced by other persons to be named in like manner, and so on continually forever.

II. And be it enacted, that such Corporation shall have perpetual succession and may have a Common Seal, with power to change, alter, break and renew the same when and as often as they shall think proper; and the said Corporation may, under the same name, contract and be contracted with, sue and be sued, implead and be impleaded, prosecute and be prosecuted, in all Courts and places whatsoever in this Province, and shall have full power to make and establish such and so many rules, orders and regulations (not being contrary to the Laws of the Country or to this Act) as they shall deem useful or necessary, as well concerning the system of education in as for the conduct and government of the said College, and of any other Institution or School connected with or dependent on the same, and of the Corporation thereof, and for the superintendence, advantage and improvement of all the property, moveable or immoveable, belonging to, or which shall hereafter belong to, the said Corporation; and shall have power to take, under any legal title whatsoever, and to hold for the said College without any further authority, license or Letters or Mortmain, all land and property moveable or immoveable, which may hereafter be sold, ceded, exchanged, given, bequeathed, or granted to the said Corporation, or to sell, alienate, convey, let or lease the same if need be: Provided always that the net rents, issues, and profits arising from the immoveable property of the said Corporation shall not at any time exceed the annual sum of three thousand pounds current money of this Province: and the said Corporation shall further have the right of appointing an Attorney or Attorneys for the management of their affairs, and generally shall enjoy all the rights and privileges enjoyed by other Bodies Politic and Corporate, recognized by the Legislature: Provided always, that no rule, order or regulation, which shall be made and established by the said Corporation in manner aforesaid shall be of any force or effect until the same shall have been sanctioned and confirmed by the said Lord Bishop or other Ecclesiastical Functionary as aforesaid.

III. And be it enacted that all the property which shall at any time belong to the said Corporation, as well as the revenues thereof, shall at all times be exclusively applied and appropriated to the advancement of education in the said College, and to no other object, institution or establishment whatever, unconnected with or independent of the same.

IV. And be in enacted, that this Act shall be considered a public Act by all Judges, Justices of the Peace, and Officers of Justice, and by all other persons whomsoever, and shall be judicially taken notice of without being specially pleaded.

V. And be it enacted, that this Act shall not extend to weaken, diminish or extinguish the rights and privileges of Her Majesty, Her Heirs and Successors, nor of any other person or persons, Body Politic or Corporate, excepting only such rights as are hereby expressly altered or extinguished.

16 VICT. CHAP. 60.
AN ACT TO AMEND THE ACT INCORPORATING BISHOP'S COLLEGE

(10th November, 1852)

Whereas it is expedient to amend the Act passed in the seventh year of Her Majesty's Reign, intituled, *An Act to incorporate Bishop's College in the Diocese of Quebec,* to confer upon the Bishop of Montreal co-ordinate powers with the Bishop of Quebec, in the Corporation of Bishop's College: Be it therefore enacted by the Queen's Most Excellent Majesty, by and with the advice and consent of the Legislative Council and of the Legislative Assembly of the Province of Canada, constituted and assembled by virtue of and under the authority of an Act passed in the Parliament of the United Kingdom of Great Britain and Ireland, and intituled, *An Act to re-unite the Provinces of Upper and Lower Canada, and for the Government of Canada,* and it is hereby enacted by the authority of the same, That the Bishop of Montreal, as well as any other Bishop or Bishops, who may be appointed for any Diocese of the United Church of England and Ireland, which may hereafter be constituted in Lower

Canada together with the Bishop of Quebec, shall hereafter constitute the first branch of the Corporation of Bishop's College; and the said Bishop shall have and possess equal co-ordinate powers in the appointment of the Trustees and of the College Council and shall have and exercise jointly all and every the powers and privileges heretofore possessed, exercised and enjoyed by the Bishop of Quebec, in the management of the affairs of the said Corporation: Provided that in case of a difference of opinion between the said Bishops, in the event of their being equally divided in the exercise of any of the powers hereby conferred upon them, the opinion of the Bishop who is senior by priority of appointment shall prevail, and his decision shall be final.

ROYAL CHARTER OF THE UNIVERSITY OF BISHOP'S COLLEGE

VICTORIA, by the Grace of God of the United Kingdom of Great Britain and Ireland, Queen, Defender of the Faith.

To ALL to whom these presents shall come, Greeting:

Whereas, by an Act passed by the Legislature of our Province of Canada, in the seventh year of our reign, intituled, "An Act to incorporate Bishop's College in the Diocese of Quebec," there was constituted and established at Lennoxville, in the Township of Ascot, in the District of Saint Francis, and within the Diocese of Quebec, in our said Province of Canada, a Body Corporate and Politic, under the name of Bishop's College, in connection with the United Church of England and Ireland, which said Corporation is, by the said Act, made to consist of: First, the Lord Bishop of Quebec, or other superior Ecclesiastical Functionary of the United Church of England and Ireland, in the said Diocese of Quebec; Secondly, the Trustees of the said Bishop's College, not less than three in number; and Thirdly, the College Council of the said Bishop's College, not less than three in number, which said Trustees and the members of the said College Council shall be named by the said Lord Bishop of Quebec, or other superior Ecclesiastical Functionary as aforesaid, and shall, in the event of their death, removal from the Province, dismissal from their office, or resignation, be replaced by other persons to be named in like manner, and so on continually forever. And whereas it is by the said Act further provided that the said Corporation of Bishop's College shall, besides other corporate powers and capacities necessary to the well ordering of their affairs, have full power to make and establish such and so many rules, orders and regulations (not being contrary to the Laws of

Canada or to the said Act) as they shall deem useful and necessary, as well concerning the system of education in, as for the conduct and government of, the said College, and of any other Institution or School connected with or dependent on the same, and of the corporation thereof, and for the superintendence, advantage and improvement of all the property, moveable or immoveable, belonging to or which shall hereafter belong to the said Corporation, and shall have power to take under any legal title whatsoever, and to hold for the said College, without any further authority license or letters of mortmain, all land and property, moveable or immoveable, which may hereafter be sold, ceded, exchanged, given, bequeathed, or granted to the said Corporation, or to sell, alienate, convey, let or lease the same, if need be: Provided always, that the net rents, issues and profits arising from the immovable property of the said Corporation shall not at any time exceed the annual sum of three thousand pounds current money of the Province of Canada; Provided, also, that no rule, order or regulation, which shall be made and established by the said Corporation in the manner aforesaid, shall be of any force or effect until the same shall have been sanctioned and confirmed by the said Lord Bishop or other Ecclesiastical Functionary, as aforesaid. And whereas, by another Act, passed by the Legislature of the Province of Canada, at a Session held in the fifteenth and sixteenth years of our reign, intituled, "An Act to amend the Act incorporating Bishop's College," it is enacted that the Bishop of Montreal, as well as any other Bishop or Bishops who may be appointed for any Diocese of the United Church of England and Ireland which may hereafter be constituted in Lower Canada, together with the Bishop of Quebec, shall hereafter constitute the first branch of the Corporation of Bishop's College.

And whereas since the passing of the said first-mentioned Act, the Corporation of the said College have, with the sanction of the Lord Bishop of Quebec, by their petition to us, humbly set forth that in pursuance of the provisions of the said Act, Bishop's College has been duly organized by the appointment of Trustees and of a College Council, and that certain statutes, rules and ordinances have been made by the said Corporation, with the approval of the Lord Bishop of Quebec; and, further, that a suitable building has been erected, and a Principal and Professors in the faculties of Divinity and of the Arts have been duly appointed, and are now engaged in the education of a number of scholars duly admitted, according to the statutes and ordinances of the said Corporation; and the said College being, according to the said Act of Legislature of our Provinces of Canada, in strict connection with the Church of England and Ireland, and supported by an endowment provided by the bounty of members of that Church and otherwise, an humble application has been made to us by the said Corporation, that we would be pleased to grant our Royal Charter for the more perfect establishment of the said College, by granting to it the privileges hereinafter mentioned.

Now know Ye that We, having taken the premises into our Royal consideration, and being willing to promote the more perfect establishment within that part of our Province of Canada called Lower Canada, of a College in connection with the United Church of England and Ireland, for the education of youth in the doctrines and duties of the Christian religion, as incalculated by that Church, and for their instruction in the various branches of Science and Literature, which are taught in the Universities of this Kingdom, have, of our special grace, certain knowledge and mere motion, willed, ordained and granted, and do by these presents, for us, our heirs and successors, will, ordain, and grant, that the said College shall be deemed and taken to be a University, and shall have and enjoy all such and the like privileges as are enjoyed by our Universities of our United Kingdom of Great Britain and Ireland, as far as the same are capable of being had or enjoyed by virtue of these our Letters Patent; and that the Students at the said College shall have liberty and faculty of taking the Degrees of Bachelor, Master and Doctor, in the several arts and the faculties of Divinity, Law and Medicine, at the appointed times, and shall have liberty within themselves of performing all scholastic exercises for the conferring of such degrees, in such manner as shall be directed by the Statutes, Rules and Ordinances of the said College; and in order that such degrees may in due form be granted in the said College, We do further will and direct and ordain, that there shall be at all times a Chancellor and Vice-Chancellor of the said University, to be chosen at and for such periods of time, and under such rules and regulations as the Corporation of the said College may, by their Statutes, Rules and Ordinances, to be from time to time passed for that purpose, think fit to appoint, and that the Chancellor, Vice-Chancellor, Principal and Professors of the said College, and all persons admitted therein to the degree of Master of Arts, or to any degree in Divinity, Law or Medicine, who, from the time of such their admission to such degree, shall pay the annual sum of twenty shillings of current money for and towards the support and maintenance of the said College, shall be and be deemed taken and reputed to be members of the Convocation of the said University, and as such members of the said Convocation shall have, exercise and enjoy all such powers and privileges, in regard to conferring degrees and in any other matters, as may be provided for by any Rules, Orders and Regulations of the said College, duly sanctioned and confirmed, as far as the same are capable of being had and enjoyed by virtue of these our Letters Patent, and consistently with the provisions thereof. And We Will and by these Presents for us, our heirs and successors, do grant and declare that these our Letters Patent, or the enrolment or exemplification thereof, shall and may be good, firm, valid, sufficient and effectual in the Law, according to the true intent and meaning of the same, and shall be taken, construed and adjudged in the most favorable and beneficial sense, and to the best advantage of our said College, as well in our Courts of Record as elsewhere, and by all and singular Judges, Justices, Officers, Ministers, and other subjects whatsoever, of us, our heirs and successors, any misrecital, non-recital, omission, imperfection, defect, matter, cause of thing, whatsoever to the contrary notwithstanding.

IN WITNESS WHEREOF, WE have caused these our Letters to be made Patent.

WITNESS ourselves at our Palace of Westminster, this twenty-eight day of January, in the sixteenth year of our reign.

By Her Majesty's Command,
EDMUNDS.

CHAPTER XLVIII.
AN ACT RESPECTING "BISHOP'S COLLEGE"
(Assented to 24th December, 1870)

Preamble.

WHEREAS the corporation of "Bishop's College" have, by their petition, prayed for legislative provisions whereby the Diocesan Synods of the United Church of England and Ireland in this province may be enabled to participate in the management and government of the said college, and it is expedient to grant the said prayer, in so far and in such manner as may be done consistently with the royal charter of the said college; Therefore, Her Majesty, by and with the advice and consent of the Legislature of Quebec, enacts as follows:

Trustees and members to be named from amongst certain persons.

1. Such trustees and members of the college as may hereafter, under the acts establishing the corporation of "Bishop's College," be named by the bishops constituting the first branch of the said corporation, shall be so named from among the following persons, that is to say: five trustees and five members of council from among a greater number of persons chosen for that purpose by the synod of the diocese of Quebec; the same number of trustees and members of council from among a greater number of persons so chosen by the synod of Montreal; a like number of trustees and members of council, for every other diocese of the United Church of England and Ireland, which may here-

after be constituted in this province, from among a greater number of persons chosen for that purpose by the Synod of such other diocese, and the remainder of the trustees and members of council from among such other members of the said United Church of England and Ireland as the said bishops deem fit; the number of such remainder to be in proportion of three trustees and three members of council for every five named by every synod;

Nomination for 3 years only.

2. The said trustees and members of council shall be so named for a period of three years only, but after that time, may be again chosen or named as aforesaid.

Annual report to synods.

3. The said college shall lay before each of the said synods annually a report exhibiting the financial and educational condition of the institution.

CHAPTER 44.
AN ACT RESPECTING BISHOP'S COLLEGE
(Assented to, the 24th of February, 1927)

Whereas the corporation of "Bishop's College", duly incorporated under the act 7 Victoria, chapter 49, as amended by the act 16 Victoria, chapter 60, has, by its petition, prayed for the repeal of certain legislative provisions and the reenactment of certain clauses in order to facilitate the proper administration of its affairs, and it is expedient to grant the said prayer;

Preamble

Therefore, His Majesty, with the advice and consent of the Legislative Council and of the Legislative Assembly of Quebec, enacts as follows:

1. The following acts, to wit, the act 34 Victoria, chapter 48; the act 63 Victoria, chapter 101, And the act 2 George V, Chapter 108, are hereby repealed.

34 Vict., c. 48; 63 Vict., c. 101, and 2 Geo. V, c. 108, repealed.

2. The corporation of Bishop's College is hereby authorized to treat any and all funds now in its hands or which may hereafter come into its hands as one fund for the purposes:

Treating of funds.

a. Of distributing proportionately over the whole any diminution in capital that may occur through depreciation or loss of any investments;

   b. Of paying out all interest or revenue received thereon proportionately at a uniform rate upon the capital of each fund,

Provided there be nothing in the instrument creating fund or trust to the contrary.

3. The convocation of the university created under the Royal Charter has always had and shall continue to have the power and authority, by rules, orders and regulations, to that end made or to be made, to regulate and fix the fees to be paid by any holder of a degree in order to qualify him as a member of the convocation of the university.

Purposes.

Proviso.

Powers of convocation of university as to qualifying fees.

CHAPITRE 130.
LOI CONCERNANT LE
BISHOP'S COLLEGE
(Sanctionnée le 28 mars 1947)

CHAPTER 130.
AN ACT RESPECTING
BISHOP'S COLLEGE
(Assented to, the 28th of March, 1947)

ATTENDU que les syndics suivants de la Corporation de l'Université du Bishop's College, régulièrement constituée une corporation en vertu de la loi 7 Victoria, Chapitre 49, modifié[e] par la loi 16 Victoria, chapitre 60, et la loi 17 George V, chapitre 44, nommément, G.H. Montgomery, C.R. chancelier, l'honorable D.C. Abbott, C.R., John Bassett, D.C. Coleman, A.S. Johnson, W.C.J. Meredith, C.R., John Molson, Walter Molson, A.A. Munster, H.A. Norton, John-H. Price, W.B. Scott, C.R., P.H. Scowen, H.H. Smith, G.M. Stearns, A.C.M. Thomson, C.R., et G.H. Tomlinson ont, par leur pétition, demandé que la charte soit de nouveau

WHEREAS the following trustees of the Corporation of the University of Bishop's College, duly incorporated under the act 7 Victoria, chapter 49, as amended by the act 16 Victoria, chapter 60 and the act 17 George V, chapter 44, namely, G.H. Montgomery, K.C. Chancellor, Honourable D.C. Abbott, K.C., John Bassett, D.C. Coleman, A.S. Johnson, W.C.J. Meredith, K.C., John Molson, Walter Molson, A.A. Munster, H.A. Norton, John H. Price, W.B. Scott, K.C., P.H. Scowen, H.H. Smith, G.M. Stearns, A.C.M. Thomson, K.C. and G.H. Tomlinson have by their petition prayed that the charter be further amended modifiée, afin de faciliter et améliorer l'administration des affaires de l'Université et de lui permettre de faire face aux exigences croissantes de son oeuvre éducative, et qu'il est à propos de faire droit à sa requête;

À ces causes, Sa Majesté, de l'avis et du consentement du Conseil législatif et de l'Assemblée législative de Québec, décrète ce qui suit:

1. *a)* Au reçu, par le secrétaire de la corporation, d'une demande par écrit signée par cinq membres au moins de la corporation, exposant les buts de l'assemblée proposée, le président convoquera sans délai, pour les affaires y mentionnées, une assemblée général spéciale de la corporation.

b) Si l'assemblée n'a pas été convoquée et tenue dans les vingt et un jours à compter de la date à laquelle la demande a été remise au président, cinq membres quelconques de la corporation pourront convoquer eux-mêmes cette assemblée générale.

c) Tout avis d'une assemblée générale spéciale devra déclarer de quelles affaires il sera traité.

2. L'article II de la loi 7 Victoria, chapitre 49 est modifié en retranchant, dans les trois dernière lignes, les mots suivants: "Pourvu toujours, qu'aucun statut, règle ou règlement fait par ladite corporation de la manière susdite, n'aura force et effet à moins qu'il ne soit sanctionné et confirmé par ledit Lord Évêque, ou autre fonctionnaire Ecclésiastique comme susdit."

3. La corporation élira son pré-

in order to facilitate and improve the administration of the affairs of the University to enable it to provide for the increased demands upon its educational work, and it is expedient to grant the said prayer;

Therefore, His Majesty, with the advice and consent of the Legislative Council and of the Legislative Assembly of Quebec, enacts as follows:

1. *a.* Upon receipt by the Secretary of the Corporation of a requisition in writing, signed by not less than five members of the Corporation, setting out the objects of the proposed meeting, the President shall forewith convene a special general meeting of the Corporation for the transaction of the business mentioned in the requisition.

b. If the meeting is not called and held within twenty-one days from the date upon which the requisition was left with the President, any five members of the Corporation may themselves convene such special general meeting.

c. Notice of any special general meeting shall state the business which is to be transacted thereat.

2. Section II of the act 7 Victoria, chapter 49 is amended by deleting from the last four lines thereof the following words: "Provided always, that no rule, order of regulation, which shall be made and established by the said Corporation in manner aforesaid, shall be of any force or effect until the same shall have been sanctioned and confirmed by said Lord Bishop or other Ecclesiastical Functionary as aforesaid."

3. The president and vice-president

sident et son vice-président parmi ses membres.

4. L'article 4 de la loi 17 George V, chapitre 44, est abrogé et remplacé par le suivant :

"4. À partir du 1er janvier 1947, les syndics et membres du conseil collégial du Bishop's College seront nommés par les Évêques sur la recommandation d'un comité de nomination nommé par la corporation en conformité avec les règles, ordres et règlements de la corporation en vigueur de temps à autre."

5. La présente loi entrera en vigueur le jour de sa sanction.

of the corporation shall be elected by the corporation from amongst its members.

4. Section 4 of the act 17 George V, chapter 44, is repealed and replaced by the following:

"4. As and from the 1st of January, 1947, the trustees and members of the college council of Bishop's College shall be appointed by the Bishops on the recommendation of a nominating committee appointed by the Corporation in conformity with the rules, orders and regulations of the Corporation from time to time in force."

5. This act shall come into force on the day of its sanction.

BILL PRIVÉ N° 119
*Loi concernant
Bishop's College*

PRIVATE BILL NO. 119
*An Act respecting
Bishop's College*

ATTENDU que Bishop's College a, par sa pétition, représenté :

Qu'il a été constitué en corporation par la loi 7 Victoria, chapitre XLIX, modifiée par la loi 16 Victoria, chapitre LX, toutes deux du Parlement canadien précédent, et amendées de nouveau par les lois 17 George V, chapitre 44 et 11 George VI chapitre 130 de la province de Québec ;

Que par une charte royale en date du 28 janvier 1853, ledit Bishop's College a été déclaré et reconnu université, sous le nom de "L'Université de Bishop's College" ;

Que des titres sont conférés au nom de "L'Université de Bishop's College" ;

WHEREAS Bishop's College has, by its petition, represented:

That it was incorporated by the act 7 Victoria, chapter XLIX, as amended by the act 16 Victoria, chapter LX, both of the late Parliament of Canada and as further amended by acts 17 George V, chapter 44 and 11 George VI, chapter 130 of the Province of Quebec;

That by royal charter dated the 28th day of January, 1853, said Bishop's College was deemed and taken to be a university under the name of "The University of Bishop's College";

That degrees are conferred in the name of "The University of Bishop's College";

Que l'emploi des mots "Bishop's College" dans le nom du pétitionnaire est incompatible avec son statut d'université;

Qu'il existe une école connue sous le nom de Bishop's College School n'ayant aucun rapport avec le Bishop's College;

Qu'un changement dans le nom du pétitionnaire ferait disparaître une source de confusion avec ladite école;

Que le pétitionnaire est communément connu sous le nom de Bishop's University;

Qu'il désire que son nom soit changé en celui de Bishop's University;

Attendu qu'il est à propos d'accéder à ladite pétition;

À ces causes, Sa Majesté, de l'avis et du consentement du Conseil législatif et de l'Assemblée législative de Québec, décrète ce qui suit:

1. Le nom du pétitionnaire est changé en celui de Bishop's University et les lois 7 Victoria, chapitre XLIX et 16 Victoria, chapitre LX, du Parlement canadien précédent, ainsi que les lois 17 George V, chapitre 44 et 11 George VI, chapitre 130, de la province de Québec, sont modifiées en remplaçant les mots "Bishop's College" partout où ils se rencontrent, par les mots "Bishop's University".

2. Sous le nom de "Bishop's University" le pétitionnaire pourra à l'avenir posséder, exercer et réclamer tous les avantages, bénéfices, droits et titres auxquels il aurait eu droit sans ce changement de nom; tous les legs ou dons qui ont été faits ou se feront en sa faveur par testament, codicille, acte de donation, police d'assurance

That the use of the words "Bishop's College" as part of the name of the petitioner is inconsistent with its status as a university;

That there exists a school known as Bishop's College School which has no connection with Bishop's College;

That a change in the name of the petitioner would remove a source of confusion with the school;

That the petitioner is commonly known as Bishop's University;

That it desires that its name be changed to Bishop's University;

Whereas it is expedient to grant the said petition;

Therefore, Her Majesty, with the advice and consent of the Legislative Council and of the Legislative Assembly of Quebec, enacts as follows:

1. The name of the petitioner is hereby changed to Bishop's University and the acts of the late Parliament of Canada 7 Victoria, chapter XLIX and 16 Victoria, chapter LX, and of the Province of Quebec 17 George V, chapter 44 and 11 George VI, chapter 130 are amended by replacing the words "Bishop's College" wherever they occur by the words "Bishop's University",

2. Under the name "Bishop's University" the petitioner shall hereafter enjoy, exercise and claim all advantages, benefits, rights and titles to which without such change of name it would have been lawfully entitled; all legacies, bequests or gifts heretofore or hereafter contained in any will, codicil, deed of donation, policy of in-

ou autrement en le désignant sous le nom de "Bishop's College" ou de "L'Université de Bishop's College", lui profiteront et lui seront reconnus sous le nom "Bishop's University", nom sous lequel il pourra recouvrer, avoir, tenir, posséder et recevoir en héritage tous les biens mobiliers et immobiliers et les droits de toute nature que légalement il peut maintenant ou pourra à l'avenir avoir, tenir, posséder ou recevoir en héritage.

3. La présente loi entrera en vigueur le jour de sa sanction.
Copie conforme au Statut de Québec sanctionné le
18 DÉCEMBRE 1958
et dont l'original est aux archives du Conseil législatif

Greffier de la Législature

surance, or otherwise heretofore or hereafter made in its favour under the name "Bishop's College" or "The University of Bishop's College" shall avail to and may be received by it under the name "Bishop's University", by which name it shall recover, have, hold, possess and be capable of inheriting all property and rights, moveable and immoveable, of any kind and nature whatsoever which it may now or hereafter lawfully have, hold, possess or inherit.

3. This act shall come into force on the day of its sanction.
True copy of the Statute of Quebec assented to on the
DECEMBER 18, 1958
the original whereof remains of record in my office

Clerk of the Legislature

APPENDIX TWO

THE CONTEXT OF THE BATTLE FOR THE CHARTER

In the early years of the nineteenth century the universities of England were under the direct and exclusive control of the Church of England, and those in Scotland were controlled to a lesser extent by the Church of Scotland established under the terms of the Act of Union of 1707. When John Strachan, Archdeacon of York and president of the Council of Education of Upper Canada, went to England in 1826 to obtain a charter "to give character and dignity" to the university he proposed to found in Toronto, it therefore seemed natural to him that his university, The University of King's College, should also be established under Church control. The charter he returned with was, he insisted, "so unconfined in its provisions that none of a character so liberal had ever passed the Great Seal of England."[1] Unlike Oxford and Cambridge, King's College was to impose no religious test on matriculants, but the Visitor was to be the bishop of the Anglican diocese, and the president and the professors who were members of the governing council were to be members in good standing of the Church of England. The university was to be endowed with 225 thousand acres of Crown land, and a grant of £1 thousand per annum was made toward the cost of the buildings.

Strachan had benefitted from a fortunate political juncture. The lieutenant governor of Upper Canada in 1827, Sir Peregrine Maitland, was a military gentlemen of High Tory prejudices who strongly backed

Strachan's initiative. In London, the Conservative administration was in disarray, Lord Liverpool having been succeeded as prime minister by Canning, who was in turn succeeded within four months by Goderich. George IV seized upon the weakness of the government to exercise stronger influence on policy and appointments than was usual. It was in this climate of opinion that Strachan's charter could be deemed liberal.

However, the Dissenter members of the British Parliament were already vigorously attacking church privilege and control in the universities of Oxford and Cambridge, and in 1829 a select committee of the House of Commons recommended amendment of the University of King's College charter to reduce church control. When King's College, London, an institution also established to teach "the doctrines and duties of Christianity, as the same are inculcated by the United Church of England and Ireland"[2] (the formal title of the Anglican Church at that time), applied in 1829 for university status, the charter granted did not give the college authority to confer degrees. After a further seven years of intense debate under the Whig administrations of Grey and Melbourne, the problem of religious control over new university foundations in England was resolved by granting a charter to the University of London, a "body of persons eminent in literature and science," to act as examiners for the granting of degrees.[3] Institutions such as King's College and the theological colleges for the training of Roman Catholic and Dissenting clergy were invited to affiliate with the University of London to present candidates for its degrees. In this context promoters of university charters for Anglican colleges who persisted in going over the heads of colonial governments to deal directly with the Crown, that is with the colonial secretary, received an increasingly cool response.

In Upper Canada opposition to the terms of Strachan's charter was immediate and intense. Anglicans were in a minority, and many of them were closely associated with the influence of the lieutenant governor and an unelected Executive Council which was the focus of political discontent in the province. Strong opposition in the legislature delayed the opening of the college, and in 1837 an act to amend the charter was passed. The judges of the King's Bench were made Visitors, and the president and professors were to be required to subscribe to only a minimal declaration of Christian belief. The college council was to include the speaker of the Legislative Assembly and the attorney-general. Since the endowment of the college was to be derived from lands which the legislature deemed to be the common property of the people, the legislature determined that the state should control use of that endowment.

Nevertheless, a great many citizens mistrusted state control of education. They did not wish to emulate the fragmentation of higher education which had resulted in the United States from attempts of the devotees of every creed and the propagandists of every party to control it, but they believed that education was a moral enterprise in which religious education must play a fundamental role. In 1836 the Methodists founded Upper Canada Academy in Cobourg, and in 1840 the Church of Scotland founded Queen's College at Kingston, to be under the control of a board of 27 trustees, all of whom had to be in full communion with the Kirk. Both groups applied in 1840 to the legislature of the newly united Province for authority to confer university degrees. When consulted, the law officers of the Crown in England had in 1839 declared that university charters could only be granted by the Crown (the British government). However, the Act of Union of 1840 had remedied this deficiency. In 1841 the Methodists obtained from the provincial legislature an extension of the royal charter granted to Upper Canada Academy to permit Victoria College to grant degrees; in the same year the colonial secretary Lord Stanley approved a grant of a royal charter to Queen's.

As the church established in Scotland by the Act of Union of 1707, the Presbyterians promptly applied to the government for a share of the endowment hitherto monopolized by King's College. The Methodists and the Roman Catholics (who had founded Regiopolis College in Kingston in 1837) followed suit. There were thus four denominational colleges in Upper Canada, all claiming state support and with a total enrolment of fewer than 50 fully matriculated undergraduates.

Solutions to the problem proposed to the Legislative Assembly by Robert Baldwin in 1843, W.H. Draper in 1846, and John A. Macdonald in 1847 failed to convince a majority of the members. Macdonald's bill offered the largest concessions yet tendered to the church parties, proposing to give, from the state endowment, an annual income of $12,000 to King's College and $6,000 each to Queen's, Regiopolis, and Victoria. The bill was strongly supported by Egerton Ryerson for the Methodists and by the Kirk, but Strachan and his party still claimed the entire endowment, and the Reform Party under Baldwin were now strongly in favour of one provincial university under secular control. Baldwin's victory in the 1848 election made this the inevitable outcome.

In 1849 the Legislative Assembly passed Baldwin's act creating the University of Toronto. Faculties of Law and Medicine were to be established, but there was to be no Faculty of Divinity. Unlike the act establishing the University of London, no provision was made for the affiliation of denominational colleges. Baldwin hoped that Queen's and Victoria would be persuaded to surrender their charters, move to Toronto, and become theological seminaries for the training of their respective clergy. In return for these concessions they were to be given some share in the government of the university but none in the income from the endowment. In 1853 University College was constituted and given complete possession of what had been the endowment of King's College.

This solution proved unacceptable to those who were committed to an intellectual climate in which scientific knowledge and theology each revealed part of an integral truth. If religious belief ceased to inform the scientific and literary instruction in the university, they foresaw that religion would cease to be part of the mainstream of the university's intellectual life. In a spirited petition against Baldwin's bill, the board of trustees of Queen's noted with regret that the elimination of the religious character of the university was the only alteration proposed in an academic program badly in need of reform. They further observed that monopoly was unacceptable to the spirit of the times—"When a wholesome and honourable competition, one great stimulus to every exertion, is removed, nothing else can supply its place."[4] Queen's refused to surrender its charter, and settled in Kingston. When Baldwin's act took effect, Bishop Strachan resigned from the Council of King's College and set about obtaining an endowment and, in 1852, a royal charter for the University of Trinity College, founded "to combine the blessings of science with the far more precious blessing of Christianity."

Meanwhile, in Lower Canada the Roman Catholic Church continued to be supported by the endowments and tithes guaranteed to it by the Quebec Act. It thereby controlled the higher education of the great majority of the population, benefitting from "the wonderful mechanism which gives [it] such advantages ... the professors receiving no salaries, working for their food, and that of the homeliest; as a consequence, an education, board and lodging included, costing only £15 a year ... the youths subjected to a constant discipline under the eye of ecclesiastics day and night."[5]

As an alternative the Royal Institution had in 1821 been granted a charter for McGill College, "deemed and taken to be a university,"[6] with authority to confer degrees in the several Arts and faculties and governed by a council composed of the governor-general, the lieutenant-governors of Upper and Lower Canada, the bishop of Quebec, the chief justices of Montreal and Upper Canada, and the principal of the college. The Royal Institution was appointed Visitor, and the Crown retained the final word in the appointment of the principal and the approval of statutes. McGill was evidently to be a university of the Establishment, but no religious tests were specified for its officers and undergraduates.

Addressing the audience at the official inauguration of McGill in June 1829, the first principal, Archdeacon George Jehoshaphat Mountain, declared that "all offices in McGill College were left freely open either to

Protestants or Roman Catholics, and students of all denominations would be permitted to attend."[7] However, in 1835, when he was about to be consecrated bishop of Quebec, Mountain felt it incumbent on him to resign as principal of McGill. He was replaced by John Bethune, Anglican rector of Montreal.

In 1837 Bethune tried to procure a revision of the charter which would have made McGill an Anglican institution, but the governor-general and the colonial office in London were unwilling to introduce any restrictions which were not in the original charter and for which there were no justifications in James McGill's will. When the Arts Faculty of McGill was at last brought into being in 1843, Bethune returned to the attack. The statutes he drew up for the governance of the college required every professor, lecturer, and tutor to promise to teach no principles contrary to the doctrines and disciplines of the United Church of England and Ireland. All members of the university were to be required to attend the parish church of Montreal on Sundays, and to be present at morning and evening prayers on weekdays.

These provisions aroused widespread resentment and caused two potential members of faculty to decline appointments. Petitions were organized in Montreal and throughout the Eastern Townships urging the legislature not to grant public funds in support of McGill College until it was determined that the institution was a non-denominational venture and administered on liberal principles. Bethune's tenure was terminated in 1846, the result of the report of a committee of inquiry and of Bishop Mountain's refusal to take his seat on McGill board of governors as long as John Bethune continued to be a member!

APPENDIX THREE

THE FACULTY OF MEDICINE

In the nineteenth century, as has been remarked, prestige and enrolment accrued to those universities which established strong professional schools. At Bishop's the training of clergy and teachers was fundamental to the university's mission as a moral enterprise and a source of liberal education. Moreover, as this training required no special facilities, it could be accomplished within the straitened financial circumstances which dogged the university during the first 80 years of its existence. Unfortunately, both the ministry and schoolteaching were badly paid professions, attractive only to those few who felt called to them. Aware of the importance the government and other potential benefactors attached to enrolment, Corporation would have liked to expand into the more popular fields, but these all required expensive facilities, and the university's endowment was not sufficient even for the faculties of Arts and Divinity. In consequence, Bishop's was unable to provide more than moral support to the schools of Dentistry, Law, Medicine, and Music that sought affiliation. Since all of these found themselves immediately in competition with the generously funded faculties at McGill, it is hardly surprising that they all eventually succumbed. One, however, the Faculty of Medicine, survived for 35 years and made a significant contribution to the medical resources available to a rapidly expanding population. Its achievements deserve to be recorded.[1]

THE FOUNDERS

On the first of February 1871 five Montreal doctors met at the home of Dr Aaron Hart David to consider the next step in their project to found a new medical school in Montreal. They were a talented group fully representative of the English-speaking community in Montreal.

Francis Wayland Campbell was the son of a Scottish printer who had established himself in Montreal as the principal printer to the Legislative Assembly and an active member of the Reform Party. After graduating M.D. from McGill in 1860, Campbell undertook the customary tour of European hospitals, passed the examinations of the Royal College of Physicians in London, and returned to Montreal in 1861, where he built up a large practice and was active as a surgeon to the militia, in particular to the units mustered to repel the Fenian raids.

Aaron Hart David was a grandson of one of the small group of Jewish merchants who had arrived in Montreal in 1760 in the train of General Amherst. After preliminary medical studies in Montreal, he left in 1833 for Edinburgh, where he graduated M.D. in 1835. By 1871 he had become a leading member of the medical profession in Montreal.

William Hales Hingston, descended from Roman Catholic Irish gentry, graduated M.D. from McGill in 1851. After the usual tour or European hospitals, during which he obtained the diploma of the Royal College of Surgeons, Edinburgh, and several other diplomas from European schools, he had returned to Montreal to practise as a surgeon, becoming an attending surgeon at the Hôtel Dieu.

Charles Smallwood had emigrated in 1833 to Canada with an M.D. from University College, London. Though he continued to practise medicine, the recording of meteorological data, which had begun as an avocation, gradually became his main interest, and by 1871 he had been appointed Professor of Meteorology (unpaid) at McGill and was internationally known for both his establishment of the McGill Observatory and his contributions to astronomical timekeeping.

The fifth member of the group, Edward Trenholme, also a graduate of McGill, was a specialist in the diseases of women and a pioneer of several gynaecological operations.

ACCESS TO THE HOSPITALS

What led these men, all but one either graduates of or closely connected with McGill, to seek to establish a second English-language medical school in Montreal—in competition with the solidly established Faculty of Medicine at McGill? To understand their motives it is necessary to

Aaron Hart David

Francis Wayland Campbell

consider the nature of the practice of medicine at the time. Insofar as this was scientific, it depended above all on the close observation of the symptoms of suffering humanity. Its essential laboratories were therefore the hospitals, and access to the hospitals was vital to any practitioner who aspired to excellence. Control over access to the hospitals was early recognized as the key to domination over the practice of medicine in Montreal.

When John Molson presented his 1819 petition to the House of Assembly for financial aid from the government to erect and endow the Montreal General Hospital (the MGH), he was vigorously opposed by Michael O'Sullivan, speaking on behalf of the medical staff of the Hôtel Dieu, who feared loss of their monopoly of access.[2] Although the petition failed, MGH was nevertheless funded by private subscription, obtained financial support from the government, and became the seat of a medical school which was incorporated into McGill University as its Faculty of Medicine in 1829.[3] By this time the medical officers of the MGH, who were also the professors of the Faculty of Medicine, had been constituted the board of examiners of candidates for a licence to practice medicine in Lower Canada. This particular monopoly was broken by a law passed in 1831 which decreed that the licensed doctors of the province would participate in the election of examiners. However, although all appointments to both visiting and resident medical staff of the MGH were made by the governors, a majority of the governors nearly always took the advice of the attending men connected with the McGill faculty, so McGill continued to control the road to professional distinction in the province.

In 1843 McGill's teaching monopoly was successfully challenged by a group of doctors closely linked with the movement for political reform in Lower Canada, who founded The Montreal School of Medicine and Surgery—l'École de médecine et chirurgie de Montréal. The founders were nearly all English-speaking, but reflecting the roots of their common political cause, they taught in both languages, each lecture being given in English in the morning and in French in the afternoon. Though several of them were Protestant, they were admitted as attending physicians to the Hotel Dieu. By 1847, however, lectures were being given only in French.

In that year the newly incorporated College of Physicians and Surgeons of Lower Canada (CPSLC) erected what it perhaps expected would be an insuperable barrier to the multiplication of medical schools in Montreal by decreeing that only candidates who possessed a university degree in medicine could henceforth receive a licence to practise. Attempts by l'École to affiliate with McGill as a second, autonomous, French-speaking Faculty of Medicine proved unfruitful, and a petition to the legislature for power to grant their own degrees was successfully opposed by A.F. Holmes, a McGill professor, on the grounds that the Faculty of Medicine at l'Université Laval in Quebec City was fully capable of meeting the needs of the French-speaking population. L'École then made an overture to Laval for affiliation, but that university refused to consider a separate corporate existence for the Montreal school. Finally, an affiliation agreement was worked out with the University of Victoria College in Cobourg, which was prepared to allow l'École its autonomy and to accept its graduates as candidates for a Victoria degree. This unlikely relationship between French-Canadian Roman Catholics and Protestant evangelicals lasted until 1890, when l'École joined the Faculty of Medicine of l'Université Laval à Montréal.[4]

When it became evident that l'École would survive, appointments to the McGill Faculty were offered to the most competent of its English-speaking professors. In a parallel move the McGill corporation elected Dr Wolfred Nelson to represent the Medical Faculty as a fellow of the university. Nelson, one of the leaders of the rebellion in Lower Canada, had been exiled to Bermuda. He had returned to Montreal and re-established himself after the amnesty of 1843 being elected in 1848 to the first of his two terms as mayor. When in the same year he was elected vice-president of the newly created CPSLC, McGill conferred an M.D. *honoris causa* upon him; his subsequent appointment as fellow provided further evidence that the McGill Faculty could no longer be identified with a conservative political Establishment.[5]

Each of the two major hospitals in the city of Montreal was thus under the exclusive control of a Faculty of Medicine, and to obtain access to these hospitals as attending physicians and surgeons was undoubtedly the primary motive of the most determined of the founders of the Bishop's faculty. Several of them also believed that, secure from competition, the established faculties had failed to keep up with progress in medical practice, and in its early years the new school offered courses and required examinations in several subjects (including public health and experimental physiology) which had not until then been taught, at least formally, by the other schools.

AFFILIATION

The first requirement for the survival of the new school was that its examinations be recognized as leading to a university degree. The founders had made a preliminary approach to Bishop's University through Colonel Thomas Edmund Campbell, seigneur of Rouville and representative of the Diocese of Montreal on Corporation. Thomas Campbell was an original. As a semi-retired British army officer, he had led the Mohawks of Khanawake in 1838 to attack the rebels at Chateauguay, and he had subsequently become military secretary to Governor Lord Sydenham and his effective agent during the election on the question of union in 1841. He was fluently bilingual, married to a French-Canadian woman, and very much attached to the rural life of French Canada. Lord Elgin, whose civil secretary he was for a time, described him as "one of the most enterprising seigneurs in the province."[6] He had continued to play an active role in the organization of the militia, in which both Francis Campbell and Aaron Hart Davis had served as senior medical officers, and it was perhaps for this reason that he was willing to support the medical school project. It was at his request that the founders met on 1 February to delegate Davis to meet the Bishop's trustees at Lennoxville and outline the plans for the new school and the proposal for affiliation. The trustees reported favourably to Corporation, and at a meeting convened in Montreal for the purpose Corporation approved the affiliation and appointed the five founding physicians professors in the Faculty of Medicine of Bishop's University. Statutes governing the new faculty were presented for consideration at a meeting of Corporation on the seventeenth of May and were formally approved at the annual meeting on 18 June 1871.

ACCOMMODATION FOR THE SCHOOL

At the first faculty meeting a committee was appointed to look for suitable accommodation for the school. Since this had to include laboratories for the dissection of cadavers and for chemical and physiological demonstrations, the task proved difficult. Though the first announcement had been circulated, stating that lectures would begin on 4 October in "convenient premises in a central location,"[7] no premises had in fact been obtained by the end of August. At last a large flat in a building on the corner of McGill and Notre Dame streets was found to be available, subject to a lease on one room which was being used for the meetings of the Chemists' Association of Montreal. On 21 September, less than two weeks before the beginning of the session, the lease was settled, including a sublet from the chemists, since their room was already furnished and well suited to general lectures.[8]

THE FIRST SESSION

During the spring and summer of 1871 the founding group had been busy recruiting new members for the faculty. Though no financial inducement could be offered, their overtures were on the whole favourably received. Unfortunately several of the founding members themselves proved equally open to persuasion. The first to leave was Charles Smallwood, who had been elected the first dean of the Faculty, perhaps because of his scientific reputation and his connection with McGill. For 15 years he had been canvassing for government support for the McGill Observatory. As ill luck (from the Bishop's point of view) would have it, he obtained in May 1871 financing from the Signal Office of the United States War Department jointly with the Canadian Ministry of Marine and Fisheries. The observatory was to become the Montreal station in the network of stations of the newly established Meteorological Service of Canada. This was the culmination of his scientific ambitions, and he resigned his medical offices in order to devote all his time to the observatory.

Smallwood was succeeded as dean by William Hingston, who was immediately faced with the problem of providing clinical teaching for the Bishop's students. He had attempted to obtain a three-month appointment as attending physician at the Hôtel Dieu for a member of the Bishop's faculty so that Bishop's students could receive clinical instruction. He reported that the nuns and the bishop were "strongly in favour."[9] However, the nuns had delegated, by notarial deed, medical control of the hospital to l'École de médecine et chirurgie de Montréal, which was strongly opposed to the proposal. Hingston hoped that a compromise could be achieved, but in the meantime Bishop's students would be allowed to purchase tickets for admission to the Hôtel Dieu clinics. McGill had proved even less accommodating. In May the registrar of the McGill faculty, in answer to an inquiry, intimated that, while the faculty had not formally considered the matter, it seemed likely that any student wishing to attend MGH clinics would have to matriculate at McGill.[10]

August brought another turn. The secretary of the Medical Faculty of Victoria College informed Dr Hingston that he could not continue to attend at the Hôtel Dieu if he remained a member of the Bishop's faculty. Hingston was ambitious—he was soon to be elected mayor of Montreal, and was eventually knighted and appointed to the Senate—and he could see no future for the new school unless its students had guaranteed access to the hospitals. He resigned from the faculty and returned to the Hôtel Dieu, vowing to obtain an appointment directly from the nuns and the right to deliver clinical lectures independently from l'École.[11]

Undaunted, the remaining members of the faculty elected Dr David as their dean, and he delivered the inaugural lecture at the opening of the first session on 4 October. Due to the difficult gestation of the institution, many of the students reported several weeks after the beginning of the term, but 25 had registered by December. Students who had earned a degree in Arts or had passed the matriculation examination for any university recognized by the Council of Medical Education of Great Britain were admitted directly. Others were required to sit preliminary examinations in English, Latin, arithmetic, algebra, geometry, natural philosophy, and one of Greek, French, or German, under the supervision of R.W. Norman. Of the first group, all but one were from the province of Quebec. Eleven came from Montreal or its environs. Twelve were of French-Canadian descent. Fees were charged per course, and the total for a first-year student would have been about $50. The session lasted for six months, from the beginning of October to the end of March, and board could be obtained in the city at from $14 to $20 a month.

Apart from seeing to the instruction of the undergraduates (and attending to their own patients), the members of the faculty had two overriding concerns during that first winter. The first was to obtain a government grant equal if possible to the grants already enjoyed by the other medical schools. A petition was drafted, and Jean-Lukin Leprohon, Professor of Hygiene, was delegated to travel to Quebec to personally press the request. It was defeated, owing, according to a member of the House, "to the combined influence of the Medical Schools in Montreal upon the Medical members of the House."[12]

The other, equally pressing problem was access to the hospitals. The MGH was indeed refusing to honour Bishop's tickets for admission to its clinical lectures. In a circular letter to the governors of the hospital dated 12 February 1872, the Faculty noted that:

> Although the Hospital is a general one, supported by a government grant and the contributions of the citizens of Montreal, yet at the present moment its full benefits for Clinical Instruction are monopolized by McGill College. This state of things is due to the fact that out of eight attending physicians, seven are Professors in that institution, and that the Clinical Lectures are delivered by their professors in the operating theatre of the Hospital, the tickets for which are refused to all, except such as are matriculated students of their college.[13]

As a solution the Bishop's Faculty suggested either limited terms for the attending physicians, so that two or more of the posts might in time go to Bishop's men, or the appointment by the governors of clinical lecturers unconnected with any medical school, as was the practice in "the hospitals of London, Dublin, Glasgow, Germany and the United States."[14] After a delay of two months the governors informed the Bishop's Faculty that they had duly considered the petition but had concluded that it was inexpedient to make any change.

The first session closed with primary and final examinations written during the last ten days of March. The statutes required candidates for the final examination to have been "engaged in medical or surgical study" for four years, but a certificate of having studied for one full year with a duly licensed practitioner permitted the student to attend for only three years. Subjects for the primary examination, usually attempted at the end of the third year, included anatomy, chemistry, practical chemistry, materia medica, the Institutes of Medicine (physiology and histology), and botany and zoology. Those for the final examination were the practice of medicine, surgery, midwifery and diseases of women and children, medical jurisprudence, pathology, and hygiene or state medicine. Candidates also had to present certificates of attendance at hospital clinics and midwifery cases, and of practice in compounding and dispensing drugs. At first an undergraduate thesis on some medical or surgical subject was required, but this was soon judged to be not useful at the undergraduate level and was discontinued in 1873.

A number of the first students had already been studying medicine for several years as associates of licensed practitioners, had satisfied the preliminary examination requirements of the CPSLC, and had been admitted with advanced standing. Several of these were deemed to be capable of sitting their final examination and defending their theses at the end of their first academic year. Six were successful, and *The Montreal Gazette* of 5 April 1872 gave a lively account of their joyful excursion with members of the faculty to Lennoxville, on a specially chartered Pullman car, to lunch with the chancellor and receive their degrees at the first medical convocation. Though there were many hurdles yet to be cleared, the Faculty could take justifiable pride in the year's achievements. As *The Gazette* remarked, "The success which has attended the bold venture of establishing a Medical Faculty in connection with Bishop's College, Lennoxville, must have surprised even the most sanguine friends of the movement." It must have been particularly gratifying to learn, from an address presented to the faculty after the examination results had been announced, that the students greatly admired the manner in which their professors had coped with the crises of the inaugural year, and were grateful for the excellence of the teaching and the invariable kindness, courtesy and friendliness of their teachers.

A NEW BUILDING

Nevertheless, it was clear that the school must have more adequate facilities. The McGill Faculty was about to move from the building on Coté Street which it had occupied since 1851 to a new and much larger medical building on campus. The Coté Street building was convenient to both hospitals, and it would have been admirably suited to the needs of the Bishop's Faculty, which made an offer to purchase it. However, the McGill school had originally moved down to Coté Street from the campus in order to be closer to the hospitals, and the governors of McGill were not about to give a rival school this advantage. (At that time, because the Montreal streets were cleared of snow, if at all, by men shovelling it into horse-drawn sleighs and there was nowhere else to put the snow from sidewalks, winter travel on foot was time consuming.) Finally Dr Robert Godfrey, one of the original members of the Bishop's faculty, purchased a lot at the corner of St George and Ontario Streets, convenient to both hospitals, and hired William Hodson to design the building to be erected there for the new school. Godfrey was a candidate for the office of attending physician at the MGH that summer,[15] so the fact that he had erected the building at his own expense and was renting it to the Bishop's Faculty remained a closely guarded secret until 1875, by which time he had obtained his appointment at the MGH and resigned to join the McGill Faculty. In October 1872 the Bishop's school took possession of the new building, the facilities of which were claimed to be fully comparable with those available to students in other Canadian medical schools.

However, clinical instruction remained a problem. Another approach had been made to the Hôtel Dieu during the summer of 1872, but access was again refused to Bishop's students. The faculty then inquired if physicians in attendance at St Patrick's hospital, the small English-speaking section of the Hôtel Dieu, might be permitted to deliver clinical lectures. St Patrick's was a public hospital receiving a grant from the government. By dint of persistent lobbying, both in the community and in the Assembly, access to clinical lectures there was at last obtained for Bishop's students. By the end of the 1872–73 session, the resistance at the other hospitals had been overcome, and Dr Godfrey, who gave the valedictory address at convocation, was able to assure the Bishop's students that during the next session they would have access to the regular clinical lectures at the MGH and the Hôtel Dieu.

The Faculty had again petitioned the government for a grant, and this time the Bishop's Corporation had been able to apply some political lev-

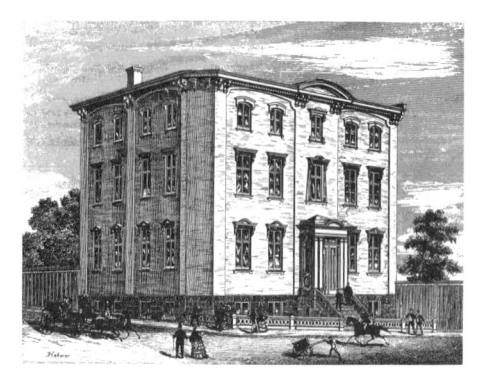

Bishop's Medical Faculty 1872   Western Hospital, 1902

erage in support of the request. George Irvine, the vice-chancellor, was Quebec's attorney-general in the Ouimet cabinet, and Joseph Gibb Robertson, the long-serving member for Sherbrooke, was provincial treasurer. In December 1872 Robertson refused to grant the second petition on the grounds that there was no provision in the budget for such a grant, but he promised that within two years the Bishop's Faculty would receive the same grant as the other medical faculties. In March 1874 a grant of $500 was voted by the Assembly, and in 1874-75 it was increased as promised to $750. It would no longer be necessary for Francis Campbell to borrow the rent from the Mechanics Bank on his personal note.

INNOVATIONS

Several of the first members of the faculty had supported the new school because they wished to introduce courses into the curriculum which were not taught at that time in the established schools. One of these was hygiene or public health. Montreal had suffered greatly from successive epidemics of typhoid fever and cholera, and Jean-Lukin Leprohon, the first Professor of Hygiene, had been active on committees established to study ways to improve public sanitation and secure a pure water supply for the city. In the first medical journal in Canada published entirely in French, *La lancette canadienne*, which he founded, Leprohon strove to promote awareness of the problems of public health among his readers, and his lectures to Bishop's students were another string to his bow. In April 1874 Montreal suffered a smallpox epidemic, and the mayor recognized the competence of the Bishop's faculty in the field by soliciting their opinion as to the best methods of treating patients in order to prevent the disease from spreading. Unhappily, despite the efforts of Leprohon and his colleagues, Montreal continued to be one of the unhealthiest cities in the western world. Resistance to vaccination exposed the population to a smallpox epidemic in 1885-86 which claimed the lives of at least 2500 Montrealers. As late as 1900 over 25 percent of all new-born children died before they were one year old, due largely to the failure of the municipal and provincial governments to secure supplies of pure water and milk and to impose compulsory vaccination.[16]

Another innovation was the equipping of a laboratory for experimental physiology. George Wilkins had been appointed the first Professor of Pathology. In August 1874 he wrote to the faculty to observe that experimental physiology had been introduced as an important element in teaching in both British and Continental medical schools, and to urge that Bishop's should be the first medical school in Canada in which physiology was taught practically. On his own initiative he had already imported instruments and apparatus from England, Germany and France, which had been developed there for experiments on animals. The idea was enthusiastically supported by Francis Campbell, who was Professor of the Institutes of Medicine, which included physiology, and the faculty accepted the proposal. Under Wilkins' stimulus, the teaching in physiology and histology included an increasing amount of experimental demonstration and of training in the preparation of tissues for examination.

At about the same time the McGill Faculty also took steps to strengthen the scientific foundations of its teaching. The prime mover there was the young William Osler, who was appointed lecturer in the Institutes of Medicine in 1874 and Professor in 1876. During his ten years of lecturing in physiology, histology, and pathology at McGill, Osler established a tradition of making use of clinical practice as a field of research as well as a pedagogical tool. In 1877 Thomas Roddick returned from Scotland to introduce Lister's antiseptic methods in the practice of surgery in the MGH. The Bishop's Faculty had thus to meet vigorous competition during its formative years.

It had also to cope with raids upon its teaching resources. In 1875 William Gardner, Professor of Medical Jurisprudence, left to take up the same Chair at McGill. The same year McGill decided to establish a Chair in Hygiene, and Robert Godfrey was persuaded to resign from Bishop's and accept appointment to the new post. As well as bringing McGill into a field that Bishop's had pioneered, the departure of Godfrey presented the faculty with a potentially serious dilemma. In 1872 they had agreed to nominate Godfrey as a candidate for election to the board of governors of the CPSLC, and Francis Campbell, who would himself have liked to be a candidate, had worked hard at the relevant meeting of the college to obtain support from McGill and Victoria for Godfrey—as a representative of the Bishop's Faculty. Though there was no formal allocation of positions on the board to representatives of the several medical schools, each attached great importance to being represented. After considerable discussion, the faculty decided to ask Campbell to see Godfrey and inform him that in their opinion, having resigned from the Bishop's Faculty, he was in honour bound to resign from the board of governors. It appears that Godfrey had not viewed the matter in that light. After taking counsel with his conscience, and perhaps also with his new colleagues, he replied that the College recognized no representation of any school and that he believed that he had been elected not as a representative of any particular interest but rather because "I was Dr Godfrey, an old and respected practitioner of this city"![17] He continued to sit as a governor of the College.

HOSPITAL ATTENDANCE

The new medical school was now seen to be solidly established, and Bishop's graduates were admitted on the same footing as those from McGill to the examinations of the Royal College of Physicians and the Royal College of Surgeons in London. However, the members of the faculty had made very little progress in their attempts to be appointed to hospital posts. From 1874 they gave first priority to a search for a hospital to which they and their students would be freely admitted. This was particularly urgent in the field of obstetrics, where it was proving very difficult to secure the minimum number of attendances at childbirth required for a licence to practise.

During their campaign to obtain access to a lying-in hospital to satisfy this need, the faculty had made arrangements with several small private hospitals to allow Bishop's students to attend their midwifery cases. One of these, the Woman's Hospital at 51 St Antoine St, was owned by William Hingston and Jean-Lukin Leprohon. In January 1875 the Faculty resolved to offer to buy the hospital, so that the Professor of Midwifery, Edward Trenholme, might have complete charge of the lying-in department and be responsible for attending all maternity cases in the public wards. By July 1876, terms satisfactory to both parties had been agreed upon, and the Woman's Hospital became the property of the Medical Faculty of Bishop's College.

The decision to buy the hospital had been precipitated by a falling-out between Leprohon and Trenholme, which the faculty had wished to resolve in favour of Trenholme, titular head of the department. However, by 1878 Leprohon and Trenholme were again at odds, and this time the faculty sided with Leprohon and asked for Trenholme's resignation. Though the minutes of the relevant faculty meetings do not give any details of the grounds for the conflict, it seems likely that it was due at least in part to Trenholme's unorthodox views on the practice of gynaecology. He has since been recognized as a pioneer in the surgical removal of uterine and ovarian tumours, but such radical intervention in the female reproductive system would have been considered controversial, if not immoral, at that time.

In 1879 the construction of the Western Hospital at the corner of Dorchester and Atwater Streets offered the Faculty an opportunity to expand the number of hospital beds it controlled. To establish a hospital to serve the rapidly growing western end of the city had been one of the dreams of the founders of the Faculty and, thanks to the initiative and determination of Major Hiram Mills, the dream was now to be realized.

The Western Hospital had been incorporated in 1874 on the initiative of a group of men prominent in business and financial circles in Montreal, led by Mills and a number of members of the faculty of the Bishop's medical school. From the beginning the project was hampered by shortage of funds. The lot on which the hospital was to be built, nearly two acres of prime land "on the outskirts of the city, with its rural attraction of salubrious air," had been expensive, and it had taken two years of canvassing to pay for it.[18] Construction began in 1876, thanks to a donation of $12 thousand from Mills, but the building was not completed until the end of 1879, when Mills put up a further $6 thousand. He offered to surrender the rights to the building for 90 percent of this sum, but the hospital corporation could not raise the money. Francis Campbell was determined that the Faculty should rent the building on behalf of Woman's Hospital; when he failed to convince enough of his colleagues to vote in favour of the move, he obtained Mills' agreement to lease the hospital to him personally for six years at an annual rent of $700. He then set about mollifying the opposition and finally succeeded in rallying most of the faculty to participate in the appointment of a board of governors for the enlarged Woman's Hospital and in the planning of the move to the new facilities.

This was at least the third occasion on which Campbell had had to pledge his personal credit in support of the school. In 1876 Robert Godfrey, citing "financial difficulties," had informed Dean David that he might be compelled to sell the Faculty building. Though he had received other offers, he would dispose of it to the Faculty for the amount which it had cost. The Faculty appealed to Corporation for funds with which to buy the building, but in the aftermath of the gutting of the college building in Lennoxville by fire and the subsequent debate over the future of Bishop's College School, Corporation was in no position to help. In April 1877 Campbell offered to purchase the building from Godfrey and rent it to the Faculty, and this is apparently what happened. Campbell had by this time identified himself as the most determined and energetic of the school's supporters, and when Dean David died in 1882 after a long illness, he was elected acting dean before being confirmed in the post in March 1883. However, when he attempted to obtain an appointment that year as attending physician at the MGH, he was defeated—narrowly—by the young Francis Shepherd, who was on his way to becoming dean of the Faculty of Medicine at McGill.[19]

THE TENTH ANNIVERSARY

The tenth anniversary of the Faculty was celebrated with some circumstance at a formal dinner held on 11th April 1881. Among the guests were the provincial lieutenant-governor, premier, treasurer, and solicitor-general, and senior members of the three other medical faculties. The following day Chancellor Heneker presided over the tenth convocation of the Medical Faculty, held in the Synod Hall in Montreal, in the presence of a large, mostly female, audience. Dean David attended but was not well enough to officiate. His place was taken by Francis Campbell, who took the opportunity to review the achievements of the first ten years and to announce the endowment of the Nelson Gold Medal in memory of Dr Robert Nelson, member of Parliament, health commissioner of Montreal during the cholera outbreaks of 1832 and 1834, physician and president of the medical board of the Hotel Dieu, one of the leaders of the rebellion of 1838, and great-uncle of Wolfred Nelson, the first student to be registered in the Faculty of Medicine of the University of Bishop's College. The donor was Robert Nelson's son, Eugene, a doctor practising in New York, and the medal was to be awarded annually for the best special examination in surgery. The adoption of the medal by an institution with such profoundly Tory roots as Bishop's was a happy indication of the political maturity the province and the country had achieved.

The Faculty could indeed take pride in the achievements of the first decade. Depending almost entirely on the financial resources of its members, it had built and equipped facilities for the pre-clinical instruction of 50 students, and in the teeth of determined opposition from the other medical schools in Montreal, it had obtained access for these students to the clinical lectures given at the MGH and the Hôtel Dieu. Though access of the members of the faculty to these hospitals was still restricted, the attending physicians at the Woman's Hospital, occupying the Western Hospital building, were all Bishop's men. The 50 beds available there for obstetrical and gynaecological patients offered exceptional clinical opportunities for students in those fields. Bishop's graduates were received in the hospitals of Great Britain on the same basis as those from McGill and Toronto, and as a measure of the school's standing in the United States, Campbell cited the achievement of Henry Chandler, first in the graduating class in 1880, in beating 21 other candidates to win a competitive examination for the post of house surgeon in the 150-bed Brooklyn Hospital.

In the early years of the school, the mother tongue of about one third of the students was French, but in 1884 the religious authorities began to exert pressure on French-speaking students to attend medical schools under Roman Catholic control. The result was a sharp drop in enrolment, and a deficit for the 1884–85 session. By the end of the decade, enrolment had more than recovered, but only a few of the students were French-speaking.

Co-ordinating the Bishop's lecture timetable with the clinical lectures given in the various hospitals was a continuing problem. The students often had very little time in which to rush from hospital to school and back, and members of the faculty, who had their patients to attend, were often late for their lectures. Atwater was a long walk from the school building, and it proved difficult to enforce attendance at the Woman's Hospital clinics. As well, the responsibilities of a professorial appointment were heavy for busy practitioners, and there was a considerable turnover in staff, often due to a breakdown in health. Nevertheless, the Faculty's activities continued to expand. The summer sessions which had been instituted in 1877 were now attracting students from other schools. A dispensary was opened in the school building in 1886, offering outpatient clinics in the diseases of women on Monday and Thursday, the diseases of children on Tuesday and Friday, and skin diseases on Wednesday. Pressure to convert the Western Hospital to a general hospital began to build among the subscribers, and in December 1888 the faculty began to look for alternative quarters for the maternity department.

HOSPITAL APPOINTMENTS

Relations with the Montreal General Hospital were gradually improving. The first members of the Bishop's faculty to be appointed to the medical board of the MGH had been Robert Godfrey, appointed attending physician, and Thomas Simpson and George Wilkins, appointed to attend the out-patients, all in 1874. At that time, J.C. Cameron was serving as assistant house surgeon, and he too had been appointed to attend the out-patients by the time he joined the Bishop's faculty in 1880. Unhappily, all these breaches in the wall proved to be temporary. Godfrey defected to McGill in 1875, and Wilkins, who had been promoted to attending physician in the meantime, resigned from the Bishop's Faculty in 1883 on his appointment to a Chair at McGill. In 1886 J.C. Cameron transferred his allegiance, to be followed the next year by Thomas Simpson. By this time, however Francis Campbell had at last obtained an appointment as attending physician to the outdoor patients and was giving a weekly clinical lecture at the MGH. In 1890 and 1891 Bishop's graduands were successful in the annual competition for the posts of resident physicians and surgeons at that hospital.[20]

As the only member of the medical board of the MGH who did not owe his appointment to McGill influence, Campbell had to cope with continual pressure and occasional harassment. In 1894 he was provoked by a particularly crude manoeuvre into public protest. The other members of the medical board had circulated to the governors, "in the interests of the maintenance of a thoroughly efficient medical service," a recommendation that J.W. Stirling, F.A.L. Lockhart, and Kenneth Cameron be appointed assistant medical specialists at the hospital. All three were lecturing in the Bishop's Faculty of Medicine, and as Dean Campbell informed the governors at their next quarterly meeting, it had been made plain to all three that if they wished to be elected, they would have to resign from the Bishop's Faculty. As dean of that Faculty, he was proud that three of its members had apparently been judged by the medical board to be the best fitted of the candidates for the posts, but he protested against the governors of the hospital being made, unwittingly no doubt, the instruments of an attempt to injure the Bishop's Faculty. The newspaper account of the meeting does not record the reply, if any, of the Board.[21] The medical editor of *The Mitre* commented, "The students of the Medical Faculty count among the students of McGill a host of friends, and these were not slow to denounce the action complained of."[22]

In the event, Cameron and Lockhart were appointed to the hospital staff and joined the McGill Faculty as demonstrators. Stirling stayed with Bishop's until 1900, holding his hospital appointments at the Royal Victoria and Western hospitals. In that year he was appointed Professor of Ophthalmology at McGill.

THE ADMISSION OF WOMEN

In March 1890 an application for admission with advanced standing from Octavia Grace Ritchie (B.A., McGill, 1888) forced the faculty to give serious consideration to the admission of women students.

Denied matriculation to the McGill Faculty of Medicine because she was a woman, Grace Ritchie had enrolled in the Women's Medical College at Kingston, which was affiliated to Queen's University. However, though several of the professors of the Royal College of Physicians and Surgeons (the medical school for men in Kingston) were well disposed toward the women and were giving them separate lectures for very small honoraria, the male medical students were actively hostile, and the clinical facilities at Kingston General Hospital did not compare with those in the Montreal hospitals. Miss Ritchie resolved to mount a second assault on the male medical establishment in Montreal.

The Bishop's Faculty would of course be unable to provide a separate course of lectures for women, so it was co-education that had to be considered. On the other hand, the Faculty was particularly well equipped to provide clinical teaching in midwifery and the diseases of women.

After a lengthy discussion, the minutes record that "the general sense of the meeting was in favour of admitting women";[23] and a committee was appointed to inquire what Miss Ritchie would expect in the way of facilities and to estimate the additional expense which would be entailed. The committee reported that a separate dissecting room would be required and could be provided at reasonable expense, but otherwise the principal difficulty would be to obtain admission for women to the clinical lectures at the large hospitals. On the other hand, Grace Ritchie had now been joined by the equally redoubtable Maude Abbott (B.A. McGill, 1890), and together they urged that the Bishop's medical school could expect to receive substantial financial support from the advocates of professional education for women in Montreal.

Ritchie and Abbott had already had some success in canvassing wealthy Montreal ladies for financial support for the medical education of women at McGill, and they had organized an Association for the Professional Education of Women (APEW), which had formally petitioned the McGill governors to approve the medical education of women in principle and to initiate a study of ways and means. However, the McGill Faculty of Medicine was adamantly opposed to the idea and refused to co-operate. Opinions among the Bishop's faculty were divided—though he was in favour of admitting women, Dean Campbell had already been quoted as doubting that they would have the nerve for surgery—but the general feeling was that the time was ripe for the admission of women, and that the potential dangers of co-education had been exaggerated. The Faculty decided to make the experiment.

By dint of personal canvassing, Grace Ritchie did manage to obtain her ticket for admission to the wards and clinical lectures at the MGH. However, having tested the waters, she warned Maude Abbott, who was in her first year of medical studies, to apply at once for her student's perpetual ticket of admission to the hospital, enclosing payment in full. Maude Abbott did so. The committee of management of the hospital, having discovered the presence of Grace Ritchie, decided that one was enough, and Maude Abbott received a receipt for her remittance but no ticket. At this point, the canvassing which had led to the formation of the APEW bore fruit. A vigorous letter-writing campaign to the governors and the newspapers, and the threats of several generous subscribers to withhold their subscriptions, forced the committee to relent in the case of Maude Abbott, but they took their case to the governors, and in May 1891 the governors resolved that no more tickets would be issued to women. The debate at the special meeting called to consider the question was extensively reported in the newspapers, and the arguments employed to persuade the governors to vote the women out reflected little

Octavia Grace Ritchie, 1888

Maude Elizabeth Abbott, 1890

credit on the speakers.[24] Happily, as one eloquent supporter of the women warned them, they had not settled the matter—they had only postponed (though, in Montreal, for 30 years!) the day of triumph.

Grace Ritchie graduated M.D., C.M. from Bishop's in 1891, Maude Abbott in 1894. Both women went to Europe for post-graduate training, where their sex raised no difficulties, and returned to Montreal for their professional careers. Dr Ritchie became a demonstrator in anatomy in the Bishop's Faculty and assistant in gynaecology at the Western Hospital, married F.R. England, another member of the hospital staff, and continued to practise and to strive for justice and equality for women throughout a long life. Dr Abbott was encouraged by a member of the McGill faculty, Charles Martin, to pursue her interest in pathology in the laboratories of the new Royal Victoria Hospital. She became an internationally recognized authority on congenital heart disease, and was invited by Sir William Osler to write the chapter on the subject in his monumental *System of Medicine*. She was also appointed curator of McGill's Medical Museum, where her work also earned her international recognition.[25]

One of the motives which led women to seek medical training in the nineteenth century was the desire to serve as medical doctors in Christian missions in foreign lands. Representative of this group was Minnie Gomery, who graduated from the Bishop's Medical Faculty at the top of her class in 1898 at the age of 23. Daughter of an Anglican clergyman who was a corresponding secretary for the SPCK, she then travelled to London for a year's training in Indian languages and customs before being posted to found a new Church of England Missionary Society hospital for women at Islamabad in Kashmir. For the next 33 years she ministered to the local population in the midst of famine, floods, and recurring epidemics of cholera, striving to gain the confidence of the Indian women in western medicine and Christian moral precepts. In 1935 she retired from the hospital and returned to England and to Montreal, but she no longer felt at home in what she found to be a materialist and wasteful society. She returned to India for two more periods of service before finally settling in Montreal, where she died at the age of 92.[26]

In spite of the edict of the governors of the MGH, women continued to enroll in the Bishop's Faculty. One or two of them managed to obtain MGH tickets through influence or by personal canvassing. For the others, clinics were established in medicine and surgery at the Western Hospital, and there was of course no difficulty in providing there the required number of attendances at obstetrical cases. However, the regulations for a licence to practise in Quebec required attendance at a hospital with at least one hundred beds, and the Western Hospital had fewer than fifty.

For the next four years the Faculty continued to admit women, and women were generally to be found among the prizewinners at convocation. However, no progress had been made with respect to obtaining admission for them to clinical instruction in the larger hospitals, and contrary to the hopes raised by the APEW campaign there seemed to be no prospect of financial support for the Bishop's school on a scale which would have enabled the problem to be solved. In 1897 the faculty resolved to admit no more women until such clinical facilities as were required by law for a licence to practise in Quebec could be made available to them. The last two women to complete their training graduated in 1900.

During the ten years since Grace Ritchie had entered the Faculty, twelve women had graduated out of nineteen who had matriculated and attended for at least one year. They had competed successfully with their male fellows, and most of them subsequently practised their profession, several with distinction. How many more might have been trained to minister to suffering humanity but for the obtuseness of the medical boards of the major hospitals![27]

STUDENT LIFE

Until the founding of *The Mitre* in 1893, only those aspects of medical student life which directly concerned the faculty were recorded. Relations between the undergraduates and the professors seem to have been commendably close. A number of petitions, most requesting changes in the schedule of lectures, and a few complaints, usually concerning irregularity in the attendance of certain professors, were taken note of in the minutes of faculty meetings, and the faculty generally tried to satisfy the petitioners. The only serious misdemeanours appear to have been committed in the course of obtaining what the Faculty calendar described as "material for dissection."[28] Before 1883 this was apparently a matter for private enterprise, and at least one undergraduate had to be allowed a year's leave of absence lest he be arrested for graverobbing. Even members of the faculty were occasionally at risk. In January 1876 Dean David had had to negotiate with an angry widower from Cornwall who, with the aid of a detective, had traced the body of his deceased wife to the Bishop's anatomy laboratory. According to the minutes of the faculty meeting at which this was reported, the detective had informed his client that it was usual in such cases to repay the Faculty the $30 which the body had cost them! The widower paid, but the story broke in the newspapers and the faculty judged it wise to reimburse him.[29] In 1883 the Legislature of Quebec enacted that bodies of persons found dead and publicly exposed or of persons who had been supported immediately before death by a government-funded institution should be delivered to the schools of medicine to be used in the study of anatomy and surgery unless claimed within 24 hours of death by a relative. Presumably this put an end to private enterprise.

One of the objects of *The Mitre* was to stimulate better relations between the several faculties of the university, and the masthead of the first issue included T.E. Montgomery, a medical student, as an associate editor. He was joined in the second issue by Maude Abbott.

For the next four years, the regular "Medical Notes" column in *The Mitre* revealed an esprit-de-corps which was remarkable given the material disadvantages under which the students laboured in comparison with their confreres at McGill. The correspondents noted with pride new courses which Bishop's was the first of the schools to make compulsory and recounted the achievements of recent Bishop's graduates in Great Britain and the United States. Relations with the students of the other medical schools in Montreal seem to have been friendly—their delegates were welcomed at the annual faculty-undergraduate dinners, and the annual theatre night was increasingly a joint enterprise with the other schools. *The Mitre* of November 1896 records, for example, that on the thirteenth of that month the medical students assembled at the school building and, carrying torches and headed by a brass band, marched to the student night at the "Théatre français." At the head of the procession walked the school janitor, "proudly bearing the Faculty banner ... on arriving at the theatre, a choice selection of songs was rendered by the students, eliciting great applause from the fashionable audience present. The floral gifts to the leading actresses were superb ... the leading actor was presented with a valuable silver-mounted cane,"[30] suitably inscribed—after which the students marched back in a body to the scene of their daily labours, no doubt content with the impression they had made!

The "Medical Notes" also included informed comment on the problems which still faced the Faculty. In June 1893 an accurate account appeared of the difficulties the women were encountering with the MGH. A year later the medical correspondent reported with alarm that McGill had decided to increase the requirements for its medical degree from four sessions of six months to four sessions of nine months, and that fees were to be raised. Everyone agreed that extension of the course was necessary, but it was pointed out that more than a third of the students had very limited means and that their earnings during the six-month vacation were indispensable if they were to continue. The correspondent urged that a course of five six-month sessions be adopted instead, and he suggested that a college as heavily endowed as McGill should not be discriminating in favour of the wealthier students. In February 1896 an editorial noted with regret the attraction which the endowed Chairs of "other Faculties" had had on some members of the Bishop's medical staff.

THE DENTAL FACULTY

In September 1892 a deputation of Montreal dentists met with members of the Bishop's faculty to discuss the possibility of opening a dental school in affiliation with the Medical Faculty.

At that time the Dental Association of the Province of Quebec controlled those practising dentistry in the province and established the requirements for the Licentiate in Dental Surgery. These included the study of basic science at university level, three years of apprenticeship in the office of a practising dentist, and examinations set by the association's board of examiners. In April 1892 the board decided that the education of dentists should be carried out entirely in an institution which it controlled, and it established the Dental College of the Province of Quebec in rented quarters in Cathcart St. W.G. Beers was the first principal and moving force behind the project, and he was supported by Hugh Berwick, a graduate in Medicine from McGill who had just been appointed staff dentist at the MGH—the first such appointment at a Canadian hospital. The college was to provide dental education in both French and English, and its graduates were to be Doctors of Dental Surgery, the degree awarded by the best American dental faculties. To this end, the college applied to Laval (Montreal) and McGill for affiliation. Laval was not interested, and McGill would not agree to call the dental graduates doctors.[31]

The purpose of the deputation in September 1892, then, was to set up a school in which the basic sciences and as much of the clinical sciences as possible were taught in a dental context and by an institution able to grant the degree of Doctor of Dental Surgery. The Bishop's medical faculty were generally in favour, and after ascertaining that the act of incorporation of the Dental Association offered no bar to the proposal the Corporation of Bishop's University gave its consent to granting the D.D.S. at the end of three years of instruction.

However, the dental practitioners of the province appear to have been divided on the issue. Those who had been involved in the founding of the Dental College still hoped for affiliation with Laval or McGill, and they successfully opposed an attempt by the Bishop's Faculty to obtain legislation licensing Doctors of Dental Surgery from any faculty in Quebec to practise without further examination. During the winter of

1895–96 dental courses were offered by both the Dental College and the Bishop's Faculty. After a second refusal by Laval and McGill the Dental College finally approached Bishop's, and satisfactory terms of affiliation were agreed upon. Theoretical and practical anatomy, physiology, and chemistry would be taught in both languages by members of the Bishop's faculty, and the specifically dental subjects would be taught by the Dental College staff. A revised bill satisfactory to the Dental Association, the Dental College, and the Bishop's Medical Faculty was then submitted to the legislature. At this stage McGill learned of the proposed affiliation and dispatched two representatives to Quebec to have the bill defeated. However, though it was referred back to committee, it survived intact and was passed into law.

In 1896 the Dental College of the Province of Quebec in affiliation with the University of Bishop's College was given official status at a special meeting of convocation on January 11, and W.G. Beers was appointed dean.[32] Beers, a remarkably versatile and energetic man, was determined to see dental education firmly established at degree level and recognized with the D.D.S. degree. His appointment as dean rallied the support of the most influential members of the profession in Montreal.

Unfortunately, his tenure was short-lived. During his first year a number of Quebec dentists, including some of his colleagues on the college staff, petitioned the dental board for an amendment to the Dental Act which would permit them to employ assistants who were not registered dental students. Feeling strongly that this would undermine the professional status of dentistry and seriously affect the opportunities for the practical training of students, Beers resigned as dean. Another source of discord was the question of how much anatomy the dental students needed. Beers urged that their study should be limited to the thorax, head, and neck, and asked for a separate examination for the dental students, and the problem was further bedeviled by the insistence of the French-speaking students that they should have their own examination and, finally, that they should be allowed to attend anatomy lectures at Laval.

During the next four years the college was administered by five different deans, and there was rapid turnover in the membership of the teaching staff. The major problem was to provide teaching of equal quality and rigour in French and in English, and it was no doubt aggravated by the inability of either Bishop's or the college to offer more than token remuneration to the lecturers.

In 1902 Dr Peter Brown, a graduate of the New York Dental College and a prominent dental surgeon practising in Montreal, became dean. After a year's experience of the difficulties of the post, he appears to have reached two conclusions: first, that the goal of providing instruction of equal quality in two languages in the same institution was not attainable with the resources at his disposal, and second, that dental education in the province must be attached to the strongest medical faculties in order to achieve the standing the profession was seeking. With two colleagues, Dr Eudore Dubeau and Dr Stevenson, he renewed contacts with Laval and McGill. As a result of these negotiations, the Dental College was closed down. In 1905 Laval established a Faculty of Dentistry granting the D.D.S. degree, with Eudore Dubeau as dean. McGill also began to teach dentistry in 1905, but the dental school functioned initially as a department of the Faculty of Medicine, with Dr Brown as the senior instructor. At first McGill still refused to grant the title Doctor to dental graduates; not until 1908 were the first D.D.S. degrees conferred at McGill.

The Bishop's Faculty of Medicine conferred its last dental degrees in 1906. Altogether, 59 men and one woman had graduated D.D.S. during the 10 years of affiliation between the Dental College and the Faculty. In spite of the efforts of the founders to offer instruction in both languages, only a small fraction of the graduates had been French-speaking. The goal had been a worthy one, but the financial resources available were never adequate to the task.

AMALGAMATION

When Bishop's had established its school, teaching in the great majority of medical schools in North America had been largely didactic. Students were given little practice in the use of such diagnostic techniques as there were, and none in scientific experiment. McGill and Bishop's had followed the Scottish and English tradition of using the hospitals for clinical instruction, but a great many medical schools in the United States had no clinical facilities. Thus it had been possible for enthusiastic individuals such as Jean Lukin Leprohon and George Wilkins to introduce courses which placed the fledgling Bishop's school in the forefront of curriculum development, and once access to the major hospital clinics had been secured, Bishop's medical graduates had no reason to fear comparison with those of the larger schools in Canada and the United States.

By the beginning of the new century, however, the situation had been transformed. The rapid development of the medical sciences—physiology, histology, biochemistry, pathology, and bacteriology—had made essential the provision of well-equipped experimental laboratories for undergraduate use, and the best medical schools were insisting on at least one year of college level study of biology, chemistry, and physics before students began their medical studies. To quote Abraham Flexner, whose report to the Carnegie Foundation in 1910 provided the impetus for revolutionary advances in medical training, "With the advent of the laboratory, in which every student possesses a locker where his individual microscope, reagents and other paraphernalia are stored for his personal use; with the advent of the small group bedside clinic, in which every student is responsible for a patient's history and for a trial diagnosis suggested, confirmed or modified by his own microscopical and chemical examination of blood, urine, sputum and other tissues, the privileges of the medical school can no longer be open to casual strollers from the highway."[33]

Dawson's tenure as principal had seen McGill established in the forefront of the teaching of experimental science in North America— equipped through the princely benefactions of W.C. Macdonald, Peter Redpath, and other Montreal patrons with excellent laboratories and endowments which made it possible to attract the best available men to fill the scientific Chairs. The McGill Medical Faculty also possessed endowed Chairs in several of the medical sciences, so it was in a position to meet the demands of the revolution in the training of medical students.

At Bishop's, on the other hand, though the faculty had from the beginning insisted on thorough training in laboratory techniques, chemistry and biology were taught by part-time lecturers, and the medical sciences were taught by busy practitioners who must have found it difficult to keep up with the rapid advances in their fields. The Faculty of Arts could provide no support, since science was still taught there as a branch of applied mathematics; nor could the university help the school to obtain endowments since, for reasons which have already been considered, Bishop's was not well-regarded by the Montreal business and financial community.

Under these circumstances, the Bishop's Faculty found it increasingly difficult to compete with McGill. When the Western Hospital decided to become a general hospital, the Faculty had succeeded in finding excellent alternative accommodation for the Woman's Hospital on Mountain Street. The new building could accommodate 20 free patients, 10 nurses, and 10 private patients, and was claimed to be the largest and best equipped obstetrical hospital east of Toronto. However, when Dean Campbell attempted to generate support for the construction of a new, larger building for pre-clinical instruction, his colleagues did not support him.

In 1894 McGill had decided to increase the length of medical studies for the McGill degree to four sessions of nine months each and to increase fees to $100 a year.[34] The Quebec Medical Act, passed in 1896, required certificates of study with a licensed practitioner for students who were not following nine-month sessions. Many of the Bishop's students had very limited financial resources, so the Bishop's Faculty did not increase its fees, and every effort was made to provide additional clinical instruction for those students who intended to practise in Quebec. However, there was a continual drain of the most promising younger members of the Bishop's faculty to McGill, and it was increasingly difficult to maintain continuity in the instruction. Enrolment was stable, and Dean Campbell continued to speak and write confidently of expansion, but in 1904 his health began to fail, and it quickly became evident that he had been the only remaining true believer. As the vice-dean, J.B. McConnell, reported to the secretary of Corporation, in order to continue, "We would need to have control of a hospital large enough for all our clinical work, money for a more suitable college building, for more equipment in the laboratories and for paying teachers in certain branches; and above all sufficient men with enthusiasm and high ideals and with small hope of pecuniary reward ... I found that we lacked these prospects in every particular."[35]

In 1903 the Trinity College Medical School in Toronto amalgamated with the Faculty of Medicine of the University of Toronto. Sir William Osler, speaking at the inauguration of the new building in which the combined schools were to operate, strongly urged the other small Canadian medical schools to join a large faculty or close down in the interest of establishing Canadian medical practice on the most advanced level.[36]

Negotiations to merge the Bishop's Faculty with the McGill Faculty were opened during the winter of 1904–05. One of the negotiators for McGill was William Gardner, acting dean, who had been one of the original members of the Bishop's faculty. In March 1905 the joint report of the negotiating committees proposed terms which were accepted by both universities. In return for an undertaking by the University of Bishop's College to surrender its right to teach and confer degrees in medicine in Montreal, McGill agreed to accept Bishop's students at equivalent level provided their matriculation standing satisfied the McGill Board of Examiners. Francis Campbell was to be listed among the McGill Professors Emeriti (with an asterisk) in recognition of his long services rendered to the profession. Those members of the Bishop's faculty who did not already hold a McGill degree would receive one *ad eundem*, should they wish to do so. A list of the graduates of the Bishop's Medical Faculty would be kept in the calendars of McGill. However, in spite of pleasant murmurs at the end of the report about increasing efficiency, consolidating resources, and promoting friendly feelings in the medical community in Montreal, McGill made no firm commitment to appoint any members of the Bishop's faculty to the McGill faculty. In fact, of the senior Bishop's men, only Andrew Macphail was appointed—to the Chair of the History of Medicine in 1907. The amalgamation thus consolidated the total control of clinical teaching in the English language which the McGill faculty had been seeking for over 50 years.[37] Andrew Macphail went on to become editor of the Canadian Medical Association journal and historian of the work of the medical services of the Canadian Forces in the 1914–18 war, in which he served with distinction in the sixth Field Ambulance. He was made a fellow of McGill in 1909 and knighted in 1918.

Shortly after this agreement had been reached, Francis Campbell died. Both his sons, one of them a member of the Bishop's faculty, had died of typhoid fever during the previous year, and his last days must have been sad indeed. Nevertheless, he had fought well and proved to be a doughty adversary for the McGill imperialists. Under his leadership and thanks largely to his energy and determination, the Bishop's Faculty had trained 246 doctors to internationally recognized standards. Canada's population was growing rapidly, and because of the rigorous licensing standards in Ontario and Quebec, the country was not, like the United States, oversupplied with medical practitioners. In these circumstances, few Canadians of the time could claim to have left a more useful legacy to their country.

APPENDIX FOUR

ENROLMENT STATISTICS

Table 1
Enrolment 1875–87

	Total	Arts	Divinity	Matriculants	Financial Assistance	Graduates In Arts	In Divinity
1875–76	20	15	5	7	17	2	—
1876–77	18	14	4	3	17	2	1
1877–78	18	12	6	3	14	7	2
1878–79	25	21	4	6	14	4	3
1879–80	29	26	3	13	13	3	2
1880–81	26	23	3	12	13	4	1
1881–82	23	15	8	3	13	8	2
1882–83	22	16	6	3	14	8	—
1883–84	25	19	6	9	14	6	3
1884–85	21	18	3	7	10	2	2
1885–86	27	23	4	10	13	8	1
1886–87	20	18	2	7	18	7	1

Table 2
Geographical Origins of Graduates in Arts and Science

	Mainland Quebec	Montreal	Other Canadian Provinces	Other	Total
1885–94	42	2	8	7	57
1895–04	50	9	18	13	90
1905–14	66	—	13	17	96
1915–22	76	1	7	3	87
1923–27	73	9	20	3	105
1928–32	115	17	29	2	163
1933–37	109	21	28	5	163
1938–42	124	28	16	4	172
1958–62	131	106	63	13	313

Table 3
Careers of Graduates in Arts

	Church	Law	Medicine	Teaching (secondary and post-secondary)	Other and unknown	Total
1854–74	39	1	1	—	25	66
1875–84	27	6	3	3	3	42
1885–94	33	3	10	3	8	57
1895–04	41	10	12	11	16	90
1905–14	37	4	2	31 (14M, 17F)*	22	96
1915–22	7	8	2	48 (14M, 34F)	22	87
1923–27	10	10	4	54 (24M, 30F)	27	105
1928–32	16	16	9	62 (28M, 34F)	60	163
1933–37	17	10	11	42 (29M, 13F)	83	163

* M = Male; F = Female.

Table 4
Sex of Graduates in Arts and Science

Period	Men	Women
1895–04	90	—
1905–14	77	19
1915–22	45	42
1923–27	65	40
1928–32	121	42
1933–37	132	31
1938–42	123	49
1943–47	102	44
1948–52	186	55
1953–57	198	108
1958–62	199	114
1963–67	383	232

Table 5
Religious adherence

	Anglican	United	Presbyterian	Roman Catholic	Other
1928–32 (Percentage of Graduates in Arts)	47	24	9	2	18
1960–63 (Percentage of Undergraduates)	52	29.5	4.5	7.5	6.5

NOTES

PROLOGUE

1 F. Ouellet, *Economic and Social History of Quebec 1760–1850* (Toronto: MacMillan 1980), 659.
2 Though the English-speaking minority ceased to dominate the government of Lower Canada at about the time of the founding of the college, it remained dominant in economic affairs in Quebec until 1960, and Quebec's French-speaking nationalists maintain that their culture is still at risk from the pressure of English-language domination of North American and international communications.
3 J.I. Little, *The Peaceable Conquest* (Burnaby, BC: Department of History, Simon Fraser University 1976), A12.
4 Ibid., A23.
5 L.P. Audet, and H. Gauthier, *Le système scolaire du Québec* (Montréal: Beauchemin 1969), 4.
6 Ibid.
7 T.R. Millman, *Jacob Mountain, First Lord Bishop of Quebec* (Toronto: University of Toronto Press 1947), 170.
8 Ibid.
9 Réal G. Boulianne, *The French-Canadians under the Royal Institution for the Advancement of Learning 1818–1829* (University of Ottawa, Master's thesis, Department of History, 1964).

10 L.P. Audet, *Le système scolaire de la Province de Québec* (Québec: Les presses de l'Université Laval 1952). Tome IV.
11 His decision may have been connected with his appointment as a judge in May 1829, when he had of course to resign his seat in the Assembly.
12 S.B. Frost, *McGill University, for the Advancement of Learning*, 2 vols. (Montreal: McGill-Queen's University Press 1980), 1:43.
13 S.B. Frost, *McGill University, for the Advancement of Learning*, 2 vols. (Montreal: McGill-Queen's University Press, 1980) 1:49.
14 Ibid., 66.

CHAPTER ONE

1 A.W. Mountain, *A Memoir of George Jehoshaphat Mountain* D.D., D.C.L. (Montreal: John Lovell 1866).
2 H.P. Thompson, *Into all lands* (London: SPCK 1951).
3 W.D. MacVean, *The Church of England and the Clergy Reserves in Lower Canada* (Master's thesis, Department of History, Bishop's University, 1947).
4 J.H. Nicolls, Letter to Harriet Mountain, 3 February 1847, Nicolls Papers, Bishop's University Archives NIC 74.
5 (Halifax) currency was an arbitrary money of account used in all the larger provinces of British North America until the decimalization of the currency in 1859. In 1841 the pound sterling was reckoned at 24 shillings, four pence currency, and the U.S. dollar at five shillings and a penny.
6 J. Graham Patriquin, *From Little Forks to Moulton Hill*, 2 vols. (Lennoxville: Bishop's College School 1978) 1:191–2.
7 Printed circular (1842). Masters Papers, Bishop's University Archives.
8 R. Montgomery Martin, *History of Upper and Lower Canada* (London: John Mortimer 1836), 331.
9 Galt was sent in 1828, at the age of 11, to the school established by Bishop Stewart at Chambly. In 1830, he returned to Scotland with his father, but it may be that his two years at Chambly inoculated him for life against education under Anglican preceptors.
10 Edward Hale, Letter to J.B. Forsyth, 4 January 1842. Hale Papers, McCord Museum, McGill University.
11 J.B. Forsyth, Letter to Edward Hale, 29 December 1841. Hale Papers.
12 Bishop's University Deed Book, 27 February 1843. Registered 7 September 1846 in Register B, vol. II, no. 987
13 Prospectus, Diocesan College of Canada East, 1842. Master's Papers.
14 Printed circular (1842). Masters Papers.
15 Edward Hale, Letter to Eliza Hale, 21 October 1843. Hale Papers.
16 *Rules, Orders and Regulations for the Conduct and Government of Bishop's College at Lennoxville in the Diocese of Quebec* with a list of Officers of the College,

etc. Sherbrooke, printed by S. Walton at the Gazette office, 1849. Bishop's University Archives.
17 A.W. Cochran, Letter to Edward Hale, 9 November 1843. Hale Papers.
18 Prospectus, Diocesan College. Masters Papers.
19 G.J. Mountain, Letter to the Secretary of the SPG, 12 October 1842. Quebec Diocesan Archives Series D, Folder 97.
20 G.J. Mountain, Letter to the Secretary of the SPG, 12 October 1844. Quebec Diocesan Archives Series D, Folder 99.
21 Lucius Doolittle, Letter to Edward Hale, 21 May 1845. Hale Papers.
22 Minutes of a meeting of the Corporation of Bishop's College, 26 June 1846.
23 Ernest Hawkins, Secretary of the SPG. Letter to G.J. Mountain, 2 March 1844. Quebec Diocesan Archives, vol. G.1.
24 G.J. Mountain, Letter to the Secretary of the SPG, 24 April 1845. Quebec Diocesan Archives Series D, Folder 99.
25 Prospectus, Diocesan College. Masters Papers.
26 G.J. Mountain, Letter to J.H. Nicolls, 17 January 1845. Nicolls Papers, Bishop's University Archives NIC 4.
27 G.J. Mountain, Letter to J.H. Nicolls, 12 June 1845. Nicolls Papers NIC 4.

CHAPTER TWO

1 Henry Roe, "Reminiscences of the Earliest Lennoxville Days," *The Mitre*, 3 (November 1895): 18.
2 Frederick Wilson, Letter to J.H. Nicolls, 4 August 1855. Nicolls Papers NIC 150, Bishop's University Archives.
3 J.H. Nicolls, Letter to Harriet Nicolls, 24 September 1852. Nicolls Papers NIC 40.
4 G.J. Mountain, Letter to J.H. Nicolls, 12 June 1845. Nicolls Papers NIC 10.
5 H. Roe, *The Mitre* 2 (June 1895): 80.
6 A.H. Crowfoot, *The Dreamer: Life of Isaac Hellmuth* (Toronto: Copp Clark 1963).
7 The Lambeth Doctorate of Divinity was conferred by the Archbishop of Canterbury on the recommendation of a bishop.
8 G.J. Mountain, Letter to J.H. Nicolls, 10 June 1853. Nicolls Papers NIC 10.
9 Crowfoot. *Dreamer*.
10 A degree *ad eundem* is conferred by a university to recognize the equivalence of a degree earned at another university.
11 Debates of the Legislative Assembly of United Canada, vol. 6, 1847, 1003–4 (Montreal: Presses de l'Ecole des hautes études commerciales).
12 J.H. Nicolls, *The End and Object of Education*. Bishop's University Library Eastern Townships Historical Collection.
13 J.H. Nicolls, *The Mitre* 2 (April 1895): 50–6.

14 Quoted by M.M. Garland in *Cambridge before Darwin* (Cambridge: Cambridge University Press 1980), 120.
15 Anon., "The Late Reverend S.S. Wood," *The Lennoxville Magazine* (Montreal: Dawson Bros.) 1 (May 1868): 206.
16 Garland, *Cambridge before Darwin*, 35.
17 SPG Archives, Rhodes House, Oxford 6/Can/LC3 134.
18 Gustavus Nicolls, Letter to J.H. Nicolls, 16 November 1846. Nicolls Papers NIC 82.
19 J.H. Nicolls, Letter to Harriet Mountain, 17 January 1847. Nicolls Papers NIC 74.
20 F.E. Judd, Letter to J.H. Nicolls, 23 December 1857. Nicolls Papers NIC 140A.
21 G.J. Mountain, Letter to J.H. Nicolls, 7 February 1848. Nicolls Papers.
22 Richard Lindsay. Letter to J.H. Nicolls. 3 June 1852. Nicolls Papers NIC 140a.
23 J.H. Nicolls, Letter to Ernest Hawkins, Secretary of the SPG, 7 May 1849. Nicolls Papers NIC 74.
24 J.I. Little, *Nationalism, Capitalism and Colonialism* (Montreal: McGill-Queen's University Press 1989), 86.
25 Philippe Sylvain. *Les difficiles débuts de l'Université Laval*. Cahier des dix, no. 36 (1971): 214.
26 James Bruce, *Letters and Journals of James, Eighth Earl of Elgin*, ed. Thomas Waldron (NY: Kraus reprint), 6.
27 Ibid., 65.
28 G.J. Mountain, Letter to J.H. Nicolls, 7 March 1855. Nicolls Papers NIC 10.
29 G.J. Mountain, Letter to J.H. Nicolls, 13 October 1854. Nicolls Papers NIC 10.
30 G.J. Mountain, Letter to J.H. Nicolls, 4 May 1855. Nicolls Papers NIC 10.
31 Convocation register.
32 *The Montreal Gazette*, 2 July 1855.
33 Ibid.
34 Ibid.

CHAPTER THREE

1 Nathanael Burwash, *The History of Victoria College* (Toronto: Victoria College Press 1927), 159.
2 Ibid., 135.
3 Hilda Neatby, *Queen's University* (Montreal: McGill-Queen's University Press), 1:76.
4 S.B. Frost, *McGill University, for the Advancement of Learning*, 2 vols. (Montreal: McGill-Queen's University Press 1980) 1:156.
5 Bishop's University Library, Eastern Townships Historical Collection, LE 3.B52N5.

6 Ibid.
7 Ibid.
8 *Dictionary of Canadian Biography* 12 vols. (Toronto: University of Toronto Press, 1966–), 12:230.
9 Frost, McGill, 1:185.
10 Minutes of a meeting of Corporation, 8 February 1854. Bishop's University Archives.
11 Minutes of a meeting of Corporation, 18 February 1855.
12 Frost, McGill, 1:196.
13 *An Act to secure the more efficient Auditing of the Public Accounts* 18 Victoria, cap. 78 Legislative Assembly of the Province of Canada.
14 G.J. Mountain, Letter to J.H. Nicolls, January 7 1856. Nicolls Papers NIC 10. Bishop's University Archives.
15 Minutes of a meeting of Corporation, 26 January 1860.
16 Frost, McGill, 1:161.
17 Minutes of a meeting of Corporation, 26 January 1860.
18 Minutes of a meeting of Corporation, 30 June 1857.
19 Minutes of a meeting of Corporation, 25 June 1859.
20 H.J. Morgan, *The Canadian Men and Women of the Time*, 2d ed. (Toronto: William Briggs 1912), 526.
21 Minutes of a meeting of Corporation, 26 January 1860.
22 Bishop's University Library, Eastern Townships Collection, LE 3.B52N5.
23 Ibid.
24 Minutes of a meeting of Corporation, 8 February 1854.
25 Minutes of a meeting of Corporation, 26 January 1860.
26 *The Mitre*, 11 (1903): 190.
27 Louis Campbell Wurtele, Diary. Bishop's University Archives.
28 The Rawson Papers 10. Bishop's University Archives.
29 Proceedings of the College Council, 9 May 1860. Bishop's University Archives.
30 Minutes of a meeting of Corporation, 25 June 1861.
31 Minutes of a meeting of Corporation, 4 October 1861.
32 Minutes of a meeting of Corporation, 24 June 1863.
33 Rawson Papers, 101.
34 Ibid.
35 Ibid.
36 Ibid.
37 Quoted in D.C. Masters, *"Bishop's University, The First Hundred Years* (Toronto: Clarke, Irwin 1950), 56.
38 W.L. Morton, ed., *Monck Letters and Journals 1863–1868*, The Carleton Library, no. 53 (Toronto: McClelland and Stewart 1970), 77–80.
39 *Dictionary of Canadian Biography*, 12 vols. (Toronto: University of Toronto Press, 1966–), 12:737.

40 Minutes of a meeting of the College Council, 19 May 1868.
41 Louis-Philippe Audet, *Histoire de l'enseignement au Québec*, 2 vols. (Montreal: Holt, Rinehart and Winston 1971), 2:17.
42 Wycliffe Jubilee Volume, 19 (cited in Masters, D.C. *The Rise of Evangelicalism*, lectures given at Wycliffe College Alumni meetings, 1960).
43 G.J. Mountain, Letter to J.H. Nicolls, October 31 1855. Nicolls Papers NIC 10.
44 C.H. Mockridge, *The Bishops of the Church of England in Canada and Newfoundland* (Toronto: F.N. Brown 1896), 244–5.
45 Minutes of a meeting of Corporation, 24 June 1868.
46 Minutes of a meeting of Corporation, 29 June 1870.
47 O. Howard, *The Montreal Diocesan Theological College* (Montreal: McGill-Queen's University Press 1963), 3.
48 Minutes of a meeting of Corporation, 18 March 1871.
49 Ibid.
50 Oswald Howard, *The Montreal Diocesan Theological College* (Montreal: McGill-Queen's University Press, 1963), 39.
51 Minutes of a meeting of Corporation, 29 June 1870.
52 Ibid.
53 Ibid.
54 Howard, *Montreal Diocesan*, 105.
55 Minutes of a meeting of Corporation, 24 June 1871.
56 Minutes of a meeting of Corporation, 18 January 1872.
57 *Dictionary of Canadian Biography*, 12 vols. (Toronto: University of Toronto Press) 11:122.
58 Minutes of a meeting of Corporation, 18 January 1872.
59 Ibid.
60 Ibid.
61 *Dictionary of Canadian Biography* 11:721.
62 Minutes of a meeting of Corporation, 26 June 1872.
63 J.D. Borthwick, *History and Biographical Gazetteer of Montreal to the year 1892* (Montreal: John Lovell 1892), 202.
64 J.H. Nicolls, Letter to the *Montreal Gazette*, 10 January 1876.
65 Henry Roe, *To the Right Reverend the Lord Bishop of Quebec, Ascension Day, 1876*. The Rawson Papers, 26, Bishop's University Archives.
66 Minutes of a meeting of Corporation, 8 June 1876.
67 J.W. Williams, Bishop's Charge to Synod. Journal of the 13th session of the Synod of the Diocese of Quebec (printed at the Daily Mercury office, 1879), 13.
68 A. Oxenden, Letter to Harriet Nicolls, August 17 1877. Nicolls Papers NIC 43/13.
69 Henry Roe, *The Dominion Churchman*, 1877 (18 October).

70 R. Mills, Letter to Harriet Nicolls, August 25 1877. Nicolls Papers NIC 43/21.
71 Resolution passed unanimously by the students of Bishop's College, 1 October 1877. Nicolls Papers NIC 40.

CHAPTER FOUR

1 J.I. Little, *Nationalism, Capitalism and Colonization in Nineteenth Century Quebec.* (Montreal: McGill-Queen's University Press 1989), 60–1.
2 J.P. Kestemann, *Une bourgeoisie et son espace. Industrialisation et développement du capitalisme dans le district de St François 1823–1879* (Thèse de doctorat, Université du Québec à Montréal, 1985).
3 J.I. Little, *The Peaceable Conquest: French-Canadian Colonization in the Eastern Townships during the Nineteenth Century* (Burnaby, BC: Department of History, Simon Fraser University, 1976), 25.
4 Henry Roe, *To the Right Reverend The Lord Bishop of Quebec, Ascension Day, 1876,* The Rawson Papers, Bishop University Archives.
5 Minutes of a meeting of Corporation, 11 September 1877. Bishop's University Archives.
6 Ashton Oxenden, *The Story of my Life* (London: Longmans, Green 1891), 217.
7 H.J.H. Petry, *The Mitre,* 4 (October 1896), 4.
8 Ibid., 5.
9 William Worthington, Masters Papers, Bishop's University Archives, Acc 83–147, Box 1.
10 S.B. Frost, *McGill University, for the Advancement of Learning,* 2 vols. (Montreal: McGill-Queen's University Press 1980), 1:177.
11 Minutes of a meeting of Corporation, 8 February 1854.
12 Minutes of a meeting of Corporation, 28 May 1880.
13 H.J.H. Petry, *The Mitre* 4 (1896): 1.
14 *Calendars of the University of Bishop's College,* 1890 and 1891.
15 Minutes of a meeting of Corporation, 30 June 1887.
16 Minutes of a meeting of Corporation, 21 April 1887.
17 Proceedings of the College Council, 29 October 1890.
18 College Council Minute Book, 1876–1896, p. 293.
19 Proceedings of the College Council, 29 October 1890.
20 The picture is preserved in the Laurie Allison Room of the University Library.
21 Reviewed in *The Mitre* 3 (March 1896): 61.
22 *The Mitre* 11 (1903): 190.
23 D.C. Masters, *Bishop's University, The First Hundred Years,* (Toronto: Clarke-Irwin 1950), 89.
24 H. Roe, *The Mitre* 2 (June 1895): 80.

25 McGill University Archives, Annual Reports.
26 J.H. Newman, *The Idea of a University*. ed. I.T. Ker (Oxford: Oxford University Press 1976), 95.
27 Ibid., 97.
28 *The Mitre* 2 (July 1895), 111.
29 J.H. Nicolls, Address to Convocation, June 1860. *The Mitre* 2 (April 1895): 50–6.
30 University Calendar, Session of 1897–98, 24.
31 University Calendar, Session of 1899–91, 24.
32 Convocation Register.
33 Unidentified newspaper account. Nicolls' Papers NIC 183/22 1887. Bishop's University Archives.
34 *The Mitre* 2 (May 1895): 73.
35 *The Mitre* 6 (July 1899): 164.
36 Minutes of a regular quarterly meeting of the Protestant Committee of the Council of Public Instruction, 3 February 1900, 367.
37 Ibid., 8 May 1900.

CHAPTER FIVE

1 Convocation Register, University Calendars and Registers of Bishop's College School.
2 *The Mitre* 30 (April 1943), 15–16.
3 *The Mitre* 9 (June 1902): 224.
4 University Calendar, Session of 1884–85, 12.
5 Chancellor's Address to Convocation, June 1892. Bishop's University Archives.
6 Minutes of a meeting of Corporation, 18 May 1906.
7 Minutes of a meeting of Corporation, 7 June 1906.
8 University Calendar, Session of 1906–07, 46.
9 Minutes of regular quarterly meetings of the Protestant Committee of the Council of Public Instruction, 14 November 1904 and 19 May 1905.
10 Ibid.
11 *The Mitre* 12 (October 1904): 4–12.
12 Ibid.
13 Ibid.
14 Ibid., 30.
15 *Dictionary of National Biography 1931–40* (Oxford: Oxford University Press 1949), 904.
16 *The Mitre* 12 (March 1905): 102.
17 Minutes of a meeting of Corporation, 9 May 1905, Bishop's University Archives.

18 Minutes of a meeting of Corporation, 21 June 1906.
19 *The Mitre* 13 (July 1906): 179.
20 Minutes of a meeting of Corporation, 20 June 1907.
21 *The Mitre* 11 (May 1904): 197.
22 *The Mitre* 15 (December 1907): 50.
23 *The Mitre* 16 (April 1909): 138.
24 *The Mitre* 15 (April 1908): 115.
25 *The Mitre* 19 (February 1912): 10.
26 *The Mitre* 17 (December 1909): 1.
27 *The Mitre* 22 (Easter 1915): 2.
28 Ibid.
29 J. Graham Patriquin, *B.C.S.: From Little Forks to Moulton Hill*, 2 vols. (Lennoxville: Bishop's College School 1978) 2:234
30 *The Mitre* 12 (November 1904): 43.
31 *The Mitre* 27 (Michaelmas 1919): 15.
32 Minutes of a meeting of Corporation, 21 April 1920.
33 *The Mitre* 26 (Convocation 1919): 10.
34 Ibid., 19.

CHAPTER SIX

1 *The London Gazette*, no. 29824 (24 November 1916).
2 *Who's Who in Canada*, 1934–35 (Toronto: International Press). 1934–35.
3 J.D. Jefferis, Personal communication.
4 A.H. McGreer, Letter to Fred Moy, 14 December 1931. McGreer Correspondence, Bishop's University Archives.
5 Report of the Principal to Corporation, 26 October 1922, McG. Corresp.
6 A.H. McGreer, Letter to John Bassett. 27 May 1935. McG. Corresp.
7 A.H. McGreer, Copy to F.E. Meredith. Meredith Papers, McGill University Archives, 4058.
8 A.H. McGreer, Letter to G.H. Montgomery, 18 November 1925. McG. Corresp.
9 Minutes of a meeting of Corporation, 8 December, 1925. Bishop's University Archives.
10 Report of the Principal to Corporation, 15 October 1925. McG. Corresp.
11 Minutes of a meeting of Corporation, 26 October 1922.
12 C.H.M. Church, Personal communication, and D. Cooper, Retrospective Correspondence I.
13 A.H. McGreer, Address to Convocation. 21 June 1928. McG. Corresp.
14 A.H. McGreer Letter to James Mackinnon, November 1930. McG. Corresp.
15 Report of the principal to Corporation. 24 October 1929. McG. Corresp.
16 A.W. Preston, *Amateur Performance* (Memoir) Bishop's University Archives.

17 A statement in support of the recommendation of an increase of the annual grant from $1,000 to $7,000 for training teachers at Bishop's University, Lennoxville. McG. Corresp. 1927 S4.
18 C. Wayne Hall, Retrospective Correspondence I. Bishop's University Archives.
19 Douglas Cooper, Retrospective Correspondence I.
20 A.W. Preston, *Amateur Performance.*
21 Marion Burt Bourne, *Alumni News Letter*, 2nd Series, no. 1 (September 1988). Lennoxville, Bishop's University Alumini Association.
22 Ibid.
23 B. Eardley-Wilmot, Alumni Newsletter, 2nd Series, no. 6 (July 1990), 6.
24 *The Mitre* 30 (November 1922): 2.
25 A.H. McGreer, Annual Report to Corporation, 1924. McG. Corresp.
26 A.H. McGreer, Letter to R.A.E. Greenshields, 7 November 1934. McG. Corresp.
27 Ibid.
28 A.H. McGreer, Letter to F.E. Meredith, 3 December 1929. McG. Corresp.
29 A.W. Preston, *Amateur Performance.*
30 J.G. McCausland, Retrospective Correspondence I.
31 Colin Cuttell, *Philip Carrington: Pastor, Prophet, Poet.* (Toronto: Anglican Book Centre 1988).
32 A.H. McGreer, Letter to R.A.E. Greenshields, 1 June 1935. McG. Corresp.
33 This had also been McGreer's view in 1929, when there had been a conflict between Dean Carrington and Professor Vial concerning responsibility for the domestic economy of Divinity House.
34 A.L. Langford, *The Development of the B.Sc. Programme* (Memoir). Bishop's University Archives.
35 Ibid.
36 C. Galarneau, *Les collèges classiques au Canada français.* Bibliothèque canadienne-française, histoire et documents. (Montreal: FIDES), 222.
37 Langford, *B.Sc. Programme.*
38 W.P. Percival, Letter to A.H. McGreer, 2 September 1937. McG. Corresp.
39 W.A.F. Hepburn, *Protestant Education in the Province of Quebec.* Report of the Quebec Protestant Education Survey, 1938.
40 P. Carrington, Letter to A.H. McGreer, 1 June 1939. McG. Corresp.
41 Minutes of the Academic Committee, 13 June 1939. Bishop's University Archives.
42 *The Mitre* 47 (February 1940): 25.
43 Minutes of a meeting of Corporation, 26 October 1944.
44 A.L. Langford, Personal communication.
45 Minutes of a meeting of Corporation, 17 May 1946.
46 *The Mitre* 19, no. 6 (1911–12): 12.

47 G.H. Montgomery, Letter to Bishop Carrington, 30 November 1946. Bishop's University Archives.
48 Minutes of a meeting of Corporation, 31 October 1946.
49 Minutes of a meeting of Corporation, 31 October 1946.
50 P. Carrington, Letter to Chancellor Montgomery. 21 February 1947. Quebec Diocesan Archives B-49C.
51 Carrington Diary. Quebec Diocesan Archives B-49.
52 A.H. McGreer, Letter to G.H. Montgomery, 12 December 1946.
53 Minutes of a meeting of Corporation, 7 February 1947.
54 Ibid.
55 An Act respecting Bishop's College, Chap. 130, 11 Geo. VI, Legislative Assembly of Quebec.
56 Colin Cuttell, *Philip Carrington*.
57 A.W. Preston, *Amateur Performance*.
58 *The Campus* 4, no. 13, (8 April 1948).
59 A.H. McGreer, Letter to W.P. Percival, 28 September 1945. McG. Corresp.
60 W.B. Scott, Letter to G.H. Montgomery, 16 May 1949.
61 Address of Chancellor Montgomery to Convocation, June 1948. Principal's Files, 1948.

CHAPTER SEVEN

1 A.R. Jewitt, "The Value of a Liberal Education." Address to Ladies' Canadian Club, 1949. Principal's Files, 1949. Bishop's University Archives.
2 *The Montreal Gazette*, 28 April 1949.
3 *The Montreal Gazette*, 30 April 1949.
4 Basil Jones, Letter to A.R. Jewitt, 21 May 1949. Principal's Files. 401 Transfer, Bishop's University Archives.
5 Minutes of a meeting of Corporation, 24 August, 1949. Bishop's University Archives.
6 B. Jones, Foreward, *The Quad*, 1950.
7 A.R. Jewitt, Letter to John Molson, 28 November 1955. Principal's Files 1303.
8 W.B. Scott, Letter to G.H. Montgomery, 16 May 1949.
9 Campaign brochure, 1948 Extension Fund. Bishop's University Archives.
10 J. Nicol, Letter to A.R. Jewitt, November 1948. Principal's Files, 1948.
11 A.R. Jewitt, Letter to Dallas Laskey, December 1951. Principal's Files, 1951: Appointments.
12 A.R. Jewitt, Letter to W.B. Scott, 2 February 1955. Principal's Files 2002 Transfer.
13 A.R. Jewitt, Letter to D.R.G. Owen, 20 December 1949. Principal's Files 1303.

14 W.R. Coleman. *Anglican Outlook and News Digest* February 1951: 14–15, March 1951:10–11.
15 Minutes of a meeting of the Executive Committee. 31 January 1952. Bishop's University Archives.
16 A.R. Jewitt. Letter to W.B. Scott, 19 January 1949. Principal's Files, 1949: W.B. Scott.
17 Minutes of a meeting of the Executive Committee, 22 January 1949.
18 A.R. Jewitt, Letter to John Molson, 29 March 1950. Principal's Files 1303.
19 A.R. Jewitt, Report to the Annual Meeting of Corporation, June 1955.
20 Minutes of a meeting of the Executive Committee. 25 April 1953.
21 A.R. Jewitt, Letter to John Bassett, 16 October 1958. Principal's Files, 1953: J. Bassett.
22 John Molson, Letter to A.L. Kuehner, 26 December 1957. Principal's Files 1303.
23 Minutes of a meeting of the Executive Committee, 3 March 1954.
24 Minutes of a meeting of the faculty, 6 January 1958. Bishop's University Archives.

CHAPTER EIGHT

1 This corresponded to the "Bac" in France, which marked passage from the *lycée* to the *université*. Men graduating from the *Collèges classiques* were two or three years older than those graduating from the *lycées*, but they were still designated as having completed their *secondary* level of education. This led to confusion in Quebec when it became necessary to establish equivalence between the B.A. of the English-language universities and the degrees (B.ès Lettres, B.ès Sciences, etc.) conferred by the French-language universities.
2 Cited in *The Campus* 11 January 1961:3.
3 Douglas Charles Abbott was born in Lennoxville, and he enrolled as an undergraduate at Bishop's in 1915 at the age of 16. Before his 17th birthday, he enlisted in the McGill Siege Battery and served in France. After the war, he enrolled in the Faculty of Law at McGill. During a distinguished career at the bar, he entered federal politics and was elected to the House of Commons in 1940. He served as minister of finance in the Canadian government from 1946 to 1954, when he was appointed to the Supreme Court. He became Chancellor of Bishop's University in 1958.
4 Arthur Tremblay, *Le ministère de l'éducation et le conseil supérieur* (Québec: Les Presses de l'Université Laval 1989).
5 Brief submitted to the Royal Commission of Enquiry on Education in the Province of Quebec by Bishop's University, 1962.
6 Edward F. Sheffield, *Enrolment in Canadian Universities and Colleges to 1970–71 (1961 projection)* (Ottawa: Canadian Universities Foundation, 1962).

7 W.P. Thompson, *The Number of University Teachers: Needs and Prospects* Canadian Association of University Teachers Bulletin 12, no.2 (1963).
8 *Report of the Royal Commission on Education.* Government of Quebec. 1964 Vol. 2, section 19.
9 Ibid., section 266.
10 Ibid., section 297.
11 Ibid., section 316.
12 *The Campus* 1, no. 1 (10 November 1944).
13 Sir James Duff, and R.A. Berdahl, *University Government in Canada* (Toronto: University of Toronto Press 1966).
14 *The Campus* 23 no. 11 (20 January 1967).
15 M. Donald, et al., *A Study of the Position of Women Students at Bishop's University.* Submitted to the Executive Committee 27 April 1967. Bishop's University Archives.
16 *The Campus* 24, no. 9 (24 November 1967).
17 Minutes of a meeting of the Executive Committee, 21 December 1967. Bishop's University Archives.
18 Minutes of a meeting of Corporation, 5 December 1968. Bishop's University Archives.
19 C.L.O. Glass, Report of the Principal to the Annual Meeting of Corporation, 5 December 1968.
20 Minutes of a meeting of the Executive Committee, 23 May 1968.
21 *The Campus* 25, no. 1 (4 October 1968).
22 Minutes of a meeting of Senate, 10 May 1968. Bishop's University Archives.
23 I.L. Campbell, Report of the Dean of Arts to the Annual Meeting of Corporation, 5 December 1968.
24 J.D. Jefferis. Personal communication.
25 *The Campus*, 24, no. 11 (25 January 1968).
26 A.W. Preston. Report on manifestation, dated 2 February, included in the minutes of a meeting of the Executive Committee, 19 February 1970.
27 Minutes of a meeting of Senate, 14 May 1969.
28 Minutes of a meeting of Senate, 27 January 1970.
29 Ibid.

APPENDIX TWO

1 J. Strachan. *John Strachan: Documents and Opinions.* ed. J.L. Henderson. (Toronto: McClelland and Stewart, The Carleton Library no. 44, 1969) p. 184.
2 F.J.C. Hearnshaw. *The Centenary History of King's College, London* (London: George Harrap, 1929) p. 70.
3 Ibid.

4 Hilda Neatby, *Queen's University*, 2 vols (Montreal: McGill-Queen's University Press, 1978) vol. I, p. 52.
5 James Bruce, Earl of Elgin, Letter to his mother (quoted in *Letters and Journals of James, Eighth Earl of Elgin*) ed. Thomas Walrond, Kraus reprint N.Y. 1969.
6 S.B. Frost. *McGill University, for the Advancement of Learning*, 2 vols. (Montreal: McGill-Queen's University Press 1980) 1.49.
7 S.B. Frost, *McGill University, for the Advancement of Learning*, 2 vols (Montreal: McGill-Queen's University Press, 1980) 1.60.

APPENDIX THREE

1 Elizabeth Hearn Milner, *Bishop's Medical Faculty, Montreal, 1871–1905* (Sherbrooke: René Prince 1985) has been an invaluable source of reference to primary material for this chapter.
2 *Dictionary of Canadian Biography*, 12 vols. (Toronto: University of Toronto Press, 1966–   ) 6:104.
3 S.B. Frost, *McGill University, for the Advancement of Learning*, 2 vols. (Montreal: McGill-Queen's University Press 1930) 1:63.
4 Ibid., 143.
5 Ibid., 148.
6 *Dictionary of Canadian Biography*, 10:131.
7 Milner, *Bishop's Medical Faculty*, 53.
8 Minutes of the Faculty of Medicine, University of Bishop's College, 26 September 1871. Bishop's University Archives.
9 Ibid., 12 June 1871.
10 Ibid., 22 May 1871.
11 Ibid., 12 August 1871.
12 Ibid., 28 December 1871.
13 Ibid., 7 February 1872.
14 Ibid.
15 Minutes of the Quarterly Meeting of the Governors of the Montreal General Hospital, 14 August 1872.
16 Terry Copp, *The Anatomy of Poverty: The Condition of the Working Class in Montreal 1897–1929* (Toronto: McClelland and Stewart 1974), 26.
17 Minutes of the Faculty of Medicine, University of Bishop's College, 20 May 1875.
18 R.C. Featherstonhaugh, *The Western Hospital of Montreal* (Montreal: Gazette Printing 1929).
19 Francis J. Shepherd, *The Origin and History of the Montreal General Hospital* (Montreal: Gazette Printing Co. 192–?).
20 Minutes of the Quarterly Meetings of the Governors of the Montreal General Hospital.

21 *The Montreal Gazette*, 10 May 1894.
22 *The Mitre*, 2 (July 1894).
23 Minutes of a meeting of the Faculty of Medicine, 3 October 1890.
24 *The Montreal Gazette*, 30 November 1891.
25 M.E.S. Abbott, "Autobiographical Sketch," *McGill Medical Journal* 28, no. 3, (October 1959): 127.
26 Milner, *Bishop's Medical Faculty*, 412–22.
27 Ibid., 406–12, 422–34. Milner has traced the careers of several other women graduates of the Bishop's medical school.
28 Minutes of a meeting of the Faculty of Medicine, 27 January 1876 and Milner, *Bishop's Medical*, 110.
29 Milner, *Bishop's Medical*, 110.
30 *The Mitre* 4 (November 1896): 19.
31 Milner, *Bishop's Medical*, 220.
32 Minutes of meeting of Corporation, 8 April 1896.
33 Abraham Flexner, *Medical Education in the United States and Canada. A Report to the Carnegie Foundation for the Advancement of Teaching.* 1910.
34 Calendar of the Faculty of Medicine, McGill University, 1895–96.
35 Milner, *Bishop's Medical*, 299.
36 *The Mail and Empire*, Toronto, 1 October 1903.
37 Minutes of the Faculty of Medicine, University of Bishop's College, 13 March 1905.

INDEX

Abbott, Douglas Charles, 253, 273, 362
Abbott, Maude, 336, 339
Abbott Hall, 263, 269
Abbott-Smith, George, 103, 163
Academic dress, 178, 210, 285
Acts relating to the University of Bishop's College; of 1843, 23, 299–301; of 1852, 43, 301–2; of 1870, 77, 305–6; of 1927, 169–70, 306–7; of 1947, 208, 307–9; of 1958, 309–10
Adams, Thomas (principal and rector): origins and education, 102–3; academic development under, 104–7, 121–3; discipline under, 103, 107, 109–10; as a builder, 111, 120; illness and resignation, 125
Allnatt, Francis J.B., 106, 161
Alumnae Society, 150
Alumni Association, 76, 146–7, 157, 159
American College Entrance Examination Board, 261

Anglican Church (Church of England), 10, 14, 16–17, 22, 35–6, 74–7, 106, 206–9
Arts, Associate in, 126–7, 135–6
Association of Professors of Bishop's University, 296
Audet, Louis-Philippe, 9, 74
Austin, Thomas, 18, 26
Aylwin, Thomas Cushing, 37–8, 52

Babin, Jérémie, 68
Baldwin, Robert, 38, 314
Banfill, Arnold Drew, 233–4
Bank, City, 6
Bank, Eastern Townships, 53, 61
Bank, Mechanics, 329
Bassett, John, 215–16, 222, 230, 244
Beaudry, P., 240
Bedford Jones, H.H., 161–3
Bethune, John, 316
Biological Exhibitions, 236–7
Bishop's Association of University Teachers, 259
Bishop's College: named, 23; opened, 30; first membership of faculty,

33–6; course of study, 38–41
Bishop's College, University of (charter), 47, 302–5
Bishop's College School: under Lucius Doolittle, 18; acquired by Corporation, 26; closed (1854), 58; reopened (1857), 60; new building on campus (1862), 66; debates over site, 83–4, 153–4; financial difficulties, 66, 94, 111, 149, 154; rebuilt after fire of 1874, 84; rebuilt after fire of 1891, 111; moved off campus, 154
Bishop's College School Association, 94–5, 109, 149
Bishop's University: named, 309–11
Bishop's University Faculty Association, 283
Bishop Williams Wing, 103, 111
Board of Governors, 158, 162
Bond, William, 79, 105
Boothroyd, Edward, 143, 201
Boothroyd, Roger, 195
Bourget, Bishop, 45–6
Bourne, Marion Burt, 179
British American Land Co., 6, 20, 21, 61, 89
British North America Act, 73–4, 245
Brodie, Nancy, 284
Brooks, Samuel, 38
Bryant, Anna, 135
Brydges, C.J., 79–81
Burt, H.C., 143, 201
Business Administration: program introduced, 241–3

Call, Frank O., 143, 150
Cambridge University, 18, 40, 91, 103, 128
Cameron, James, 95, 334
Campbell, Ian, 285, 293
Campbell, Francis W., 318, 329–30, 332–4, 336, 346–7
Campbell, Thomas E., 322–3
Campus, The, 240, 253, 268, 277
Canada, United Province of, 6, 11
Canadian Association of University Teachers, 271, 283
Canadian Officers' Training Corps, 182, 199

Canadian Union of Students, 276
Carrington, Philip, 189–90, 198, 206–9
Casault, Louis-Jacques, 44
Catholic, Roman, 7–10, 14, 16, 38, 45–6, 73, 90, 256, 314, 315, 333
Centennial Theatre, 273, 386
Champlain Regional College, 295
Chapel of St Mark, 87, 111–12
Chapman, Edward, 18, 33, 36–7, 112–13
Charter, royal, 44–7, 302–5
Chauveau, Pierre Joseph-Olivier, 73
Childs, Sydney, 190, 227
Church of England: see Anglican Church
Churchwarden Club, 144
Clarke, Lewis, 231
Clergy Reserves, 16–17, 44
Cochran, A.W., 23
Cochrane, Matthew, 91, 95
Coleman, D.C. 192
Coleman, W.R., 229–30
College Council, 23, 42, 62, 64, 107–10, 121
Collèges classiques, 7, 193–4, 258, 266
Collège d'enseignement général et professionnel, 265–6, 295
College Frying Pan, The, 64
College of Physicians and Surgeons of Lower Canada, 321
Collegial government, 271–2, 281, 293–4
Colonial Church and School Society, 37
Compton Ladies College, 123, 145
Conseil des universités, 288, 296
Constructive Report, 157–9
Convocation: membership, 49; public meetings of (1863), 50–2; (1895) 117; (1914), 150–2; (1967), 273–5; (Medical), 326, 333; delegation of powers to Senate, 272
Corporation: established, 23; composition, 23–5, 43, 77–9, 169–170, 206–8
Coulter, Bruce, 254
Curriculum development, 104–7, 121–2, 142–4, 172–6, 227–8, 259

INDEX

David, Aaron Hart, 318, 324, 332
Davidson-Davies Chair, 100
Dawson, William, 57, 113, 345
Deane, Philip, 294
Debating, 41, 64, 145, 251, 263
Deep Purples, 265
Dental Association of the Province of Quebec, 342
Dental College of the Province of Quebec, 343
Derick, Carrie M., 150
Devoir, Le, 253
Dewhurst, James, 178
Dewhurst Hall, 179, 263
Discipline, undergraduate, 64–5, 107–10, 239, 268–70, 275–8
Divinity, Faculty of, 105, 143, 189–90
Divinity degrees (Synod), 106
Divinity House, 104
Doctor of Dental Surgery, 343
Dominion College of Music, 121, 144
Donald committee, 275
Doolittle, Lucius, 17–21, 26, 49, 50
Dramatic Society, 144–5, 179, 185, 263
Duff-Berdahl report, 271, 294
Dunn, E.A., 132, 142
Dunn, John, 240
Duplessis, Maurice L., 196, 208, 222, 249
Duval, Errol, 242

Eastern Townships, 4–6, 89–90
École de médecine et de chirurgie de Montréal, 321–2, 324
Education, Graduate School of, 176, 203, 267, 290
Education, public: Royal Institution for the Advancement of Learning, 9–10, 12; Syndics, Act 10; McGill College, 12; Public Instruction, superintendent of, 11; department of, 73; Council of, 73; Protestant committee, 126, 136, 176 195–7; consolidation of school districts, 177; Hepburn committee, 195–7; Parent Commission, 256–8, 265–7; Ministry of 257, 287–8, 295
Elgin, Lord, 44–7
Elliott, Ezekiel, 23, 25

Evangelical (Anglican) party, 74–5
Executive Committee of Corporation, 170, 225, 228, 230, 239, 241, 243–4, 277, 281
Executive Council (Quebec), 22, 23

Farwell, William, 135
Federal financing for universities, 244–6
Financial appeals, public: first (1843), 20; for salaries, (1846), 37; (1849), 43; (1859), 65–8; to restore the endowment (1880), 99–100; building extension fund, 104; Jubilee fund, 118; Hamilton memorial, 120; Diamond Jubilee, 150; (1924), 170–1; (1936), 192; (1948), 222; (1958), 244; Bishop's 70, 273; Opportunity fund, 297; Learning for Life, 297
Fires: (1874), 83; (1876), 84; (1891), 111
Fry, Marion, 228
Fulford, Francis, 43

Galt, Sir Alexander T., 20, 69, 352
Gauthier, Germain, 278, 288
Gazette, Montreal, 50, 203, 219, 326
Gérin-Lajoie, P., 256, 257
Gibbins, H. de B., 140
Glass, C.L. Ogden (principal): origins and education, 251; appointments by, 253–4; expansion under, 258–62; residence life under, 263, 268–70, 275–8; resigned, 280
Godfrey, Robert, 327, 330
Gold medal, Nelson, 333
Gomery, Minnie, 339
Governors general, 69, 117, 150, 171, 172, 205
Grant, G.M., 114
Grants, government, 38, 44, 59, 111, 125, 148, 150, 171, 222, 273
Gray, James, 228, 247, 291
Greenshields, R.A.E., 184
Growth, 243, 258–9
Gummer, C.F., 144, 149
Gymnasium, 120, 153

Hale, Edward, 22–3, 63, 81

Hall, Grant, 99, 154, 171
Hall, Robert, N., 97
Hamilton, Charles, 71, 100
Hamilton, H.F., 131, 143
Hamilton, John, 128, 170, 184
Hamilton, Robert, 83, 100, 120
Harrold, T.C., 27
Harrold Chair of Divinity, 100
Harrold Lodge, 87
Hatcher, A.G., 174
Hawkins, A. Ernest, 27, 43
Healy, Dennis (principal), 293
Hellmuth, Isaac, 34–6
Heneker, Richard W., 61, 79–80, 84, 94–5, 102, 125–7, 128–31, 134
Hepburn Report, 195–7
High School of Montreal, 60
High School Teaching Diploma, 174, 193
Hingston, William, 318, 324
Holme, L.R., 122, 126
Home, Maurice, 174, 193, 194
Hôtel Dieu de Montréal, 324
Howard, J.G., 26
Howard Ferguson Cup, 205
Hudspeth, R.N., 143

Jackson, Grace, 231–3
James, Cyril, 203, 245
Jefferis, Jeffrey D., 203, 240, 290
Jellicoe, Sydney, 231, 290–1
Jesuit estates, 45
Jesuits, 7
Jewitt, Arthur Russell (principal): origins and education, 213; conflict with Dean Jones, 219–21; academic development under, 227–9, 234–7; defence of Dean Coleman, 229–31; collegiate life under, 238–41; policy for growth, 243–4; program in business administration, 241–3; illness and resignation, 246–8
Johnson, Andrew S., 237, 247
Jones, Basil, 190, 203, 205, 220–1

Kaufman, Fred, 240
Kuehner, Albert L., 174, 193, 227, 246, 261
Kuehner Hall, 273

King's College, Upper Canada, 312–13
King's College, Windsor, 23, 106

Lafontaine, Louis-Hippolyte, 37
Langford, Arthur N., 194–5, 236–7
Laskey, Dallas, 228, 279, 291
Laskey, Marie, 228
Law, Faculty of, 97
Legislative Assembly: of Lower Canada, 9, 10, 11; of United Province of Upper and Lower Canada, 6, 23, 37–8, 313–14; of Quebec, 328, 343
Legislative Council of Quebec, 106
Leprohon, Jean-Lukin, 329, 331
Lesage, Jean, 249
Library, 148–9, 231–4
Lieutenant governors, 8, 117, 146, 333
Lloyd, Christopher, 187
Lobley, Joseph Albert (principal): origins and education, 91; principal of the MDTC, 93; endowment rebuilt, 99–100; rector of BCS, 102; illness and death, 102
Lodge, New, 148, 166
Lodge, Old, 42, 120
Logan, Sir William, 64, 70
Loyalist, United Empire, 36, 171
Loyola College, 181

Mabbutt, James, 276
McCausland, J.G., 189
McConnell, J.B., 346
McCord, John Samuel, 49
MacDermot, T.W.L., 253
Macdonald, John A., 314
McDonald, S.J., 181
McGill University: admission to the Bar, 105; art of teaching, 121; A.A. examinations, 126–7; Faculty of Medicine, 321–2, 324, 327, 330, 334–5, 344, 345–7; and graduate school of education, 203
McGreer, Arthur Huffman (principal): origins, 164, 166, 168; renewal of Corporation, 169–70; financial campaigns, of 1924, 170–1; of 1936, 192; academic development under, 172–6, 192–5;

INDEX

on Protestant committee, 176–7, 195–7; conflict with Dean Carrington, 189–90, 198; 1939–45 War, 199–205; secularization of Corporation, 295–8; his legacy, 209–12
McIntosh, Louise, 228
Mackay, A.O., 273
McKenzie, Margaret Stewart, 104
Mackinnon, C.G., 234, 244
Medicine, Faculty of, 97, 317–47; building, 327
Meekran, R.J., 145, 153
Meredith, F.E., 171, 184
Michell, H. 201
Miles, H.H., 33, 64, 68–9, 70–1, 82
Ministry of Education: see Education, public
Mitchell, C.W., 131–2
Mitchell, William, 259
Mitre, The, 123, 135, 139, 145, 153, 341
Molson, J.H.R., 120
Molson, John Henry, 217, 227, 230, 242
Monck, Frances, 69–70
Montgomery, Georges H.S., 171, 207, 208, 212
Montreal Diocesan Theological College, 77, 105–6
Montreal General Hospital, 321, 324, 327, 334–5, 336
Montreal Ladies Educational Association, 134
Montreal School of Medicine and Surgery, 321
Moore, A.H., 136, 148
Morris, Lt-Col W., 21
Morris, William, 142
Morris House, 111
Motyer, Arthur, 228, 263, 273, 291
Mountain, Bishop George Jehoshaphat: origins, 13; first principal of McGill College, 14; Bishop, 14; founder of Bishop's College, 17, 21, 22–5, 27–9; petitioner for royal charter, 44–7; founder of See of Montreal, 43; death, 74
Mountain, Harriet, 42

Mountain, J.J.S., 104
Music, Faculty of, 114, 121, 144

National Conference of Canadian Universities, 245
Nelson, Wolfred, 322
Newman, J.H., 75, 115
Nicol, Jacob, 170, 227
Nicolls, Jasper Hume (principal): origins and education, 28; first year as principal, 30–3; relations with faculty, 33–7; canvassing, 37, 43, 65, 66, 69; teaching load, 71–2; rector of BCS, 71; professor of divinity, 70; Evangelical attack on, 79–82; enlargement of chapel, 87; death, 87
Norman, R.W., 82, 325
Norton, Harry, 225

Ordinands, syllabus for, 198–9
Osler, William, 95, 330, 346
Owen, Eivion, 175
Oxenden, Ashton, 76–7
Oxford University, 28, 166, 169, 172, 213, 251

Parent Commission, 256–8, 265–7
Parergon Society, 145
Parrock, Richard A. (principal): professor of classics, 112; principal, 142; and the alumni association, 147–8; academic development under, 148–9; and BCS, 149, 153–4; resigned, 156–7
Paterson, Alex K., 293, 294
Patridge, D.C., 243
Penhale, Alfred, 238, 261
Plante, J.P., 281–3
Pollack, Maurice, 226
Preston, Anthony W. (principal): lecturer and professor of classics, 185–7; dean of Arts, 246; vice-principal, 281; principal, 281–4
Price, Evan J., 95, 120
Price, John H., 273, 297
Public Relations, 136–7, 170–1

Qua, N.C., 150, 152
Quebec City, 3–4, 21, 28, 37, 43, 146

Queen's University, 113–14, 314–15, 335
Quintilian Society, 42

Racine, Bishop Antoine, 90
Ramsay, Thomas K., 81, 107
Rawson, Christopher, 66
Raymond, W.O., 174–5, 227
Read, P.C., 93
Reid, C.P., 23, 99
Residences: Old Arts (McGreer), 26, 120; Divinity, 104, 111; New Arts, 178; Norton, 225; Pollack, 225; Mackinnon, 244; Abbott, 263; Kuehner, 275; Munster, 273
Rhodes, William, 95
Rhodes Scholars, 159, 187, 251, 261
Richardson, A.V., 149, 201, 227
Ritchie, Octavia Grace, 134, 335–9
Robertson, J. Gibb, 95
Roe, Henry, 30–1, 71, 83, 84–6, 87, 109–10
Ross, J.K.L., 153–4
Rothney, W.O., 175–7, 203
Routh, H.V., 137
Royal Institution for the Advancement of Learning, 9–10, 12
Royal Rifles of Canada, 199–200
Royal Victoria College, 134
Royal Victoria Hospital, 335, 339
Rusk, W.J., 122, 126
Ryerson, Egerton, 55

St Francis College, 59
St Lawrence and Atlantic Railway, 53
Sancton, Andrew, 276–7
Sauvé, Paul, 249, 251
Scarth, A.C., 71, 84
Scholarships, 100, 238, 261
Science, programs in, 150, 174, 192–5, 236–7
Scott, F.G., 98, 135, 136, 139, 148, 159
Scott, F.R., 159–61
Scott, W.B., 148, 217, 219–21, 244
Scowen, Philip, 225, 233, 243, 261, 288
Senate, 272, 283, 285, 291
Setlakwe, R., 240
Sewell, S.C., 34
Sheffield, Edward, 258

Sherbrooke, 5, 21, 53
Sherbrooke Academy, 11, 127
Sherbrooke Gas, Water, and Electric Light Co., 61, 117
Simpson, Thomas, 95, 334
Slack, George, 23
Smallwood, Charles, 318, 324
Smith, D.D., 294
Smith, Garth, 238
Smith, Hollis, 25
Smith, Oswald, 122, 126, 131
Smith, Rocksborough, 162, 163, 175
Smith, Sylvia Burt, 228, 238
Society for the Promotion of Christian Knowledge, 25, 37, 104
Society for the Propagation of the Gospel in Foreign Parts, 13, 15, 27, 44
Stanstead Seminary, 12
Stewart, Bishop Charles James, 12, 17
Stewart, J.C., 152
Stigma affair, 107–10
Strachan, Bishop John, 312, 315
Stringer, Don, 238
Students' Association, 156, 278
Students' Executive Council, 179, 238, 275, 278, 280
Synods, 76–7, 169

Tambs, R.C., 76, 82, 84
Taylor, Maria C., 135
Teaching, art of, 121
Tenure, 107
Thaler, Roderick, 228
Thompson, J.H., 52, 66
Thorneloe, Bishop George, 82, 109
Tomkins, Lyman, 246
Tomlinson, G.H., 225
Tomlinson, G.H. Jr, 195
Trenholme, Edward, 318, 331
Trustees: duties, 23; first appointments, 23; synods to appoint, 77; bishops to appoint, 169–70; Corporation to nominate, 208

Union générale des étudiants du Québec, 276
Université Laval, 45–6

Vial, Frank G., 143

Victoria College, University of, 55; Faculty of Medicine, 322
Visitors, The, 23, 39, 103, 221

Waitt, T.B. (principal), 135, 140
Walker, William, 49
Wars: (1914–18), 150–3, 159; (1939–45), 199–201
Watkins, B., 112
Western Hospital, 331–2
Whalley, A.G.C., 227
Whewell, W., 39
Whitney, James Pounder (principal): origins and education, 128; conflict over A.A. examinations, 135–6; academic development under, 131–2; women admitted to lectures, 132–5; resigned, 139

Wilkins, George, 329–30
Williams, Bishop J.W.: headmaster, BCS, 60; elected Bishop of Quebec, 66; collaboration with Galt, 74; defence of the endowment, 83
Woman's Hospital, 331
Women undergraduates, 132–5, 145–6, 179–81, 238–9; in residence, 269–70, 275–8; in Faculty of Medicine, 335–6, 339–40
Wood, S.S., 17, 28, 40
Wurtele, L.C., 63–4

Yarrill, Eric, 200
Yates, N.P., 104
Yearwood, Peter, 277

Bishops College Lennox